HOLDING ON AND HOI

Jewish Diaries from Wart.....

Examining the diary as a particular form of expression, *Holding On and Holding Out* provides unique insights into the experiences of Jews in France during the Second World War. Unlike memoirs and autobiographies, which reconstruct life stories, diaries record daily occurrences without the benefit of retrospect, describing events as they unfold. In *Holding On and Holding Out*, Anne Freadman explores themes of identity and time, considering as well how the pre-persecution lives of diarists shaped the way they viewed their wartime experiences.

Holding On and Holding Out closely follows two individuals, Raymond-Raoul Lambert and Benjamin Schatzman, from the first entries in their diaries to the final ones written before each man disappeared into Nazi extermination camps. Through an investigation of these and other select diaries, Freadman assesses how individuals used their diaries to record their daily lives under Nazi persecution, waiting for the end of the war with a mixture of hope and despair. Some diarists used their writing to bear witness not only to the terror of their own lives but also to the lives and suffering of others. Some used their writing to memorialize those who had been killed. All used their writing as a way to leave behind traces of themselves, to assert, "I live; I will have lived."

ANNE FREADMAN is Honorary Professorial Fellow in the School of Languages and Linguistics at the University of Melbourne.

Holding On
and Holding Out

Jewish Diaries from Wartime France

ANNE FREADMAN

UNIVERSITY OF TORONTO PRESS
Toronto Buffalo London

ISBN 978-1-4875-0753-4 (cloth)   ISBN 978-1-4875-3644-2 (EPUB)
ISBN 978-1-4875-2519-4 (paper)   ISBN 978-1-4875-3843-5 (PDF)

Library and Archives Canada Cataloguing in Publication

Title: Holding on and holding out : Jewish diaries from wartime France /
Anne Freadman.
Names: Freadman, Anne, 1944– author.
Description: Includes bibliographical references and index.
Identifiers: Canadiana (print) 20200177788 | Canadiana (ebook) 20200177931 |
ISBN 9781487507534 (hardcover) | ISBN 9781487525194 (softcover) |
ISBN 9781487536442 (EPUB) | ISBN 9781487536435 (PDF)
Subjects: LCSH: Holocaust, Jewish (1939–1945) – France – Personal narratives.
| LCSH: World War, 1939–1945 – France – Personal narratives. | LCSH: Jews –
France – Biography. | LCSH: Jews – France – Social conditions – 20th century. |
LCSH: Jews – France – Diaries – History and criticism. | LCSH:
French diaries – History and criticism.
Classification: LCC D804.195 .F74 2020 | DDC 940.53/180922 – dc23

University of Toronto Press acknowledges the financial assistance to its
publishing program of the Canada Council for the Arts and the Ontario Arts
Council, an Ontario government agency.

Canada Council   Conseil des Arts
for the Arts   du Canada

ONTARIO ARTS COUNCIL
CONSEIL DES ARTS DE L'ONTARIO
an Ontario government agency
un organisme du gouvernement de l'Ontario

Funded by the   Financé par le
Government   gouvernement
of Canada   du Canada

Canadä

Contents

Preface

The project of this book stands apart from that of others that study Jewish diaries from the Holocaust. The work of historians, for example, may draw on diaries to illustrate their accounts of events known from documentary evidence, or to reveal the personal dimension of these events. Such historiographical uses of diary archives have an important place in the painstaking construction of our understanding of Nazi persecution, but the place I carve out in this book is somewhat different. My focus is the experience of individuals, to which end I study diaries as a particular *genre* of writing. I take 'genre' to refer 'to a conventional category of discourse based on a large-scale typification of rhetorical action.'[1] Where some scholars of the painful and significant issues raised by the Holocaust might decry this approach as mere formalism, my view of form is that it is functional, providing the means whereby writing can do its work. This is a rhetorical view of genre,[2] where rhetoric is the study of the effects and consequences of acts of discourse.

I start by contrasting diaries and autobiographies. These two genres differ in at least the following respects. First, a diary is written from day to day, whereas an autobiography is written retrospectively. The latter tells the story of how the writer got to the point at which she or he decides, or is able, to write it. This is the point in time from which the writing proceeds, and it determines the temporal perspective on the events that led there. In the case of memoirs of the Holocaust, the writer *has survived*, whereas the writer of a diary cannot know whether this will be the outcome or not.[3] Second, an autobiography has an ending, to which its narrative leads; diaries are rarely completed: they stop, interrupted by events. Third, an autobiography tells the story of a period of time; a diary is written sporadically – sometimes, but not always, on a daily basis – so the significant unit of time is the day or the few days since the last entry. Diaries are thus made of gaps and fragments. While continuity may be disturbed or disrupted by the strategies of autobiographical writing, discontinuity is the very condition of the writing of a diary. Fourth, the entries of a diary are dated, with these dates referring both to the entry and, by means of such deictic adverbs as 'today' and 'yesterday,' to the events recounted. The time elapsed between the event and the entry, typically short, allows the emotions generated by the event not merely to be named, but shown in the writing – its rhythms, its silences, its failures to name.[4] Fifth, while in both genres the narrator and the protagonist are nominally identical, the temporal relation between the two is different in each, the diary often being written in haste; hence, too, the point of view, the organizing perspective of the narrator, is different. Because of the brief lapse of time between the events and their recording, the narrator of a diary is using the writing typically as a means of collecting herself or himself, whereas the writing of a memoir or autobiography aims to organize the events into a coherent narrative. 'Collecting' contrasts with 'recollecting' and implies the shattering, disconcerting, or alienating effect of the experience on the self. Finally, in a diary these events that shatter, these attempts to collect, are ongoing; the writing reports them as they happen. A diary records *living*, however imminent the threat of death.

These contrasts locate my book on a different street, though it is neighbouring, from that of a fine book by Amos Goldberg, which also uses first-person writing in an exploration of what happens to narrative identity under conditions of trauma.[5] Notwithstanding his acknowledgement that a diary 'is a text written without the perspective that would enable the organization of the events into a single narrative,' Goldberg evinces doubt as to the status of diaries as a genre on the grounds that they have 'neither thematic nor structural rules.'[6] For this reason, he collapses diaries with autobiography into an overarching category, 'the autobiographical genre,' which consists of 'life stories'; in the Holocaust, he claims, these demonstrate the struggle between the constituting impulse of narrative and the disintegration of trauma. Thus, where he acknowledges that it inheres in the very project of an autobiography to 'constitut[e] human identity as a narrative identity,' he uses the characteristic features of a diary to argue that the 'life-story' of trauma enacts a story of disintegration.[7] This is a persuasive argument concerning what happens to the person. But what is a 'life-story'? Is it the retrospectively recounted autobiography, told with its peripeteias and its turning points on the route taken to its arrival point? Is it the biography of a life cut short that we as readers construct from the material of a diary, with or without ancillary documents? Or is it the putative now impossible life-story sometimes referred to in memory or fantasy by diarists? Diaries are not emplotted;

their narrative mode is that of the episode and the anecdote. Hence, they cannot 'unravel' a plot projected or constituted by one of these other genres; nor are these always already discontinuous, fragmentary texts 'dismantled.' *Mutatis mutandis,* the same argument applies to the 'identity-creating characteristics of the life-story.' Trauma may well, as Goldberg argues, 'demolish the most basic parameters necessary for the constitution of inner identity,' but we will see that diary writing presents its own means for maintaining the first person.[8]

These means depend on the *sine qua non* of discourse; this is, deixis.[9] 'I,' 'here,' and 'now' are mutually implicated, each presupposing the other for its definition; together, they constitute the deictic centre of utterance. This is the mechanism from which flows all discourse, whether or not 'I' is erased in the third-person conventions of historical writing or made explicit in the first-person genres. This place is the condition of possibility for 'there' and 'then,' 'this' and 'that,' for the meaning of the tenses, for the adverbs and prepositions that establish place in space, and for some verbs of motion and exchange. Hence the deictic centre sets in motion the whole apparatus of reference. The full range of egocentric and extrovert foci of attention is governed by the same mechanism. To read a text as proceeding from this point is therefore to read the network of spatial and temporal relations of the writing 'I' with the world in which and about which it writes. Indeed, this network is both 'the subject-matter and the structure of diary-writing.'[10] My analysis of 'identity' follows from this fact: identity is a function of these relations. As they shift and disaggregate under conditions of radical change, such as those of Occupied France, so do we read in the diaries stories of adaptation and resistance as the writing 'I' seeks to withstand the threats it faces to the continuity of self. The 'I' who writes a diary uses it as a means of not collapsing, rewriting its embeddedness in the complexity of its others. Accordingly, my method of analysis of the matter of identity differs from analyses of 'narrative identity,' which frequently rest on the assumption of a separate, if not isolated, 'inner' subject of its stories. Chapters 1 and 2, on this topic, draw systematically on the use of pronouns, the relationality they necessarily imply, and their referential scope. To read a diary *in extenso* is to read the story these pronouns tell.

Likewise, my analysis of the topic of time rests on the uses of tense and its relationship with the fragmented, but linear and chronological, composition of the diary. This analytical strategy produces quite different findings from analyses that rest on narrative sequence. Trauma 'destroys temporal continuity,' Goldberg writes, and hence 'erases the difference between present and past.' For him, this 'stops time' in a 'static present' 'identical to the complete absence of the present.'[11] These are the

premises for his analysis of time in his corpus. Mine contrast markedly
with them. To be sure, many of the diarists register the traumatic disruption of a life-plot to which Goldberg draws our attention.[12] But they
do so in the course of writing their day-to-day efforts to live through the
disruption, however radical it might be. Hence, in chapter 3 – 'Making
It Last' – living through the present is of the essence. It is not 'static.'
Continuously redeploying the deictic mechanisms described above, the
writing 'I' reinstates itself in time on each occasion the writer makes
an entry. I agree with Goldberg that the past is erased by the present,
but not that the present is 'absent'; on the contrary, the present is the
time of survival, the assertion of the writer's continuing presence in the
uncertainty of what comes next: '*I am here now.*' Accordingly, my focus is
the experience of this present. Hence, I read the deictic adverb 'now'
through the phenomenology of temporal experience, which I elaborate
in chapter 4.

It also follows from my reliance on deixis that I take the diaries as
acts – acts of utterance, discursive acts. However, the characteristic discursive properties of diaries are adaptable to a variety of circumstances,
and hence lend themselves to a variety of acts. The majority of diarists
I consider in this book write in a situation of social erasure: they have lost
the place that would enable them under normal circumstances to leave
a mark, however modest, on the world they have lived in. In most cases,
the diaries are their only means of leaving a trace of their existence.[13]
This trace registers the erasure and defies it; the act is assertive: '*I live; I
will have lived.*' In many of these cases, the diary is also a bequest and, for
many, an act of witness: an assertion that demands acknowledgement,
a bequest that demands to be honoured, witness that demands to be
witnessed in its turn. The reader of these diaries takes on the responsibility of assuring a future foreclosed to the writers. This, in turn, raises
the issue of addressivity. While it is often assumed that diaries have no
addressee, the diaries I discuss demonstrate the error of this assumption.
In the immediate, they might be written to someone concrete, whether
it is the writer or the addressee who is missing or arrested; often they are
addressed to children in the future or, less concretely, to whomsoever
might find them, and, ultimately, to the anonymous reader who will fulfil
the task the writing assigns them.

'Close reading' is not the name of a method so much as a portman-
teau term for many techniques and strategies for 'listening' attentively
to a text. Each technique selects from the multiplicity available those
patterns and networks of textual features that best serve its purposes.
I have outlined the kind of selections I make; they start from the grammar of discourse, aiming to grasp the enunciative acts performed by

the writing. They do not stop at the grammar, since those acts – the enactment of identity (chapters 1 and 2) and the insistent persistence of the self (chapters 3 and 4) – involve the complex experience of living through menace. Counting myself as addressed by these diaries, committed by the very fact of taking them up to fulfilling their demands on me, I am governed, in the chapters that follow, by what Hélène Berr calls the 'distressing effort,' the 'painful undertaking,' the 'arduous task of telling the stories,'[14] and, like her pursuit of this undertaking, mine in this book is pervaded by the ethic of witnessing.

A Note on the Corpus

Many but not all of the diaries I use have been published. Their titles vary among 'Journal,' 'Cahiers,' 'Carnets,' but these are usually conferred in the editorial process. Likewise, the manuscript diaries use a variety of designations such as 'ce cahier,' 'mes notes,' 'mes papiers,' 'mes mémoirs' (this notebook, my notes, my papers, my memoirs). I use the term 'diary' to cover all these cases, taking them to be broadly synonymous, on the condition that the text is written in distinct entries, sequentially over time, and in the first person. The items of my corpus have been selected for their illumination of the topics of time and the self.

This book is not a survey; hence, the corpus does not purport to cover all French Jewish diaries from this period. Reference to others can be found in a volume by Alexandra Gabarini.[15] Some of my readings make reference to memoirs[16] as well as diaries, and on two occasions I tell stories from diaries written by non-Jews.[17]

I express my gratitude to the families for authorizing reference to the two unpublished diaries: Germaine Léon (Archives du Mémorial de la Shoah: DCCCXXIX–1), and Saül Castro (held by the family).[18] Apart from these two, I have not studied the manuscripts of my corpus; all other references are to published – hence, readily accessible – books.

Acknowledgments

Acknowledgments are a genre of mourning as well as gratitude. Both are due in first place to the people whose precious writings are the subject and the *raison d'être* of this book.

Thanks to the librarians at the Mémorial de la Shoah in Paris, for their help in locating obscure material and for helping to obtain permission from the families of the diarists. In this respect, I acknowledge my debt to Madame Markoff, daughter of Jeanne Léon, and Madame Berthelet and Franck Berthelet, daughter and grandson of Saül Castro. Franck Berthelet generously granted access to his transcription of Castro's diary, which is otherwise unavailable, and to some pages of the manuscript.

Thanks to my stalwart friends who read drafts and offered thoughtful advice as well as practical help: Irena Blonder, John Frow, Jeannine Jacobson, Jeffrey Minson, Frances Muecke, Francie Oppel, Lesley Stern, Janna Thompson. I thank you all, among many other interested and concerned friends, for sustaining me during the process. I have also been sustained with fun and love by Nutmeg and Cinnamon, who were my constant companions until their dear lives ran out, and by Bosi, who is with me now.

I miss, as I recall, Sylvia Lawson's impassioned talk of writing in the world. That's what we do it for, she would say. Special thanks to the members of the 'Trauma and Narrative' reading group, for searching questions and the refusal of simple answers. Thanks to audiences at the University of Manchester, the University of Queensland, the University of Melbourne, and the 'Iconicity East and West' conference at Rikkyo University, where I presented early versions of some of this work. An overview of the argument regarding French Jewish identity, with some additional material, was published under the title 'From Assimilation to Jewish Identity' in *French Cultural Studies* (28, 1: 54–66).

For the inestimable gift of his string of worry-beads, I thank Stathis Gauntlett.

Parisa Shiran helped prepare the manuscript for submission to the press, and Peter Cowley helped with the copy edit. Thanks to you both. I could not have done it without your generous and intelligent work.

Ross Chambers accompanied this project from its inception until his death. His inspiration and encouragement, the rich interchange I had with him over the years, pervade the book. I wish I could thank him, but thanks would never be enough.

HOLDING ON AND HOLDING OUT

Introduction

Ce journal entrera ... dans la postérité des miens. Ce sera toujours ça de sauvé.

This diary will be passed down to my family's posterity. This at least will be saved.
— Albert Grunberg, diary entry, 26 January 1943

On 24 September 1942, at 8:05 in the morning, three French policemen came to arrest Albert Grunberg, a Jew, a hairdresser, and a communist *Résistant*, at his home in the rue des Écoles in Paris. He gave them the slip, and from then until 23 August 1944 he remained in hiding in a neighbouring building where a hidden room had been made ready for him in case of need. His benefactor was the concierge, Mme Oudard, who brought him his meals and the daily newspaper, kept a vigilant eye on the other residents of the building, and from time to time went up for a chat over a clandestine coffee. When it was safe, she shepherded his wife up the stairs, sometimes to stay the night. For some months during those two years, his brother also stayed in the little room. The brothers were close, having been orphaned at an early age. This brother, Sami, who had been interned in the Jewish camp at Compiègne,[1] was a troubled soul without Albert's emotional and intellectual resources.[2] Life then was particularly cramped, and not particularly serene. Generally, however, Albert Grunberg was alone; he had one tiny window that he could not open for fear of detection, and he could not see the street, let alone go down to take the air. Sometimes, he writes, his room felt 'like a cage' (24 January 1943, 89), and he adopted the prisoners' habit of marking the time remaining until the hoped-for end of his confinement. For two years, he held on and held out for his own liberation, and the liberation 'of all who are oppressed' (3 January 1943, 73).

He kept up his morale by writing a diary, explaining that it miti-gated the solitude: 'La douleur qui se tait est funeste. C'est pourquoi il m'arrive parfois d'écrire une page telle à [*sic*] celle-ci. Cela me soulage' (7 January 1943, 74–5; Unspoken suffering is deadly. That's why I some-times write a page like this one. It makes me feel better). He had never written anything like this before and is apologetic about his spelling and his style, although it is lively and entertaining, and often witty. Writing helped him wait, and it would help him remember the good times as well as the bad: 'En attendant, mon Journal m'est d'un très grand appui moral. Quelque chose ne va pas, vite mon journal. De m'y épancher cela soulage ma peine. Suis-je content, vite je note l'objet de mon contente-ment. Cela fait balance' (18 May 1943, 172–3; While I wait, my Diary is a great moral support. If something is amiss, quick, to the diary! It soothes me to pour out my heart. If something makes me glad, just as quickly I note down what it is. That balances things out). Having decided to keep a diary, he finds more reasons to be pleased: 'Je me félicite ... de les avoir ainsi fixés, mes souvenirs [...] Car il importe pour moi que je me souvienne' (27 April 1943, 161; I am pleased with myself for having set down my memories. For it is important to me that I remember). These memories, here called his memoirs, will be a gift to acquit the debt he feels he has incurred toward his wife and Mme Oudard. In the diary he records the minutiae of his existence, as well as everything he learns about events in the outside world.

The room was situated behind the apartment of some sympathetic neighbours who were not usually in Paris. They allowed a hole to be drilled in their wall to enable Grunberg to plug in a radio. 'Si je n'avais pas eu la radio, je me demande ce que je serais devenu car c'est elle qui me prend la plus grande partie de mon temps' (3 January 1943, 72; I don't know how I'd have managed without the radio, because I spend most of my time listening to it). Using earphones, he heard performances of theatre and music, sometimes the broadcast mass (for the music, not the sermons), and a great deal of propaganda. He had an acute sense of what not to believe, and his running commentary on it is sometimes very droll. He learned from Radio France, for instance, the secret of Louis XVIth's death: the king had been assassinated by the Jews, or perhaps – this from the pro-Nazi publication *L'oeuvre* – by the ancestors of the cur-rent pretender to the throne. 'C'étaient certainement des Juifs aussi [...] À remarquer que les Bolchéviques ne sont pas dans le coup' (21 January 1943, 87; No doubt the Jews gave them a hand. Note that the Bolsheviks were not part of the plot'). He also listened to broadcasts from several other sources – notably New York, Switzerland, London; these broadcasts allowed him to fill in the gaps left by the censored news on the official

French stations.[3] For these reasons, and despite being cut off from his comrades, he was better informed both about the progress of the war and about the killing machine in operation in the east than many other people. On 9 July 1943, he provides a remarkable summary of what he knows of the Nazi methods, ending with an account of Jan Karski's report to the British authorities, which he has heard on the BBC.[4] Comparing the persecution of the Poles (of whom he believes 20 to 30 per cent were to be eliminated) with that of the Jews, he writes: 'Pour les Juifs ce n'est pas compliqué, il s'agit plus simplement de les exterminer totalement de façon à ce qu'il n'y reste plus trace sur la surface de la Terre! C'est pourquoi l'extermination est systématique et se fait dans le silence' (9 July 1943, 195; It's not a complicated calculation for the Jews; they are simply to be totally exterminated so that no trace remains of them on the surface of the Earth! That's why the extermination is systematic and carried out in secret). Following this passage, he writes a message to his sons: 'Robert! Roger! Mes enfants! Rappelez-vous! Rappelez-vous toujours! Rappelez-vous durant toute votre vie le martyre que les ennemis de votre race et de votre nation ont fait et continuent de faire subir à vos contemporains!' (ibid., 195–6; Robert! Roger! Children! Remember! Always remember! Remember your whole life long the martyrdom inflicted on your contemporaries by the enemies of your race and of your nation!).

Grunberg's diary maintains his sense of self in this period of enforced inactivity with very restricted human interaction. It records the perpetual present of a life in waiting; writing it keeps him sane; it is a bequest, and hence a deferred communication; and it sends this message to future generations: never forget!

The diaries studied in this book are, like Grunberg's, written by Jewish people in wartime France. They tell stories of waiting, and of struggling to maintain a sense of self – of what it is to hold on and hold out in the face of extraordinary forces. The book is composed of four chapters, each of which develops an aspect of two central topics – 'time' and 'the self' – which come together as an account of the self in time. The diaries have in common the purposes formulated by Grunberg, yet they have singular stories to tell, in that each is marked by the circumstances under which it was written – the space and the place, the moment and the times. The personal experience of these circumstances is the focus of each chapter.

Nevertheless, a general introduction is in order. The extermination of European Jewry affected a far smaller proportion of French Jews than of any other occupied country,[5] but all French Jews were affected by the powers and the powerlessness of the Vichy government, and it is to this experience that most of the diaries refer. Some but by no means all of the texts I have studied were written in camps; because France had no ghettoes, none parallel the famous diaries from Eastern Europe. The circumstances of the diarists vary considerably, but for all, the diaries were motivated by the period of the occupation or by specific situations determined by it. Some, like Grunberg, were in hiding and remained safe. Some envisage a future filled with grief or, alternatively, the dream of a new era. Grunberg continued his diary until the liberation of Paris, when, on 26 August 1944, he tells the story of his return home. He appends a concluding entry on 2 October: 'je veux conclure' (I want to conclude), he writes, doing so with premature optimism concerning 'l'avènement des Soviets en France' (the advent of Soviet [rule] in France) (2 October 1944, 352). Other diaries are suspended at the moment of arrest, deportation, or death. Their writers were women and men, young and old, rich and poor, people from old established and from recently arrived families, resistance militants and small-c collaborators, fervent Zionists and vehement anti-Zionists, Jews by government decree and Jews by loyalty or conviction and faith.

My focus on the two topics, time and the self, is determined by the diary taken as a genre. The mutual interconnections of these topics will provide the answer to a question implied by any study based on a specific genre: what does this genre, in this case a diary, tell us that other kinds of document – even other first-person testimonial genres – do not tell us? Let me introduce my answer in abstract and general terms, before turning to the specificities of the texts. I take time and the self to be structurally constitutive of the diary. First, time: a diary tells us what it feels like to live in 'this' present with 'this' recent past and to anticipate an unpredictable but fearsome future: it records the experience of time. It does so by means of the convention of dating the entries, which ties the occasion of an event to the time of writing about it. If the series of events shows the writer subject *to* the march of history, the series of entries shows her or him subject *of* reflections on that history. As we read through a diary, we read its writer – subject in both these senses – through time. A diary discloses the temporality of selfhood. Second, diaries are a practice of the self, the first person reflecting upon their experience as it affects their sense of who they are. The self is the centre of that experience, its agent perhaps, in some measure, but also its product, continually constituted by it, continually changed by it. Hélène Camarade notes that the diary is structured as 'a site for the encounter of the self with its world.'[6] This is what a diary tells us: not only the subjective account of a series of events, but the record of a person experiencing their world – their time and their times. What we learn in diaries from the brutal period of the Nazi Occupation of France is more, and other, than illustrations of an already known – or otherwise knowable – context. 'I do not need to describe the historic events ... the acts of violence, our depression,' wrote Victor Klemperer following *Kristallnacht,* 'Only the immediately personal and what concretely affected us.'[7]

Klemperer is drawing a strict distinction here between the writing of formal history and the writing of diaries. While there is no doubt that 'personal diaries offer a valuable source for modern and contemporary history,'[8] the distinction between the two genres rests on the diary's focus on a history lived as experience by the person engaged in writing the account. The diary records not only the external event but also the means of knowing it, and centrally, its intimate effects. The conditions of the writing are part of that story, as is the precariousness of the diary's existence. This first-person perspective is exactly what is erased by the conventions of formal historiography. To counter the 'flattening' effect of this erasure, Saul Friedländer, for example, has used diaries extensively in his splendid 'integrated' history of the Nazi era, writing of the diaries he uses that, 'as a source for the history of Jewish life during the years of persecution and extermination, they remain crucial and invaluable testimonies.'[9] He goes on to write that diaries bring 'voices' to historiography: 'the individual voice has been mainly perceived as a trace,' he writes, but 'suddenly arising in the course of an ordinary historical narrative [...] [it] can tear through seamless interpretation and pierce the [...] smugness of scholarly detachment and "objectivity."'[10] By quoting diaries throughout his narrative, he seeks to 'disrupt' 'the business of usual historiography' that 'domesticates and "flattens"' the story that it tells.[11] Amos Goldberg takes issue with Friedländer's ambition here, on the grounds that the mass media in the twenty-first century are pervaded by individual voices: the device is too familiar for our emotions and intellectual habits to be disrupted by it.[12] I am less concerned with disrupting our 'emotions and intellectual habits' than with the capacity of diaries to disrupt the conventions of historiography: as long as they serve as sources within these conventions, they contribute to the wider history but remain subservient to it. Thus, even when they disclose the personal effects or idiosyncratic interpretations of particular events, they do not tell their own story. Their story is the lived experience of the person at the centre of that life who is also the writer of that record.

Notwithstanding some loose usage in English, 'experience' and 'event' are not coextensive. According to the Shorter Oxford Dictionary, an event is the source of experience: 'Actual observation of or practical acquaintance with facts or events considered as a source of knowledge';

'knowledge resulting from ... what one has undergone.'[13] Experience is the junction of a raw occurrence with interpretation or reflection, the mediation of the one in and by the other.[14] The 'raw' is unsayable, but it can be indexed by pointing to moments of inarticulacy. To demonstrate this, I quote from the diary of Friedel Bohny-Reiter:

> Nous avons de la visite. Deux Suissesses qui travaillent dans un de nos homes. En traversant avec elles l'Îlot J, je prends conscience à nouveau de la misère de la vie de camp. Quelles impressions cela laissera-t-il à nos visites de l'extérieur? Elles étaient de plus en plus silencieuses – je me suis rappelé mon premier jour au camp.[15]

> We have visitors. Two Swiss women who work in one of our homes. As I cross J Compound with them, I see with new eyes the misery of camp life. What will be the impression left on these visitors from the outside? They grew more and more silent – I recalled my first day at the camp.

The passage records an encounter; it is speechless. The two Swiss women are struck dumb. In relation with them, Bohny-Reiter positions herself as 'experienced' by recalling her own first encounter with the camp. Back in her room at the end of that first day, she had reflected on what she had seen:

> Yeux ouverts ou fermés – je ne vois rien que d'immenses yeux d'enfants affamés dans des visages marqués par la souffrance et l'amertume. Et encore des yeux d'enfants qui défilent devant moi comme dans un film. Il n'y a qu'un jour que je suis ici, il me semble que c'est une semaine.[16]

> My eyes can be closed or open – I see nothing but the enormous eyes of starving children, their faces marked by suffering and bitterness. And more and more of them, children's eyes filing before me as if in a film. I've only been here for one day and it already feels like a week.

In this passage, Bohny-Reiter's diary clarifies for us a significant process. What she describes is not a real scene – it is a spectre, haunting her. We might say that she translates it, first moving it out of her head by means of an analogy ('like a film'). This first day, a single day, plunged her into a new, all-engulfing, and utterly confounding reality, so that the time of the encounter could not be measured; the moment of reflection retrieves real time and disables – with 'il me semble' (it seems to me) – the unreality of her sense of duration. Note the persistence of the past in the present, notwithstanding the fact that her sense of practical common-sense reality reasserts itself. Yet the first sight of these starving children is already a memory as she writes, and it is writing that transforms it, interpreting it, then reflecting on the difference between two states of consciousness – what it felt like, and what she knows – about the children, 'starving,' 'suffering,' 'bitterness,' and about the difficulty of processing this as reality. Note that the encounters recounted are events in her work as a nurse; the reflections emerge in the act of writing.

This lapse of time and this necessary juncture between event and reflection constitute together the typical composition of a diary entry. Strictly speaking, diaries are not contemporaneous with the experiences they record: whether at a remove of five minutes, an hour, several days, or even months, the writing always follows the event. However, they are written progressively, in fragments, accompanying the living of the life. It follows that they reflect upon the events they record progressively, in fragments, and frequently with changes of understanding motivated by various factors as they proceed. This is what Raymond-Raoul Lambert, writing of André Gide, calls 'la pensée qui chemine'[17] – thinking as it treads its path. It records and reflects upon what has happened, apparently randomly.

Yet that random path tells a different story from the stories told in the entries taken singly. The reader is able, where the writer is not, to take a diary as a whole: to do so is to seek a certain piecemeal but progressively constructed coherence, which I take as its 'project.' To explain this, I note that any diary has a recognizable function or purpose, such as an aide-mémoire or the notes of the journalist planning a report.[18] It is customary to distinguish sub-classes of diaries on this kind of pragmatic or functional basis; however, since the diary is able to turn itself to any number of purposes, the effort to classify – necessarily predictive – is inevitably inadequate to its task. The idea of a project is offered as an alternative. To this end, I stress the singularity of the responsiveness of any diary to the perpetually modified engagement of the diarist with the world of her or his experience. As the note taking becomes more selective, more preoccupied, as the record keeping becomes more urgent, as the diarist envisages the possibility that life may end prematurely, she or he comes to envisage the possibility that keeping this record may be their only future-directed undertaking, the only projection of the self beyond the present. Then the writing of the diary takes on the quality of a project, telling its own story pervasively across the entries. I read the projects of two individual diaries in chapters 2 and 3, whereas chapters 1 and 4 rely on selected entries from a variety of diaries.

The focus on identity rests on the observation that the personal and collective history of the Jews of France was severely disrupted by a crisis in their sense of belonging. I study the *experience* of that disruption in everyday life. What were the events that effected it, and what reflections on those events do we find in the diaries?

These questions require a preliminary discussion of the term 'assimilated' and its opposite, 'foreign': this is a highly charged distinction. Although 'assimilated' is sometimes used for a class distinguished from foreign Jews – and hence used to political ends – assimilation is more properly considered an intergenerational process. The writers of the diaries I consider span this process; some came from families established in France for several generations, while others had migrated in the early decades of the twentieth century, or their families had done so. People in this latter category were assimilated in the minimal technical sense that they were citizens of France. Whether from the former or the latter group, whether speaking French from birth or as a second language, all wrote in French and hence envisaged a French-speaking readership.

The logic of assimilation had been fostered by the Napoleonic policy under which not only were Jews granted full citizenship, but they were also expected to assimilate to the point of invisibility.[19] Yet the very notion of assimilation was ruled out by the Vichy laws, which classed as exclusively Jewish everyone who had previously enjoyed this status, making them all too visible and depriving them of their rights as citizens of the French Republic. This book is about the consequences of this policy for a small number of Jews, who, because they wrote about them, can be taken to speak for the large number of others who did not. These consequences directly affected their material living conditions, their friendships, their professional activities, their political choices, and their daily lives; they affected how they lived through the years of the Occupation and how they envisaged the future; and they caused great physical suffering, sometimes unto death. The experience of these consequences is the matter of their diaries and is investigated in chapters 1 to 4.

The Vichy laws tore asunder two parts of the assimilated identity – French and Jewish – provoking in some cases a conflict between them and an inner struggle to integrate them in some alternative resolution. For this reason, 'identity' turns out to be a key problem in the diaries. The term 'identity' slips easily into contemporary discourse; it slips even more easily out of precise conceptual grasp. This is partly due to the presupposition that it is some 'thing' or essence that lies at the core of a self. My argument against this presupposition will be elaborated in chapter 1. Instead, I consider identities to be the provisional outcomes of events and practices of identification. It follows that these events can be narrated; accordingly, chapter 1, 'Narratives of Identity,' tells stories of these events. An experience of identification occurs when what happens to form or to assault the person's place in society enters the space of the reflective self. This formulation follows from the discussion of 'experience' above. The diary is a privileged genre for exploring this process. Constitutively written in the first person, a diary is a practice of the self, whether its focus is introspective or turned outward. Read chronologically, a diary tells the story of the self through time and in history. If particular entries recount particular experiences of identification, then the series can be read for their progressive accumulation, and their upshot in what is commonly called identity. Yet, day by day, experience by experience, diaries display the paradox of identity: contingencies make and unmake what we fondly believe to be the core of our being. Diaries invite us to study identity, at the same time as opening up the very notion of 'identity' to critique and interrogation. This leads me to prefer the term 'self' to that of 'identity' in the following chapters, in which I study the social place of a person (chapter 2) and the maintenance of the bodily self (chapter 3). These issues take us well beyond the categories of belonging and exclusion that arise under 'identity.'[20]

If the crisis of identity referred to above deprived the Jews of France of their place in French society, what is a self without a place to be itself? Chapter 2, 'The Place of the Self,' studies the diary of Raymond-Raoul Lambert. Losing his place, he invented a substitute, in a defiant but doomed project to maintain a public self that could influence for the better the fate of his fellow Jews. Lambert's diary discloses the gradual but inevitable drama of his failure. This story is usually told as an episode in the public history of French Jewry; in the diary, it is the story of a man's experience. I have appropriated the motto he adopted for his struggle – *tenir et durer*[21] (holding on and holding out) – for the title of this book.

Time is a condition of possibility of experience, hence of the processes of formation, adaptation, maintenance, and indeed disintegration of the self.[22] Lambert's motto is equally apposite for a quite different kind of struggle – that of Benjamin Schatzman, interned for eight months in French concentration camps. In his diary, Schatzman writes almost exclusively of the processes that undermined his health and the tactics he adopted for physical survival. This struggle is the topic of chapter 3, 'Making It Last.' It is commonly said that selfhood is reduced to a suffering body by the brutality of conditions such as these; however, the reflective practice of a diary supports a shift to agency. In Schatzman's diary, we read a self who draws on all its resources to care for itself.

Presupposed in experience, time is not merely transparent to some other phenomenal content; it, too, can be an object reflected on and known. The writers of these diaries are necessarily the products of their accumulated past experience, yet they have landed in times for which that experience has not prepared them. With exceptions, it is rare for them to recall their past. They are confined in the present, the 'now,' which William James represents as having 'a prow and a stern.'[23] What is 'now' when the sum of previous experience is all but irrelevant, and plans are unable to be made? This is the topic of chapter 4, 'Narratives of Time.' Again, the formal conventions of the diary, with its punctual entries, written sequentially over time, each referring to more or less short spans, make it the privileged genre for exploring the experience of time. Furthermore, in the circumstances recorded by these diaries, continuity is the burning question: neither does life continue as it always has, nor can life be predicted to continue beyond today. Yet in these diaries, we come to know resistance against the forces of discontinuity and disaggregation, and persistence toward some future – 'survival' is the better term. Whether or not the writer survived the carnage, the long-term survival of the text depends upon us, its readers. These diaries are acts of witness; they enjoin on us 'the responsibility to be responsive'; in their afterlife, they 'are sites of discursive interchange' in which our role is both to mourn and to continue the authorial project.[24] Hence my title: *Holding On and Holding Out* – for one more day, one more entry, and for a reader.

Chapter One

Narratives of Identity

Une identité n'est jamais donnée, reçue ou atteinte, non, seul s'endure le processus interminable, indéfiniment phantasmatique, de l'identification.

Identity is never given, received, or reached, no, there is nothing but the interminably long-suffered process of identification, inconclusive, phantasmatic
— Jacques Derrida, *Le monolinguisme de l'autre*

Introduction: The Experience of Identity

Brought up and educated under the ideals of the secular republic, or drawn to them in their decision to immigrate and seek citizenship, French Jews were faced in 1940 with what we would now call a problem of identity. Their bond with France was shaken, if not shattered, by the advent of anti-Semitic policies initiated by the Vichy government, modelled on those of Germany. Under the *Statut des Juifs*, they were considered primarily as Jews, rather than as French people.[1] In the terms of the discourses current in France at the time, universalist assumptions were no longer available to them, nationalist assumptions were foreclosed, and they were stigmatized by the opprobrium of particularism. How did they experience this manipulation of their allegiances? With fear, self-evidently, and rarely effective adjustments of their living arrangements; sometimes they responded with disbelief and a naive faith in the willingness and ability of 'France' to protect their rights as humans and as French nationals. Some found it deeply offensive; some fled, some joined the Resistance, and some looked to their Jewish background for a sense of belonging no longer available from elsewhere. For all, it was dramatic, not only because of the threats to life and limb that it entailed, but also because it shook to the core their understanding of their place in the world. Following

Derrida's admonition (above), I shall argue that their place in the world was established, and hence undermined, by *experiences of identification.*

Their place in the world had been defined by the Enlightenment ideals of the secular republic under which religion was deemed to be an entirely private affair, and the relationship of individuals to France was defined by their citizenship. The principles underpinning the constitution of the successive republics countenanced no group allegiance, whether falling outside or contained within the nation. The history of the term 'identity' in France should be understood in this context. Before the war, identity had not been a topic of discussion; the word, with the acceptation we now attach to it, was barely used, except for such things as identity papers and other official documents, where the mention of one's nationality was mandatory; but this is the administrative use of 'identity,' the term and the concept. However, for a small proportion of the French population between 1940 and 1944, identity papers, ration cards, and the outer clothing all had to carry the term 'Juif'; this status supervened over their nationality. Jews who had acquired French citizenship after 1927 had their naturalization rescinded.[2] Furthermore, the *Statut des Juifs* of 1940, and its revision of 1941, did not distinguish between French-born Jews and immigrant Jews;[3] in practice, this assimilated the former to the latter. The native-born Jewish population found this failure to distinguish them from more recent arrivals deeply offensive, sometimes insisting on the distinction on nationalist and xenophobic grounds.[4] If anti-Semitism represents a grouping called 'the Jews,' the *statut* – along with parallels elsewhere in Europe – transformed this representation into the conditions of legal and administrative action, with real consequences on the social organization of persons and their relations with each other and the state. The 'J' label entailed origin and destiny, restrictions on behaviour and activity, on property rights and professional status, on the use of city spaces and public transport, on access to goods and services; and it underpinned the right of others to behave toward Jewish people outside the standard social norms and indeed the laws that applied with respect to the general population.

Grouping and labelling these people, placing them outside the reach of French law and subjecting them to the 'laws of exception,' conferred on them an 'identity': this fact – this event or series of events – determines all further experience of the self for the writers of the diaries I discuss. For this reason, my first step is to investigate 'identity.' In order to do so, however, I am bound by the confusions besetting this topic to engage in a theoretical aside.

It is generally acknowledged that the earliest use of 'identity' as a technical term of psychology appears in the work of Erik Erikson, and that it converged with the problematic of identification in anthropology and sociology.[5] Identity, following Erikson, is a matter internal to the individual, whereas 'the sociologists ... tend to view identity as an artefact of interaction between the individual and society.'[6] For this reason, sociologists preferred the term 'identification,' implying 'a process, continuously created and re-created ... held together by the slender thread of memory.'[7] Evidently, the premises of the psychology-inspired tradition of theory are less appropriate for understanding the socio-political experience of identification of the Jews of Europe than are the sociological premises, so it is the latter that will direct my analyses.

It is unhelpful that the convergence of the two traditions has resulted in a convergence of terminology, and that, despite the relative clarity of the term 'identification,' the expression 'the sociology of identity' has become usual. The North American account of the sociology of identity derives from philosophic Pragmatism, from C.S. Peirce, for whom the individual and society – and indeed, the world at large – are bundles of habits interacting with one another, resisting one another, or modifying one another on occasion. This idea was taken up and developed by G.H. Mead.[8] It is a significant counter to the essentialist assumptions that sometimes underpin the psychological accounts of identity. In it, the self is 'active, multiplex and changeable.'[9] Accordingly, it pervades the background of Erving Goffman's account of self-presentation.[10] Both Goffman and Erikson were working in the same period, with the groundwork for each account published in the 1950s. Goffman analyses self-presentation in terms of a theatrical framework. Human life is theatre, 'with front stage and backstage areas, props, sets, audiences, and teams of performers ... The parts are learned through emulation and identification with parents and peers.'[11] Under this analogy, a 'performance' may be defined as all the activity of a given participant on a given occasion that serves to influence in any way any of the other participants.[12] Goffman's work is open to criticism in important respects, but it is heuristically useful in the description of the everyday behaviours that constitute the self. I shall therefore draw on it, modifying it – particularly in light of the work of Judith Butler – in my discussion of some of the stories in chapter 1.[13] Starting with stories of acts and practices of identification, I move to others in which behaviours of self-presentation are more prominent.

There is another reason for my decision to opt for a sociologically oriented account of the self rather than a psychological account of identity, with its reliance on interiority. When the two kinds of theory converged in the mid-century, they revived the topic of ethnic identity. This occurred with the reciprocal influence of Margaret Mead's work on national character and Erikson's theorization of the relation between 'ego identity' and 'group identity.'[14] Identity, Erikson writes, is sometimes understood as 'a conscious sense of individual identity,' sometimes as 'personal character,' sometimes as 'ego synthesis,' and sometimes as 'the inner solidarity with a group's ideals and identity.'[15] These formulations are nothing if not tautologous, but they also point to the conceptual problem at the heart of theories of, or appeals to, identity. Not only does the term's history show the convergence of different theoretical traditions and the confusions that arise therefrom; not only, as has argued Vincent Descombes, does the notion of collective identity betray an unwarranted analogy between a community and a person;[16] but the Eriksonian view of identity is tainted with the same assumptions as those that inspired Nazi racism.

'Identity' is also a problem of language: the nominal form reifies it, requiring that it be located, and tending toward its essentialization. Hence, though stated by Erikson to be a psychic *process*, it is, or is to be found in, the inner core of an individual, and is 'an essential aspect of a group's inner coherence';[17] this 'thing' is 'located *in the core of the individual* and yet also *in the core of his communal culture*, a process which establishes, in fact, the identity of those two identities.'[18] These are dubious assumptions, providing further reason to focus on the verb – to identify – whether used in the first person, as the claim *to* an identity, or in the second person, as the attribution *of* an identity *to* someone else.

The stories in this chapter are arranged in two sets: the first comprises narratives of identification in which a 'we' is constituted or dissolved, asserted or denied, challenged or consolidated. The second set comprises narratives of performance, where identity is a praxis, a way of being in the world.

A Pronoun Tells Its Stories: 'We'

Whereas we may think of 'identity' as that which is proper to an individual, 'identification' does not occur within, or affect, an isolated 'I': it is relational. Spoken by a first person, 'we' identifies the speaker with a group and dissociates that group from others: 'my identity is my identification with those with whom I say we.' This is so regardless of the grouping from which it is spoken: for example, the Nazis constituted the Aryan race by expelling from it Jews (and others), thus, as Valentin Feldman writes,[19] giving shape to a heretofore disparate 'Jewish community' and thereby creating the conditions of a new 'we,' contested or adopted as the case may be.

The stories in the next three sections of this chapter exemplify a range of responses among Jewish people in France to the conditions created by the *Statut des Juifs*. In all of them, 'we' is the site of what Derrida refers to as 'identity trouble.'[20] One is an escapee, one is an internee, one is a resistance activist. Within the general framework of Nazi and Vichy anti-Semitism, they experience this trouble variously, representing it and responding to it accordingly.

Léo Lania

Born in Ukraine but settled in Vienna and subsequently Germany, an assimilated Jew, journalist, screen writer, and left-wing intellectual, Léo Lania fled following the Nazi takeover in 1933 and took refuge in France. Like many German and Austrian political dissidents and Jews in France, he was interned as an enemy alien during the Phoney War. With a group of friends, he escaped from the camp, eventually crossing the demarcation line between Nazi-occupied France and the so-called Free Zone. This is what he writes in his memoir of this period:

> We had been living in false hopes [...] There – under German rule – we could count on the help of the French people [...] With them, we formed a common front against the Nazis. We were not alone.
> Here, in 'free' France, we were again enemies. We were subjected to special laws, constantly threatened with arrest and internment. And now our persecutors were Frenchmen.[21]

A line, of the most arbitrary kind, separates France into two spaces, organizing the territory into two regimes of control. Under these two regimes, people, ordinary people, manifest quite different anxieties about their self-interest. 'There,' the French people could be relied on for help, the loan of bicycles, gifts of food, guidance as to safe routes through the countryside, shelter, and medical attention; 'here,' no such support was forthcoming. Its opposite was more than probable. 'We were again enemies' writes Lania, whereas 'there,' we counted as friends. The line, a geographical line between one group of French people and another, changes who these escapees are in relation to 'the French.'

If Lania and his friends had imagined that by crossing into the Southern Zone they were crossing into freedom, they were quickly disabused. They had crossed into the Vichy-controlled zone and were therefore subject to an anti-Semitic and xenophobic regime the equal of the one they had fled in 1933. Not only they, but anyone offering them help, was subject to arrest. In this respect, the line of demarcation made no difference to their prospects at all. Indeed, it was drawn on nationalist lines, between the German occupation and a simulacrum of French sovereignty, and nationalist sentiment was not helpful for a fleeing for-eign Jew. Repeating, so to speak, the gesture of fleeing into the France of their political ideals, they discovered a different France.

The 'I' of writing speaks for the little group of escapees; the question is where 'we' stands in relation to 'them.' It would be tempting to think of the line of demarcation as a metaphor for categorization and othering, but this is approximate at best. The escapees are 'othered' on both sides of the line – on one side by the Germans, on the other by the French. What happens in this case is that 'the French' themselves are othered, or not, by the Germans, and this changes the relational dynamic. On one side of this line, 'we' is joined with the French to form 'a common front' – 'we were not alone.' On the other side, 'we' is disjoined from the French, is excluded from this grouping, and flees in fear of persecution from it: 'we were again enemies.'

'We' is a complex pronoun. Its function is rarely confined to the plu-ral of 'I,' sometimes including an addressee ('I' and 'you'), sometimes including 'they.' Lania's story recounts a point of trouble concerning exactly this issue: in the Occupied Zone, 'we' is set to expand to include 'they': we were not alone; we formed a common front. In the 'Free Zone,' 'we' has no such potential.

Identification occurs at the point where 'I' joins with a group to speak and act as 'we.' 'We' is de-constituted at the same point, where a disjoin-ing such as we read in this story operates a further identification. The potential for a larger, more inclusive 'we' is cut off at the line of demar-cation. This effect is positional and provisional.

Nevertheless, the story is more complex than the pronominal usage that results from it. If we posit the unspoken 'we' on the other side of the equation, we must ask why the escapees met with hostility. What was it about them that identified them as a danger for the French of the Southern Zone? What is it about crossing this line that makes the common lot – the Occupation with its attendant threat – unrecogniz-able as common? While I do not discount self-interest as a factor, let me speculate that it has to do with the symbolic charge associated with crossing a boundary. Lania and his comrades had crossed two bound-aries, the first fleeing the Nazis in their homelands, the second from north to south in France. They will be refugees for years following this, or dead, or arrested anew. Time and again in these stories we will find references to 'wanderers,' 'foreigners,' and *apatrides* – stateless peo-ple – the last term was to become official parlance after the war. These terms evoke the wandering Jew, but the issue is more acute than refer-ence to a mythic status would suggest. The person with no homeland is not merely uprooted, she or he is 'rootless,' the precise opposite of the fascist/nationalist account of what it is to be 'native': rooted in the soil, in a language, in a culture, in a nation. By definition divested of such rootedness, having no homeland, boundary crossers have no identity, least of all 'here,' among 'us.' Wanderers with no 'identity' (in this sense) are a danger for a settled group, because 'we' don't know how to 'place' them, or where.

This view is amply borne out in my next story, in which an assimilated French Jew works vigorously to dissociate himself from the 'foreign Jews' with whom the *Statut des Juifs* identifies him. His discourse is that of xenophobic France; the voice he adopts is itself an act of identification with the French population, from which, as he puts it, the *statut* had torn him. Published following the Liberation, addressed principally to other assimilated French Jews and to the non-Jewish French population (blame falls squarely on the Germans, not on the Vichy government), it is also, no doubt, an act of fealty.

Jean-Jacques Bernard

The first memoir of internment in the French camps was written by Jean-Jacques Bernard, a prominent playwright of the mid-century, and son of Tristan Bernard, who had also been prominent in the world of the theatre.[22] I stress that, like Lania's, this is a memoir, not a diary. It therefore lacks the dimension of experience through time that will be my principal focus. Nevertheless, it is a precious if disquieting document, serving to demonstrate the poverty of the discourses of identity available to French Jews of the period, thus showing *a contrario* the inventiveness of those individuals who worked around, beyond, or on, this range, rather than being confined within it. Bernard's memoir proclaims an identity that does not shift one iota during, or as a result of, his experiences.[23]

Bernard was arrested on 12 December 1941 in what is known as the *rafle des notables* (the round-up of prominent people). The Nazis had demanded a thousand Jewish arrests in reprisal for an attack on some German officers, but the French authorities were able to find only 732; they made up the numbers with internees from Drancy camp. The notables were the very paragon of the professionally successful assimilated population; the Drancéens were mainly 'foreign.' The 732 'French' included men from the pre-war political elite as well as university professors, engineers, dentists, and judges; there were some lawyers, but many of these had been rounded up and sent to Drancy in August of that year. The Paris bar was rid of its Jewish members through these two operations.[24] Bernard notes how many of the Compiègne internees knew one another, and how surprised he was to discover that one or another of them was Jewish. Of this group Bernard notes:

> tous ces hommes étaient restés volontairement à Paris, ayant pesé les risques: [...] J'entrevis ce jour ce qui fut la grande constatation de mon internement: c'est que, chez la presque totalité de ces Français, aucun sentiment de race n'existait. Ils se jugeaient atteints comme Français et uniquement comme Français.[25]

> having weighed up the risks, all these men had stayed in Paris deliberately: [...] that day [the first] I glimpsed the general truth that was confirmed during my internment: this is that these Frenchmen had no sense of race. They felt that they had been attacked as Frenchmen, and solely as Frenchmen.

I note the use of the term 'Français,' the name of a nationality; in this apparently unremarkable passage, Bernard contrasts it with 'un sentiment de race.' Indeed, throughout his text, Bernard is incapable of conceptualizing the problem of identity outside the opposition between nation and race. It is noteworthy that, when a certain Mme Aronson wrote to him about his book, she insisted on 'race' as the criterion for his arrest:

> Dans le camp de la mort lente il n'y avait que des gens appartenant à ce que les racistes appellent LA RACE JUIVE. Il y avait dans ce camp des gens de tous les pays, déjà ou pas encore assimilés, des intellectuels ou des artisans et des industriels, des bons et des mauvais, mais tous appartenant à la même RACE. (Annexe – 'Correspondance avec ses lecteurs,' 296)

> No-one was in the camp of drawn-out death save those belonging to what the racists dub THE JEWISH RACE. There were people of every nationality, some already and some not yet assimilated, intellectuals and manual workers and industrialists, good people and bad, but all belonging to the same RACE.

Bernard's insistence on nationality simply missed the point, she wrote (294); the internees were a multi-national group whose members, at different stages of assimilation, were all treated alike. But Bernard cannot acknowledge that assimilation is a process. One was born French, or not; there were 'the French' and the others. In his second response to this correspondent, he claims that it was she who had missed this point: 'Je ne crois pas que vous puissiez imaginer ce que fut le sursaut national des Français de Compiègne devant la volonté allemande d'arrachement. C'est là-dessus que j'ai voulu mettre l'accent' (298; I do not believe that you can imagine the shock of national indignation among the French at Compiègne at the German determination to tear us out. That's the point I wanted to stress). Note the word 'arracher' (to tear out): it is a violent action, somewhat like uprooting. We were being torn from the nation. For this reason, Mme Aronson's point is indeed entirely lost on Bernard; it is beyond him to understand that 'nation' is no more natural, no deeper, than race.

The issue she grasps, and that he fails to understand, is that 'nationality' is acquired, cultural identity is learned, and 'race' was the central concept of the Nazi discourse. For him, 'race' is a fiction because, as he puts it, he found no trace among his fellow internees of 'un type juif caractérisé, au sens où on l'entend généralement' (42; of a Jewish type, in the sense in which it is generally meant). He means genetically determined physical racial characteristics. The only kind of collective identity he recognizes is national. Further, it is significant that he blames the Germans for tearing these people from the national fabric. We know from many sources that the distinction between 'French' Jews and 'foreign' Jews was home-grown, and that it operated as a formal category in Vichy policy throughout the Occupation.[26] Bernard's difficulty in acknowledging French responsibility in this matter is tellingly characteristic (67–8), not only of a certain proportion of assimilated Jews under the Occupation who persisted in believing, in the face of the evidence, that an increasingly powerless Vichy government could or would protect them, but also of the subsequent difficulty the French showed in acknowledging the role of the Vichy authorities in the persecution.[27]

Bernard's whole discourse is dominated by his claim to innate identity, based on his identification with where he was born; this is what he means by French 'national identity.' It serves as a kind of bedrock for him and determines his incapacity to include himself with the 'foreign' Jews in the camp in the pronoun 'we.' The materiality and consequentiality of 'race,' however, is that it could be posited and produced discursively, through a logic of birth and lineage, through legislation, police and paramilitary powers, and a sophisticated administrative apparatus.[28] Not understanding this, Bernard's memoir relies on an ontology opposing his 'inner' identification, which he considers as the truth, and these identifications from the outside whose reality he persists in denying. The first response of many to a summons or visit from the German authorities was often similar to Bernard's: 'Que voulaient-ils?' he wondered. 'Perquisition? Arrestation? J'avais souvent pensé à de telles éventualités. *Je n'y croyais pourtant pas beaucoup. On ne pouvait rien alléguer contre moi*' (28, emphasis added; What were they here for? A search? Or an arrest? I had often thought about some such eventuality, *but I didn't believe in it much. There was nothing they could allege against me*). Likewise, many were simply perplexed, thinking that perhaps they had been picked up in error; and many, like him, thought they would be protected by some legality, their nationality,[29] or their war record: 'On avait fait récemment un recensement des anciens combattants juifs, un autre recensement où l'on avait *séparé les Français des étrangers*. Tout cela *nous* donnait une assurance peut-être précaire, mais une assurance pourtant' (28, emphasis added; Lately there had been a census of Jewish returned soldiers, and another *separating French from foreign Jews*. All this reassured *us* somewhat, albeit no doubt with little certainty).

These Vichy administrative categories – more honoured in the breach than in the observance – correspond to his own, so he believes them: Bernard's 'we' is confined to French Jews who had fought for France. Nevertheless, he does have a sense of what he calls 'une âme collective' (53), uniting 'tous ces hommes' in the solidarity of internment; but this 'human we' quickly divides along national lines. Observing that the *notables* were a very homogeneous group, Bernard believed he could speak for them all collectively – until the Drancéens arrived. At that point, 'we' is sorely troubled. For Bernard, the difference between the two groups is that the Central European Jews believed in a 'Jewish community,' whereas the French did not. In the following passages, it is worth pausing to consider his use of the terms 'community' and 'society'; both are contrasted with the implied 'nation':

> Les *étrangers* transférés de Drancy étaient presque tous des Juifs d'Europe centrale, des apatrides qui, chassés de leur pays, étaient venus demander l'hospitalité de la France, mais gardaient au fond du coeur *le sentiment d'une communauté juive*. Ce sentiment était généralement inconnu et même repoussé de la plupart des *Français* arrêtés avec moi. (66, emphasis added)

> The *foreigners* transferred from Drancy were almost all Jews from central Europe, stateless people who had been driven from their countries and who had sought hospitality from France. Nevertheless, deep in their hearts they nursed *the idea of a Jewish community*. Generally, this idea was unknown to the French people arrested with me, or was even rejected by them.

In this respect, the non-French Jews are doing the Germans' work:

> Le but des Allemands était clair: on arrête sept cents Français, on les mêle à trois cents étrangers; on brasse ces mille hommes et on a un embryon de *société juive*. Si ce dessein machiavélique trouva un écho naturel chez les Juifs d'Europe centrale – et comment en aurions-*nous* voulu à ces malheureux de se raccrocher à ce phantasme? – , il n'éveilla chez *les Français* que refus,

indignation ou révolte [...] Tout ce qui tendait à *nous écarter* de la communauté française nous blessait. (66, emphasis added)

The aim of the Germans was clear: take seven hundred Frenchmen, stir
them in with three hundred foreigners, mix the thousand together, and
you have the embryo of a Jewish society. It was a Machievellian scheme; if
it naturally appealed to the central European Jews – how could we hold
it against these unfortunate people if they clung to this phantasy? – it was
met with rejection, indignation, and revolt among the French [...] We were
injured by anything that could set us apart from the French community.

The *nous* that emerges in this passage is motivated by the 'revolt'
against identification with a group of 'foreigners': we were French; we
refused the device that tore us from the French community. It is as if
any identification with the foreign Jews would reinforce the logic of
their arrest: Bernard resists this with a force equal to, and deriving from,
his impotence against it. Note that he does not so much as notice the
implications of the word *apatrides*. As Mme Aronson was to point out to
him, these people were Czech, Polish, Russian, Hungarian, or Turkish
nationals: foreigners, he implies through his oversight, they were primarily Jewish; they identified, so he claims, with a 'Jewish community.'
If they were foreign, they were Jews, and, if Jews, they were foreign. The
anti-Semitic gesture creates the Semitic collective, defining who could be
excluded from it. Bernard repeats this logic: slipping seamlessly from a
'Jewish community' to a 'Jewish society' and then to a 'Jewish nation' –
and hence from an informal grouping to the spectre of Zionism and
a nation based, as he thinks, on race – this is an 'arbitrary creation,' a
phantasy shared by these unhappy people, and emphatically not by 'us.'
'We' are French nationals, 'nés et élevés en climat français, avec tout ce
que ce climat comporte de tradition latine et même chrétienne' (66;
born and bred in French climes, with the Latin and even the Christian
tradition that comes with it). Maurice Goudeket, husband of the writer
Colette, and interned in the same round-up, applauded Bernard for this
sentiment in the letter he sent in acknowledgement of the book: 'Je ne
sépare pas l'amour profond que j'ai de ce pays d'une sorte d'adoption
du catholicisme' (Annexe, 276; I cannot separate the deep love I have of
this country from a kind of adoption of Catholicism). I am less interested
here in the adoption of Catholicism than in Bernard's expulsion from,
we might say, his national heart of any possibility of identification with
the foreigners. To his close confidants he declares, 'il est bien entendu
que, si je devais périr dans cette aventure, je serais mort pour la France;
je ne veux pas être revendiqué comme victime par le judaïsme' (66; it

goes without saying that if I should perish in this mishap, I would have died for France; I do not wish to be a victim claimed by Judaism as one of its own). *Mort pour la France* – the supreme patriotic status.

Stressing that the internees were united in their common suffering by 'la fraternité humaine' (67; human brotherhood), Bernard juggles with three terms – race, nation, and the universal – 'refus de solidarité sur le plan juif, solidarité sur le plan humain' (110; rejection of solidarity at the Jewish level, solidarity on the human level). Under a standard republican discursive regime, 'race' must be discounted as particularist. Bernard's arrest among seven hundred of his ilk was a crime against Frenchness, not a crime against humanity (a legal category that, of course, had yet to be created):

On comprendra que, sur le plan juif, un fossé se soit presque instantément creusé. Leur acceptation, ou plus exactement leur appel du judaïsme, leur aspiration vers la nation juive nous paraissaient aller exactement dans le sens de la volonté allemande, heurtaient dans ses fibres les plus profondes *notre attachement ancestral* à la France. (67, emphasis added)

My readers will understand the gulf that opened up in the domain of Jewishness. Their acceptance of Judaism or, more precisely, their call to it, their yearning for a Jewish nation, seemed to us to go in exactly the same direction as the German will, offending *our ancestral attachment* to France at its deepest.

Un fossé – a gulf: it is much deeper than a 'line.' Whereas 'they' 'aspire' to a Jewish nation, 'we' are ancestrally attached to the French one. I note the word 'ancestral,' which will be used by Jacqueline Mesnil-Amar to opposite effect. In both cases, it gestures to an identity story attaching the individual to an imagined past, locating him or her among others, allowing the 'I' to give 'we' a substance beyond the local and occasional.

Let me return briefly to Bernard's collapsing of a Jewish 'community' into a Jewish 'nation.' Nazism had created a Jewish identity, and belonging to it was a terrible thing. The threat is experienced by Bernard on two levels. First, there is the physical and emotional misery of arrest and internment. Second, there is the matter of grouping: with no sense of belonging with his 'foreign' co-religionists, being treated as one of them is, for him, as we have seen, an 'uprooting'; indeed, this is the title ('L'Arrachement') of the first chapter of his memoir. Does he even count as French?[30] Taken together with the Zionist view that the establishment of a Jewish state was the only solution for the Jews of Europe, this threat underlies both the telescoping of a Jewish 'community' with a Jewish 'society' and then 'nation,' and the intense rejection of this

rationale that we read in Bernard. In one sense, he is right. In the early
days of Nazi rule in Germany, and of the occupation of France and
other countries, ethnic cleansing took the form of forced evacuation
of diasporic Jews and their concentration in some geographical region
elsewhere. If Zionism could count as the project of shelter and refuge
for persecuted Jews all over Europe, it could also count as a geopolit-
ical solution for getting them out of the way. A certain Kadmi Cohen,
interned in Compiègne at the same time as Bernard, went on (in 1943)
to mount a case to the effect that the Vichy regime should support the
Zionist project because the establishment of a Jewish state would contribute directly to the realization of the government's aims.[31] Prior to that, in
1942, Xavier Vallat (commissioner for Jewish affairs) considered a proposal that there should be 'an international agreement defining Jewish
nationality, locating Jews in their own state somewhere, and conceding
to those who chose to be left behind only the status of foreigner.' He
remarked that 'it will be the victor's business, if he intends to organize a
durable peace, to find the means, worldwide if possible, European in any
case, to settle the wandering Jew.'[32]

Zionism as a solution for each side of this deadly dispute? God forbid.
Yet here we have the prospect of the 'wandering Jew,' the archetypal
boundary-crosser, finally 'rooted,' albeit somewhere else. Bernard was
by no means the only Jewish intellectual to argue against Zionism on
these grounds. For Victor Klemperer, Zionism and National Socialism
sprang from the same source in Romantic political philosophy,[33] and
many took a position against Zionism in order to argue for the dignity of diaspora Jewry. Not so Bernard, who was caught on the horns
of the dilemma constituted by opposing 'nation' to 'race' and then
discounting the latter in the name of universalism – as did his cousin,
Jacques Ancel, a historian, who gave a talk in the camp on 'the formation of the idea of a nation.' At the end of it, a member of the audience
asked him what he thought about 'a Jewish nation.' Ancel's reply was
'coupante et catégorique: "Il n'y a pas de nation juive!"' (108; categor-
ical and trenchant: 'there is no Jewish nation!'); he was applauded by
the majority of his listeners. Ancel's answer was, writes Bernard, 'un
réconfort pour nos coeurs français' (ibid.; comforting for our French
hearts). When one of his co-internees responds to this event by saying
'nous ne sommes Juifs qu'à partir du moment où on nous le reproche'
(111; we are Jews only when they besmirch us with it), it could have led
to an understanding of the politics of identity; but Bernard thinks of
this comment as a 'réaction sentimentale, purement humaine' (ibid.;
a sentimental, purely human reaction), meaning, I imagine, that it
is not based on a well-thought-out theory of nationhood such as the

one expounded by Ancel. Some time later, in the infirmary, Bernard engages in conversation with a Turkish boy, 'un jeune garcon aux yeux vifs, au type oriental bien marqué ... Ce Juif-là avait quelque chose de musulman. N'était-ce pas naturel? Mais qu'on parle après cela de nation juive!' (168; a bright-eyed young boy, very oriental looking ... One might have taken this Jew for a Muslim. No surprise in that. And then they talk about a Jewish nation!). Here 'race' is marked by a physical type; a 'nation' would purportedly be based on racial homogeneity. We recall his first assessment of the mass of men arrested with him, the homogeneity of their appearance indicating for him that there was no physical type that marked the Jews (42).

In order to keep the peace in Compiègne, the French Jews had made a rule to the effect that all 'delicate issues' be avoided in public conversation, but this Turk was a newcomer, and he did not know:

> Et que disait ce musulman ... Du moins, ce Turc? ... Il disait avec une ironie provocante: 'Ah! Ne cherchez donc pas, nous sommes des Juifs, des Juifs, des Juifs!' [...] Me dressant sur mon lit, je criai avec force: 'C'est faux. Nous n'acceptons pas cela. Nous sommes ici des Français, et rien d'autre. Nous ne sommes pas des Juifs, mais des Français. (169)

> And what did he have to say, this Muslim ... this Turk, rather? With provocative irony, he said: 'What do you imagine? We're Jews, Jews, Jews!' [...] I rose up in my bed and shouted: 'That's wrong. We don't accept that. We're French and nothing else. We are not Jews, we're French.'

Bernard was somewhat contrite about his outburst to the Turk, not for its content but for its tone. But this tone – evident in some of the other anecdotes concerning the same problem – betrays the intensity of a personal investment in refusing to count as a Jew.[34] When, after the war, Bernard converted to Catholicism, he proclaimed himself 'un Juif chrétien' (Annexe, 293; a Christian Jew); nothing during this period of crisis enables him to say that he was 'un Français juif' (a Jewish Frenchman). The gulf had been dug: one or the other, but not both. 'La véritable solidarité des Français de Royallieu s'établit donc sur une dénégation, sur un refus' (111; The true solidarity of the French at Compiègne was based on a denial, a refusal): 'Nous ne sommes pas Juifs' (we are not Jews).[35]

The complexities of Jewish social assimilation could be lived in other ways. There were French Jews for whom, as Mihaïl Sebastian writes, being Jewish was not a position from which one could resign.[36] My next story shows the opposite of Bernard's rejection – identification with an ancestral, rather than a national, 'we.'

Jacqueline Mesnil-Amar

Born to a prominent assimilated Jewish family, Jacqueline Mesnil-Amar, like other *résistants*, did not keep a diary of her militant activities. The dangers of leaving a paper trail are all too evident. However, in 1944, her husband was arrested, and it was then, on 18 July, when the Liberation was all but certain, that she started to write.[37] Sometimes addressed to her husband, the diary recalls more detail of her resistance activities than would have been possible in a diary written earlier in the Occupation. In a passage written on 6 August 1944, she evokes the period of the capitulation: there were former friends of her father's, whom she had once known as his dinner guests, now finding their way in the politics of Vichy, and there was 'cette débâcle de mon coeur, cette déroute de ma vie' (52; this collapse, this rout of my heart and my life).[38] There follow some brief and moving portraits of notable people, then this shocking question: 'Et souvent je me demandais: "Mes amis me protégeront-ils de mes ancêtres?"' (53; And I wondered frequently if my friends would protect me from my ancestors).

The question is virtually anti-Semitic in its assumptions, as if the latter – the ancestors – were the very source of the danger from which her friends would save her. With whom could she identify? Certainly not, at this stage, with her Jewish heritage. In this passage, the word 'friends' refers to the older generation of power and influence – 'sénateurs, députés, journalistes' – (52; senators and members of the house, journalists). She is evoking a period four years prior to the time at which she writes (54); the context of the sentiment is the beginning of the Occupation, and we should read it accordingly. Writing at the end of that period, Mesnil-Amar *quotes* her question, to show the identity work done in the intervening years. In the same entry, she asks: 'En cette première nuit d'espérance, pourquoi surtout se rappeler ... le reste? Le drame que nous avons vécu, heure après heure, jour après jour, le drame des Juifs, le nôtre, le mien' (55; Why, on this first night of hope, should I remember ... the rest? The drama that we have lived through, hour after hour, day after day, the drama of the Jews, our drama, mine). Note the insistence on *nous*, and on 'my' place in it. She sums up the process she has been through as follows:

L'obsession juive prenant le pas sur l'obsession française en dépit de nous-mêmes, creusant sa plaie secrète, travaillant lentement, insidieusement, laissant sa profonde érosion sous la chair, dans nos âmes, faisant peu à peu de nous ces espèces d' 'étrangers' dans leur pays, ces Français 'différents,' furtifs, trop modestes, ou braqués, toujours à vif, ces gens à part,

instables et mouvants, sans travail, sans poste, liés entre eux par les liens
inavouables de la complicité et de la peur. (55)

Despite ourselves, slowly, insidiously, the Jewish obsession took over from
the French obsession, carving out its secret wound, working its way deep
into our flesh and our souls, gradually turning us into 'foreigners' in their
own country, French people but 'different,' furtive and self-effacing, or
always on the *qui-vive*, always raw, unstable, adrift, without work, without
positions, bound by the inadmissible bonds of complicity and fear.

Three points strike me in this passage. One, to which I shall return
below, is the 'presentation of self in everyday life'[39] of 'ces Français différents.' The second is the struggle recorded between 'l'obsession juive'
and 'l'obsession française' – that is, preoccupation with the Jewish issue
and preoccupation with the French national issue, whatever 'we' may do
or think. An unattested but imaginable 'we' referring to French assimilated Jews is here pulled apart, its two components competing for attention. As a result, 'I' identifies now as some kind of foreigner. Yet, third, at
the very point where this obsession injures us, 'turns us into foreigners,'
the pronoun changes: 'faisant ... de *nous* ces espèces d' "étrangers" dans
leur pays' (making ... of *us* some kind of 'foreigner' in *their* country):[40] the
portrait of French Jews continues in the third person. Superficially, this
is an effect of writing from the observer's point of view, yet it also enacts
the drama of othering that the sentence recounts. The 'Jewish obsession'
is responsible for the injury; deprived of their place in French society,
the Jews experience a 'troubling' of their identity, unsettling them, making them 'instables et mouvants' (unstable and adrift).

In the same passage, still recalling this process, Mesnil-Amar alludes to
the recent history of French Jewry, noting how comfortable it was to live
as if the Dreyfus affair had never happened, evoking with more than a
touch of irony the comfortable middle-class life 'we' led, *bien assis* – not
just seated, but settled – in our chairs and our social roles. Our civic
separation, our alienation, she writes, 'nous a fait Juifs, lentement, du
dehors, nous qui l'avions si bien oublié' (made us into Jews, we who
had forgotten it so thoroughly, slowly, from the outside), finally touching
'notre conscience bourgeoise si paisible' (our peaceful middle-class consciousness) (57). This process of identification from the outside has an
unexpected consequence: 'je ne sais quoi de mystérieux et d'ancestral,
presque d' "habitué" à cette sorte de malheur, a soudain levé au fond
de nos âmes!' (ibid.; a sudden, a mysterious, ancestral 'je ne sais quoi,'
something that was almost used to this kind of calamity, rose up in our
souls!). No, we must say, recalling the first passage I quoted, our friends

could not save us from our ancestors: they are there, ready to return. The identification 'from the outside' has operated an anamnesis; identification 'from within' is the outcome.

We read from Stuart Hall this suggestive comment concerning the 'inward' dimension of identity: 'Identities are the names we give to the different ways we are positioned by, and position ourselves in, the narratives of the past.'[41] Three 'narratives of the past' are at work in Mesnil-Amar's account. The first is the story of the occupation of France – let us call it the national story; the second is the 'ancestral' story of the Jews; and the third is that of assimilated Jews during, and following, the Dreyfus affair. In the first, she led a 'normal life' at the beginning, when her experience was no different from that of thousands of other Parisians among whom she had fled south. At this point, she suggests, she was obsessed with the situation of France: then, 'on faisait semblant d'être comme les autres' (55; we pretended to be like the others). This involved living in denial ('notre incompréhension'), but this in turn involved 'une vie bizarre, divisée' (55; a strange, divided life). Then, when the *Statut des Juifs* was adopted, 'On nous prit nos biens, notre métier, et, pire que tout, notre rôle de citoyen, notre cher rang social, si durement acquis en trois quarts de siècle. Et puis, sur [*sic*] la pression allemande, notre liberté, notre vie' (56; They took our property, they took our professions, and worst of all, they took away our role as citizens, our beloved social place, obtained at such cost in the course of seventy-five years. Then, under German pressure, they took our freedom and our lives).

They took away our role as citizens: this is her version of Jacques Helbronner's observation of the practical valuelessness of French citizenship for Jews under Vichy law.[42] Little by little, Mesnil-Amar writes, it is this – 'notre "séparation," notre aliénation intime de toute vie civique' (57; our 'marginalization,' our deep alienation from all civic life) – that made us Jews, putting an end to our true life in a travesty of life as outlaws and pariahs, making us beg for a shred of security and a corner of homeland (57). The exchange of one identity for another is not simple: the loss of citizenship sets off 'trouble,' represented by Mesnil-Amar through the metaphor of 'travesty.' These are still French people, their national identity disguised, their *errance*, their *fuite* – their wanderings and their flight from danger – giving them the appearance of statelessness. At the same time, the Jewish story emerges through identification with the ancestral story of a habit of persecution that has lasted, as Mihaïl Sebastian writes, for 'a few millennia': 'I have read "Esther's Letter" in the English Bible, and today Racine's *Esther*. (This too is a way of celebrating Purim!) Three centuries, a few millennia – and our story is still the same. What a fantastic mystery!'[43]

Compare Léo Lania's account of an episode that took place in the camp before his escape:

> The pious Jews celebrated Chanukah (Feast of the Maccabees). The last time I had seen a Chanukah celebration was as a little boy in the house of my grandparents. Now, torn between emotion and embarrassment, I sat among the bearded old men and listened to the cantor intoning prayers in a language I did not understand. Childhood memories rose up in me, and added nothing to my good humour.[44]

We had forgotten we were Jewish, writes Mesnil-Amar; my memories returned, writes Lania, I was torn between 'emotion' (my identification with the world of my grandparents) and embarrassment (my identification – through ignorance of Hebrew – with the secular, political world of my friends). Importantly in these two episodes, the identification operates through time. Identity is not merely a matter of present positionings or of relationality in social space. If it is in part an effect of address and representation,[45] these must be understood complexly, beyond the framework of a communicational dynamic. If Lania is 'represented' in this episode, it is in a language he does not understand, and in a memory he does not welcome; if he is addressed, it is by his past, in a ritual he participates in – he does not tell us how or why. 'Interpellation' would be a better term. This is what many Jewish religious rituals do: they rehearse a story in which the participants are required to position themselves alongside the historical or legendary protagonists, forming a transhistorical 'we' – the 'children of Israel.'

In his memoir, Lania leaves it at this. A dim memory has troubled his identity, as if he had left aside childish things – ritualized Jewish memorial practices – when he became an adult, believing in the grand secular narrative offered by Enlightenment modernity and swallowed whole by the left-leaning intelligentsia of which he was a prominent member. Mihaïl Sebastian does something more complex. At the time in the Jewish calendar when he would celebrate Purim with his family (22 March 1943), he reads the story of the festival in two versions, one biblical (but in the English translation because he is learning this language) and one from the classical canon of French literature, as if to reassert the place of Jewish stories in the literary culture of Europe. This is a riposte to anti-Semitism, which insists that it has no such place: Sebastian's reading and his reflexions upon it constitute his own act of identification as a European Jew, finding a European way of 'celebrating Purim.'

For Sebastian, 'three centuries' take their place alongside 'a few millennia,' thus counterbalancing the interpretation of the ancestral story as a destiny with a gesture toward the real cultural history of retellings, appropriations, of Jewish stories. Like him, and unlike Bernard, here Jacqueline Mesnil-Amar does not allow the trouble to mime the terms of the persecution – either French or Jewish, national or trans-national, *bien assis dans notre pays* or wandering. I have already remarked on the use of the metaphor of travesty, where participation in the national story is not lost, but disguised. This is one way for the two 'identities' to co-exist, in turbid non-transparency. However, arranging the two stories considered thus far as the two terms of a dialectic, we find them resolved in a third story, which is repressed by the opposition between the other two. When Mesnil-Amar evokes the Dreyfus affair, it is not only as an episode in the ancestral story but also as a story of France and of what it is to be Jewish in France. As she tells it, we *forgot* about the Dreyfus affair because we were so comfortable. The comfortable settledness, the social successes, and the middle-class houses (57) represent an amnesia made possible by the homogenizing discourses of the secularist Third Republic, which disguised the complex ideological forces over which it believed it had triumphed.[46] Repressed, these forces returned under Vichy. When Mesnil-Amar tells this story, it works to sublate the alternative between a French identity and a Jewish one; it is an act of identification that locates 'we' in a national history and reinterprets the national story accordingly. The struggle for citizenship for minority groups that she alludes to is an identificatory process not merely for the Jews in France but, just as significantly, for France. The historical subtlety evident in this resolution was lost on many French Jews of the period.

Nor, however, does it represent a definitive theoretical position achieved through the deliberate application of the dialectical method. Mesnil-Amar's ideas on this matter are purveyed in a diary, a genre characterized by fragmentary reflexions: we should no more expect consistency in this genre than we would expect it in experience, or in subjectivity. We may look for conclusions, but there are none. Instead, we find our diarists looking for ways of processing the complex realities of their experience, trying out interpretations and formulae drawn from multiple discursive sources. Thus it is that some twenty pages further on in her diary, Mesnil-Amar returns to the dominant binary opposition between French and Jew, settled and wanderer, rooted and rootless. In this passage, she has taken her young daughter to play in the gardens and is sitting with a certain Mme L., also the wife of a resistance activist who has been arrested. Mme L. is not Jewish. (In the following passage,

the antecedent of the pronoun 'y' is 'le pays qui nous environne' [the
country that surrounds us].)

> J'y ai souffert comme elle du destin de la France, mais j'ai porté tout au long
> le poids d'un autre destin, d'un destin millénaire ...
> Et je regarde cette femme assise, étrangère et semblable à moi, figée à
> ce sol par tant de racines, dans le passé et l'avenir, et à ses côtés je me sens
> mouvante et transitoire, venue de très loin dans les siècles, avec cet autre
> visage secret, qui est aussi moi, et me vient d' 'ailleurs,' de je ne sais où, de
> nulle part, et malgré moi *je suis aussi la soeur de tous ces enfants d'Israël*, que
> je ne connais pas, les étrangers, les inconnus, les traqués. (8 August 1944,
> 72–3; emphasis added)

> Like her, I have suffered from the fate inflicted on France, but the whole
> time, I carried the burden of another fate, a millennial destiny ...
> Watching this settled woman, seated beside me, so like me and so
> unfamiliar, held fast in the soil by so many roots both past and future, I
> feel unstable, impermanent; I have come from the distance of centuries
> with my hidden face: it too is me, but it comes from elsewhere, I don't
> know where, from nowhere, and despite myself, *I am also the sister of all
> those children of Israel* whom I don't know, strangers, unknown to me,
> hunted.

Again, *assis* refers not only to the posture of the woman beside her, but
to Mesnil-Amar's focus on the number and depth of her roots in France
and French history. This contrasts with her own sense of transience –
'mouvante et transitoire' – in a phrase that recalls "instables et mouvants"
quoted above, an internalization of the story of exile, recalling *l'errance,
la fuite* of a previous passage, and the uprooted escapees of Lania's story.
Remarkably, the term *étranger* – foreigner or stranger – is used first for
Mme L., then repeated several lines below for 'the children of Israel'
whom she does not know, foreign or strangers to her as she sits in a
temporary 'we' with another woman so like herself: 'comme des millions
d'autres femmes sans nouvelles, Mme L. et moi, nous attendons, nous
attendons ...' (8 August 1944, 73; like millions of other women without
news, we wait, we wait ...).
    Mesnil-Amar is caught between this woman, with whom she identifies
on this occasion, and 'mes compagnons de misère, frappés comme moi
par notre fatalité' (ibid. my companions in misery, struck, like me, by
the fatality of being us). On the same park bench, in the same situation
and the same sunshine, 'j'y ai cherché plus loin des vibrations plus profondes qu'elle n'a pas eu à percevoir' (ibid., 72; I sought an echo from

further afield than she could access). Notice, again, the 'hidden' face, the one disguised for interactions with non-Jews – her fellows in one story, strangers in another. It is telling, too, that she *sought* her connection with the ancestral story. Not everybody did; they were too concerned with asserting the differences between themselves and the 'foreign' Jews who, like Léo Lania, had sought refuge in France from the Nazi threat.

Mesnil-Amar herself cites an example, evoking

> La voix si distinguée de monsieur S., industriel de l'Est, exaltant sa stupeur dans le jardin de l'hôtel, à Vichy, après le premier Statut des Juifs: 'C'est insensé! Une mesure semblable ne peut pas s'appliquer à des Français, pas à des Israélites français! À des Juifs étrangers, peut-être, mais pas aux Juifs français! C'est inconcevable! Une véritable spoliation ...!' Pauvre monsieur S. On fit tellement mieux. On nous prit nos biens ... (etc.) (6 August 1944, 56)

> Monsieur S., an industrialist from the East [of France], in the Vichy hotel after the first *Statut des Juifs*, his oh so distinguished voice loudly proclaiming: 'It's madness! That sort of measure can't be applied to French people, not to French Jews! To the foreign Jews, maybe, but not to French Jews. It's unthinkable! It's outright rapine ...!' Poor monsieur S. They did better than that. They robbed us of everything ... (etc.).

By no means all French Jews – or all European Jews, for that matter – heard the call of the ancestors, or would heed it. For them, the national story was far more compelling. The 'we' of the Jews – identification with the millennial destiny, sisterhood with strangers from elsewhere – could be refused, in favour of 'fraternity' with the French – even when that fraternity was refused them by the other component of 'we.' Nor was the 'we' of victimhood the source of a 'we' that would necessarily override the differences within French Jewry, between assimilated Jews and foreign Jews.

Taken together, the three stories of 'we' I have told outline the complex issues of identity experienced by Jews in France under Vichy. Secular and modern though they all be, Léo Lania represents exactly what separates Bernard from Mesnil-Amar. Whereas Mesnil-Amar embraces identification with Lania's condition, Bernard refuses it; his desperate reiteration of his Frenchness echoes the xenophobia of France in the period, acting to identify him with the country of his birth. Bernard's denial of his Jewishness cannot be separated from this. His vehemence in discussion with the Turkish boy, and again with Mme Aronson, reveals a kind of horror at the possibility that he may be both. It is as if the claim to purity, to ancestral rootedness in the 'climes' of France, is invoked as a talisman against danger. But this danger is not adequately represented by his internment. Yes, the conditions at Compiègne were draconian, causing death and acute suffering, but when Bernard bears witness, it is to what he calls in a later article a 'fruitful lesson' he drew from this experience: persecution, he writes, could serve to 'clarify one's ideas and define one's position': 'Les Français enfermés avec moi ... comme moi, ne savaient penser que français. Ils ne savaient pas penser juif' (78; Like me, the Frenchmen locked up with me could only think as Frenchmen. They were incapable of thinking as Jews'). He later predicts that most of the foreign Jews, or at least their children, will loosen their hold on Jewish 'particularism' as they integrate with 'us.' But there will be others, those who hold fast to their Jewish ways and ideas: 'ceux-là seuls, on pourra dire d'eux qu'ils ne sont pas assimilables, parce qu'ils ne sont pas Français' (195; of these, and only of these, can we say that they are not assimilable, because they are not French).

The contrast with Mesnil-Amar could not be more marked. There is a Jewish story, and she is part of it, not only because she is Jewish, but because two recent manifestations of that story are also significant episodes of the French story. Hers is an account of a nation constructed from the intertwining of people with different histories, and an account of the processes of identification affected by the vicissitudes of those histories and of that intertwining. Mesnil-Amar knew, as Bernard did not, that she joined in the 'we' of two discrepant groups, and she invoked the ancestral story in order to understand how 'we' could be 'foreigners in *their* own country.' Bernard, hurt though he was by this very fact, never accepted that it was a fact; nor did he seek to understand it. And so he never learned *not* to ask whether his friends would protect him from his ancestors: acknowledging that they had not, he was just puzzled, and thought they should. Where Bernard claims to have only one 'face' – not recognizable as the 'Jewish' 'type' – Mesnil-Amar accepts that she has two, each operating in different situations, neither more authentic than the other.

At the heart of these contrasts, then, we find contrasting assumptions concerning identity. For Bernard, 'appearance' – which I use as a generalization over 'face' – is the outward expression of an inner truth. Certainly he is confused as to whether this inner truth is genetic – an effect of race – or whether it is the effect of assimilation, but, in his account, the appearance of his chosen group of assimilated Frenchmen conveys the depth of their Frenchness, while the appearance of the Turk betrays his foreignness: swarthy, he could pass for a Muslim, but, asks Bernard, isn't this 'natural'? The question of appearance thus parallels in Bernard's view the assumption that identity lies in the individual's soul and shows, if at all, only in the non-particularity of that person's face and bearing.

It is therefore a matter for the person alone. Mesnil-Amar starts from the opposite assumption: her face depends on whom she is with; it both derives from and serves her interactions. Hers is a social theory of identity.

This brings me to my second collection of stories. They invite me to take up the issues raised by the metaphor of travesty, disguise, appearance, and face.

Narratives of Performance

On peut changer de moi comme on peut changer de visage.
Pour s'en apercevoir, il suffit de revêtir une capote de soldat.

Changing your self is like changing your face.
To see the truth of this, you need only put on a soldier's cap.
                                    – Valentin Feldman, *Journal de guerre*, 3 January 1940

Jean-Jacques Bernard (fin) and Jacqueline Mesnil-Amar (bis)

For all his belief in interiority, Jean-Jacques Bernard was a man of the theatre: 'en caleçon' (29; wearing only his underpants) when the Germans arrived at his door, he had dressed quickly, but carefully. He would be kept, he thought, for a day, or perhaps overnight; the worst he expected was an interrogation: 'je me disais que j'allais sans doute être interrogé. Aussi, par un souci de tenue [...] j'avais mis mon costume neuf, un chapeau neuf, mon meilleur pardessus et mes meilleurs souliers' (30; It was likely, I thought, that I would be interrogated. So, concerned with my bearing, I had put on a new suit, a new hat, my best coat and my best shoes). Wearing the right costume, he would deliver his lines persuasively, showing in his self-presentation the incongruity of the situation: Me? Here? 'Vous êtes sûr qu'il n'y a pas d'erreur?' (28; Are you certain there is no mistake?). With the tricks of his trade, and the accoutrements of the prosperous middle class, he had evidently decided to perform his status. It didn't work.

En caleçon, Bernard was vulnerable because his underclothes gave him no way of influencing the view others had of his place in society. He dressed, therefore, in the costume of his class and standing, indistinguishable from others of his kind. But he was distinguished as a Jew, not by the star, which had yet to be instituted, but by administrative practices such as the census, and stamps reading 'J' on the ration-cards. Later, in the camp, his costume long discarded or in tatters, we find him reduced to a pair of clogs, a beret, and a shawl (123); a famished, freezing body, he was unable to occupy any role – assert it, yes, but not perform it persuasively. Hence the anger he shows to the Turk: it is triggered by impotence. In the camps, the internees were deprived not only of food and shelter, not only of their milieu and their loved ones, but of the very conditions under which the practices of identity could be exercised. Their minimal dress marked them as members of the camp population; they had no identity but this.

'Les hommes ... naissent nus, mais ils vivent et meurent tout habillés' (Men ... are born naked, but they live and die fully dressed), wrote Jacqueline Mesnil-Amar on 20 August 1944 in a nice calque on Rousseau (112). Formulated as if it were a proverb, the observation draws our attention to the importance of appearance as a means of being in the world, of living and dying as fundamentally social processes. Let us take Mesnil-Amar's insight as a *topos* for reflecting on identity, and let us gloss it by calling on the work of Erving Goffman.[47] This gloss will take the matter of 'dress' as a metonym for the arts of self-presentation, in which, for Goffman, 'a "performance" may be defined as all the activity of a given participant on a given occasion that serves to influence in any way any of the other participants.'[48] In light of the complex mechanisms of identification at work under Nazism, we may question the applicability of Goffman's theory to the situation of Jews: they had no influence, no social agency. However, it is precisely for this reason that Goffman's work can get us started on a social and cultural account of identification practices. For it is not enough to say that Jews under Nazism were stripped of their identity, as if we knew what this meant. What they lost was the self-presentational means to intervene in the definition of the situation: they could not 'engender' 'the impression of reality among those among whom' they found themselves. They could not 'control the conduct of others, especially in their responsive treatment of [them].'[49] In Goffman's account, this capacity relies on having a stage, an audience, a team with whom to play, and, above all, a play in which the part has its place. This play is the plan for co-operation and thus presupposes a shared universe in which the performance 'exerts a moral demand' on the other participants, 'obliging them to value and treat [the performer] in the manner that persons of his kind have a right to expect.'[50] Presumably, these are Bernard's predictions when he appears at the police station, but he has no control over the situation he finds himself in, because he and his interrogators were not in the same play: the part he has learned relies on the assumption that he has social agency, while his interrogators are there in order to deprive him of exactly that.

Nevertheless, under most circumstances – notably not arrest and internment – dressing the part of the invulnerable could result in a modicum of success in evading the imposition of identity. To illustrate this, we may adduce the portrait given by Jacqueline Mesnil-Amar of her father, Jules Perquel.[51] Both her parents continued to live in Paris, but they were in hiding, moving from safe house to safe house. Her father 'refus[ait] obstinément de porter l'étoile' (stubbornly refused to wear the star):

> Dire que chaque matin, à heure fixe, dans ce quartier d'Auteuil – ici même –, papa sort et fait ses courses, avec une ponctualité intraitable – vestige de sa puissance défunte – et cette sihouette dangereusement reconnaissable de vieux Parisien, un peu 'militaire en retraite ...' On le voit, claudiquant sur sa mauvaise jambe, appuyé sur sa canne, bien vêtu, coiffé de ce drôle de chapeau un peu allongé que connaissait naguère toute la Bourse, saluant ses voisins, parlant aux femmes et aux enfants, souriant, affable, l'œil très bleu, cet oeil auquel rien n'échappe. Qui pourrait croire, à voir passer ce vieux monsieur tranquille et décoré, que la Gestapo est venu huit fois à son domicile et qu'à chaque instant, à chaque tournant de rue, la Mort l'a guetté? (17 August 1944, 96)

> Just think! Every morning at the same time, in this very district of Auteuil, father goes out to do his errands, with his unwavering punctuality – a vestige of his former power – and this dangerously recognizable silhouette – the elderly Parisian with something of the 'retired military man.' You can see him limping on his bad leg, leaning on his cane, well dressed, on his head that oddly shaped, somewhat elongated hat known to the whole of the Stock Exchange, greeting his neighbours, speaking to the women and children, smiling, affable, his striking blue eyes that miss nothing. Who would believe, seeing this calm, elderly gentleman wearing his decorations, that the Gestapo has come to his lodging eight times, and that Death has never ceased to lurk around every corner, waiting for him?

Notice the 'vestige of his former power' – a particular socio-economic power associated with his class and his profession – readable from his 'punctuality' but also from his habits of public courtesy and from his careful attention to dress. Something in the self-presentation of this 'calm, elderly gentleman' gives the lie to the image of the hunted Jew as he defies the daily threat. That it is a rhetoric, however, adopted as a strategy for public appearance, is recognized by his daughter, who also sees him in private:

> Un Lorrain, un Parisien? Bien sûr, et avant tout. Et pourtant ... quand je monte parfois le soir, et que je le surprends penché sur sa radio, maniant doucement les boutons, la pale lumière du crépuscule tombant sur son front, sur ce visage lucide de vieil homme, un petit calot sur la tête, parce qu'il a froid, un châle sur les épaules, je le vois tout à coup, dans un

reflet ancestral, une lueur à la Rembrandt ... un Juif, comme son père, ses ancêtres. (17 August 1944, 96–7)

From Lorraine? Parisian? Of course, before all else. And yet ... sometimes, when I go up to see him in the evenings and come across him bent over the radio, adjusting the dial, the pale light of dusk illuminating his forehead and his clear-sighted old man's face, wearing a little cap because he's cold, and a shawl over his shoulders, that's when I see in him an ancestral image lit as if by Rembrandt ... A Jew, like his father, like his forebears.

Goffman would analyse the old gentleman's performance in the street as relying on 'front': this may include such things as 'insignia of office or rank; clothing; ... posture; speech patterns; facial expressions; bodily gestures.' Such things are managed by 'expressive control' exerted in order for the performance to 'come off'; on this control depends the belief of the audience in the performance.[52] The arts of self-presentation exert rhetorical control, a means of influencing others. They depend upon what we call self-possession, in defiance of possession of the self by others. This is lost at the point of arrest, but not in other, less threatening situations. At home, Monsieur Perquel is 'backstage'; there, his daughter describes him as an old Jew who resembles his ancestors.

The theatre analogy appears to imply that the father's performance is a fiction, as if the part he was playing was not truly his. On this reading, the actor is distinct from his role, speaking words provided by an author, wearing a costume, and placed in a décor designed to maintain the illusion, the whole set in train when the curtain rises and completed when the curtain falls. But this reading is based on the assumption that playing a part is necessarily false. Thus, from the Nazi point of view, the Jews of Europe were just pretending to be like everybody else; the function of the yellow star was, at least in part, to disable what these specialists in racial identity took to be camouflage.

While Goffman takes the backstage to be the place where preparations for the performance are made, where the team comes together and plays out the conditions of its coherence, the analogy of the theatre carries unfortunate baggage. For many, it implies that there is a real person under the costume, an agent with its own desires and fears who manipulates the role. Goffman's account of the presentation of self does little to dislodge the difficulty that arises in many accounts of identity whose conceptual framework relies on the dichotomy of surface and depth, outer and inner. True, he reverses the presupposition deriving from the tradition of the soul, according to which identification from the outside is inauthentic, imposed by society for its own ends on an authentic inner reality that demands to be recognized. Yet this same dichotomy haunts Goffman's analysis even as he seeks to dismantle it. Distinguishing between the self as performance and the self as performer, he comes close to a dialectical resolution: the body is a mere 'peg' on which 'something of a collaborative manufacture will be hung for a time,' while the self as performer is 'psychobiological,' yet seems 'to arise out of intimate interaction with the contingencies of staging performances.'[53] Nevertheless, the resolution is not complete, but, before I turn to an account that pushes it further, I want to return to Jacqueline Mesnil-Amar, whose reflections on her own experience require us to consider the multiplicity of roles performed by a social body and attached to a proper name. Jacqueline Mesnil-Amar's analysis of identity allows for 'two faces' and 'two worlds' (23 August 1944, 122), neither more real than the other.

In practice, when we ask, 'Who was Jacqueline Mesnil-Amar?,' the answer is given in a biography: starting with the information provided by the civil administrative use of the term 'identity,' we go on to find a list, or a narrative, of what she did during her life. She gives such a list when, with the approach of the Liberation, she ponders what it will mean for 'who she is' when she is no longer engaged in Resistance activities:

> Un instant le destin m'a traînée à sa suite, pauvre petit acteur, sur une scène trop grande, dans un vaste théâtre, pour jouer un petit bout de rôle, mon rôle de traquée, mon rôle ancestral, un instant l'Histoire m'a portée sur ses ailes et prêté sa lumière, et mon âme a battu toute proche de Paris, couchée sur Paris, et mes fibres ont vibré toutes proches de celles de ma race, à jamais emmêlées. Mais c'est presque fini. La fin approche, le rideau va tomber. Me voici bientôt rejetée à mon propre destin, rendue à mon angoisse à moi, à ma vie, ma petite vie, nouée, fermée, comme toutes les vies. (23 August 1944, 129)

> For a brief moment I, a poor little actor on a stage that was too big, in a huge theatre, I was hauled in by destiny to play a bit part, the role of the hunted, my ancestral role; for a brief moment History carried me on its wings and lent me its light, and my soul lay with Paris, beat in time with Paris, and the fibres of my being throbbed with those of my race, enmeshed with them for ever. Now it is ending. The curtain will fall. Soon I'll be back in my own small destiny, returned to my personal anxieties, to my life, my little life, closed and tied up, like any life.

In Mesnil-Amar's hands, the metaphor of the theatre serves to delimit the time and space of the dramas in which she has participated, one being that of the Resistance (*la lumière de l'Histoire*, Paris), the other being that of the Jews (*ma race*). Her 'petite vie ... fermée, comme toutes les vies' is not some authentic reality in contrast to these two dramas, but a small stage, contrasting with the large stage of historical events. Like many women who lived through the war, Jewish or not, in France or elsewhere, she expects to return to the smallness of domestic life, a personal destiny that, because, as she thinks, it has no audience, is unlikely to register in the events that make 'History' with its capital letter. Witness the 'sacrifice' she is prepared to make of her 'personal ambitions' (ibid.).[54] This life has been suspended for a time. Thus, the war brought with it three roles: wife and mother, resistance activist, Jew.

Although she envisages that her life will return to its pre-war norms and forms following the return of her husband, her experiences will have changed her, will have changed her husband, and will have changed their sense of their place in the world. In a passage from one of her post-war articles recalling the day of the Liberation of Paris, she outlines the practices of identification and their effects:[55] false papers gave a superficial 'similitude,' the yellow star marked difference, we were foreigners without a place. Our deep identity,[56] she writes, retrieving the nativist discourse, came from being like other people in the city of our birth. 'Mais les joies sont brèves' (But joy is brief). She, her husband, and other former Jewish *Résistants* from their group decided to 'break the wall of silence' surrounding the fate of deported Jews, forming le Service central des déportés israélites (the Central Service for Jewish Deportees) with the aim of searching for survivors and tracing information concerning those who had perished.[57] Mesnil-Amar's articles, reproduced with her published diary, first appeared in the monthly bulletin of this organization. Its work was very significant. For my purposes, it shows how Mesnil-Amar's list of roles changed in response to circumstances. She did not, as she had feared, return to the small stage of domesticity; this new stage allowed her to bring together her marriage, her Jewishness, her activism – and notably, her writing. This was her response to survivors who had known 'l'envers de la médaille appelée Civilisation' (the other side of the coin called Civilization) and who demanded that the world be told: 'Et nous avons raconté, pour tous ceux qui ne savaient pas ... Et nous avons raconté aussi pour tous ceux qui avaient oublié. Et nous avons rassemblé quelques-uns de ces articles pour tous ceux qui oublieront' (So we told the stories, for those who did not know ... And we told them too for those who had forgotten. And we have brought together some of those articles for all those who will forget).[58]

More striking even than the fact that her own roles had evolved in this way is the preposition she uses in this passage. While the survivors use 'à' ('racontez-leur' [tell them]), she uses 'pour.' We told these stories *for* those who didn't know, *for* those who had forgotten, or, in the future, *for* those those who will forget. This 'for' represents her new relationship with France. It is not oppositional, and it is not polemical; it is a preposition of solidarity, as if her audience needed the stories she tells. But this audience is 'they,' distinct from 'we.' 'La divine similitude' (heavenly sameness) is flawed.

Recalling Stuart Hall's formulation – 'identities are the names we give to the different ways we are positioned by, and position ourselves in, the narratives of the past' – we can say that the flaw derives from the following asymmetry: 'we' share the French story – the war, the Occupation – but the French do not share 'ours' – the fate of the Jews. For Jacqueline Mesnil-Amar, they must be made to do so. What these witnesses were asking of the French was effectively to modify their identification with the recent past, but too many people had profited from the expropriations, and too few people were prepared to include in their 'we' a group who had been defined as lying outside it. Their 'own' stories may well have included stories of forced labour (sometimes considered to be the 'real deportation'), but they did not include, and for decades could not include, the active participation of the Vichy government in the destruction of the Jews of France. The immediate post-war period in France saw a resurgence of anti-Semitism in some quarters, and even in Resistance circles it was deemed preferable not to refer specifically to the Jewish question.[59] The Gaullist Resistance was a nationalist movement, and to the extent that it dominated post-war ideology and policy, it defined a national 'we' that brooked no division. It was only at the very end of the Gaullist period – with Max Ophüls's *Le chagrin et la pitié*[60] – that an alternative to the Resistance myth was told. The Jewish story of France was officially acknowledged only by the last of the Gaullist presidents, Jacques Chirac, in 1995.[61]

Narrative memory – the stories that position us alongside those who do, vis-à-vis those who do not, share the same past – does not command Goffman's attention. This is because his 'teams' are locked into an inexplicit and ill-defined notion of the current circumstances. Thus, for example, Mesnil-Amar's barricade builders are a motley group, leading her to exclaim joyfully 'C'est la levée du peuple de Paris jailli des profondeurs!' (23 August 1944, 125; this is the people of Paris rising up from the depths!), but this unity is as fleeting as 'our' common identity with 'la société, la France.'[62] The barricade builders are a team, assembled for a punctual task. Its members come from all milieus and all walks of life, but they have different histories; some may well be 'the sons of collaborators' (23 August 1944, 125). This team gives each member a role, but it does not give them an identity. This point makes it clear that we should avoid any conflation between the theatrical analogy and 'a play,' where the latter is singular, punctual, and occasional. Mesnil-Amar's biography shows that she acts on different stages with different audiences, sometimes in parallel, and sometimes serially, with one performance preparing her for another. The presentation of self in everyday life does not imply that there is a true or authentic self that puts on and takes off a mask, but that costumes, props, and so on are the means of social presence and hence of action.

So I will pursue the analogy until it reaches the limits of its usefulness. Men are born naked, but they live and die fully dressed. Nobody could be more different from Jules Perquel than Valentin Feldman, yet the diary of the latter provides me with a further somewhat parallel opportunity to explore the issue of self-presentation and the use of performance to occupy a place, albeit a place of refuge.

Valentin Feldman

The son of Russian Jewish parents, an immigrant from an early age and naturalized in 1931, Valentin Feldman did indeed have several 'faces.' Well known among the young Paris intelligentsia, he was on track for an academic career in philosophy before volunteering for the army. Following his demobilization, he was a teacher in the national education system, and his hidden face was that of a communist activist in the Resistance, for which he was executed at Mont-Valérien in July 1942.[63]

Feldman's intellectual trajectory had led him to identify as a free thinker; while he did not repudiate them, his Jewish origins were not important to the way he thought about himself:

> Je ne croyais guère à la destinée du judaïsme. Je me suis toujours foutu, et au fonds [*sic*] je me fous encore royalement, du judaïsme et de sa destinée [...] Mais un fait demeure: tous les grands juifs ont commencé par se libérer du judaïsme: le Christ, Marx, Spinoza, Bergson – toute proportion gardée entre ces noms. Mais il n'en reste pas moins vrai que c'est comme 'juifs' qu'ils ont été 'recensés' par l'histoire. Et que chaque fois que le pharaonisme s'installe dans le monde, il fait aux juifs une condition d'esclaves.
>
> Que c'est peu drôle, peu drôle, de faire le martyr sans la foi. (9 October 1941, 218)

> I really didn't believe in the destiny of Judaism. I couldn't give a damn, and it's the same now, about Judaism and its destiny [...] But one fact stands out: all the great Jews started by freeing themselves from Judaism: Christ, Marx, Spinoza, Bergson – I don't mean to equate these names. But even so, it remains true that history has counted them as Jews. And every time pharaonism takes hold in the world, it reduces the Jews to slavery.
>
> It's no fun, no fun at all, to be a martyr without faith.

In this passage, Feldman, the philosophic rationalist, relies on a distinction between *destinée* construed teleologically – God's will for his people – and the fate of Jewish people in history: if the former is an article of Jewish belief, the latter is martyrdom without faith, and it is a 'fact.' This is his version of the 'millennial' story of Mihaïl Sebastian and the ancestral memory of Mesnil-Amar. Feldman is forced – forced because, like a string of famous Jews, he is 'free' of religious faith – to consider his own place in this story by the rise of official anti-Semitism. By the date of the passage above, he is about to fall under the provisions of the *Statut des Juifs*.[64]

The *statut* was promulgated on 3 October 1940, but Feldman learned of it through the press a couple of weeks later. He records his reaction on 21 October: 'Statut raciste en France (en France!!)' (219; A racist law in France (in France!!)). It provided, among other things, that no Jew could be employed as a teacher. From this date until 15 August 1941, his status in the education system remained ambiguous, although he was being actively investigated. It is of some interest to follow this process through the diary.

He receives the first intimation of imminent dismissal from his position from a notice in the press reported to him by a pupil:

> Averti donc par un élève, averti lui-même par un journal, j'avertissais le surveillant général pour qu'il avertisse le Principal. Pour moi, point de doute: c'était une révocation. Mais quand on révoque, on notifie, tout de même, à l'individu louche qu'il n'est pas digne de fonctionner comme fonctionnaire. Et 48 heures après la notice publiée dans la presse locale, le dit individu ignore quelle est sa condition. (6 January 1941, 230)

> So then, notified by a pupil, himself notified by a newspaper, I notified the supervisor so he could notify the Principal. But surely, when one revokes an appointment, one gives notice to the suspect individual that he is not worthy of serving as a servant of the state. And 48 hours after the publication of the notice in the local paper, the said individual still does not know what his status is.

This report turns out to have been a false alarm, but what will happen next? 'Nommé dans un lycée ou promu chômeur? ... Et quand je me crois révoqué, je ne le suis pas encore tout en l'étant probablement' (ibid.; Appointed to a *lycée* or promoted out of work? Believing myself dismissed, I am not yet dismissed, and at the same time I probably am). Several days later, a letter from the school bursar (on an unconnected matter) implies that he is still on the payroll (10 January 1941, 231). The next day he is informed that, in a case of mistaken identity, he had been taken for somebody else who was 'atteint par le statut des juifs' (21 January 1941, 235;

affected by the *Statut des Juifs*), and in another letter, a month later, that
he is 'maintenu à titre "précaire"' (7 February 1941, 244; maintained in
his position without guarantees). This rather absurd episode inaugurates
a period of waiting and complying with administrative procedures.

These procedures were undertaken to check if he too should be identified as a Jew – that is, whether his appointment to the national education
system could be maintained. While continuing to work in the school, he
must provide his family tree (13 February 1941, 248):

> Mon agonie administrative est vraiment d'une lenteur désespérante.
> Me voici encore dans une classe à surveiller une composition de philo,
> banalement, comme si la France n'était pas fasciste, comme si mes ascend-
> ants et les ascendants de tous mes ascendants étaient de simples cauchois.
> (10 March 1941, 256)

> The process of my administrative death is desperately slow. Here I am, still
> in a classroom, supervising a philosophy test, as if France was not fascist, as
> if my ancestors and the ancestors of all my ancestors were born and bred
> in Caux.

Here, his dismissal takes on the status of a future death, imminent yet
held up by administrative bungling: 'Une nouvelle demande rectorale
de renseignements sur mes ascendants – envoyée il y a plus d'un mois'
(11 March 1941, 259; Yet another demand from the rectorate, sent a
month ago, for more information about my ancestors). By the end of
April, he is certain that his 'révocation peut enfin arriver' (28 April 1941,
277; dismissal might happen at long last) by week's end, but we learn in
June that the ministry had repeatedly lost his file (20 June 1941, 294). He
is finally dismissed in August (15 August 1941, 300).

Feldman had immigrated with his mother when he was seven years old,
leaving Russia in 1922; we can surmise that some of the official papers
documenting his family tree had been left behind, perhaps lost in post-
revolutionary chaos. In doubt was the 'race' of his paternal grandfather. Early
in the saga, the rectorate had made a decision, which was then overturned:

> Le fin mot de l'histoire est bien l'erreur du Rectorat sur ma 'douteuse'
> ascendance. De ce point de vue l'affaire est réglée: il n'est point question
> de m'éliminer comme juif puisqu'on ne saurait me donner (l'expression
> est à retenir!) 'le nombre de grands-parents requis' (24 January 1941, 236)

> The key to the story is indeed the mistake made in the rectorate about my
> 'dubious' ancestry. From this point of view, everything is sorted out: there

is no question of using Jewishness to throw me out because they are unable to give me (note this expression) 'the required number of grandparents.'

It was technically tricky, this application of the criteria for Jewishness:

> Les Anglais ne bombardent pas Dieppe; mais Ministère et Rectorat bombardent le collège de notes me concernant. Une de plus vient d'arriver. On me demande, outre des pièces justificatives que nul ne saurait fournir, moi moins que quiconque, mon 'arbre généalogique' (*sic*), en même temps que celui de mon conjoint (re-*sic*). (11 February 1941, 245)

> There is no English bombardment in Dieppe; but the college is bombarded by the ministry and the rectorate with notes concerning me. Another has just arrived. What do they want from me? Apart from documents that nobody could provide, least of all me, they want my 'family tree' (*sic*) as well as that of my 'spouse' (re-*sic*).

Accordingly, he produced two superb family trees (13 February 1941, 248), but doubt persisted. Whatever could be proved, or not, concerning the questionable grandfather (2 May 1941, 279), it would make no difference in the end: 'Cette histoire de ma révocation est d'un ridicule achevé. Elle finira bien comme elle doit finir. Mais qu'elle finisse, nom de Dieu! Et une bonne fois pour toutes.' (24 March 1941, 262; This business of my dismissal is completely absurd. It will end up the way it must end up. But God, let it end once and for all). Finally, it did: 'Vu le "Patron." Ce sera pour le 15, la grande disponibilité. Et ce n'est plus du "changement" qu'il s'agit cette fois; c'est de la *rupture*' (12 August 1941, 301; Saw the 'Boss.' They will let me go on the 15th. This time, it's not a matter of 'change,' but of being barred from the service).

By this time, the technical difficulties had been eliminated by a change to the 'definitions' – the criteria for counting someone as Jewish. Feldman's comment goes to the heart of the matter: 'la race est bonne enfant dans ses rapports avec le législateur' (9 May 1941, 282; race is not troublesome for a lawmaker). Identity is not a matter of essence: it is produced by administrative practices that could, moreover, be changed, at whim, or in the interests of efficiency.

If identity, one's identity in history, is produced by acts and practices, then the J-label is 'merely' – I use the adverb with all due care – an instrument. It was not always used, and sometimes it conflicted with others whose punitive provisions were devised on other grounds. In the specific case of France, definitive identification was effected by the ways and means of killing.[65] Feldman did not die as a Jew: that brought about

only his 'administrative death.' He would be executed in reprisal for
a Resistance attack, which – in another twist of mistaken identity – he
had not in fact committed.[66] But he was indeed a communist and had
been implicated in other actions. Following one of his reprieves as a
Jew, 'l'Inspecteur d'Académie m'a demandé de lui fournir toutes sortes
de détails sur mon ex-activité politique. "Tout cela n'est rien, fit-il, l'essentiel est de n'avoir pas été communiste"' (24 January 1941, 236; The
Inspector asked me to provide all sorts of details about my former political activity. 'All this is nothing, quoth he, the main thing is not to have
been a communist'). So his communist face – comprising, among other
things, his scorn for bourgeois mores – was the one he kept hidden, and
the most effective way of doing so was to maintain his public persona as
respected teacher in a provincial secondary school. This was made possible by keeping hidden his Jewish face. And so we find him in surprising
company, first working with the community defence, guarding German
cables (18 January 1941, 233). He seems to have charmed the boots off
the good people of Dieppe, to have persuaded them of his good character by the consummate performance of his role. He spent time in 'distinguished company,' as if his honour could not be doubted. One of his
excursions is a tour of the cemetery with the respectable Mme Dagne,
whom he paints as pious and deeply bourgeois and with whom he has
merciless fun. In the privacy of his diary – this is where he is backstage,
on display as irreverent communist intellectual, for himself if not for his
intimates – the jokes allow him to de-identify with her after spending the
afternoon appearing to do the opposite:

> Mme Dagne connaît bien le cimetière: elle y fait halte toutes les semaines,
> en allant voir sa mère – (sa mère vivante, qui n'est pas encore en terre,
> mais, ce faisant, une politesse à la mère de la mère qui, elle, est si j'ai bien
> compris en terre, s'impose d'elle-même, comme une visite pieuse qu'une
> âme pieuse ne se refuse pas). (17 March 1941, 259)

> Mme Dagne is well acquainted with the cemetery: she stops there every
> week on her way to see her mother – (her living mother, not yet in the
> earth, but on her way, it would not be polite not to visit the mother's mother
> who, if I've got it straight, is in the earth, because piety has its rules).

I pause to remark that Mme Dagne's habits, too, are practices of identity –
obeying the rules of courtesy with weekly visits both pious and sociable. They are regular, and they maintain social belonging across space
and through time; death does not diminish them: 'Parmi les tombes à
Dieppe avec Mme Dagne, on se sent à l'aise comme dans un salon de

thé. Elle connaît les familles, les occasions qui les ont menées là où elles
sont et resteront' (ibid.; Among the gravestones of Dieppe with Mme
Dagne, one feels as comfortable as one would in a tea-room. She knows
the families, and the occasions that sent them to their present and future
resting place). This is about having a place: Mme Dagne explains that
the municipal council has offered concessions in the cemetery to anyone who is a victim of the bombing. 'What a godsend that would be
for a wanderer like me. Holy ground for eternity,' comments Feldman
(ibid.). Unlike Mme Dagne, whose place is assured by the past and into
the future, but like other Jews in France in this period, Feldman is a
'vagabond,' '[un] éternel passant, jouissant d'un provisoire permis de
séjour' (5 November 1941, 223; ever a passer-by, his residency permit
only provisional). But if Mme Dagne performs her place through the
company she keeps, so can he. We take up his story:

> La propriétaire de la Maison Dorée me fit savoir qu'un agent de police
> me recherchait. Et le lendemain, les élèves ... me confirmèrent cette in-
> formation. On a beau avoir sa conscience pour soi, une visite de la police
> ne fait pas plaisir. Antécédents? Antécédents biologiques dits 'ascendants'?
> Ce n'était qu'un mandat, indemnité de repli. Et avec l'agent de police j'ai
> bu, aux Tourelles, un petit 'anjou' sec. Quelles fréquentations! Dieu de
> Dieu, quelles fréquentations! (17 March 1941, 260)

> The owner of the Maison Dorée informed me that a policeman was look-
> ing for me. And the next day, this was confirmed by the students. It's not
> enough to have a clear conscience; a visit from the police is not a pleasant
> prospect. Antecedants? Biological antecedants known as 'ancestors'? It was
> nothing but a postal order, in compensation for the mistaken dismissal. So
> I went for a drink with the policeman, we had an *anjou sec* at the Tourelles.
> What company I keep! God in Heaven, what company!

The raconteur needs his initial alarm in order to make the most of his
punchline. He had been expecting his dismissal, duly carried out with
bureaucratic punctiliousness, but the unexpected police visit could easily have meant worse: arrest and internment. There is genuine fear here.
Masking it, Feldman's mordant humour is evident throughout the diary,
nowhere more so than when he tells identity stories. In these months,
when he is under such serious pressure from the authorities, he accu-
mulates them:

> Et pour finir, dimanche après-midi, un 'thé-conversation' chez un voisin
> rouennais, un percepteur! [...] Et la femme vaporeuse et *milovidnaïa*

[charmante] du percepteur qui m'a dit d'un ton approbateur: 'Au lycée
Corneille, les élèves parlent de vous qui vous êtes engagé: M. Feldman, *quel
exemple pour la jeunesse!*' (*sic*, re-*sic* et sur-*sic*). Me voici proposé à la légende
de la *gens* honorable. Cimetière avec une dame pieuse, 'anjou' avec un
agent, thé et légende avec un percepteur, et des parties d'échecs avec des
soldats allemands et un inspecteur de la sûreté. Tant de belles fréquenta-
tions m'impressionnent. Qui l'eût cru? (ibid.)

And to finish up, Sunday afternoon, 'tea and sympathy' at the house of
a neighbour in Rouen, a tax collector! [...] Whose wife, charming and in
the clouds, said to me approvingly: 'The students at the lycée Corneille
talk about you, Monsieur Feldman; you volunteered. *What an example for our
young people.*' (*sic*, re-*sic*, *sic* again). Look at me, candidate for a legendary
role in the tribe of respectability. Cemetery with a devout lady, *anjou* with
a policeman, tea and legend with a tax collector, and chess with German
soldiers and a security inspector. I am impressed by all this fine company.
Who would have thought it?

He has mastered his technique for not standing out in an environment from which he is deeply alienated. However, the company he keeps
will not keep him. All these anecdotes tell stories of blending in, of keeping company with the enemy. He appears to have a place, but it is in the
here and now, guaranteed neither by his past nor into his future, and
potentially undermined by his place in other company. The company
one keeps – the keeping of that company – is indeed one of the daily
practices of identification, and because it is a practice, it is open to *feinte*,
to pretence. In the next example, he had gone as an observer, to see for
himself the strength of right-wing Catholic *bien-pensant* participation in
proclaiming true French identity.

Hier, – place du Vieux-Marché où je suis allé dans l'après-midi, histoire
de me rendre compte, une assez belle manifestation, typiquement
bourgeoise [...] Tous ces vieux messieurs, aussi ces dames de l'A.F. [l'Action
française] avaient répondu à l'appel de Jeanne [...] c'est bien la première
fois de ma vie que je me trouve dans une foule ayant Jeanne d'Arc pour
objet d'unanimes pensées. Il n'était pas donné à tout le monde de suivre
Maurras et Doriot dans leurs pérégrinations annuelles. Et il n'est point
dans mes habitudes de forcer le destin. (12 May 1941, 283)

Yesterday – the Old Market square: I went there in the afternoon, to see for
myself; a fine demonstration of the bourgeois kind [...] All those old gentlemen, the ladies too, from the A.F. [Action française], had heard the call of

Joan [...] But it is surely the first time in my life that I have found myself in a crowd thinking in unison about Joan of Arc. Not everyone gets the chance to follow Maurras and Doriot [prominent French fascists] in their annual pilgrimages. Nor is it my style to tempt fate.

The procession is itself a performance of identity in two senses, both in the literal theatrical sense and in the Goffmanian adaptation of that sense. It is ritualized, staged, put on for an audience, and it also serves to proclaim and enact the 'we' of its participants. Feldman's comment shows both these dimensions: he is there to observe – wondering, no doubt, who is in the crowd and gauging the support for l'Action française – and he appears to have participated, at least to the extent of showing the crowd that he is 'with' them. Being there, however, is a feint: in all these anecdotes, he performs like a fully paid-up member of a community that would exclude him if only his other faces were known.

Note, however, that nowhere in these passages does he in fact write 'nous'; the diary serves as a place in which he can dissociate from the people with whom he has acted. They are 'they,' he is 'I,' and the implied addressees of the diary, his 'we,' are those who would understand the jokes – his partner and his comrades in arms, let us suppose. And Valentin Feldman himself, as he writes to rehearse his day and enjoy his performance, at the same time as performing his backstage self. These people would not feel betrayed by his participation in this right-wing community because they would understand the why and the how of this complex play of identities, but the right-wing community would most certainly feel betrayed by discovering that an outsider had masqueraded as one of them.

When Goffman considers the issue of masquerade (mystification, misrepresentation, impersonation, and so on), he overlooks the possibility that one may have to adopt a role as a matter of life and death. I assume that it is for this reason that Goffman's analysis is framed in moralistic terms: one is 'sincere' or one is 'cynical.' The cynic is one who may experience 'a kind of gleeful spiritual aggression from the fact that he can toy at will with something his audience must take seriously.'[67] Perhaps this would be his analysis of Feldman's jokes. But the presupposition of such an analysis is exactly the one we have already found haunting Goffman's work, notwithstanding his attempts to lay the ghost: there is a real person with motives and emotions underlying the presented self. Ultimately, this makes the theatrical account unsatisfactory, not only because moral categories of this kind have no sociological underpinning, but also because the presupposition shows the limitations of Goffman's analysis taken as an account of identity. It continues to be the case that, for him,

identification practices and the reality of the inner person remain distinct, with the latter ultimately responsible for both the mastery of the
role and for its truth – by which is meant not only the extent to which the
actor convinces the audience and himself, but also its underpinnings,
some emotional, spiritual core that remains untheorized. This perpet-
uates the tradition of the 'soul' – for which, I believe, 'identity' is the
secular substitute.

We might look to Judith Butler's radical critique of identity to find a
way out of this difficulty.[68] Since she is concerned with sexual identity,
there are some limits to drawing an analogy with the situation that concerns me here – that is, the imposition of the J-label and the unwilling
compliance of those who were subject to it. Nevertheless, it is well fitted
to describing two aspects of this situation: the mechanisms of power that
enforced it, and the forms of resistance that became available through
these mechanisms. Further and more specifically, I am persuaded by
Butler's revision of the notion of performance by which she makes it
converge with 'performativity.'

Butler's revision of Goffman moves through a reworking of Foucault's
account of an 'aesthetics of existence,' which Stuart Hall glosses as 'a
deliberate stylization of daily life; ... its technologies are most effectively
demonstrated in the practice of self-production, in specific modes of conduct, in what we have come from later work to recognize as a kind of *performativity.*'[69] Importantly, in Butler's work, the performative is not a show
for an audience but, following Austin's use of the term,[70] the production
of real effects: the illocutionary act does not describe a state of affairs,
but 'makes it so'; all performative acts *change* the environment in which
they are uttered. They are acts with force, effective because, following
Derrida's account of citation and iteration, they are not owned by a single
actor or occasion. Hence, the effects are not punctual and not ephem-
eral; they are 'tenuously constituted through time.'[71] Indeed, repetition
is 'the mechanism for the cultural reproduction of identities'; they are
'tools' lying about, inert but potent, 'where the very "taking up" is enabled by the tool lying there.'[72] And they are deeds, with no doer behind
them; the 'doer is variably constructed in and through the deed.'[73]

As we have found with our examples, if identificatory acts, gestures,
and presentations of self are practices of performance, then they can be
mimicked, but this does not mean that all identity performance is mim-
icry. Butler's work has sometimes been construed as implying just that,
because of the prominent place of the concept of parody in her account
of impersonation. If 'gender is impersonation,' she writes in *Bodies That
Matter*, does that mean that one puts on a mask or persona, that there
is a 'one' who precedes that 'putting on'?[74] No, because 'the practice by

which gendering occurs, the embodying of norms, is a compulsory practice, a forcible production';[75] if 'embodying is a repeated process ... one
might construe repetition as precisely that which *undermines* the conceit
of voluntarist mastery designated by the subject in language.'[76] It cannot be achieved by a simple act of will. Let us apply this analysis first to
the practices of identification perpetrated by the anti-Semitic authorities
and then to the forms of resistance we have found in our examples.

The force of the J-label was achieved precisely through repetition: the
census, the file system, the notices on businesses, the ration cards and
other identity papers, and the imposition of the star, the last being worn,
and thus shown, repeatedly, on every occasion the Jewish person left the
house. The labelling continued in acts of arrest, in the bureaucratic procedures we have seen in the case of Feldman and in his dismissal. It was
pursued in arrest, in further categorization in the prisons and camps,
in deportation, in the destination of the convoy, and finally in the selections. On the part of the person submitting to these forms of labelling,
it was sometimes incorporated in posture and behaviour: witness the
contrast between Jacqueline Mesnil-Amar's father's mien in the street,
and the 'furtive and self-effacing' Jews she describes elsewhere (6 August
1944, 55). However, there can be no question of the formation of desire
in these cases. We might say that 'incorporation' was achieved by internment (its effects on the body), by killing, and by the plundering and
abuse of corpses, but not by a living performance. In place of any bodily
investment of the J-identification, anti-Semitism resorted to caricature.

This brings me back to the performance of Mesnil-Amar's father and
that of Feldman. In each case, we have two personae, two roles, two
modes of behaviour – two, because what might have been a single mixed
entity under another dispensation has been divided by the categoriza-
tions at work. In neither is one a mask manipulated by a soul-like entity;
in each case, the agency is produced as an effect of the relation between
the two: one needs protection, the other provides the tools. It finds those
tools 'lying around' in the repertoire accumulated from the identification practices appropriate to, and appropriated by, the performance of
a place in society, now in the past and no longer licit. In the case of
Feldman particularly, the persona is not centrally constituted by looks or
dress, by acts or gestures, although such props are used punctually to reinforce the impression: the central ingredient is the company he keeps –
the 'place' in society he continues to occupy while he must (or can). By
contrast, Mesnil-Amar's father, although walking at ease along the street
(of a *quartier* where he lives in hiding), no longer frequents the stock
exchange or welcomes establishment personalities to his table. Both
men live, precariously and for the nonce, on two sides of the boundary.

   This boundary is formed by the process of 'abjection,' by which, Butler
argues, something originally part of a 'we' identity is ejected and trans-
valued 'into a defiling otherness.' This is what happened under Nazism.
The bodily metaphor is adapted to political use: 'cultural and hegem-
onic identities' are founded and consolidated by the exclusion of some
Other or set of Others, thus constituting 'a border and boundary tenuously maintained for the purposes of social regulation and control.'[77]
However, borders are necessarily ambiguous places, enabling escape *into*
the crowd as well as from it; it is this ambiguity, the very instability of a
border that requires constant shoring up, that make resistance and subversion possible. I turn now to an example in which the impersonation
of abjected Jewish identity is performed to politically subversive ends.

Françoise Siefridt

'Je me promenais sur le Boul' Mich' avec Paulette, arborant chacune une
magnifique étoile jaune de notre fabrication. J'avais écrit sur la mienne
"papou"' (I went for a walk on the Boulevard Saint Michel with Paulette,
each of us sporting a splendid yellow star we had made. On mine I had
written 'Papuan').[78] This is the opening of Françoise Siefridt's diary,
which covers the period of her internment, from 7 June (the date on
which the wearing of the star was enforced) until 31 August 1942; on her
arrest, she was first taken to the caserne de Tourelles, then transferred
to Drancy. She was one of a small number of non-Jewish people – many
of them, like her, devout Christians – to adopt this form of protest: she
records seven at Tourelles (13 June 1942, 99) and ten in Drancy (20 June
1942, 104), none of whom expected that their protest would earn them
arrest.[79] Their action was not concerted, it was spontaneous, and, as
with those engaged in building barricades and other informal resistance
actions, they were a motley group:

> C'est dans mon dortoir que se trouvent toutes les Aryennes qui ont porté
> l'étoile. Il y a une vieille dame de la bourgeoisie, digne et respectable, une
> employée des postes fiancée à un Juif, deux employées de bureau dont l'une
> a un petit garçon, et son mari prisonnier en Allemagne, une fille-mère qui
> travaillait dur pour élever seule son petit garçon, une dactylo, une march-
> ande de journaux. Cette dernière n'a peur de rien. C'est un vrai moineau
> de Paris. Quand on lui demande sa nationalité, elle répond: 'Parisienne
> pur-sang.' (13 June 1942, 99)

> I'm in the dormitory with the other Aryan women who wore the star. There's
> an elderly middle-class lady, dignified and respectable, a postal clerk whose

fiancé is Jewish, two office workers, one of whom has a little boy, and whose husband is a prisoner in Germany, a single mother who has worked very hard to bring up her little son, a typist, and a newspaper vendor. This last is fearless; she's a true Parisian. When you ask her her nationality, she replies: 'Pure bred Paris.'

A bond is formed among the 'amis des Juifs' (friends of the Jews). A young man signals to her on her arrival at Drancy, identifying himself as one of the same grouping: 'Nous nous faisons des signes qui veulent dire que nous sommes amis, puisque enfermés pour la même raison' (13 August 1942, 132; We signal to each other that we're friends, because we're locked up for the same reason). Extending her fellow feeling beyond the bounds of this group, she writes of her relationship with the other internees in her dormitory, then beyond: 'Dans ce camp, il règne une atmosphère à la fois de bouge et de camaraderie' (13 August 1942, 134; the atmosphere of this camp is like that of a slum, but with a sense of companionship).

The expression *ami/e des Juifs* is a formal label, invented to deal with this group of protesters. Their action wreaked havoc on the identity boundaries established by the Gestapo. At the outset, the carceral system recognized three categories of prisoners, using the geography of the prison to separate them, and imposing on each a different punitive regime. There are the political prisoners, the common-law prisoners, and the Jews. To start with, Siefridt is placed with the first of these, where she sketches both the membership of the groups and the relations among them (9 June 1942, 95), but two days later she is taken out of the political group and placed with the Jews (11 June 1942, 96). Later still, the Jews are segregated, and a new category created: 'Ce matin, les dix Aryennes qui sont au camp pour avoir porté l'étoile jaune le 7 juin reçoivent l'ordre de porter l'étoile juive, et une banderole avec l'inscription "amie des Juifs"' (20 June 1942, 104; This morning, the ten Aryan women who are in the camp for wearing the star on 7 June have been ordered to wear the Jewish star, with a banner reading 'Friend of the Jews'). At the beginning of July the size of the banner is increased (6 June 1942, 113).

What the Gestapo intends as a device to name and shame the protesters works in practice quite otherwise. It identifies them exactly as they wish to be identified, and proclaims solidarity with their fellow internees. It also dissociates them from the silent collusion of sections of the Catholic Church,[80] and identifies them for others of like mind. For the Jewish women with whom she shares a dormitory, Françoise Siefridt is an enigma. They hesitate to form a 'we' with her; their response to her action shows the extent to which they have internalized the abjecting identification imposed on them: "'Pourquoi as-tu fait cela pour nous? ... Tu ne sais pas que nous ne sommes pas des jeunes filles comme les autres. Nous avons une tache, nous. Comment as-tu pu nous estimer? C'est un malheur actuellement d'être juif'" (13 August 1942, 133; 'Why did you do that for us? ... Don't you know we're not like the other girls? We are stained. How could you value us? These days it's bad luck to be Jewish'). This is a composite quotation, evidently, but its elements are eloquent: we're not like others, we are stained, how could you respect us? They reveal what is meant by 'friend': through this act of self-inclusion, the protesters identify with the Jews, they are marked in the same way, they do not disdain them, they share their misfortune. Something more poignant is meant, too, as the protesters set about looking after orphaned and sick children (15 August 1942, 137ff.). The children are being prepared for deportation: 'Je cause avec eux,' writes Siefridt. '"Alors, vous êtes mon amie...?" me disent-ils' (16 August 1942, 139; While I chat with them, they say to me 'So you're my friend?').

When Françoise Siefridt and her fellow protesters adopt the star, they subvert the boundary that abjects the Jews, joining the Jews in that abjection, lending them dignity. They are doing something similar to the parodic performances that interest Judith Butler. The boundary is shown to be precarious, needing to be shored up, reinforced by oppressing the friends by the same means as those to whom they are friends, and forcing an increase in the numbers included in the rejected category, thus making nonsense of its logic. We can see in this act and its sequels the opposite of the other kinds of boundary crossing we have observed in this chapter – both evasion and flight (Lania), and blending into the crowd (Feldman, Jules Perquel). In these cases, a boundary is crossed in order to find safety; in the case of the wearers of the star, it is crossed in the opposite direction. But in both cases, the porosity of the border is tested, proved, by performance.

There is, however, a significant difference between the two cases. It pertains to what Feldman calls the company one keeps. By keeping company – identifying – with the other prisoners, Siefridt can write that 'en prison les amitiés se nouent rapidement et prennent tout de suite tout notre être' (18 June 1942, 102; in prison, friendships form quickly and immediately take hold of us totally). The investment of 'all our being' in solidarity with the population of prisoners is probably what Goffman calls 'sincerity.' Butler gives us a more satisfactory analysis. Feldman keeps certain company only instrumentally, and opportunely, knowing that these relationships cannot last beyond his discovery, and dis-identifying from these worthy people in his diary. While Siefridt's action is voluntary and deliberate, it interacts with the operations of power that control the

environment in which it is conceived and carried out. The doer is constructed by the deed: wearing the costume of the friends of the Jews is
performative, where proclaiming makes it so.

The Slender Thread of Memory

There arises from the stories I have analysed a persistent question, one
that I have equally persistently evaded. This is the question of continuity.
Erikson insisted that continuity was essential to identity, and the problem of the sociological analysis is precisely that the account it presents
would be fragmented and occasional, were it not for 'the slender thread
of memory.' We have seen that Goffman's notion of 'teams' in which
roles are taken up is insufficient to deal with this problem. Two problems
arise from this notion of continuity: (1) If memory underpins the continuity of selves across the radical changes undergone by the people we
have discussed, what is memory? What is the repressed that interpellates
Léo Lania; what returns in Jacqueline Mesnil-Amar's ancestral 'nous'?
(2) What is the memory Mesnil-Amar's father carries of who he has been,
in his bearing, his manners, his refusal to wear the star? I have adduced
the *topos* of the stories that position us for the first of these questions;
for the second, I can adduce the Peircean idea of the person as a bundle or 'network' of habits.[81] Peirce's view displays evident connections
with the function of 'reiteration' in Butler's account of identity. Culled
from Peirce's admittedly fragmentary comments, this serves as a means
of unpacking Goffman's 'psychobiological peg.'[82]

A 'man's Real Self, or True Nature,' writes Peirce, 'the very springs of
Action in him,' are 'habits.'[83] Habits are conservative, but are not static:
hence 'the self is a sign in the process of developing,' not a discrete
entity but a coordination of 'ideas' developing relationally, with habits
accreted from past experience and challenges to those habits requiring
adjustment to meet the future.[84] The capacity of the organism 'to take
and to lose habits' rests in its 'limitless capacity ... to learn.'[85] Note that
Peirce invokes an 'organism': 'the human body with its unique capacities plays an *indispensable* role' in survival and adaptation.[86] It is logically
and empirically necessary to the acquisition of self-consciousness, which
Peirce takes to be indispensable to any account of the self. I note that the
writing of a diary is a concerted and systematic act of self-consciousness.

Taking these ideas into account, the last story in this chapter allows
me to recapitulate many of the themes I have discussed in the foregoing
stories, while at the same time broaching the question of continuity. We
will see that the slender thread of memory is a great deal more complex
than we might first expect. At the end of his memoir, Jean-Claude Stern

writes, 'Maintenant, je vais essayer de vivre' (Now, I will start to live).[87] The sentence marks the radical discontinuity in his life recounted in the preceding pages; in it, 'maintenant' refers to the historical present, a moment bringing one period to an end and inaugurating another: not so much 'life,' but 'living,' is written into a tentative, though resolute future. It challenges an enquiry into the experience of identity to ask how there was a 'je,' an 'I,' that could undertake this task of starting over. What is it that accounts for the continuity between past and future that is asserted against all odds by this sentence?

That there is an 'I' who can tell the story is another thing. In support of a broader argument concerning 'the history of the person,' Nikolas Rose points to the production of personhood through a diversity of technologies, including discursive genres such as autobiography and biography: 'Memory of one's biography is not a simple psychological capacity, but is organized through rituals of storytelling, supported by artefacts such as photograph albums and so forth.'[88] This is amply attested by the circumstances in which Stern's story was written: it was put together from his diary and a series of conversations with his daughter, these conversations being recorded and then edited by the two interlocutors working together, with the diary not retained integrally but used as a basis for the events of a particular period. All of it is written in the first person, but this first person is an artefact of the editing process. It is important to bear in mind that not only the impression of resilience and courage, but the very continuity of this first person, are effects of these practices. Looking back, the first person constructs the coherence of his life story – he is the agentive locus of his habits.

Jean-Claude Stern

Born in France and brought up in a household that observed traditional Jewish practice, Jean-Claude Stern was mobilized as an army communications technician, then demobilized following the *débâcle*. After a period working in the South, he joined a *maquis*. He kept a diary during his period as a French soldier and for a short time afterwards, but not during his Resistance years. The story of his first contacts with the Resistance provides a clear demonstration of the constitution of a 'we.'

The story proceeds through the use of pronouns, which starts from an isolated Jew looking for a contact ('un pauvre type comme moi, un juif isolé' [July 1941–December 1942, 57; a poor sod like me, an isolated Jew]), and ends up in *nous* (we). The *nous* takes some time to emerge, going through several steps to conjugate its two members. When he refers to a comrade, Delente, 'he and I' is not yet 'we' in the first stages as they circle around one another (58); the narrative uses the impersonal third-person 'on.' Then 'il me propose de l'accompagner' (59; he suggests I go with him), and 'lui et moi' (he and I) is used with the first person plural. The *nous* is used as the actor when 'he' and 'I' are part of a larger group comprising other members of the cell. When these others disappear into the woods, 'lui et moi rentrons' (he and I go back to town). Still 'he' and 'I' are distinct, with a first person plural verb. Then *nous* is established: 'Delente m'apprend alors que ces maquis *nous* concernent, tous les deux ... une confiance totale et réciproque exist[e] désormais entre *nous*' (61; emphasis added; then Delente tells me that these cells are the business of *both of us* ... from then on, there is total trust between *us*).

The caution displayed in this passage of nearly four pages in length – recounting 'des mois de travaux d'approche' (58; months of circling around one another) – is required to build the group. This process entails patrolling its borders; trust between its members cannot be established without taking every precaution against spying and leaks. There are several instances of infiltration, none of them fatal, but all of them representing danger (e.g., August 1943, 67). Clandestine activities necessitated a total break with the outside world, so even personal communication with others beyond the group must cease. Stern buries his identity papers, and finds himself with no name, no address, no work, no safe place to live in (67) until false papers and work with a comrade provide him with cover. He has no further contact with his family; after the Liberation, he will discover that they were all deported and killed; even the family apartment had been stripped of all its contents (August 1944– December 1945, 124).

Stern's identification with the Resistance was exclusive; the 'we' he had formed with Delente, and then with the wider *maquis* of the area, entailed total rupture from all other groups to which he had been attached previously. In order to understand what this entailed in practice, we must return to the outbreak of the war. He had been employed in paid professional work for the first time in 1939, having qualified as a communications engineer. All his schooling had been in France; his father and uncle were professionally trained, as an engineer and as an architect, respectively, and both were decorated veterans (January–June 1941, 56). From his early youth, he identified as a Jew and as a Frenchman, where 'la France' is symbolized primarily by its military heroes and army (1919–36, 11). Brought up in 'cette ambiance "ancien combattant"' (this veteran atmosphere), with a traditional Jewish education alongside the secular school he attended (ibid.), he had minimal interest in politics and was simply puzzled by his parents' cautious response to the election of a

government led by Léon Blum. The significant thing to note here is the
contrast between the sixteen-year-old, for whom the elevation of a Jew to
high public office is a subject of pride, and his parents, who believe it to be
a risk not worth taking (1919–36, 13). Their caution recalls Mesnil-Amar's
sketch of modest, furtive, self-effacing Jews. They understood more of what
was happening in Germany at the time than their children did (1919–36,
12), and no doubt wished to protect them from fear. No doubt, too, they
had memories of the Dreyfus affair, but, even as the bad news became
more insistent and the danger more imminent, the young Jean-Claude
did not feel threatened. Words were not acts in his understanding:

> Complètement absorbé par mes études et mes activités de radio amateur,
> je n'ai aucune conscience du jusqu'auboutisme des 'Mort aux Juifs!' qu'on
> entend et voit écrit partout sur les murs de Paris. Je ne me sens pas vraiment
> concerné. C'est pour moi comme 'À bas machin!', 'Vive truc!' Des mots et
> non des actes. (14)

> Totally taken up with my studies and my amateur activities with the radio,
> I am completely unaware of just how far 'Death to the Jews!' will be pushed.
> You hear it and see it written all over he walls of Paris, but I don't feel it's
> about me. I'm sure they're words, not acts, like 'Down with whatsit!' and
> 'Long live whosit!'

Notwithstanding their awareness of anti-Semitism, the parents also
felt protected by their Frenchness. With respect to the awareness of
their son, the passage below reveals some ambiguity: the first sentence
shares the parental optimism in its assertion that his family is not greatly
affected, whereas the second does not; and the last paragraph is clearly
written in hindsight.

> Le Statut des Juifs, signé par le gouvernement de Vichy, affecte peu ma
> famille: les anciens combattants de la Grande Guerre 14–18, comme mon
> père et mon oncle, se sentent intouchables. Ne sont-ils pas Français, an-
> ciens soldats aux nombreuses médailles, bons travailleurs, l'un ingénieur,
> l'autre architecte, tranquilles pères de famille payant leurs impôts, toujours
> respectueux de la loi?
>   En réalité, ils sont totalement inconscients du danger. L'horreur qui les
> guette est tellement inimaginable qu'ils ne l'imaginent pas. (January–June
> 1941, 56)

> Signed into law by the Vichy government, the *Statut des Juifs* has little effect
> on my family: returned soldiers from the Great War, like my father and my

uncle, feel protected. Aren't they French, former soldiers covered with medals, good workers, one an engineer and the other an architect, quiet-living family men who pay their taxes, law-abiding citizens?

In fact, they are totally unaware of the danger. The horror that awaits them is so unimaginable that they cannot imagine it.

Notwithstanding the need to hope for the best, the son is concurrently taking stock himself: 'J'assiste à la prise de conscience des gens par rapport à la France Libre, à ma propre prise de conscience' (ibid.; I note people becoming aware of the Free France movement, I note it in myself). It is time to find a way to act.

Nevertheless, his childhood 'admiration pour les héros de Verdun' (1919–36, 11; admiration for the heroes of Verdun) is so strong that, even in 1940, following the capitulation, he believed with many others in the wily old man, sure that 'le maréchal Pétain joue un tour de cochon aux Allemands sur le plan militaire' (ibid., 42; Marshal Pétain is playing a dirty military trick on the Germans). Later still, he remained convinced that 'seul Pétain peut éviter une capitulation plus complète encore. Ayons confiance en lui comme en De Gaulle' (December 1940–January 1941, 52; only Pétain can avoid total capitulation. Let's believe in him as well as de Gaulle.) It is remarkable that the text contains no explicit repudiation of this habit of faith in the 'hero of Verdun.'

Thus far, we have discerned three constituent features in Stern's bundle of identifications. One is this idealized faith in the military. The second is identification with his Jewish religion; the emotion generated by this – following his pride in the elevation of Léon Blum – becomes shocked disappointment as he discovers he is excluded from a certain idea of France. The third is his identification with France. All three are formed in early childhood, all three are deeply bound with his familial relations, and none is readily open to revision. His idealization of France, however, is 'finished' with the advent of the *statut*: 'Je suis donc, à cause de ma religion, interdit d'accès à de nombreux métiers, des portes se ferment devant moi ... Liberté, Égalité, Fraternité, la devise de la France dont mon maître parlait à l'école, c'est fini' (July 1941–December 1942, 47; So because of my religion, I am excluded from numerous occupations, doors are closing in my face ... Liberty, Equality, Fraternity, the motto of France I learned to understand from my primary school teacher, it's done for.)

The *statut* represents a betrayal of the France that is represented by its motto and emblematically symbolized by the brief success of Léon Blum.[89] As we watch Stern in the course of his engagement in the Resistance, his identification with this betrayed France cannot be disentangled from his identification as a Jew. Thus, for example, in his early teenage years, having joined the French Jewish Scout movement, he rejects the Zionism of his comrades:

> J'apprécie toutes nos activités et pourtant je me bagarre souvent car, pendant les camps, on hisse deux drapeaux: l'un français, l'autre israélien. L'État d'Israél n'existe pourtant pas encore! Je considère ce dernier comme secondaire. Et je rouspète. Je ne veux que le drapeau tricolore, le seul. (1919–36, 12)[90]

> I enjoy all our activities, yet I often get into fights because at these camps, two flags are raised: the French flag and the Israeli flag. Long before the existence of the state of Israel! It has secondary importance for me. And I protest. I want only one flag, the *tricolore*.

We can surmise that Stern was motivated to join the Resistance by something more complex than nationalism. His future in France had been precluded by the *statut*, and he had become an outcast: 'Pire que tout, j'ai beau me regarder dans la glace, examiner mes mains, mes bras, etc., je ne vois aucune différence avec mes copains. Pourtant, je suis désormais un exclu' (September–October 1940, 47; Worst of all, looking in the mirror, examining my hands, my arms and so on, I see no difference between me and my friends. But I am now an outcast.) The 'mirror' is the trope of self-recognition. It is here that he experiences for the first time the cleft between what he sees and what others see when they look at him. He does not 'see' a Jew so much as a French soldier, but his administrative identification will ensure that the mirror no longer gives an image of the real. 'J'ai un cafard abominable,' he writes. 'Je m'endors avec difficulté' (ibid.; I am dreadfully depressed; I have trouble getting to sleep). Nevertheless, apart from a family emergency,[91] there is little to indicate that his Resistance activities are specifically motivated by his Jewish allegiance, and because of his clandestine existence, there is no Jewish practice possible between 1941 and 1944. Outcast, then outlawed, his personal, and thus his Jewish, identity are not restored until the Liberation, the latter evident from the fact that he was married in a synagogue.

Stern's life thus displays something that must have been the case for many people – the persistence of deeply rooted habits of belief at the same time as a radical discontinuity of his identity vis-à-vis the world of his daily activities. This latter is marked by the hiding of his identity papers for the purposes of clandestine activities – 'Maintenant, je n'ai plus de nom, de date de naissance ni d'adresse, plus de travail ni de logement' (August 1943, 67; From now I have no name, no date of birth, no address, no work and nowhere to live) – and the taking of a false name (68). Any exclusive identity is a precarious base for a future when the role is over. He gives up all contact with his family and receives no news of them for some time before their arrest. His bond with his family appears to have been very strong; it is broken in practice by his clandestine existence and then by their fate. Even the pillaged family apartment contains no object that could serve as a memento except for a single crumpled photograph of his little niece. How – with what or whom – did he identify in this void?

The answers to this question all rely on retrieving some elements of continuity with his previous life. First, he joins the army; this involves a change of costume. The day of his demobilization, 19 January 1941, is marked by giving up his military kit, a fact that brings him back into ordinary society: 'habillé en civil, une véritable métamorphose, je rends mes derniers vêtements militaires aux autorités et touche ma solde' (December 1940–January 1941, 54; dressed in civvies, it's a complete metamorphosis; I return the last of my military clothes to the authorities and get my pay). The last notes in the diary of this period as a soldier show him dreaming of rejoining the army 'si c'est pour flanquer à la porte, une bonne fois pour toutes, les gars d'en haut et à droite, comme on dit. Et Vive la France!' (January–June 1940, 55; if it's for throwing the squatters out once and for all, and long live France!). When he does so, in August 1944, it is with the Free French forces. Under orders from his superior officer to 'reprendre ma véritable identité' (August 1944–December 1945, 122; take back my true identity), he drops his *nom de guerre* – 'ce jour-là, le capitaine Auguste disparaît définitivement' (ibid.; that day, Captain Auguste disappears for ever) – and he is dressed again in a 'tenue quasi militaire' (123; something like a military uniform). Costume has been a cover for him; it now matches his 'true identity.'

The expression 'true identity' refers to the information contained in his identity papers and in his civic files. This is his family identity – his name and his officially recorded genealogy. The family itself cannot be restored, but, once his name is re-established, he can claim the family apartment. This is the second thread of continuity. 'Je retrouve simplement le droit de louer à mon nom l'appartement de mon enfance. Et il me faudra, bien entendu, verser au propriétaire les loyers impayés depuis l'arrestation de mes parents, les loyers de 1943–44' (August 1944–December 1945, 124; Without much trouble I claim back the right to take the lease on my childhood home in my own name. Of course, I have to pay the landlord the unpaid rent since the time of my parents' arrest, rent from 1943 to 1944). Notice the importance of the name here and, significantly, that of paying the arrears in rent. On first sight, this demand is shocking, but we should note that, by complying with it, he is able to claim, and to make good that claim with the landlord and the legal authorities, that the apartment has continued to belong to his family, and hence, he to it. If his life-long address stands for a habit of place, it brings with it habits of occupying and circulating in its spaces, and in the spaces of which it constitutes his quotidian centre.

The third thread is his profession. From a very early age (we can presume he was around ten years old), he was obsessed with 'the wireless': 'je me passionne surtout pour la TSF ... – la radio de l'époque' (1919–36, 11; my great passion was for the wireless – the radio at that time). The passion continues as a hobby (14), and then as his professional vocation: his first employment is in the research laboratory of Radio City (1937–40, 15). This is also his role in the army (ibid., also September–October 1940, 46–7), while after the defeat, he finds ways of listening to the BBC (December 1940–January 1941, 51) and sorting out technical problems for others who also want to listen (January–June 1941, 55). He finds appropriate skilled work and uses it for both official and unofficial purposes (July 1941–December 1942, 57), and it is in this position that he meets Delente. By the end of 1942, with the occupation of the Southern Zone, there are strict prohibitions placed on radio technology and on the expertise and training needed for it; Stern steps into the breach (autumn 1942–winter 1943, 64), mastering the FM technology used by the Americans, then training comrades in it; it was a technology so new that it was unknown in France. His skills in radio technology continue to be useful to the Resistance (1944, 99, 101, 102–3, 106ff, 112 ff), and it is he who first gets the news of the Normandy landing (110–11). When he joins the Free French forces, radio communications are again his responsibility (August 1944–December 1945; 122 ff, 124).

The fourth thread of continuity he manages to retrieve is with a girl-friend, met in June 1943 through the good offices of his uncle and cousin in the Southern Zone. She had been his wartime penfriend, but the relationship had evolved. He had been able to inform his parents then of his decision to marry her. The match has family sanction, and their life is to be lived in the family home. For the ceremonies, they are appropriately costumed, he in his 'costume military uniform) and his bride 'ravissante en robe de lainage marron et chaussures à semelles de bois' (August 1944–December 1945, 125; lovely in a brown wool dress and shoes with wooden soles), both dressed in memories of the war that is not yet over.

All these threads of continuity rely on material practices. There is nothing ineffable, no soul, no psychic core that needs to be invoked in order to explain the persistence of the 'I.' But there is memory, both shared and archived. First, Stern is with his Resistance comrades when he meets up with the French Forces of the Interior; his identity is grounded in his membership in a team. When the colonel urges him to reclaim his 'true identity,' continuity is established by linking two sets of records – his original military record and the shared memory of his work in the Resistance – forming the basis of a renewed career: 'Maintenant, mon histoire se confond avec celle de l'armée française' (ibid.; Now my history cannot be disentangled from that of the French army). Second, the reclaiming of the family home depends both on his identity papers, which establish his place in the family, and on the entirely material transaction of paying the arrears in rent; the memory here resides in documents and their use, this in turn being governed by practices of the law. Third, the continuity of his skill set should be understood as a bodily memory, an intellectual training translated into the hands, the tools they take up, and their dealings with equipment. This body can carry its memory from team to team. And fourth, there is the marriage, with its tenuous connection to his parents, the new family established in the place, the very place, of the lost family: I am not alone, he writes, my wife's family is now mine (ibid.)

There is a 'we' in all the strands of this story of survival; at no point do we encounter an isolated 'I,' never is identification lodged in interiority. The first *topos*: my identity is my identification with those with whom I say 'we.' This connects with Goffman's idea of the 'team,' but teams are punctual, occasional, and can be dispersed. Shared memories, and collective practices, are required for the company I keep also to keep me. There is performance – notably the performance of his technical skills, the performatives of the marriage ceremony, and no doubt also those of the other legal decisions involved and of his appointments as captain and then as commander of his company (August 1944–December 1945, 123–4). The second *topos*: man is born naked, but he lives and dies fully dressed. We can take this now to mean all the trappings of his role, its equipment, its embodiment in skills and gestures. From the genealogy of the birth certificate to the epitaph with its stylized biography, Goffman's 'psychobiological peg' is in all cases incorporated and materialized. There is no membrane separating the self-hood of the self from the ramified network of memory practices by which it is situated – identified – in social space and time.

The third *topos*: 'Identities are the names we give to the different ways we are positioned by, and position ourselves in, the narratives of the past.'[92] These narratives, whether those of a single life or of a collective history, are repeated and ritualized. In the home (father's war) and in the schoolroom (the national motto), these too are performatives that situate the child in a story of belonging. In the case of Jean-Claude Stern, the operative narrative of the past is that of the heroes of Verdun; he spent his childhood believing in their legacy, and his war years fighting

to revive it. Positioning himself in relation with that story, he identifies as
his father's son, an enlisted man, a Resistance fighter, and then an officer:
'maintenant, mon histoire se confond avec celle de l'armée française'
(August 1944–December 1945, 125; now my story is one with that of the
French Army). When Stern looks in the mirror of his memoirs, he sees
a soldier; as he takes up his habits in the stripped apartment, he uses
this place to start again; then, writing his memoirs with his daughter, he
fulfils the promise of the *topos* of continuity.

In the following two chapters, I study the diaries of Raymond-Raoul
Lambert and Benjamin Schatzman, respectively. Together they demonstrate the struggle to maintain the self: the former in the strategic adaptation of professional habits involving self-conscious identity positions,
and the latter in systematic adaptive techniques to survive the conditions
of a concentration camp. These too are practices of continuity.

Chapter Two

The Place of the Self: The Diary of Raymond-Raoul Lambert

J'ai honte de mon impuissance. Mais il faut rester là pour avoir vu.

I am ashamed of my impotence. But I must stay where I am in order to have seen.

J'aurai le droit de parler après la guerre.

I shall have the right to speak after the war is over.
    – Raymond-Raoul Lambert, 11 October and 18 December 1942

Introduction

Diaries and memoirs are self-conscious practices of the self, differing one from the other in that, where memoirs are retrospective, diaries are written progressively, accompanying the living of a life. The former are public performances: recall Jean-Jacques Bernard, who writes to proclaim his Frenchness, and for whom that proclamation is designed to give the lie to the Jewishness for which he was punished. Likewise the composite text of Jean-Claude Stern, which acts as a mirror in which he watches himself in the role passed down from the inherited script of 'France.' Both texts present retrospective narratives in which outcomes and upshots are fully consistent with beginnings and middles. Diaries, by contrast, display the back-stage: I recall Valentin Feldman, whose hidden face is given expression in his diary; it gives him a clandestine space in which to perform his proscribed persona. In this chapter, the writing of a diary will again command my attention; in this case, the diary serves as a means to prepare and rehearse – in both senses – the public role.

   In the stories I have told in the previous chapter, a frequent trope has been that of place. If, as Jacques Derrida writes, it is nonsense to think in terms of 'having' – and hence of 'losing' – one's identity, it makes good sense, on the other hand, to speak of having, occupying, making, or losing one's place.[1] A refugee such as Léo Lania, fleeing across borders, is placeless as well as stateless, 'wandering,' as in the myth of the transnational Jew. In her use of the same trope, Jacqueline Mesnil-Amar opposes it to 'settled,' but for her it is a condition forced on the Jews by persecution – it is not the natural condition of 'the Jew,' as a Xavier Vallat, who wished to 'settle them' in Palestine, would have it. Jean-Jacques Bernard asserts his roots in France and complains that he is treated like the Jews who are just passing through. We recall Valentin Feldman's wry comments in the cemetery: a wanderer, with only a temporary visa, shown an eternal resting place and told of the grant of a burial plot in perpetuity: what a godsend that would be. Then there is Jean-Claude Stern, without identity papers, and therefore, without an address, eventually laying claim to his family home and settling there. Since identity papers – among other kinds of official certificates – carry a personal address as part of a person's administrative identity, we might say that the trope of place has force in modern civic administrative practices. It is, in fact, a complex mix of literal and metaphorical assumptions. To have a place is to belong. It entails community relations and social roles, habits of movement around a space. Indeed, I suggest that this trope gathers into itself all the *topoi* of identity I have discussed in the previous chapter. To explicate the place of a person is to say who they are.

The Jews of Europe lost their place in ways that varied considerably from circumstance to specific circumstance. In this chapter, I investigate the experience of the loss of place, and the struggle against this loss, in the case of Raymond-Raoul Lambert, who remained in prominent public life until his arrest in August 1943. He did not survive.

Background

One of the 'personnalités marquantes du monde juif d'avant-guerre' ('outstanding personalities of the Jewish world pre-war'); 'one of French Jewry's important leaders from the 1930s through the war years'; 'this extremely important Jewish leader'; 'arguably the most important French-Jewish official in contact with the Vichy Government and the Germans during the war': the prominence of Raymond-Raoul Lambert in Jewish life in France is undisputed in the major specialized histories.[2] This is not to say that his actions during the war were not controversial; they were, in fact, highly contentious. However, twenty years of historiography have made a difference to these debates. From the time he and his colleagues were excoriated as 'collaborators'[3] to the most recent assessments, there has been a considerable shift.[4] A moderate summation of the controversy is given by Julian Jackson, who writes of Lambert that he 'had once enjoyed the confidence of many leading French politicians' and that his diaries 'testify to his good faith, decency, and tragic naivety.'[5] It is not my task to reassess the politics of Lambert's work, although I will, perforce, allude to the contemporary as well as the retrospective controversy from time to time. My business is with his diary, and thus, with its writer's account of his experience. Before I come to it, however, it will be necessary to provide some context, introducing not only the organization for which Lambert took special responsibility during the war years but also the people with whom he had dealings.

Raymond-Raoul Lambert was born in 1894 to a long-established French Jewish family, originally from Metz, but living in Paris by this time. He attended the Lycée Rollin and served with distinction in the Great War, being awarded the Croix de Guerre for his actions at the battle of Chemin des Dames. He joined the French civil service and served as a representative on the Allied Rhineland High Commission, where he earned 'the respect and admiration of Germans and French alike.'[6] He was appointed for a time as deputy to Edouard Herriot and held a position in the Ministry of Foreign Affairs. A pan-Europeanist, he sought to further *rapprochement* between Germany and France after the war, showing a keen interest in political developments in the two countries and alert in the 1930s to the rise of anti-Semitism. He remained convinced that France could not go in the same direction, and the diary shows how shocked he was to learn that it had. In addition to his civil service work, he was a rising Jewish intellectual voice, writing regularly in Jewish periodicals and acting as editor-in-chief of one of them, *L'Univers israélite*. He is principally known, however, for his work on behalf of Jewish refugees throughout the 1930s; this was both welfare work and political work aimed at building bridges between the native French Jewish population and the newcomers, as well as negotiating on policy issues with successive governments. Deeply committed to this project, he served first as the general secretary of the Comité national de secours (the National Relief Committee) then following that, in the same role for the Comité d'assistance aux réfugiés (the Refugee Aid Committee; CAR). The history of the work of these and other associated organizations, their internecine dissensions, and the policy settings that conditioned them, is the subject of Vicki Caron's fine book *Uneasy Asylum*.[7] This history is important for understanding Lambert's struggles with the right wing of French Jewry, and in particular with the Paris Consistory[8] and its vice-president, later its president, Jacques Helbronner.[9]

The Comité national closed in 1935. According to Caron's analysis of the debates leading to this outcome, this was a decision taken deliberately by the 'hardliners' such as Helbronner. Seeking to 'prove once and for all that French Jews always put their French interests above their Jewish interests' – that is, to prove their unalloyed loyalty to France – this faction preferred to 'abandon all efforts on behalf of the persecuted victims of Nazism' rather than be seen as encouraging further numbers with excessive generosity.[10] The closure of the Comité national precipitated the marginalization of the hardliners from the practicalities of the issue, and the creation of the CAR, in which 'a more moderate leadership ... represented above all by Raymond-Raoul Lambert' took policy in a different direction: 'the principal aim' of the Comité national, writes Caron, '[had been] to get rid of the refugees,' whereas the CAR 'believed that French Jews had a moral obligation to help their persecuted coreligionists' and to seek constructive solutions for their settlement.[11] The hardliners did not persist in their opposition: 'the policies of French Jewish notables vis-à-vis the refugees underwent a dramatic transformation during the mid-1930s.'[12] However, there remained deep divisions within French Jewry on 'a range of issues,' but, with the moderates in charge, 'stubbornly refus[ing] to abandon the refugees, even though that stance pitted them against their own government,' a significant degree of consensus was eventually achieved.[13] Lambert's role in this transformation was considerable: he achieved major improvements in the organization of the relief work and the political negotiations required to keep it running, and hence, considerable success affecting thousands of people; he was unafraid to confront the government, but never lost his belief in France. Nevertheless, he failed to achieve his major aim, which was the adoption of a *statut des étrangers*, which he envisaged as a legally binding policy on immigration and the granting of refuge. In the light of this failure, he developed the principles that guided him in the work he was to do under the Vichy régime: these were to 'hold on and hold out' and to maximize small victories. No matter how inconsequential it might seem, 'every act of relief' contributes, he wrote, to the alleviation of 'immense suffering'; as such, it is 'indispensable.'[14]

These principles are consistent with his view that 'there exists no grandiose project, nor any constructive solution that might be capable of saving all the unfortunates who have pinned their hopes on our organizations.'[15] Lambert was a pragmatist who, in 1941–42, negotiated with the Vichy government to form, under its auspices, the Union générale des israélites de France (the General Union of French Jews; UGIF). At the instigation of the German authorities, this brought together under a single umbrella all the secular Jewish organizations in France. The Nazis envisaged a total unification of Jewish life under one administrative bureaucracy, on the model of the *Judenräte* of Eastern Europe, but there are numerous respects in which the UGIF did not resemble its model, and its role remained limited:[16] in practical matters it did not act on behalf of the occupying or Vichy authorities, but it did attempt to use the Vichy framework to continue its benevolent work.[17] It was Lambert who insisted that it should not conduct police work and who obtained an undertaking from the authorities to this effect. Because of the demarcation of France into two zones, there were two separate branches of the UGIF, whose internal structures and policies remained distinct. Lambert was in charge of UGIF-sud.[18]

The disputes in which Lambert was embroiled converge on this point. First, after he assumed a prominent role in the UGIF-sud, the internal dissensions in the French Jewish world resurfaced, taking the form of what Caron calls 'bickering over questions relating to leadership and representation.'[19] Helbronner, in particular, accused Lambert of taking over the representation of French Jewry without regard for the Consistories (whose bailiwick was limited to religious affairs); Lambert did not claim to do so, and eventually managed to persuade all concerned that he had no such ambition. But there remained considerable distrust between the two men – both, as Cohen puts it, 'blessed with inflated egos' – so it was difficult for them to work together on any practical matter, notably on forming a common front for dealings with the government.[20] Second, for Jewish Resistance groups, communists, and activists of other stripes, the 'legalism' espoused by the UGIF and its willingness to work within the framework set out by the Vichy authorities were nothing less than Jewish collaboration. This is the position argued by Maurice Rajsfuss and, more moderately, by Jacques Adler; Cohen and Caron provide a more nuanced view. As I read the scholarship on this and related matters, it seems clear to me that Rajsfuss's view is informed, on the one hand, by the widespread discrediting of UGIF policies and practices during the final year of its operation,[21] and on the other by the stark opposition between resistance and collaboration that prevailed in French historiography until the 1980s.[22] Besides, of the person himself, it is important to acknowledge that, even if Lambert was not a Resistance militant, this is not equivalent to condemning him as a collaborator.[23] While it is plain that he did not engage directly in Resistance activities, it is equally plain that he was unstinting in his efforts to support refugees and immigrants, and, where possible, to save any Jews at risk in the Southern Zone.[24] He was, I believe, motivated from the outset by his work prior to the outbreak of the war.[25] It is not for me to adjudicate the rights and wrongs of his actions, but rather to read those actions as performing – enacting – the identity of a 'Jew of France' that was becoming progressively less viable as the obstacles it encountered became more insurmountable. He could not, in the end, 'make it so.'

A Jew of France

Losing a Place

Like many others, Lambert asserts an identity that conjoins 'French' and
'Jewish': 'J'ai donc des craintes pour l'avenir de mes enfants, et j'ai des
craintes particulières en tant que français et que juif de France' (10 May
1941, 100; 'I fear for the future of my children, and my fears are particularly those of a Frenchman, a Jew of France' [38]).[26] He asserts his 'clear
desire to remain both an excellent Jew and an excellent Frenchman'
(30 November 1941, *Diary*, 76). Can he do so in an environment in
which any such formulation designates nothing but a mixed category?
For Lambert, these are declarations of assimilation, but what is assimilation, or integration, when mixity is the very incarnation of the evil that is
to be cast out of a racist Europe?

For Jean-Jacques Bernard, the mixed category is the site of a contradiction that demanded resolution; choosing 'Frenchness' over 'Jewishness,
he ultimately converted to Catholicism. Another remarkable case is that
of Henri Bergson, writing on 'the Jewish problem,' whose proclamation
of his 'Jewish solidarity' is followed by his concern that it should not run
counter to the 'national interest.' This was written in 1907, in the context
of a critique of anti-Semitism; Lambert quotes it gratefully (17 June 1942;
Diary, 172). He would never know that Bergson was to be the object of
an unpleasant, though short-lived, controversy on precisely this point.
A brief digression is in order.

In 1938, Bergson again formulated his sense of solidarity, this time in
a codicil to his will. In it, he reiterates his conviction that there was no
contradiction between being Jewish and Christian; accordingly, he would
have converted (and was widely believed to have done so), had it not been
for the rise of 'la formidable vague d'anti-Sémitisme qui va se déferler sur
le monde' (the fearsome wave of anti-Semitism that is about to break over
the world). Wanting, as he writes, to remain within the ranks of the persecuted, he nevertheless asks that a Catholic priest officiate at his funeral.[27]
Here was his public solidarity, and here, too, was his spiritual allegiance:
the one was social and political, the other was a matter for his soul. Yet
Bergson, who (like Spinoza) had incurred the wrath of some sections of
religious Jewry, considered these people to be his enemies. This enmity
is the background for two contentious sentences in the codicil. The one
that interests me is a parenthesis to the effect that anti-Semitism was provoked 'en grande partie, hélas, par la faute d'un certain nombre de juifs
entièrement dépourvus de sens moral' (largely, I regret to say it, by the
wrongs of a certain number of Jews entirely lacking in morality). When

his widow allowed the codicil to be published in *Le Journal de Genève* in 1941, she censored this damaging parenthesis. She was undoubtedly alert to the use that could have been made of it under Vichy, and she published the censored version anew, with a commentary, in a collective volume in memory of Bergson in 1942, also published in Geneva.[28] However, a different version, with the deletions restored, appeared in some newspapers in the Southern Zone, some time between these two approved versions. Finding them in 1947, a certain Léon Baratz became exceedingly angry. He trusted the censored version, using it to denounce the restored version. The offending sentences, he asserted, 'do not exist in the will' and had been interpolated to falsify Bergson's intentions.

It is clear from the title of Baratz's article ('Deux "juifs-chrétiens": Henri Bergson et J.-J. Bernard') that the principal point of his polemic is to oppose the attitude of Bernard with Bergson's solidarity.[29] His fury was reignited on the occasion of the doctoral defence of a Mme Mossé-Bastide, whose thesis clarified the issue of the interventions in the will and Mme Bergson's intentions in the matter. This defence was reported in *Le Monde*. Baratz wrote a long letter to the paper reiterating his view that the damning parenthesis was an anti-Semitic interpolation, as well as his view of 'ces crypto-juifs,' 'ces juifs entièrement assimilés ou mieux, dissimulés' (these crypto-Jews,' 'these Jews who are not so much assimilated as hidden), such as Bernard, whom he here denounces for his '"brimade" antisémitique tant qu'anti-sioniste' (anti-zionist, nay anti-Semitic outburst). The letter was not published.[30] Instead, *Le Monde* published the codicil as Bergson had written it.[31] The controversy – Mme Bergson's politically dictated discretion, Baratz's post-persecution fury – indicates how deeply the question of Jewish identity in France had changed in the disastrous intervening years. The issue of Jewish solidarity had completely overridden what had been the crucial issue pre-war, that of assimilation.

Assimilation, for Bergson and Bernard, and also for Victor Klemperer in Germany and many others, entailed accepting Christianity. What was it for Raymond-Raoul Lambert, who pledges never to renounce his Judaism in any way (6 November 1940; *Carnet*, 86; *Diary*, 24)?

> Dans l'histoire du judaïsme français la loi d'hérédité a été corrigée par la loi d'adaptation, étant donné la puissance d'assimilation du milieu national. Rien d'étonnant donc à ce qu'Israël en France soit moins absolu, plus fondu dans la nation muliforme comme dans ses types humains que partout ailleurs. (29 March 1942, 163)

> In the history of French Jewry, given our national culture's assimilating powers, the law of heredity has been mitigated by the law of adaptation. So it

is not surprising that the boundaries of 'Israel' in France are less clearly defined and tend to blend into this multifaceted nation with its many ethnic types, more than anywhere else. (112–13)

For Lambert, assimilation is a historical, a cultural, process, effected as much by the social environment, by the 'power' of the nation to assimilate its migrants, as by their cultural adaptation. This is entirely consistent with his understanding of anti-Semitism, that a society can refuse to exercise that power, 'considering' or 'seeing' Jews as eternal foreigners: 'On utilise la passion xénophobe, réveillée par la défaite et les restrictions, et on considère les Juifs, incapables de s'intégrer dans la communauté française, comme des individus éternellement étrangers dans tous les pays' (22 June 1941, 108; 'Xenophobic passions aroused by our defeat and the restrictions in force were exploited, and Jews were considered incapable of being integrated into the French community but rather seen as individuals who are eternal foreigners in every country' [47]).

Notice that, on this view, assimilation is different from what we might call 'conjugating' French and Jewish. In the structure of conjugation, one member or the other can be sloughed off. Thus Maurice Barrès expects that French Jews would, over time, either recant or simply lose their Jewishness and become freethinkers, and Bergson considers his Jewishness to be a matter of solidarity, not of confession.[32] The other side of this coin is for French Jews to be divested of their Frenchness. Thus, as Lambert writes, 'Il se peut donc que, dans quelques jours, je sois un citoyen diminué, que mes fils, français de naissance, de culture et de foi, soient brutalement et cruellement rejetés hors de la communauté française' (2 October 1940, 83; 'So it is possible that within a few days I shall see my citizenship reduced, and that my sons, who are French by birth, culture, and faith, will find themselves brutally and cruelly cast out of the French community' [20]). The point for Lambert was to be a 'French Jew' (10 May 1941; *Diary*, 38), as one would say 'a French Catholic' or a 'French Protestant.' Yet under anti-Semitism, France, as he sees it, had not exercised its assimilating powers, so the law of adaptation was disabled. As a result, the mixed category disaggregated into the conjugated formulation – French *and* Jewish (see, for example, 30 November 1941; *Diary*, 76). In a moment of despair, Lambert wonders if the only solution is resolution of the dilemma into its two terms, the national identity so reviled by Bernard, and the confessional identity bestowed by conversion: 'Mais il faut que je prenne garde à moi-même, car, aux heures de découragement, je ne vois que deux solutions parallèles au problème juif: le sionisme ou le baptème dans la dispersion' (2 July 1943, 233; 'But I must watch myself, for in times of discouragement I can see only two parallel solutions to the Jewish problem: Zionism, or baptism in the diaspora' [193]).

He will not give in; immediately following the formulation of this despairing dilemma, he calls on the source of a particular definition of the nation: 'au secours, Barrès!' ('Barrès, help!') (ibid.). This is the Barrès of *Les diverses familles spirituelles de la France*, first published during the Great War, and republished in 1930.[33] Lambert notes on 2 December 1941 that he reread it. In that work, Barrès makes the case that patriotism is the higher faith in which French diversity can find its unity, illustrating this with 'témoignages' from young heroes at the front. To open his chapter on the Jews, Barrès writes:

> Une grande affaire d'Israël dans son éternelle pérégrination, c'est de se choisir une patrie. Il ne la tient pas de ses aïeux; il l'acquiert alors par un acte de volonté, et sa nationalité est sur lui comme une qualité dont il se préoccupe de prouver qu'il est digne.
> Beaucoup d'israélites, fixés parmi nous depuis des générations et des siècles, sont membres naturels du corps national.[34]

> In its eternal wandering, a major concern for Israel is to choose a homeland. It does not inherit it from its ancestors; it acquires it through an act of will, and its nationality is born aloft like a quality of which it is concerned to prove it is worthy.
> Many Jews, established among us for generations and for centuries, are natural members of the national body.

A nationality that a Jew must 'prove that he deserves': the rest of the chapter displays examples of young men who did just this during the Great War. This must have resonated with Lambert; rereading Barrès is especially moving in the present circumstances (2 December 1941; *Carnet* 135). Like Barrès, for whom nationality is 'an act of will,' Lambert pursues his own course, intent on being 'an excellent Jew and an excellent Frenchman' (30 November 1941; *Diary*, 76). A Jew who exerts this act of will becomes a 'natural member of the body of the nation': this metaphor must have been balm to the heart of someone who felt 'cast out' from the bosom of France. But reading on in Barrès, we might wonder if this 'natural' membership has any great force, for those who are truly French have an 'unreasoning, almost animal love' of 'their fatherland,' something like the 'attachment they have to their mother.' By contrast, Jewish patriotism is a 'decision,' a contract, an act of will, and an intellectual choice.[35] Such acts are insufficient foundation for national unity; they lack the parental bond. The contrast he relies on lies between an intellectual choice and the unreasoning animal attachment to a territory. Note again the stress on the 'familial' in Barrès's contrast between new arrivals and other Jews who are 'enracinés depuis des siècles et des générations dans le sol de la France et mêlés familièrement aux bonheurs, aux malheurs de la vie nationale' (rooted in the soil of France for centuries and generations, participating as in a family with the joys and sorrows of the nation). Only this latter group is 'implanted' in France. This distinction was highly influential. The split among native French Jews on refugee and immigration policy during the 1930s can be attributed to it.[36]

Rooted in the soil: this is what Lambert believes about himself. The 'nation' – not 'pure' or homogeneous as in racist theories, but able to inspire in the diversity of its 'families' a 'love' that holds them together – that is what gives him a place.

> La France ne peut tout accepter et ce n'est pas pour rien que, depuis plus d'un siècle, mes parents se mêlent à son sol, - que j'ai fait deux guerres. Je n'imagine pas pour me femme, pour mes fils, pour moi-même, la vie sous un autre climat, un déracinement qui serait pire qu'une amputation. (15 July 1940, 72)

> France cannot accept just anything, and it is not for nothing that the bones of my family have mingled with its soil for more than a century – and that I have served in two wars. For my wife, my sons, and myself, I cannot imagine life in another climate; pulling up these roots would be worse than an amputation. (9)

It is a literal place, one that he cannot imagine leaving; yet he fears just that (16 May 1941; *Diary*, 40): the future in this country would see his sons become pariahs (4 June 1941; *Diary*, 41), like the stateless Jews 'now wandering or interned in France, who have never succeeded in becoming integrated into the nation' (20 December 1940; *Diary*, 26). Indeed, he literally loses his home (14 July 1940; *Diary*, 20). 'Roots' are a metaphor, yet they also refer to the soil: land ownership is likely to be a problem for his sons (15 June 1941; *Diary*, 43), and he has 'graves to care for' (9 October 1940; *Diary*, 22). 'From now on,' he frets, 'anything is possible: the next thing they could do is desecrate our cemeteries' (5 October 1941; *Diary*, 74). In another moment of despair, he wonders if it would be possible for him to give up this symbolism:

> Nous aurons appris du moins à mépriser définitivement les biens meubles et à douter – ce qui est grave – de l'enracinement des familles ... Est-ce possible? Quand je souffre d'être diminué par la loi, je songe, pour mes vieux

jours à une maison sur une colline – ailleurs qu'en France ... Mais je sais
bien que cela ne serait pas possible! (18 December 1942, 202)

> We shall have learned at least, once and for all, no longer to care about
> goods and furniture, and – what is more serious – to have doubts about
> putting down roots as families ... Is this possible? When I am suffering un-
> der these humiliations by law, I dream of spending my old age in a house
> on a hill – somewhere other than in France ... But I know very well that it
> wouldn't be possible. (159)

And indeed, it was not – not possible for him to envisage that eventuality
with any conviction. At the beginning of the very next entry in the diary,
he plans on retiring to the Côte d'Azur (*Diary*, 3 January 1943, 161).

In this light, it is telling that, when his daughter was born on
27 January 1942, he gave her 'un prénom d'affirmation et d'espoir'
(11 February 1942, 149; 'a name expressing affirmation and hope' 95),
the most French Catholic, the least Jewish name he could have thought
of: Marie-France. It is as if he had planted her. Deportation and death
put an end to it, to the symbol, to his place in France, and to this deeply
rooted family. The baby was under two years old.

'We'

That 'the bones of my family have mingled with its soil' is neither merely
a historical fact nor merely metaphorical. It is the grounds for Lambert
to write 'we' of his place in the national community, and it is in his pronominal usage that we can watch him losing that place. When Lambert
reads the news of the *statut*, he records 'l'un des plus attristants souvenirs
de ma vie' ('one of the most grievous memories of [his] life'):

> Il se peut donc que, dans quelques jours, je sois un citoyen diminué, que
> mes fils, français de naissance, de culture et de foi, soient brutalement et
> cruellement rejetés hors de la communauté française... Est-ce possible? Je
> ne puis y croire. La France n'est plus la France. (2 October 1940, 83)

> So it is possible that within a few days I shall see my citizenship reduced,
> and that my sons, who are French by birth, culture, and faith, will find
> themselves brutally and cruelly cast out of the French community ... Is this
> possible? I cannot believe it. France is no longer France. (21)

He has learned that 'France is no longer France,' and, like many others, he is at first tempted to blame the *statut* on the Germans in order

to exonerate the French. Nevertheless, he knows he is making excuses;
a year later, in 1941, he was to write that it didn't help to recall that
Hitler was in command (15 June 1941, *Carnet*, 104; *Diary*, 43). By education a proficient Germanist, and clear-sighted about the threat posed
by Nazism, he sees the emerging truth of Vichy as an offence against an
entire history. On 19 October 1940, when he reads the text of the *statut*
in the press, he writes of his shock, as what he names, remarkably, his
'illusions' crumble:

> Le racisme est devenu la loi du nouvel État. Quelle honte! [...] toutes mes
> illusions s'écroulent! J'ai peur non pour moi, mais pour mon pays [...] Où
> dort en ce moment la pensée libre de France ...?
>
> J'ai pleuré hier soir comme l'homme qui, subitement, serait abandonné
> par la femme qui a été le seul amour de sa vie, le seul guide de sa pensée, le
> seul chef de ses actions. (85)

> Racism has become the law of the new state. What a disgrace! [...] All my illu-
> sions are crumbling around me. I am afraid, not only for myself, but for my
> country [...] Where is it sleeping, the liberal thinking France is known for?
>
> Yesterday evening I wept, like a man who is suddenly abandoned by the
> wife who has been the one love of his life, the one guiding light to his think-
> ing, the one leader whom he has followed in his actions.* (23)[37]

A 'wife': is this the 'almost animal' love to which Barrès refers? I think
not. This is not a territorial belonging but the cleaving to a 'certain idea'
of France, which counts in this analogy as his 'guiding light,' the 'leader
whom he has followed in his actions.' I note in passing the gendering of
the fatherland as a mother. 'France,' in the words of du Bellay, 'mère des
arts, des armes et des lois' (France, mother of arts, of arms, and of laws):
as we will see below, it will never lose the first of these attributes for him,
but it has forfeited all claim to the others. Henceforward, Lambert persists in identifying himself with the historical France that could stand for
these ideals, while he dissociates himself from the France of the present.

If 'we,' the Jews, or his own family, mingled with French soil in the
past, that mingling no longer has force among the living. There are the
French, and there are the Jews: 'these people,' as he writes disdainfully,
and 'ourselves.' A rather dramatic discussion with a state official marks
the moment when he realizes this:

> Après la paix, ai-je dit, il faut une solution territorialiste pour les apatrides
> car la Palestine n'offre qu'une solution partielle. Et vous? m'a-t-il dit, avec

une certaine cruauté, que ferez-vous? Mais je reste et je resterai français,
ai-je répondu. Et j'ai en vain attendu la parole d'accord qui m'eût prouvé
qu'entre *ces gens et nous* il n'y avait pas le mur d'incompréhension bâti par
l'action tenace de l'Allemagne. (2 August 1941, 121–2; emphasis added)

When there is peace, I said, there must be a territorial solution for those who
are stateless, as Palestine offers only a partial solution. And you? he asked
me rather cruelly, what will you do? Why, I am and shall remain French, I
replied. And I waited in vain for a word of agreement, which would have
proved to me that there was not, between *these people and ourselves*, a wall
of incomprehension built by the tenacious actions of the Germans. (62;
emphasis added)

Yet still he tries to exonerate 'his country' by blaming the occupier,
until, on 5 October 1941, he reports that 'sept synagogues ont sauté à
Paris au lendemain du Grand Pardon. Je n'aurais jamais cru que, dans
mon pays, le fanatisme pût un jour se manifester d'une telle façon!'
(131; 'seven synagogues were blown up in Paris the day after the Day of
Atonement. I would never have believed the time would come when, in
my own country, fanaticism would manifest itself in such a way!' [74]).
'Where is France now?' he asks on learning of the massive round-up
known as the *rafle du Vel d'Hiv* (21 July 1942, 127). The truth of France
is in the past: 'the reality of the country is not its legal reality' (128);
he hopes against hope that it may reappear in the future. On the same
day as registering the *rafle du Vel d'Hiv*, having also witnessed a 'first
mass demonstration against Laval and Hitler,' he expresses the belief
that 'France will rehabilitate itself.' 'I still have hope for my country'
he declares (ibid.), quoting Péguy's discussion of the Dreyfus affair in
support: '"It is not just our honor, the honor of our whole people in
the present [that we defend]; it is the historical honor of our people,
the honor of our ancestors and of our children"' (ibid.). Nevertheless,
'my country has dishonored itself' (6 September 1942; *Diary*, 127); '*our
nation* is being lost and a culture is being allowed to die' (3 November
1942; *Diary*, 150; emphasis added). If 'we' refers to the national 'we'
with which Lambert identifies, this identification is increasingly weak-
ened by the 'loss' of the nation, the 'death' of its culture, and hence of
the place – 'my country' – he has claimed as his own. This is not to say
that Lambert ceases to identify as French, but that the country that is
capable of casting his sons out of the national community is no longer
'France.' The entry of 3 November 1942 quoted above marks the
end of this 'we.'

During the same period – roughly 19 October 1940 to 11 November 1942, when the Germans occupied the Southern Zone – 'we' increasingly refers to the Jews.

Un ami m'écrit: On ne juge pas sa mère, même quand elle est injuste. On souffre et on attend. Ainsi dev*ons-nous*, Juifs de France, courber la tête et souffrir. Je suis d'accord. Je ne puis toujours croire que tout cela soit définitif [...] Attend*ons*. Mais, sans cesser d'être français, accept*ons* l'épreuve et ne reni*ons* rien de *notre* judaïsme. (6 November 1940, 85–6; emphasis added)

A friend wrote to me: You don't pass judgment on your mother, even when she is being unfair. You suffer and you wait. Thus *we, Jews of France*, are supposed to bow *our* heads and suffer. I agree. I still cannot believe that all this is definitive [...] *Let us* wait but, while never ceasing to be French people, *let us* accept this ordeal and never renounce *our* Judaism in any way. (24)

The *statut* 'has really shaken up my inner life,' Lambert writes on 20 December 1940 (*Diary*, 25); surely this episode is just 'an eclipse, an interruption, of the freedoms that are necessary for modern man' (ibid.). While at the start this 'we' refers to the Jews of France, as it does above, it comes to refer more broadly: 'I am being made less than' French; 'it hurts me terribly, but it makes me suffer even more when I realize that there are truly stateless Jews' (26), 'pariahs,' 'wandering or ... interned,' 'living on the margins of our society' (ibid). He does not yet write 'we' to include himself with these people: 'I fear for the future of my children, and my fears are particularly those of a Frenchman, a Jew of France' (10 May 1941; *Diary*, 38). Yet the prevailing anti-Semitic discourse makes no distinction between one group of Jews and another, and Lambert's response to this grouping is to re-appropriate it. If 'international solidarity' (2 August 1941; *Diary*, 62) is an anti-Semitic reproach, it is also the basis for his sense of responsibility toward the refugees, and an enlarged Jewish 'we' is the outcome. Reporting a discussion with Xavier Vallat, the commissioner for Jewish affairs, he writes, 'En zone occupée, me dit Vallat, la situation va devenir pour les Juifs chaque jour plus tragique. Il a l'air d'en vouloir aux Allemands de *nous* rendre sympathiques par l'excès de leurs persécutions.' (3 October 1941, 130; emphasis added; 'Vallat told me that in the Occupied Zone the situation of Jews will only become more tragic by the day. He looks as though he is annoyed with the Germans for gaining sympathy for *us* with their excessive persecution' *[73; emphasis added]).

This was the crucial conversation in which the idea for the UGIF was first broached: it was to be a 'unified Jewish Community' in which 'our work in the Free Zone' could continue (ibid.). As we know, this organization was conceived by the Nazis as part of the bureaucratic apparatus of persecution. However, there is no doubt that Lambert saw it as an opportunity for fostering solidarity between French native Jews and refugees. Thus he wrote a note to himself, which he copies into the very last entry of the diary, the day before his arrest:

> Note retrouvée sur le rôle que j'entendais faire jouer à l'UGIF (1941): Diffuser dans les rangs du judaïsme et dans le pays, par rayonnement, l'esprit de solidarité et d'entraide, contribuant ainsi à créer dans nos communautés l'élite morale nécessaire au progrès. (20 August 1943, 238)

> Found a note from 1941 on the role I intended having the UGIF play: to spread through the ranks of Judaism and throughout the country, by our influence, the spirit of solidarity and mutual assistance, thus contributing to the creation within our communities of the moral elite that is needed to make progress. (199)

This is the tragedy of the UGIF, this attempt to reappropriate an administrative logic, to translate it into the terms of a moral logic. Some have called it Lambert's naivety: the stakes were high, and Lambert was gambling. Commenting further on Vallat's proposal, he writes, 'On ne peut refuser puisqu'il importe pour les travailleurs sociaux de continuer d'abord à agir. J'accepte puisqu'il est l'instance légale. Mais j'espère ainsi être mieux placé pour présider un jour à la liquidation de ce Commissariat' (3 October 1941, 131; 'We cannot refuse since the important thing in the first place is for the social workers to carry on. I accept it from him because he is the legal authority. But I hope this will put me in a position, some day, to preside over the liquidation of this Commissariat' [73]). Not only was he intent on using the UGIF for the urgent purpose of maintaining welfare work, he was also dreaming of the defeat of the regime that had required its formation. Being close to its organization, he thinks, knowing its ways and means from the inside, might eventually allow an assimilated French Jew – himself – to turn the tables 'some day' on those who had disassimilated him, on the Commissariat for Jewish Affairs that had torn the Jews out of the French polity to administer their lives and their deaths under a law outside the law. This is a fantasy of revenge.

The passage quoted above from the last entry of the diary concludes as follows: 'Le secours matériel est un ultime moyen destiné à faire face aux événements imprévus ou à remédier à des situations qui dépassent les possibilités familiales ou individuelles. L'aide morale est plus précieuse

et souvent plus efficace' (20 August 1943, 238; 'Material aid is a means
of last resort, intended for use in facing unexpected occurrences, or in
situations that are beyond the resources of families or individuals. Moral
support is more precious and often more effective' [199]). Lambert has
been able to dispense only the former: it was the more urgent, but not
the more important, of his objectives. We should recall that the disunity
of French Jewry had been the problem with which he had struggled for
a decade. It had done enormous harm. If identifying the Jews was a tool
of oppression, creating the conditions for the Jews to identify *as* Jews
was, for Lambert, a moral and political necessity. It is in this light that
I understand his willingness to go along with the creation of the UGIF,
and the struggles with the Consistory that ensued. Lamenting these conflicts toward the end, Lambert writes that 'it is with my fellow Jews that
I have the greatest difficulties' (21 March 1943; *Diary*, 173–4). Jewish
unity remained elusive,[38] and the Jewish 'we' refers either to his allies or
to Jews in general; the pronominal identifier is not used to claim a place
among the group – the native French Jews – to which sociological criteria
would predictably assign him.[39]

I Myself

The bureaucratic parameters for the role Lambert was to play in the
UGIF were the responsibility of Vallat's office, although some details
were negotiated between Vallat and Lambert (28 December 1941; *Diary*,
84).[40] But to the details of the script and the performance, Lambert laid
personal claim. This claim is made in terms of a set of values that informs
all his decisions and his judgments. They define his representation of
himself as a moral agent. That representation relies in the first place on
the way the individual 'I' sets himself in contrast with the two principal
'we' groupings I have discussed above: one is France; the other, French
Jewry. With both, he singles himself out in opposition to the absence
of significant moral qualities he discerns in them: consistently, he con-
demns their powerlessness, lack of courage, and passivity. Thus he writes
in his first entry that he was witness to 'the disarray and paralysis of my
country's central nervous system' (12 July 1940; *Diary*, 67). Likewise, he
was to write a year later: 'French Judaism has become spiritually para-
lyzed' (22 June 1941; *Diary*, 44). We can construe 'paralysis' as an inability to act; he contrasts this with his own capacity for action, which has
precedents in his pre-war career (11 December 1941; *Diary*, 79–80).

   Throughout the diary, we find a collection of lexical items that cluster around these ideas: 'action' and 'inaction' are echoed in 'energy'
and 'activity' versus 'lethargy' and 'passivity,' among others. This cluster

pervades the diary. It is the key to Lambert's moral self-definition. If there is a 'total absence of the heroic view of life' (8 March 1941; *Diary*, 36), if the 'wretched people of France' are 'so deep in lethargy that they do not even sense this affront to their entire history,' it is a specific affront to 'notre génération de la grande guerre' (16 May 1941, 102; 'our generation of the Great War' [*Diary*, 39]), and thus to him personally, distinguished in a particularly bloody battle. 'Où sont donc, sous ces conditions, l'honneur et la dignité?' (18 March 1941, 97–8; 'Under these conditions, where are honour and dignity?' [*Diary*, 34]).

As we might expect, the early parts of the diary are principally concerned with the capitulation of France. He records his impressions of a generalized sense of defeat, in response to which he writes that he has been 'thinking a great deal about [the] need for the rebirth of morale in our country' (15 July 1940; *Diary*, 6). Accordingly, he sends a memo to his superior officer, Colonel Pascot, now in the ministry: 'every former soldier' must be turned into 'a factor of energy within the national community' (*Diary*, 7), and he suggests a series of topics for morale-raising talks. This is a commanding officer speaking, someone who continues to take responsibility for his men at the time of the disaster; it is also someone who is prepared to advise his superiors, who sees it as his task to contribute practically to the national recovery.

The topics he suggests are themselves of interest: 'France has never been crushed by military defeat,' 'the spiritual mission of our country remains independent of the vicissitudes of history,' 'victory makes nations soft, defeat regenerates them' (15 July 1940; *Diary*, 8–9): not feeling crushed and having a spiritual mission are early clues to his view of himself; even 'regeneration' foreshadows his sense of rejuvenation through action. He knows his history, and draws on it for exemplary stories of *redressement* (recovery); at this point, still the soldier, still the patriot, he lists Pétain along with others who 'have been greatest in serving France ... in its darkest days' (15 July 1940; *Diary*, 9). He believes this memo never arrived. Later, in Vichy, he makes a similar suggestion to General Bührer, again with no response (16 July 1941; *Diary*, 57).

The memo has two modes of existence and perpetrates two distinct discursive acts. Addressed to Pascot, it is advice: there is a job that needs to be done. This is an attempt to act on the national stage, and it outlines the role Lambert saw himself playing. In the form in which we read it, it is copied into the diary, where we see him auditioning for this role and rehearsing it. I use 'to rehearse' both prospectively and retrospectively: 'to go through, or practise (a play, a piece of music, a ceremony etc.) in preparation for public or actual performance' and 'to perform again or repeatedly as if practising; to exercise.'[41] In this double sense, 'rehearsal' is a central function of diaries, and is prominent in Lambert's. It allows him both to refine his tactics and to assess his actions and their outcomes. Throughout the diary, Lambert rehearses what it means to be Lambert.

Recopying the memo into his diary gives him the opportunity to rehearse his own values, while the rehearsal of historical precedents in uplifting talks for the troops is intended to remind them of the sources, and to model the best, of the national character. 'The dominant mood in many areas reminds me of the psychosis of May 1917' (15 July 1940; *Diary*, 7). The memo contrasts 'moral action' with the 'lack of energy and enthusiasm' that he discerns in the troops (ibid.) and the carelessness with respect to such matters that he discerns in the national leadership. There is a need to instil in the troops the 'will to take part in the national community's struggle for recovery' (ibid., 6). Let us add 'will,' 'struggle,' and 'participation in the national community' to our lexical cluster: the first two of these are the opposite of the capitulation and the armistice. Reflecting months later on the causes of the defeat, he lists 'lack of collective will and enthusiasm in the country. No energy at all among the leaders' as key factors (8 March 1941; *Diary*, 38). Aside from the national 'we' that Lambert identifies with – a 'we' that shares the historical references he draws on – he writes as if his concern with the rank and file corresponds to a shared objective: 'le but poursuivi' (15 July 1940, 70; 'what we are trying to achieve' [*Diary*, 7]).

But was this objective truly shared? Five days later, he records observations that illustrate the problem: 'Les militaires se vengent de la défaite comme ils peuvent' (20 July 1940, 73–4; 'the soldiers take revenge for the defeat in any way they can' [*Diary*, 10]), adding that 'the general in command is a worthy descendant of the one who played billiards in 1870' (ibid.). Again, we find what is lacking in the leadership – the need to learn from history and the failure to do so – as well as the contrast with himself: 'Is it wrong of me to speak humanely to the men, and not to give my instructions to the warrant officers in a threatening tone?' (20 July 1940; *Diary*, 11). 'I' has already begun to stand out from 'we.' A year after the defeat, he writes that he is 'enraged [...] to belong to a nation that is so powerless today' (10 May 1941; *Diary*, 37); and, a month later, 'I feel ... for the leaders of this country [...] an immense and profound contempt' (15 June 1941; *Diary*, 43). If France 'legally expels [him] from its bosom' (4 June 1941; *Diary*, 41), he in turn is 'nauseated' by the opportunism of its officials (6 July 1941; *Diary*, 51). Contempt, rage, nausea: the depth and force of his emotion are a measure of the intensity of his identification with France. Its behaviour is 'abject' (27 March 1942; *Diary*, 107). He rejects it, as if expelling it from his own being.

His condemnation of the Jewish leadership is, if less drastic, no less emphatic: 'Les Juifs de France n'ont pas eu, après la détresse de juin 40, ni les chefs ni les défenseurs qu'ils méritaient. Les guides spirituels sont sans voix et sans courage' (24 February 1941, 92; 'Since the calamity of June 1940, the Jews of France have had neither the leaders nor the defenders they deserve. The spiritual leaders have lost their voices and their courage' [28]). 'Courage' is the major quality lacking in these leaders: 'M. Helbronner ... kept his head down before the *statut* was published, when he should have been courageous' (30 November 1941; *Diary*, 76), while he imagines himself 'envied' for the courage he shows (11 December 1941; *Diary*, 79–80). Later in the same entry, he records that, following a particularly heated exchange in a meeting with the consistory, 'some friends ... told me that the chief rabbi ... gets jealous when he sees himself being eclipsed by courageous members of the laity' (ibid., 82).

Courage is what he finds in himself, by contrast with these others who cannot even recognize courage when they see it: 'Ceux qui nous attaquent devraient plutôt nous applaudir, car c'est nous qui luttons ! [...] C'est nous qui faisons preuve de courage à travailler dans ces conditions' (25 May 1942, 169; 'Those who are attacking us should be applauding us, because it is we who are carrying on the struggle [...] We are the ones who are showing courage in working under such conditions' [120]). If military defeat was in part caused by 'incompetence' and the 'lack of will on the part of the leaders' as well as by a 'lack of collective will' at the national level (8 March 1941; *Diary*, 35), then 'will' staves off defeat by continuing the struggle. For Lambert, 'the conscious will' is 'a miracle' (27 March 1942; *Diary*, 106); he calls on his own will frequently and congratulates himself on maintaining it (ibid., 109).

His strength of will has sustained him, enabled him to 'resist' – that is, to 'carry on the struggle' – and, coupled with 'energy' and focus, has helped him to withstand fear – the fear of bombing raids long ago, and the fear of the Nazi round-ups in Marseilles in early 1943: 'Nous sommes passés par des émotions que jamais je n'oublierai. Mon énergie et ma volonté, la conscience de mes immenses responsabilités m'ont calmé et guidé. J'ai été fort, et j'ai été utile (1 February 1943, 206; 'We have been through emotions such as I shall never forget. My energy and my willpower, and the awareness of my immense responsibilities, have kept me calm and guided me. I have been strong, and I have been useful'* [163]). Standing fast, continuing to act – this is the 'heroism of struggle' in warfare, and in his 'war' with the consistory, whose leaders he indicts when he sums up his two struggles – for the welfare agencies, against the 'Jewish Princes' – in the evident awareness that the final entry in his diary is indeed likely to be final: 'Ils ont préféré leur confort à l'incertitude et

à l'héroïsme de la lutte ... Il était plus facile de protester et de s'abstenir
que se maintenir en agissant ... C'est le but assigné à l'action qui justifie
les attitudes (20 August 1943, 238; 'They preferred their own comfort to
uncertainty and the heroism of struggle ... It was easier to protest and to
abstain than to stand fast through action ... Attitudes are justified by the
purpose attributed to action'* [199]).

Making a Place

If Lambert was in a position to act, it is because he had made a place for
himself. Powerlessness and inactivity were anathema to him, and, shortly
after his demobilization, he took up his old work with the Comité d'assistance aux réfugiés (9 October 1940; *Diary*, 21).

Looking forward, he imagines a task for himself that also continues his
engagement from before the war: 'Après la paix je voudrais collaborer à
l'œuvre qui permettra de résoudre en France le problème des étrangers
et de l'immigration. J'ai quelque expérience' (6 July 1941, 112; 'When
there is peace again, I'd like to work with others on resolving the problem of foreigners and immigration in France. I have some experience'
[51]).[42] The idea for this role seems to have emerged at the same time as
a visit to Vichy; certainly it is recorded in the same entry: 'Je suis rentré
hier d'un voyage à Vichy où j'ai repris contact avec les autorités ... J'ai
beaucoup vu et beaucoup entendu, beaucoup appris en cinq jours et j'en
reviens fort optimiste' (6 July 1941, 112; 'I returned yesterday from a trip
to Vichy, where I renewed my contact with the authorities ... I saw and
heard a great deal, and learned a great deal, during the five days there,
and I've come back quite optimistic'* [51]). This seems to have been an
initial fact-finding visit, but 'renew' suggests that he is picking up where
he left off previously. The next visit, recorded ten days later, tells us more:
he maintains his contact with his 'friends' in Vichy (16 July 1941; *Diary*,
55). These people are contacts from his past professional life. Only some
are described as 'friends' individually. In this group, we find some Jewish
people: 'my friend Pierre Bloch, the young socialist deputy from l'Aisne'
(ibid., 56),[43] and 'Spanien – my friend from school and Tour d'Auvergne
Street – who is defending Léon Blum' (58). Others are close to Vichy
government circles: Lieutenant Colonel Pascot (by whom he was 'warmly
welcomed' [55]); Rochat ('whom I knew from the days of Delbos and
Geneva' [56]); Guichard ('whom I knew as a ship's lieutenant in Bonn'
[57]); Fourcade ('shiftier and more opportunistic than ever' [57]);
General Blairot, (who 'received me with the warm welcome I expected
from him' [57]); and Fouques-Duparc, mentioned in the report of the
previous visit as 'my friend' (6 July 1941; *Diary*, 51). Only the last on this

list 'has kept a clear conscience and sound judgment' (16 July 1941; *Diary*, 57). This comment suggests that Lambert has no illusions about these people's views on the Collaboration: he simply maintains his networks.

Apart from Spanien, who later joined his team of workers at the UGIF, there are two government officials on this list with whom he maintains a friendship. One is Fouques-Duparc: on 27 March 1942, Lambert notes a 'long and delightful conversation' with him (*Diary*, 111), and he dines with him again later that year, noting that he has 'aged greatly' (3 November 1942; *Diary*, 150), making no further comment about his 'clear conscience and sound judgment.' The other is Pascot, who had been his commanding officer in the army, and who '[was] really becoming a friend' (21 July 1940; *Diary*, 18). With Pascot, he has a warm and candid relationship:

> J'ai dîné avec mon colonel Pascot, commissaire général aux Sports, c'est-à-dire ministre dans le gouvernement de 'collaboration.' En temps ordinaire et sans le Statut, je serais son chef de cabinet. Mais il reste mon ami. En toute sincérité je lui ai dit les scrupules qu'il aurait dû avoir de faire partie d'un ministère aussi suspect à l'opinion publique, et à juste titre. Sa femme, avec le bon sens de la Française patriote, enrage. (5 May 1942, 167)

> I dined with Colonel Pascot, the general commissioner for sports, which means he is a minister in the 'collaborating' government. In normal times, I would have been his ministerial secretary. But he is still my friend. I told him in all sincerity that he should have had scruples about being part of a ministry that is so suspect in the eyes of the public, and I was right to do so. His wife, with the good sense of a French patriot, was furious.* (117)

His candour with this man does not diminish over the months, but insight into him evolves. In July, he notes that together over dinner they listened to Pierre Laval's 'infamous speech' of 22 June 1942: 'J'ai dîné avec Pascot pour entendre le discours infâme de Laval: "Je crois à la victoire allemande" aurait suffi, mais il a dit: "Je souhaite la victoire de l'Allemagne." Il se condamne à mort, ai-je dit à Pascot qui n'a malheureusement pas compris (8 July 1942, 175; 'to say "I believe Germany will be victorious" would have been enough, but he said "I hope Germany will be victorious." "He's writing his own death sentence," I told Pascot, but unfortunately he didn't know what I meant' [126–7]). Nevertheless, he maintains his friendship with him. He sees Pascot again in November, when he notes the 'selfishness and cowardice' that allow his 'friend' to 'accept servitude' (3 November 1942; *Diary*, 150). Yet this insight does not break the friendship.

We might be as puzzled by Lambert as he is by Pascot's 'psychology' (ibid.). Observing the utter 'powerlessness' of the French government following the occupation of the South, knowing what he knows about the internment camps and the deportations, in the thick of negotiations with the commissariat, 'the Gestapo, the Commission on Employment, the National Security, the Refugee Service, and the administrative office of the president of the Council of State' (16 April 1943; *Diary*, 177), he still seeks out Pascot for lunch and notes of him that 'he remains a loyal friend' (ibid.). Evidently, the loyalty is reciprocal, and no level of insight into Pascot's collusion with the dishonor of France has the power to weaken it. In order to understand this, we should note that Lambert had written to Pascot on first reading news of the *statut*: 'I have received from Commandant Pascot, my former boss, to whom I had written of my sorrow on the day after the *Statut* was published, an admirable letter,' which he then copies into the diary (20 December 1940; *Diary*, 25). The anti-Semitic laws, Pascot assures him, do not 'correspond to the deep sentiments of the French people.' 'I am very much with you ... in the painful circumstances you are enduring,' Pascot writes. 'Have patience. This only increases the friendship I feel for you' (ibid.). Pascot appears to separate his active collaboration from this bond, and so does Lambert. For the latter, it is no doubt a thread of continuity in a world disrupted.

On the busy visit to Vichy, reported on 16 July 1941, Lambert makes a new contact:

> Avec Pierre Bloch, mon ami [...] j'ai vu Xavier Vallat, Commissaire aux Affaires Juives qui nous a reçus cordialement. Curieux entretien! Pour accepter un tel poste il faut ne pas être un philosémite et avoir bien peu de conscience pour accepter – quatre jours par semaine à Paris! – les directives de l'Allemagne. (116)

> With my friend Pierre Bloch [...] I went to see Xavier Vallat, commissioner for Jewish affairs, who received us cordially. A strange conversation! To have accepted such a position one cannot be a philo-Semite, nor can one have a strong conscience to be able to take orders from Germany – for four days a week in Paris!* (56)

In this case, Lambert does not need time to formulate an accurate assessment of Vallat. He is clear-eyed from the outset. The man who 'received us cordially' is an anti-Semite and an active contributor to the dishonour of France under collaboration.

Immediately following the passage above, Lambert goes on to write, 'Vallat nous considère, nous, comme des camarades' ('Vallat considers us, us, as comrades'). Note 'us,' and note the seductive ploy in Vallat's approach: 'we,' he seems to have said, are not on opposite sides. Having established this, Vallat explains that 'he does not want any Jews in the administration, in politics, or in banking.'

> Pour l'avenir de nos enfants, il nous conseille d'attendre et de les orienter vers les métiers manuels ou vers la terre. Il nous promet qu'en zone libre nos biens ne seront pas touchés, me demande des renseignements sur les œuvres, demande à me revoir et s'émeut au tableau que je lui fais des camps d'internement, mais, dit-il, le domaine de la police n'est pas le sien. (16 July 1941, 116)

> Concerning our children's future, he advises us to wait, and to steer them towards manual trades or working on the land. He promised us that in the Free Zone our goods will not be confiscated, and asked me for information about the [social work] projects; he asked to see me again and was touched by the picture I painted of the internment camps, but he told me he has nothing to do with police work. (56)

This advice concerning 'our children's future' is exactly what Lambert rails against elsewhere (see, e.g., *Diary*, 29 October 1940, 23; 15 June 1941, 43; 2 August 1941, 61). He notes the condescension then passes on to practical business. The relationship is established.

In early October 1941, he records 'a long visit with Xavier Vallat in response to his summons. Very proper' (3 October 1941; *Diary*, 73) By this stage, the proposal for the UGIF has been formulated, and discussions concerning its implementation are proceeding. Lambert records his ambivalence along with the predictable excuses for Vallat:

> J'ai revu deux fois à Vichy Xavier Vallat. J'ai le regret de constater qu'il a confiance en moi et me consulte comme le travailleur social le mieux au courant des œuvres juives et le moins suspect au point de vue français. Il est soumis à une pression énergique des autorités d'occupation et n'accepte en vérité que d'être un exécutant. (30 November 1941, 133)

> I have been back to Vichy twice to see Xavier Vallat. I am sorry to realize that he trusts and consults me as the social worker who knows most about the Jewish agencies, and as the least suspect person from the French point of view. He is under strong pressure from the occupying authorities and has really agreed only to carry out their orders. (76)

Vallat's 'trust' is a double-edged sword: Lambert is considered in some quarters to be 'Vallat's man' (11 December 1941; *Diary*, 80) and a

'Quisling' (18 April 1942; *Diary*, 115). He is able to dismiss these accusa-
tions, first by relying on his own pragmatic assessment of the situation –
'*L'union des Juifs* se fera, avec, sans ou contre nous' (30 November 1941,
133; 'The Union of Jews will be created with us, without us, or against
us' [76]) – and, second, because the new organization will give him a
desirable role: 'Je suis le seul capable d'en être le secrétaire général.
Tâche lourde et bien grave. En songeant à l'avenir, avant d'accepter je
ne consulterai que ma conscience' (30 November 1941, 133; 'I am the
only one capable of being its secretary general – an onerous and very
serious task. With an eye to the future, before I accept it, I shall consult
only my conscience'* [76]).

From the phrase 'before accepting it,' we can infer that the role has
been offered by Vallat and, hence, that the judgment that Lambert is
'the only one capable' is part of Vallat's pitch. Lambert sees himself in
the commissioner's eyes, finds his abilities confirmed, and then asserts
this judgment as his own. This is the dynamics of narcissism; it rests on a
deep, unacknowledged insecurity. Whether this insecurity is hard-wired
in Lambert's personality is not my concern: it is enough to attribute it to
a moment in history when a rising star of France's public administration
is now a 'pariah' (15 June 1941; *Diary*, 42; 22 June 1941; *Diary*, 44). Vallat
has told him that there should be no Jews in the administration or in politics, and Lambert notes elsewhere the other professional areas in which
he has achieved some prominence – the military, writing – from which he
is now excluded. He has been cast out from all the arenas in which he has
performed. His competence in his roles, his actions, his achievements,
the public recognition, are now in the past, fixed, arrested – remembered
or forgotten – but no longer able to be built on. This pinpoints a major
element of the crisis for Lambert. Not only constructed of already accom-
plished acts and practices, identity must be projected ahead of the present; however, Lambert acknowledges, 'we should no longer consider our
desires to be elements of reality' (4 June 1941; *Diary*, 40). His sense of
what he has done, and of what he is capable of, may be unimpaired, but
it has no future. None, that is, until Vallat offers him one.

Should we assume, then, that his acceptance of the role was not in
genuine doubt? I think not. Lambert is quite aware of the moral quandary it puts him in: 'Dois-je me réjouir ou me lamenter?' (30 November
1941, 133; 'Should I rejoice or lament?'* [77]), he wonders, aware that
to accept this onerous task would be a serious act. Recall his desire to
participate in the eventual 'liquidation' of the commissariat. But he
knows that this fantasy of revenge is less likely than other outcomes, and
he notes drily that the 'leaders – appointed by decree – of French Jewry'
are 'Vallat's future victims' (2 December 1941; *Diary*, 78). 'Can we accept

being the executors of those in power?' he asks (ibid.), before resolving his dilemma in typically pragmatic terms:

> Mais je crois que nous ne pouvons accepter de représenter les Juifs de France pour autre chose que pour les questions sociales et philanthropiques, que nous ne pouvons, nous-mêmes, taxer nos coreligionnaires, que nous ne pouvons disposer nous-mêmes de fonds saisis chez les nôtres et que, dans tous les cas, notre travail technique ne doit pas signifier que nous acceptons le principe des lois d'exception. (12 December 1941, 135)

> But I think we cannot accept to be the representatives of the Jews of France in anything other than social welfare and philanthropic issues, ... we ourselves cannot impose taxes on others of our faith, ... we ourselves cannot distribute funds confiscated from our people and ... in any case, the fact that we are doing this technical work should not suggest that we accept the principle of the law of exception. (78)

Note the clear drawing of boundaries with which Lambert defines his role: the restriction of his domain of responsibility to social welfare; the refusal to collect taxes or to use confiscated funds; and the definition of his work as 'technical,' thereby separating it from any putative ideological position. It was optimistic to hope that others would see it in this way; nevertheless, in this passage, he rehearses the stipulations that he eventually got Vallat to accept (28 December 1941; *Diary*, 84–5). They will guide his actions.

If he was seduced by Vallat, Vallat was also, it seems, seduced by him, no doubt by the qualities of clarity and firmness that we see in the passage above, but also for the considerable negotiating and organizational skills he was to deploy in the practical work. Nevertheless, initially, the mutual seduction seems to rest on the very simple matter of peer-group recognition. In marked contrast to his sketches of others associated with the commissariat, Lambert appreciates Vallat's manners. He is 'well brought up' and 'cordial' (16 July 1941; *Diary*, 56) as well as 'proper' (7 September 1941; *Diary*, 73); he 'trusts and consults me' (30 November 1941; *Diary*, 76); and 'he proved his loyalty to me' (28 December 1941; *Diary*, 85). Later, he notes, 'Vallat, as always, [was] very open and frank with me' (8 January 42; *Diary*, 90). On 13 February, Lambert 'had a telephone call at the office from Vallat. He congratulated me on the birth of [my daughter] and asked after Simone. This is very proper diplomacy!' (18 February 1942; *Diary*, 101). The fact that the two men shared the same objectives and trusted each other as colleagues, even covering for each other as necessary, is demonstrated at the height of the disputes

Lambert had with the consistory, during which time (December 1941 to March 1942) they communicated behind the scenes like two plotters against the forces that threatened to scuttle their plans. The impending loss of this relationship was very worrying for Lambert. That there was considerable trust between the two men is implied in the report Lambert writes following the conversation in which Vallat passes on the news that he is to be removed from his office. The word is that Darquier de Pellepoix is likely to succeed him. The two men share their opinion of this latter:

> Darquier de Pellepoix, un antisémite de réunions publiques, connu pour ses escroqueries et ses maladies, se donne déjà comme son remplaçant et la presse de Paris cite son nom. Ce serait une catastrophe! Vallat le dit, le sait, et espère que le Maréchal ne cédera pas ... Moi aussi, car mieux vaut savoir ce qu'on a ... (27 March 1942, 162)

> Darquier de Pellepoix, an anti-Semite of the rabble, known for his swindles and his illnesses, is already announcing himself as Vallat's successor and being mentioned in the press in Paris. What a disaster that would be! Vallat says so, and hopes the Marshall won't give in ... I hope so too – better the bird in one's hand ...* (110)

But to what extent was Vallat 'in his hand'? Lambert had succeeded in instituting a federated structure for the welfare agencies in the South, thus ensuring their relative autonomy (25 May 1942; *Diary*, 120) – hence the possibility used by some of them to engage in covert Resistance activities. He had also largely controlled the choice of members of his council (11 Feburary 1942; *Diary*, 96) and had obtained acceptance of the administrative stipulations mentioned above (28 December 1941; *Diary*, 85). Regarding the last-minute hesitations of the consistory, Lambert and Vallat were indeed 'comrades in arms,' with Lambert relying on the commissioner for tactical support. Lambert assuredly was helping Vallat do his job, but Vallat in turn gave him everything he wanted – even including the choice of bank for the UGIF funds. Lambert's immediate objective throughout was to ensure that government restrictions and the anti-Semitic laws not disable the work of the agencies; throughout their negotiations, he did everything in his power to protect the Jews from colluding in their own persecution.

The demise of Vallat is directly attributable to his alleged lack of rigour towards the Jews – in Lambert's words, he was not sufficiently 'under the German heel' (27 March 1942; *Diary*, 162) – and it is certainly a plausible hypothesis that the Germans, too, feared that Vallat was 'Lambert's man.'

Supposing this to be the case, Lambert's very success turned against him and his objectives when Vallat was replaced by 'that fool called Darquier de Pellepoix' (5 May 1942; *Diary*, 117). Darquier's incompetence was soon recognized by his superiors and by the Germans, with disastrous consequences for the Jews.[44]

Lambert records his first meeting with Darquier, where it is revealed that the new commissioner has already been sidelined from responsibility for the deportation measures (11 October 1942; *Diary*, 141); Lambert remarks only that he has been granted further insight into the administrative disorder of the regime. This entry also records notes made from a visit to Vichy in August; the conversation with Darquier was followed by Lambert's final visit to Vallat, who had by then vacated his position: 'je revois Xavier Vallat dans un bureau de domestique à l'hôtel du Parc. Il me confie que "'désormais les Boches charrient un peu trop!" De plus en plus curieu' (11 October 1947; *Carnet*, 187) ('I go to see Xavier Vallat in a domestic staff office in the Park Hotel. He confides in me that now "the Boche are going a bit too far." Curiouser and curiouser!' [*Diary*, 141]). This is evidently a social call: Xavier Vallat was his 'friend' (8 January 1942; *Diary*, 90); the visit of 11 October 1942 brings the relationship to an end.

As Lambert was useful to Vallat, so was Vallat useful to Lambert. Richard Cohen and others have pointed out, however, that the relationship cannot be reduced to a simple calculation. Genuine respect had grown up between them, and some warmth; they had worked closely together. If it is the case that Lambert is seduced into accepting the role and working with Vallat because it offers him a way of being himself, it is also the case that his identity is bound up in his competence, and that the role he accepted gave him a way to use it to pursue objectives on behalf of the people most in need. As in the case of Pascot, however, I believe that this friendship points to a deeper stake. No matter how deep the chasm that had grown between what had become two poles of his identity –'an excellent Frenchman, and an excellent Jew' – Lambert was intent on maintaining both, and his friendships in Vichy, as well as his work, confirmed for him that he could do so.

Another way of doing so was the pattern of his itineraries around the Southern Zone. He shuttled back and forth between Marseilles and Vichy, nearly always stopping in Lyon to continue discussions with the consistory and with UGIF colleagues on the way. We can count at least twenty-three visits, sometimes at the rate of two a month, in the course of eighteen months before the beginning of 1943. Consider that the train trip took twelve to fifteen hours each way. To take one example of the frenetic activity that this involved, I cite the trip of 27 July 1942: arriving in the evening of that date, he has meetings on the following two days, as well as attending to administrative business, leaving Vichy at dawn on 30 July. He meets Helbronner at the station in Lyon, then arrives in Marseilles at 6:30 p.m., holds a meeting at 7 p.m., and leaves again for Vichy at midnight, holding a strategy meeting with his colleagues on the train. He gets to Vichy at 3 p.m., stays until 2 August for appointments, then stops for two meetings in Lyon (6 September 1942; *Diary*, 129–30). This travelling was necessitated by the bureaucratic demands of his position, but we can also take it as a metaphor: the two components of his identity were separated in time and in space, as well as ideologically and in terms of a radical power differential. Lambert, who saw himself as a diplomat, made them talk to one another as if, in his person, they could make common cause.

These journeys were also a practice of place. Aside from the visits to Lyon and Vichy, Lambert travelled extensively to camps, homes, and orphanages in the Southern Zone. Many of these visits are not specified except in lapidary notes – 'I have been travelling a lot' (20 June 1943; *Diary*, 188) – but the trip from Marseilles and back, from 30 May 1943 to 3 June 1943, took him to Toulouse, Limoges, Périgueux, Thiviers, and Bergerac on 'a tour of our institutions and a meeting on technical matters' (22 June 1943; *Diary*, 190). He did some travelling with the family, to give them and himself a break from the intense activity and the anxieties caused by round-ups and raids in Marseilles, and he also travelled to Grenoble several times, notably at the end of April 1943 for 'the founding of the Centre for Jewish Documentation [CDJ], an illegal and clandestine organization whose main purpose was to collect documents on the period of the War. Lambert was considered one of the founders of this organization.'[45] What is evident in all these travels is that the territory marked out becomes a space of recognition: 'Well, well ... so they know me in Vichy' (20 August 1943; *Diary*, 198), while in Grenoble 'they are thinking of asking me to play a specific role in [the CDJ in the] future' (16 May 1943; *Diary*, 178–9). There is even grudging recognition from Jacques Helbronner, who 'said to Albert Lévy in Lyon last Sunday that I'm quite intelligent but a lightweight, not enough depth' (27 March 1942; *Diary*, 105), and who wrote to Lambert to congratulate him on his courage after one attempted intervention (13 February 1943; *Diary*, 216). 'In hard times,' he remarks drily after being received at the consistory, 'one makes peace' (17 August 1943; *Diary*, 196). He reports fulsome recognition following the tour around the institutions: 'I was received as the boss ... I was received as a king ... I was treated both as boss and friend' (22 June 1943; *Diary*, 190). He is deeply gratified when the 'Joint' asks him 'to be their director for France. I accepted in principle, but I refused to resign as general director of the UGIF at this time of greatest danger' (29 November 1942; *Diary*, 153).[46]

This is what he has become – the place he now occupies – 'un person-nage de premier plan dans le judaïsme français' (11 December 1941, 135; 'a central figure in French Jewry' [79]), as he sees it. This is what enables him to act, and it is in action that he recognizes himself, indifferent to the fact that he is 'discussed and attacked by some and flattered and encouraged by others' (79): 'L'action enivre et satisfait' (8 January 1942, 147; 'Taking action is intoxicating and satisfying' [93]). His self-recognition is jubilant:

> Action, action, vive l'action! et quelles sont mes responsabilités! Hénaurmes! J'en souris et ce sourire peut me convaincre de la réussite finale ... 'Jeune officier plein d'allant,' disait ma citation de l'autre guerre. Je reste le même et sauverai les Œuvres juives, malgré les vieux. (27 March 1942, 158)

> Action, action, long live action! And what responsibilities I have! Ginor-mous! It puts a smile on my face, and my smile makes me believe that we shall succeed in the end ... My citation from the first war called me 'a young officer with plenty of drive.' I remain what I was, and I shall save the Jewish charities in spite of the old men.* (105–6)

'Je reste le même': this is the deep stake accompanying his efforts to save the Jewish welfare agencies. But could his action save any Jews? Certainly Lambert tried very hard to avert deportations; his success was minimal. In the last months, once the South had been occupied and the round-ups in Marseilles and other southern centres were in full swing, we find Lambert frequently rehearsing his actions. Eventually he is forced to make a distinction between action as such – 'I am acting, this is what matters' – and the effectiveness of his action. In this dreadful period, he comes up against the kind of power of which he has no understanding and no experience, facing which he has no strategies and few tactics. Against it, however intense his energy – and, we must say, his courage – he is ineffectual. Learning this, he will ultimately learn his place.

Learning His Place

The first hard lesson seems to be the loss of financial autonomy. The UGIF bank account had been established under government control, and the agencies that comprised the union had had to relinquish their funds to the central account. This entry is remarkable:

> Le jour où, avec Gaston Kahn, nous avons remis à Couturier les fonds de no-tre Comité, incorporé dans L'Union, nous en aurions pleuré! Ce soir-là, j'ai compris que le Statut nous diminuait vraiment et que c'est nous qui faisons preuve de courage à travailler dans ces conditions. (25 May 1942, 169)

The day when Gaston Kahn and I had to turn over to Couturier the funds of
our committee, now incorporated into the *Union,* we felt like weeping! That
evening I understood that the *Statut* really was diminishing us, and that we are
the ones who are showing courage in working under such conditions. (120)

Displaying the structure of 'experience' (see the discussion of this concept
in the Introduction) in which an event gives rise to subsequent reflection
in which its meaning becomes clear, the entry shows that only now does
Lambert truly understand the effect of the *statut,* as if he had believed that
the influence he had exercised over the institution of the UGIF would
somehow preserve it from this loss of autonomy. He learns in this moment
the effect of his actions, as if he had earlier been blinded by the intoxica-
tion of action as such. Further, his assertion of 'courage' is wilfully blind to
the relation between decisions he makes and the way they will be used: it
separates practical consequences – a focus on cause and effect – from the
moral qualities of the actors, focusing exclusively on the latter.

His place may well have been 'at the centre of French Jewry,' but
on 21 July 1942, in the light of 'redoubled persecutions' and the mass
arrests and deportations of that month, he compares himself 'to someone in Alsace under the heel of Germany' (*Diary,* 128). In August, he
was 'involved ... in the efforts to stop' the first deportations from Les
Milles. Because of this, 'and because I don't think I have shown any lack
of courage,' he notes down the series of events (6 September 1942; *Diary,*
128–9). His efforts were fruitless, but he continues to assess himself on
his moral qualities rather than on outcomes. Thus he writes:

J'ai agi, j'ai pensé, je suis satisfait de mon action et l'avenir me récompen-
sera. Mais les heures et les journées passent sans que je trouve le temps de
noter mes pensées. L'action reste impérieuse; il faut une volonté tenace
pour reprendre contact avec soi-même. (21 September 1942, 181)

I have been acting and thinking. I am satisfied with my actions, and my
reward will be in the future. But hours and days go by in which I can find no
time to record my thoughts. Taking action remains the urgent imperative,
so it requires a strong will to stay in touch with oneself. (133–4)

In this passage, 'action' counts as the opposite of keeping his diary, so
the following notes are delayed until 4 October 1942.

Je forme une équipe sociale de l'UGIF qui monte au camp des Milles pour
prendre 'les dernières volontés' des déportés qui partiront dans deux ou
trois jours. En protestant par écrit contre les déportations, j'accepte de

répondre à la Préfecture qui nous demande de mettre dans les wagons le campement et les vivres qui adouciront un tant soit peu les rigueurs du voyage. (182)

I formed a group of UGIF social workers to go up to the camp at Les Milles to record 'the last will and testament' of the deportees who will be leaving in two or three days. While sending written protests against the deportations, I also resigned myself to responding to the Prefecture's request that we put camping equipment and food aboard the railway cars to mitigate, if ever so slightly, the hardships of the trip. (135)

Here, he turns his efforts to mitigating the hardships of the voyage because he is powerless to prevent it. Not only under the heel of Germany, he is submitting to the 'requests' of the prefecture. Moreover, 'je rappelle Vichy au téléphone, mais en vain. On ne veut ni me voir là-bas, ni même me parler par téléphone ici' (183; 'I tried again to call Vichy, but in vain. They didn't want to see me there, or even talk to me here by telephone' [136]). His place is indeed diminished.

Undaunted, he addresses his representations to the prefecture:

Vendredi 7 août: Jour de lutte avec Spanien. Mes équipes sociales ont fait un travail de galérien, mille fiches sur les individus menacés de déportation. On travaille la nuit au bureau.

Samedi 8 août : Je remets les fiches à la Préfecture. Elles sauveront certaines familles. Je demande qu'on nous laisse au moins les enfants. À 18h30 j'apprends que nous en sauvons 66. (183)

Friday, August 7: A day of struggle for Spanien and me. My teams of social workers had been slaving away and gathered a thousand files on individuals threatened with deportation. We were working at night at the office.

Saturday, August 8: I brought the files to the Prefecture. They will save certain families. I asked that at least the children be left in our care. At 6:30pm I was told we could save sixty-six of them. (136)

From here on, Lambert measures his successes – the people he saves from deportation – by counting them: 66 out of 1,000 (above); 'a few ... But I have the feeling that their fate has only been deferred' (11 October 1942; *Diary*, 138); 'a few more' (142); 'one' (143–4). By the end of this one long entry, he reports that 16,000 Jews have been deported (the editor's note suggests that the number is more likely to have been 9,000 by this date).[47] On 26 March 1943, he reports that he 'was able to have two old people released' (*Diary*, 175); none were saved from the transport of

24 January of that year (1 February 1943; *Diary*, 169). Most entries report failures. In January 1943, the raids and arrests in Marseilles become ever more numerous, but a train load of deportees bound for Compiègne may be brought back; on 13 February 1943, he reports that it 'will probably come back' (*Diary*, 172), but on 16 April 'the train to Compiègne isn't coming back – and the people from Marseilles have been deported' (178).

These numbers appear deliberately unemotional. Returning to Les Milles with Lambert and Spanien for the August 9 convoy, we read:

> Mon équipe prend 'les dernières volontés' des futurs déportés. Dans la cour de la huilerie transformée en camp d'embarquement la fièvre monte. Regards de ceux qui vont partir et m'interrogent avec anxiété. Vais-je les sauver? Je me raidis pour ne pas être ému. Je remets les fiches à la Préfecture. On sauvera les enfants de 2 à 15 ans. Est-ce humain? Les parents nous les confieront pour qu'ils échappent à l'enfer. L'après-midi, au bureau, on prépare le matériel qui équipera les wagons. Matériel de fortune comme pour un radeau de sauvetage: cuvettes, bouteilles, quarts, seaux ... Dans la campagne provençale d'une paix désespérante et stérile, à deux pas des forêts brûlées, la tuilerie avec son horloge et ses fenêtres difficilement bouchées et devant la petite gare des Milles, gardées par des policiers en armes. Il faut montrer patte blanche pour traverser le passage à niveau. Toutes ces déportations sont organisées loin des villes pour que le crime passe inaperçu. (11 October 1942, 184)

My team records the 'last will and testament' of people who are about to be deported. In the courtyard of the oil filling station, which has been turned into an embarkation camp, anxieties are rising. The eyes of those about to depart question me in their anguish – am I going to save them? I stiffen to ward off the emotion. I take the files to the Prefecture. Children aged two to fifteen will be saved. Is this humane? Their parents will entrust them to us so that they may escape this hell. During the afternoon, in the office, we prepare the equipment, makeshift equipment, as if for a life raft: metal bowls, bottles, drinking cups, pails ... here in the desperate and barren peace of the Provençal countryside, a few steps away from the burnt forest, in the tile factory with its clock and its windows with holes imperfectly stuffed, in front of the little Milles railroad station, guarded by armed police. We must identify ourselves in order to step across the level crossing. All these deportations are organized far from the cities so that the crime will not attract notice. (137–8)

The juxtaposition of 'am I going to save them? I stiffen' shows Lambert, powerless and emotional as he witnesses the unbearable, but determined to maintain his capacity for practical action.[48] Equally, the juxtaposition of the 'Provençal countryside' with what is being perpetrated in it reveals a Lambert having to learn – again – in this very 'climate', that 'France is no longer France.' The next day is a 'heartrending spectacle':

> Des cars enlèvent 70 enfants aux parents qui vont partir le soir. J'ai obtenu que les enfants partent avant pour ne pas assister à l'appel des parents ... Mais quelle scène dans le soleil brûlant! Il faut retenir les pères et les mères quand les cars quittent la cour. Quels cris et quelles larmes, quels gestes des pauvres pères qui, avant la déportation définitive, caressent le visage d'un fils ou d'une fille comme pour en conserver l'empreinte au bout des doigts! Des mères hurlent de désespoir et personne ne peut retenir ses larmes. (18 May 1943, 184)

> Buses are taking away seventy children from parents who are to depart that evening. I have arranged for the children to leave first so they will not see their parents subjected to the roll call ... but what a scene, under the blazing sun! We have to hold the fathers and mothers back as the buses leave the courtyard. What wailing and tears, what gestures as each poor father, faced with the moment of deportation, caresses the face of a son or daughter as if to imprint it on his fingertips! Mothers are screaming in despair, and no-one can hold back tears. (138)

Holding back the parents, holding back their own tears, their 'action' has come to this: 'I am ashamed of our powerlessness' (139) Yet he 'hope[s] against hope' and returns the next day 'to try for more rescues. The condemned people are now glad to see me coming. They know that through my intervention some people were spared' (ibid.). Then –

> Le 1er et 2 septembre, je remonte aux Milles puisqu'un départ est prévu pour le 3 et je tiens, avec Spanien, à tenter d'opérer quelques sauvetages. Mais la police s'énerve et le chiffre n'est pas atteint ... Dans la nuit du 1er au 2 on fait l'appel des partants et l'on meuble les wagons dans un désordre inhumain. Des enfants sont portés dans le train sans lait. Les scènes de désespoir se multiplient. J'ai honte de mon impuissance. Mais il faut rester là pour avoir vu. Des gens que j'ai sauvés des deux premiers départs sont repris cette fois sans aucun examen. (11 October 1942, 188)

> On September 1 and 2 I go back to Les Milles, where another transport is scheduled to leave on the 3rd, and try, together with Spanien, to rescue a few more. But the police are growing irritated, they haven't filled their quota ... during the night of the 1st, roll call is held and the wagons are filled

in a chaotic way unfit for human beings. Babies are carried aboard without
any milk. There are increasing scenes of desperation. I am ashamed to be
so powerless, but I must stay to have seen this. People I have saved from the
first two transports are now being taken.* (142)

The man of action can do nothing but watch – 'to have seen this' –
condemned to acknowledge his own 'powerlessness' and to feel
'ashamed.' Note the clause 'I must stay to have seen this': not only does it
defy the intention for the deportations to pass unnoticed, but, by means
of its tenses, it also projects into a future beyond the event the bearing
of witness. His enraged contempt for the powerlessness of France finds
a fearful echo here. Such scenes, he goes on, 'marquent de honte un
régime' (189; 'are the mark of a shameful regime' [144]): 'Le plus triste
c'est la méprisable lâcheté des fonctionnaires' (189; 'The saddest part
is the contemptible cowardice of the officials' [144]) who cannot even
acknowledge their own disgust at what they have to do.

Lambert, as we might expect, refuses inaction, and refuses to be like
these others. He distinguishes himself by an act of desperate bravado. 'Je
ne tiens plus' (11 October 1942, 189; 'I can't stand it any more' [143])
he writes, as he recognizes an individual among the crowds selected for
deportation; it is Fischer, a publisher originally from Vienna, and decorated by France. He pushes apart the guards: 'je [le] prends par le bras
et le place derrière moi' (189; 'I grab his arm and put him behind me'
[143]) – protecting him with his own body. It is the action of a soldier.
Then, putting the whole episode behind himself, he goes on with his
practical duties.

He has discovered his lack of power, yet he is undefeated: 'Je me retrouve aussi décidé que dans mon observatoire du Chemin des Dames;
j'ai vingt ans' (29 November 1942, 196; 'I am still as determined as I was
in my lookout post at the Chemin des Dames; I feel like a twenty-year
old again'* [151]). The military analogy is pervasive in these months:
'all our agencies now recognize me as their boss, and my office is turning into a military HQ in full swing' (ibid., 153); 'I am in the battlefield' (18 December 1942; *Diary*, 157); 'we have to keep fighting and not
desert the fort of the agencies the moment they are in danger. I cannot
become now what I have never been, someone who runs away' (ibid.).
Then come the raids in Marseilles in January 1943: he makes three visits to the prefecture, starting on 23rd, where he is not received until
25th, in an attempt to intervene on behalf of those already arrested, and
to prevent further arrests. No information or response is forthcoming
until the 26th, when he learns that 'the French police no longer have
any power over matters concerning you. All Jews are to be arrested' (1

February 1943; *Diary*, 166). All he can do is send telegrams to Vichy and wait for the power struggle between the French police and the Germans to be settled. He gains a hearing from the French, but no satisfaction, and the convoys are supervised by the Germans: the 'police chiefs of Marseilles became the purveyors or the instigators, conscious or unconscious, of German policy' (ibid., 169). In March, he notes, 'I was not able to get them to allow our delegates to enter the internment camps' (26 March 1943; *Diary*, 176). After some of the UGIF staff have been arrested, and the organization is threatened with having to give up its 'foreign' workers, Lambert makes representation to Vichy to save them (16 April 1943; *Diary*, 177). Full of people needing support, his own office is raided (6 May); sixty are arrested. He saves 'five or six' and makes representation on behalf of nursing mothers; he obtains one further release. In June, he learns of the arrest of a further eighteen Jews in Aix; he obtains the release of eight of them (29 June 1943; *Diary*, 192). In July, he is 'hoping to halt the collective arrests of Jews in Marseilles' (2 July 1943; *Diary*, 193). In August, 'fifty-one adults and thirty-eight children in Marseilles' are released, thanks to his efforts – 'I can be proud of that' (18 August 1943; *Diary*, 197). He tries to intercede – 'but with no hope of success' – on behalf of André Baur, his opposite number from the UGIF-nord (ibid., 197–8). These numbers testify to his unrelenting efforts, but they are very small.

From the episode at Les Milles, he has learned the limits of his power, but, within these limits, there are still some things he can do. He uses the diary to reassure himself with a mixture of objective fact and the rhetoric of contrast with which we are familiar. Thus, of his last meeting in Vichy (with Jacques Guérard, secretary to Laval) he notes:

> Quant à la question juive, il ne peut rien pour humaniser les mesures. Nous sommes abandonnés à nous-mêmes et ne pouvons espérer qu'en l'action locale et en se fondant sur la fiction de la zone libre. Ma politique est la seule rationnelle. Sur mon bureau, une fiche en évidence: au 16 août j'ai obtenu à Marseilles la libération de 51 adultes et 38 enfants. Je puis être fier. Si, sur le plan général, Laval avait agi avec autant de méthode! Mais il ne sait pas l'allemand. (18 August 1943, 237)

As for the Jewish question, he cannot do anything to make the measures at all humane. We are left to our own devices and have no hope other than through action at the local level based on the fiction of the Free Zone. The policy I have been following is the only rational one. On my desk is a piece of paper that proves it: on August 16 I obtained the release of fifty-one adults and thirty-eight children in Marseilles. I can be proud of that. If only Laval had been acting, across the board, with such a well-calculated method! But he doesn't know German. (197)

If Laval's failures include his linguistic ignorance, they are also due to his inability to act with a 'well-calculated method.' The contrast with Lambert is pointed. First is the latter's proficiency in German, which stood him in good stead in his dealings with individual German officials, both in Marseilles and in Vichy, and even got him out of trouble with an officious Gestapo officer (12 August 1943; *Diary*, 196). Second, 'Bien rares sont ceux qui savent ce qu'ils veulent et qui veulent ce qu'ils savent' (3 January 1943, 206; 'those who know what they want, and who want what they know, are very rare' [163]): this differentiates Lambert from the French leadership (servile), from the Jewish leadership (impotent and indecisive), and from those whose courage consists only of romantic dreams of heroic conquest. In contrast to such ineffectual individuals, he boasts that he has 'an excellent system' (17 June 1942; *Diary*, 121); 'well oriented' is another term for this (1 February 1943; *Diary*, 163), as is 'clear-minded': 'Clear-minded judgment is the most precious of qualities for the man of action' (3 January 1943; *Diary*, 163; see also 12 July 1943; *Diary*, 194).

Then there is his capacity for calm: 'I go on calmly arranging our departure' he writes of the demobilization of his troops (12 July 1940; *Diary*, 5). As he makes his arrangements for handing over the welfare agencies' accounts, 'I give orders calmly and clearly, knowing where I am going and where I want to go' (17 July 1942; *Diary*, 121). During the November 1942 raids, 'the feverish emotions of the people around me make me even calmer and more composed' (29 November 1942; *Diary*, 151), and, in the same entry, 'we are under curfew and in mourning, the mass of people numb with indifference, but in our circles is a particular anxiety. I am becoming more and more calm' (152). In response to the January raids in Marseilles, he writes 'we have been through emotions such as I shall never forget. Through energy and willpower, and the awareness of my immense responsibilities, I have kept calm and well oriented. I have stayed strong and been useful'* (1 February 1943; *Diary*, 163). On 19 June 1943, a 'fearful day,' he was told by SS officer Bauer to expect reprisals against the Jews for a terrorist attack: 'I told him I would wait for him calmly and with a good conscience' (20 June 1943; *Diary*, 188). The situation worsens by the day; the following month he writes, 'I remember my composure as a soldier in 1916, during the terrible April offensive that was my baptism by fire' (9 July 1943; *Diary*, 193), but maintaining one's composure under such circumstances 'takes a lot of energy' (12 July 1943; *Diary*, 194). Eventually, he admits to being 'a bundle of nerves' (17 August 1943; *Diary*, 195). Yet even at this point, he does not give up.

The question is why. Did he never truly learn his place? Donna Ryan puts the question in this way: 'How could someone like Raymond-Raoul Lambert continue to see himself as the protector of the Jews, both French and foreign, even after the Nazi occupation of the city?'[49] Did he indeed see himself this way? Ryan's characterization is questionable. As against this, he professes disdain for Stendhalian heroics. The diary shows that he simply did what he could, saved the few who could be saved, and kept to his motto: 'Tenir et durer' – 'To hold on and hold out.' The question is rather how he was able to persist in the face of the odds. Richard Cohen seeks an answer in Lambert's personality, arguing that, by 18 December 1942, 'he appears to have been at this stage so deeply invested in his hubris and direction that the growing awareness of the impending disaster could not alter his determination.'[50] This seems unfair in the light of Lambert's own note of that very date: 'I am in the battlefield [...] We have to keep fighting and not desert the fort of the agencies the moment they are in danger. I cannot become now what I have never been, someone who runs away' (18 December 1942; *Diary*, 157). The decision is again that of a soldier. We have seen, moreover, that he was not deluded as to the nature of the France he was in, and that 'hubris' is not an apt description of a man who was 'ashamed at [his own] powerlessness' in the deportation yard at Les Milles. Indeed, Cohen's editorial note interprets these events as a tipping point, 'as if suddenly the balance between his professionalism and his innermost feelings was shattered, and he "reacted like a madman,"' pointing out that Lambert's action in saving Fischer was 'a moment of clairvoyance in which he sensed that, as a Chevalier de la Légion d'honneur himself, he too could be deported from his beloved France.'[51] We might ask, then, if holding back his tears and getting on with business made him lose sight of what he knew. It is unlikely: he wrote the relevant diary entry two months after the events. Lambert's own answer reads as follows: 'My instinct is to have absolute faith in the future, and duty compels me to be the last to leave the ship' – this, even with its consequence: 'My wife and children are not to be separated from me' (29 November 1942; *Diary*, 153). Even in August 1943, he is still 'weighing up' his responsibilities towards his family 'in the face of an uncertain future' (17 August 1943; *Diary*, 195). He was certainly an optimist: good news from the war gives him hope, but good news conflicts with the events in Marseilles: 'One day we think we will be back in Paris for Christmas [...]; another day we are dreading being deported to Poland' (12 July 1943; *Diary*, 195). The dread is outweighed by the optimism that can be discerned in the time frame envisaged – 'in spring 1944' matches the 'six months' he gives himself in the previous entry (9 July 1943; *Diary*, 193). He was also a military man, prepared to die in battle, the opposite of 'the general [...] who played billiards in 1870' (20 July 1940; *Diary*, 10). He was at his post 'in the field of battle, as we say nowadays' (21 March 1943; *Diary*, 174); he would not desert it.

Why, then, did he not save his wife and children? The decision is all the more perplexing in light of his indefatigable efforts to save the children of deportees. His concern with his family's safety is uppermost throughout the diary, from the moment of the defeat of France onwards: 'J'ai connu la plus atroce des inquiétudes pour le sort de ma femme et des trois fils qui sont toute ma vie et désormais toutes mes raisons de subsister et de lutter' (12 July 1940, 67; 'I have been dreadfully worried about the fate of my wife and my three sons [... They] are my whole life and my only reason now to go on living and struggling' [3]). In his diary, Lambert makes it clear that his family sustains him: 'L'avenir peut être sombre, les épreuves à venir bien redoutables, je me sens le courage de tout affronter, au milieu de ma petite famille' (24 July 1940, 82; 'The future may look dark, the ordeals to come ominous enough, but I feel I have the courage to face anything, when I am with my little family' [19]). His place was with his family; he could not give it up.

Could not, because the literal, flesh-and-bones family is also highly symbolic. Recall the familial bonds of nationhood in the Barrésian discourse. The 'family romance' informs his gender identity, which, in turn, we can speculate, informs the way he conceived his public role. The man of action ashamed of his tears – and of his impotence against a ruthless power – 'king,' 'boss,' the military man who refuses to leave his post: this is a certain ideal of manhood. Moreover, the biography of Lambert shows him stepping into the vacancy left by the death of his father: the good son becomes father to himself and husband to his mother: her memory, he writes, 'takes the place of a religion for me' (27 March 1942; *Diary*, 108). When his country betrays him, and he feels as he would had he been abandoned by the woman he loves, the good husband struggles to redeem her honour, and the good father calls his daughter 'France.'

A Place in Books

Reading

Thus far, my investigation of the trope of place has been confined to geographical place and its imaginary, and to social place and its enactment. However, Lambert's diary is more than a report of his engagement in historical events. He was 'a man of action,' but he was also an intellectual, one whose place in the world was explored through reading and writing. This was one of the guarantees of continuity in his life. He read constantly throughout the period of the diary, and he regularly made notes about his reading. He read current affairs, literary studies, history, and political pamphlets. He read randomly, and he pursued projects. He used books as a safe space, and as a means of reflecting on himself and on the events of the world he lived in. Recovering the kind of attention necessary for reading has saved him from the stupor caused by the *débâcle* (20 July 1940; *Diary*, 11). He reads 'to keep [his] mind alert' (9 October 1940; *Diary*, 22), to 'wash [...] away the impurities of life' (20 December 1940; *Diary*, 26), to recharge his energies (30 November 1941; *Diary*, 77), to console himself and to give him insight into himself (27 March 1942; *Diary*, 108). Reading Julian Huxley's *What Dare I Think?* 'gives [him] courage for present trials and expectations for the future' (11 May 1941; *Diary*, 39). He reads to get ideas for further reading, to seek 'a helpful tonic at this time,' and to enhance his own writing (16 May 1943; *Diary*, 179). Most importantly, whatever he is reading and whatever he draws from it, he reads to maintain his active participation in French culture: 'Although the exception proves the rule, I go to French springs to quench my thirst' (3 October 1941; *Diary*, 73).[52] Hence the significance of the following:

> Enfin un excellent recueil d'essais philosophiques et politiques, paru au temps où l'on avait le droit de penser: *La France et la liberté*. De telles pages (Valéry, Francis Delaisi) donnent foi en l'avenir.
> On en a bien besoin en ce moment, surtout quand on fréquente, comme moi, des fonctionnaires dont l'opportunisme, trop souvent, donne envie de vomir. (16 July 1941, 112)

> [I have read] an excellent collection of philosophical and political essays ... *La France et la liberté*. Readings like these (Valéry, Francis Delaisi) give one faith in the future.
> That is really what we need just now, especially when, like me, we must meet with officials whose opportunism too often makes me want to throw up.* (51)

Jewish writers were also important: Henri Franck, for example (30 November 1941; *Diary*, 133), and one of his most significant reading projects is to 'go back to Bergson.' He takes this decision having read Gilbert Maire's *Bergson mon maître* 'qui me pousse à relire Bergson de plus près car he crois que j'y trouverai ce que j'attends depuis de longues années' (17 June 1942, 171; which is pushing me to reread Bergson more closely, because I can see that I will find there something for which I have been waiting for many years, not a certainty but some fresh light on my thoughts' [122]). Some two weeks later, he notes that he has begun with *Le Rire* and believes he has found in it the 'method' he seeks; 'À mon âge, Bergson convient parfaitement' (1 July 1942, 173; 'Bergson is exactly right for me at my age' [124]). I shall return to his use of Bergson below.

Reading is a discipline that takes him out of the intensities of the present moment, providing the reflective space in which those intensities are recorded as experience. Current events are inserted into a longer time frame and a wider interpretive space. Likewise, his reading can reinforce, or provoke him to revise, the moral code I have discussed above. The full range of his uses of reading is displayed in an early entry; here he tells us that the list is 'a bit of everything, without being very choosy or methodical'; yet the choices show a certain coherence. He makes notes on eight books he has read just to 'keep [his] mind alert' (9 October 1940; *Diary*, 22). At several points, he notes the reflections on the present these books have inspired, and almost all of them display connections with the preoccupations we have discerned in the diary: the 'courageous' lines of Claudel, the 'lucid critique' of Maxence, Schlumberger's 'critique of military heroics,' and the contrast between heroism and cowardice. Most importantly, the last shows him seeking to understand the present through reading history. It is a three-volume manual in the history of foreign policy:

> J'ai lu, avec passion – car je suis à l'âge de l'Histoire – le premier tome du *Manuel de politique étrangère* (1610–1789) d'Émile Bourgeois. Quelle puissance on acquiert à comparer nos épreuves aux années tragiques déjà connues par les peuples et les nations! J'éprouve le besoin de lire des œuvres de philosophie historique. (25 May 1942, 168)

> I was excited – because I am the right age for History – by the first volume of Emile Bourgeois' *Manuel de politique étrangère* (1610–1789). What power it grants one to compare our ordeals with those of the tragic years that peoples and nations have already known! I'm feeling the need to read some books on the philosophy of history.* (118)

From his reading of the second volume of the treatise by Bourgeois, he makes a direct comparison between Napoleon Bonaparte's 'dreams of the east' and present-day German expansionism (1 July 1942; *Diary*, 124).

Learning from history marries the 'inner life' to the public role. His reading confirms that there might be alternatives to the policy of 'bowing and scraping' to the conqueror. He finds the model for this attitude in a book on Richelieu:

> J'ai lu de mon ami Fouques-Duparc, *Le Troisième Richelieu*, monographie remarquable et pleine de vie. On peut négocier avec le vainqueur, quand on est vaincu, sans se soumettre et sans accepter le joug. Quelle différence avec l'amiral Darlan surnommé à Paris l'amiral Courbette! (16 [*sic*] July 1941, 112)

> I read *The Third Richelieu* by my friend Fouques-Duparc, a remarkable monograph, very lively. One can negotiate with conquerors, when one has been conquered, without submitting to them, without putting oneself under a yoke. How different this is from Admiral Darlan, whom the Parisians call 'Admiral Bow-and-Scrape'! (51)

Certainly this lesson was one he believed he could apply to his own dealings with the occupying authorities. A second model, one that might surprise us, is Talleyrand, the 'prince of diplomats'; he admires his lucidity and his pragmatism: 'Talleyrand me plaît comme un chef' ('I like the kind of leader I find in Talleyrand'); 'Il peut être pris comme modèle ... dans mon action au sein des groupes juifs' (22 October 1942; 193; 'He can serve as a model ... for me in my work with the Jewish groups'* [148]). The book is a biography, by definition the story of an individual and of his role in 'constructing great events.' This is the 'great man' view of history; it informs almost all of Lambert's accounts of the events he lives through, and especially his view of leadership. Thus, searching history for the motives of the leaders is a search for a certain mode of explanation. However, Lambert makes no note on the explanations proferred by the book; rather, he registers admiration for its subject and is apparently seduced by his style of leadership. If Talleyrand 'can serve as a model ... for me and my work,' it is not because the parallel is compelling but, I suggest, because Lambert seeks in Talleyrand an image of strategic cleverness, strength of will, and success, on to which he projects himself. It is by no means irrelevant to this interpretation that he read the first book on this historical figure in late October 1942, shortly after he wrote his reports on the deportations at Les Milles, and the second one in June 1943 in the thick of the Marseilles actions, when his own capacity to influence events was reduced almost to nil.

This use of reading for models implies adapting the information to a different situation: 'my work with the Jewish groups.' Lambert draws an analogy 'without modesty' to underscore his 'satisfaction' with the work he had done in the previous year (22 October 1942; *Diary*, 148)

Later he writes: 'Je n'atteins pas cette grandeur, mais je me rapproche de lui quand, malgré les angoisses qui devraient m'abattre, malgré mes écrasantes responsabilités, je tiens à ma solitude et à l'ordonnance de ma toilette, chaque matin au réveil' (29 June 1943, 232; 'I do not measure up to his greatness, but I compare myself with him, when, despite the anxieties that threaten to lay me low, despite my overwhelming responsibilities, I insist on my time alone and on the precise routine of my *toilette* each morning when I wake up' [192]). It is striking that he draws a parallel not only with the work of the professional public servant but also with the private man.

To take Talleyrand as a model is a highly selective process. He sets aside his pettiness, and his betrayals, to find that there is a lot to learn in 'sa volonté et sa conscience du réel' (29 June 1943, 232; 'his willpower and his awareness of what is real' [191–2]). 'Willpower': this is the tell-tale point of identification, as is the 'awareness of what is real,' by which I understand Lambert to mean a capacity not to be deluded or duped. But if Talleyrand was a patriot and a 'distinguished character,' he was also subject to 'base infatuations' and capable of 'betrayal'; Lambert treats the portrait as an array of moral traits from which he can pick and choose at will. Only on some such premise as this is his identification with the talents of Talleyrand sustainable.

Writing

Reading in this way is a practice of the self; books are the company he keeps. By contrast, writing has a projected audience. I have suggested that in writing his diary, Lambert rehearses his role, practising for it, or reviewing how it played out. Part of the rehearsal function is to plan his future books, of which he notes several in the course of the diary: mentioned twice, a memoir of his mother, which he has begun to write for his sons (17 July 1941, 119; *Diary* 59; see also 27 March 1942, 160; *Diary* 108). Another writing project, mentioned once, and probably as a joke, was one on 'these gentlemen in the Consistory' (21 July 1942; *Diary*, 127); finally, 'my great postwar book, which I am beginning to carry in my head, "The Drama of the Jews"' (2 July 1943; *Diary*, 193). Apart from the last, clearly envisaged as a major work of history, the material for these could have taken their place in his memoirs, for which the diary comes to serve as an aide-memoire (2 March 1943; *Diary*, 173).

Whether for his intended books or not, keeping the diary quickly takes on the function of making a record for the future: 'Il me faut noter les détails de la comédie pour moi-même, et pour l'avenir, comme au temps où je consignais par écrit les vicissitudes de mes démarches avant de quitter Bonn pour le Quai d'Orsay' (11 December 1941; 135–6; 'I should write down the details of this comedy for myself and for the future, as I did with the ups and downs of the actions I took before leaving Bonn to move to the Quai d'Orsay' [79–80]). The 'comedy' refers to his difficulties with the consistory. In addition, like other memoirists, the record keeping allows him to document his side of the dispute: 'Il me faut, pour mémoire, noter rapidement ce qui s'est passé avec Xavier Vallat depuis ma dernière entrevue. Mes souvenirs doivent rester précis car les individus sont jaloux et méchants' (28 December 1941, 138–9; 'I must quickly write down for the record what has been happening with Xavier Vallat since my last interview with him. I must be precise in remembering because individual people are jealous and mean' [84]).

This political function persists through the diary to the end. Lambert has his eye firmly on the account of the formation and the work of the UGIF that will go down in history: 'Mes notes me serviront peut-être un jour à écrire *Dix ans de diplomatie juive*' (8 January 1942, 145; 'perhaps one day I should use my notes to write *Ten Years of Jewish Diplomacy*' [89]). Using his 'notes' to write a memoir of his work as a diplomat from 1933 onwards would allow him to include not only his current dealings but also the full span of his work on the refugee problem. It is evident that, for him, his difficulties with the consistory are seamlessly continuous with his disputes with the right wing of French Jewry long before the Occupation; this was the premise for his actions, and for the disdain in which he held his opponents. The book, with its prophetic time span of 'ten years,' would have given him scope to write the history on that basis, and not merely to settle scores. This plan demonstrates the difference between a book planned for publication and a diary, for we continue to find in the diary barbed personal comments concerning 'the old mandarins' (29 March 1942; *Diary*, 111) and 'mémento pour servir à l'histoire de l'UGIF et de la mauvaise foi des dirigeants du judaïsme' (8 July 1942, 174; 'some notes for the sake of the history of the UGIF, showing the bad faith of the Jewish leaders' [125]). The difference between *Ten Years of Jewish Diplomacy* and this idea for an alternative book, and the fact that the latter has no title, demonstrates the same thing. An entry 'about writing a book that would get back at them,' made when relations between Lambert and the consistory were at their worst, expresses exasperation, not a plan (21 July 1942; *Diary*, 127). Ultimately, however, we find Raymond-Raoul Lambert revealed in the pages of his diary more clearly than he would have been in the story of his fights. It is the only book he left. In the same way as the projected book on his mother, he writes it to preserve his memories for his sons.

   The diary falls into three broad periods: the defeat, the formation of
the UGIF, and the deportations from the South. The first extends from
12 July 1940 until 22 June 1941. It comprises his reflections on the defeat
and the armistice, on the passing into law of the *statut*, and his return to
social work. On 16 July 1941, he records his first trip to Vichy, and the
period from that date until 6 September 1942 is concerned principally
with the negotiations with Vichy and the 'bickering' with the consistory.
August 1942 sees the first of the deportations from Les Milles, although
Lambert does not record that event until the entry of 4 October 1942.
This period until the last entry (20 August 1943) comprises the takeover
of the Southern Zone by the Germans, and Lambert's frantic activities
to try to save people from deportation and to 'mitigate the suffering'
of those who could not be saved. As he becomes more and more busy
in the second period, he notes that his time alone, for 'writing down
my thoughts day by day' – for being 'introspective' – for getting 'back
in contact with myself' is both more precious and reduced (2 March
1942; *Diary*, 106). His decision, then, is to 'spend half an hour on it every
morning, before going to the office' (105), and 'to write before reading'
(106). Despite that commitment, 'I have been neglecting this diary' and
'I have forgotten to record the events of my last trip to Vichy' (17 June
1942; *Diary*, 120–1). In the third phase, the pressure becomes far greater,
and the entries cover longer periods of time: 'I shall quickly note here
what I have done and seen for over a month' (6 September 1942; *Diary*,
129); these notes continue in the entries of 21 September and 4, 11, and
15 October. Again, on 29 November, he makes notes on the past three
weeks (*Diary*, 151), but on 7 December he despairs, 'When shall I ever
have time again to write and to think?' (*Diary*, 156), a fear confirmed on
18 December: 'So much is happening that it has kept me from writing
down my hopes and anxieties' (*Diary*, 157). By 21 March, 'the intensity
of action scarcely allows me any time to myself, even to write down every
evening how far I got that day' (*Diary*, 173); it is in this entry that we read
his intention to keep notes for the sake of his memoirs. 'In the midst of
all this action,' he writes on 16 May, 'I have not been able to write down
what I've seen, what I've suffered, for myself and for others' (*Diary*, 178).
He has been kept from 'writing down [his] daily reflections' and again
promises himself 'not to let so many days go by without getting back
to [the diary] again' (22 June 1943; *Diary*, 189). At the end, when he
acknowledges that he is 'a bundle of nerves,' he 'no longer [has] the
energy to take up [his] pen' (17 August 1943; *Diary*, 195).
   The effect of not keeping his diary is that 'my thoughts run through
my fingers like water' (2 June 1943; *Diary*, 189). He fears that 'what [he]
has done and seen' may be lost to memory. It is during this last period

that the loss of his memories becomes a preoccupation. The following passage is especially poignant in this light:

> J'ai eu 49 ans il y a huit jours et je m'en étonne ... Il faut songer bientôt à poser les premières fondations de ma retraite ... C'est à ce moment que j'ai appris par Chaplain qu'on a déménagé toute ma bibliothèque, mes chers livres, mes chers papiers, mes chers souvenirs de famille, mes lettres de guerre ... (18 August 1943, 237)

> I had my forty-ninth birthday a week ago, which astonishes me ... Soon I shall have to think about making plans for my retirement ... It was at that very moment that I learnt, through Chaplain, that my entire library [in Paris] has been cleared out, my precious books, my precious papers, my precious family mementoes, my wartime letters ... (198)

He fears the loss of his memories, not because this would be the loss of his past, which in any case leaves its 'tracks on my life' (22 June 1943; *Diary*, 189), but because it signifies their loss for the future. Hence the importance of the two books for which he makes plans in the final period – his memoirs (21 March 1943; *Diary*, 174) and 'The Drama of the Jews' (2 July 1943; *Diary*, 193). Neither, we can presume, would have shown Lambert as witness as we see him in the diary.

In the early parts of the diary, witnessing ranges from his emotional reflections on the disarray of defeated France to his amusement at the chaos of the Vichy bureaucracy: 'Les secrétaires posent des dossiers sur les bidets des salles de bains transformés en armoires. Aux murs des notes dactylographiées car le papier a repris ses droits' (2 October 1941, 130; 'The secretaries keep their files on top of the bidets in the bathrooms. There are typewritten notes pinned to the walls for paper is back in use' [130]). 'Dans ce désordre de palace réquisitionné les huissiers veillent à chaque étage, mais, si l'on arrive avant les heures de travail, on peut, avec un peu d'assurance, entrer partout, tout voir, tout lire, tout emporter ... (3 October 1941, 130; 'In this mess of a requisitioned palace, every floor is guarded by porters, but if you come before working hours you have only to look a bit self-assured to get in anywhere, see and read anything, and even take it with you ...'* [72]). Perhaps no passage in the diary gives a more revealing insight into his capacity for seeing a situation clearly and summing it up quickly for the possibilities it offers for tactical action.

However, no such possibilities are evident in the reports from Les Milles. 'I would need a book to write it all down,' he writes despairingly (4 October 1942; *Diary*, 140). No matter how much detail he observes, how much trauma he sees, how much brutality he witnesses, there is no action he can take and no way of taking advantage of what he knows. He is ashamed to be so powerless; he can only watch what happens as '40 humains qui n'ont commis aucun crime, parce qu'ils sont juifs sont livrés par mon pays qui leur avait promis asile à ceux qui seront leurs bourreaux [...] Je ne puis assister à chaque sortie du camp et me cache pour pleurer' (11 October 1942, 185; '40 human beings who have committed no crime ... [are] delivered up because they are Jews, by my country which had promised them asylum, and handed over to those who will be their executioners [...] I cannot watch each group leave the camp, I hide where I can weep' [139]). Nothing could have challenged his moral code as deeply as this. A man who felt shame for the behaviour of his government and contempt for its leaders, Lambert – the tireless fighter for the right of asylum – would never have imagined himself in this position.

Nor does he report being in that position again. Admittedly, he was prevented from witnessing the worst of the brutality in the following months by being excluded from other camps and deportation yards (1 February 1943; *Diary*, 168). The experience of the powerless witness is rarely again the place from which he writes. The overwhelming impression given by the last year of the diary is one of energy. Even at Les Milles, 'I try in vain to telephone Vichy in the hope of saving something, or a few people. They told me no one is there' (4 October 1942; *Diary*, 136). However, unlike France, he did not accept defeat. The remainder of the diary is remarkable for its focus on things done, and throughout, the diary itself bears witness to what that work entailed. 'During the afternoon, in the office, we prepare the equipment to be placed in the railroad cars, makeshift equipment, as if for a life raft ' (ibid.). He tries for more rescues, he pleads 'with more energy' (11 October 1942; *Diary*, 139); in Vichy, he makes 'three requests with an energy that surprises even [him]' (141), he goes back to 'rescue a few more' (142), and physically saves Fischer (143). He lunches with a 'pure patriot who does not lay down his arms [and who] gives [him] courage' (3 November 1942; *Diary*, 149). He keeps his team well in hand (29 November 1942; *Diary*, 153) and they continue their practical work. His responsibilities increase (7 December 1942; *Diary*, 156). He has 'unpleasant business' to do in Vichy (18 December 1942; *Diary*, 157). He engages in feverish action (3 January 1943; *Diary*, 161) for the rest of the diary. Telegrams, letters, interviews, heated discussions, reorganizing the agencies under orders from the Germans (21 March 1943; *Diary*, 175), negotiating with the Vichy officials and with the German authorities, spending months 'of anxiety, of ordeals and actions difficult to carry out' (16 May 1943; *Diary*, 178). But he is 'satisfied' and 'proud' when he secures some concession or obtains releases: he has 'not had to blush at [his] efforts' (ibid.); nor will his sons 'have to be ashamed of their father' (ibid.). He clings to his ideals, even 'if everything crumbles around us' (27 March 1942; *Diary*, 109), comparing the endurance of these ideals 'to the persistence of certain features in the landscape, this sunlit kaleidoscope unreeling past the window of my train compartment' (ibid.). He would find that there were no windows on the last train: where was France – his place – now? Two years previously, fearing for the future of his sons, he had asked, 'Quelles armes leur donner ...?' (10 May 1941, 100; 'What weapons can I give them ...?' [38]). In the absence of the memoirs he was never to write, his diary bequeaths to his sons – who would never read it – a model.

Thinking as It Treads Its Path

The choice of Richelieu and Talleyrand as models might tempt us to conclude that Lambert was simply, but preposterously, vain. Yet the diary gives us matter for a more nuanced reading. He read for many purposes, but above all, to learn. One of the things he learned about was keeping a diary. Of the major writers of the first half of the twentieth century, two in particular are important for Lambert's diary: Henri Bergson and André Gide. Both were enthusiasms for the young Lambert, and he returns to both during the period of its writing. Bergson is the philosopher whose special focus is the self in time; Gide is the writer of a diary that was Lambert's constant companion as he wrote his own.

Noting that 'Bergson is exactly right for me at my age' (1 July 1942; *Diary*, 124), Lambert feels the need, as he did with other 'enthusiasms,' to reread certain pages before proceeding. He returns to Bergson for guidance: 'Je crois, cette fois, que j'ai trouvé la méthode que j'attendais depuis longtemps, que je soupçonnais la vraie pour enrichir ma vie intérieure et qui sait? pour me formuler les commandements de sagesse, puisque je ne suis ni croyant ni incroyant' (1 July 1942, 173; 'I think this time I've found the method for which I have been waiting for a long time, which I suspected would be the true way of enriching my inner life and, who knows? would formulate wise commandments for me, since I am neither a believer nor an unbeliever' [124]). In evidence here is the serious reader's habit of association, of making two books converge on the site of a personal preoccupation. The final sentence surely comes from Gide: 'I console myself by reading André Gide's *Journals*, picking up pearls such as, "I am someone who does not believe; I am not impious." Yes, Gide has helped me to see within myself more clearly' (27 March 1942; *Diary*, 108). This convergence is helpful to us for understanding what kind of a project the diary was for Lambert. In Bergson's

Laughter, Lambert finds some 'moving passages on joy and cheerfulness'; he intends to pursue his study (21 July 1942; *Diary*, 127). If he did, it is not recorded in the diary; nevertheless, we can speculate that he derives from his earlier reading of *Matter and Memory* a rationale for keeping the diary.[53] For Bergson writes that, whereas our 'character' is the condensation of our whole life's experience, the conscious mind prefers to keep the past at bay.[54] Accordingly, for Lambert, the diary is a 'protest': 'Ma volonté de conserver ce carnet n'est-elle pas une protestation contre la conscience de l'effacement nécessaire des détails de ma vie passée et l'affirmation de la volonté d'en conserver la trace pour la direction de ma vie intérieure?' (1 July 1942, 173; 'Isn't my determination to keep this diary a protest against the awareness that the details of my past life will necessarily fade, and the expression of my will to preserve its traces to guide my inner life?' [124]). Bergson will, he hopes, counter the aestheticism of Barrès, which has influenced him to 'worry more about superficial ordering than about respect for time and for life' (ibid.).

'Time and life': this conjunction points to the generic nature of a diary. It is also a direct allusion to the Bergson of *Creative Evolution*, in which memory is given the function of explaining why time is not just a succession of discrete instants. His argument makes a claim for the constitutive place of memory in identity formation, but Lambert alludes to an account of forgetting, and Bergson closes the paragraph with an important distinction: if the whole of our past 'pushes' us in certain directions, determining tendencies of action and desire, only a small part of that past is 'represented.'[55] Otherwise, the mechanisms of the brain are designed to consign the past to the unconscious mind, selecting for use in the present only what can serve us in the situation we are in.[56]

Keeping a diary counters this tendency by not selecting what it collects. If memoirs – and the use of diary notes for projected memoirs – stake a claim to one's place in history by making strategic choices within the available material, diaries are archival in nature: they keep everything. André Gide tells us – and told Lambert – that the training of one's memory for and by the writing of a diary is a discipline, designed to counter the tendency to forget noted by Bergson. 'Tenir au jour le jour ce carnet: bonne discipline, dont je me suis toujours bien trouvé' (Keeping this notebook from day to day: it's a good discipline, which has always served me well).[57] For Lambert, we can surmise that keeping the diary – quickly, between two trains, or carefully transcribed in a hotel lobby waiting for his room to be prepared – is likewise a discipline in memory, its notes recorded to increase the range and detail of his represented experience. 'I must recall things in order, as in an appointments diary, so as not to forget anything' (28 December 1941; *Diary*, 90).

This exercise has the advantage of making more experience available to Lambert for understanding his desires and motivations – or his hopes and his fears. It allows him to use his memories – of events or of his reading – for guidance. Hence, as we have seen, he learns from Bergson to preserve his memories to 'guide' his inner life; likewise, Gide's diary is 'full of lessons' (2 March 1942; *Diary*, 102). These 'lessons' may include the 'discipline' of diary keeping, of which Gide also notes that 'la morne notation des faits' (the dreary noting down of [little] facts) has value as a training exercise.[58] Other lessons may be of a moral or emotional nature: 'Gide has helped me to see within myself more clearly,' writes Lambert (27 March 1942; *Diary*, 108), and he follows Gide in seeking guidance not from doctrine, but from reading and reflecting: 'Yet to me, all orthodoxies are suspect. (André Gide, *Journal*, 1933, 1157).'[59] It is a poignant fact that this inscription is to be found inside the cover of Lambert's final notebook; the editorial note tells us that it was written there on the day before his arrest.

Keeping a diary is a far humbler exercise than writing one's memoirs. It is more revealing, more disarmed and disarming; its rehearsal function implies that it does not parade for a public audience. Indeed, one of the conventional tropes of the genre of the diary is the friend:

> Empaytaz m'écrit: 'Je pense que tu as fort à faire et que ton poste actuel doit être particulièrement lourd, mais quelle satisfaction morale, au prix même d'un labeur écrasant, que de penser qu'on fait œuvre utile et qu'on rend service à toute sa collectivité.' Son amitié l'a éclairé. (9 July 1943, 234)

> Empaytaz wrote to me: 'I expect you have a great deal to do and that your present position is particularly onerous for you, but how satisfying it must be morally, even at the cost of enormously hard work, to think one is doing something useful and serving one's entire community.' His friendship has brought him this understanding.* 194)[60]

This letter, like others that Lambert quotes, must indeed have been sustaining. Correspondence – which involves both reading and writing – is yet another grounding practice, especially with a close friend with whom all his youthful literary enthusiasms were shared. Lambert resolves to keep up this correspondence at the same time as keeping his diary regularly: both are forms of intimacy, both cheer him (12 July 1943; *Diary*, 194). Not quite a 'dear diary' moment, the parallel between writing to a friend and keeping the diary is nevertheless quite explicit here. We can look to Gide for the moral dimension of this trope: 'Si ces carnets viennent au jour, plus tard, combien n'en rebuteront-ils pas, encore ... Mais combien j'aime celui qui, malgré eux, à travers eux, voudra demeurer mon ami!' (If one day, in the future, these notebooks are published, there will be many people who will be turned off by them, although ... But how I love the one person who, despite them and because of them, still wants to be my friend!).[61]

Despite them, because of them: we can take this passage as 'guidance' for the reading of diaries. The record of an individual's experience is addressed to (the figure of) a trusted friend, curious, interested, accepting of the writer's foibles, not fooled and not judgmental. Above all, this reader would keep it company along the path it treads.

Chapter Three

Making It Last: The Diary
of Benjamin Schatzman

Je ne vois qu'une chose à faire: faire l'impossible pour en sortir vivant.

I see only one thing to do: do the impossible to get out alive.
                                – Benjamin Schatzman, letter, 22 September 1942

Introduction

The previous chapter tells the story of a very public man who sought
to have his proclaimed identity as French and Jewish recognized by the
Vichy government, and to use that recognition to maintain his capacity
to act for the welfare of his fellow Jews. We turn now to the fate of a very
private man whose struggle, equally desperate, was focused exclusively
on his own survival. The 'self' in this story concerns neither the categories of identity nor, indeed, the matter of place: it is too late for both.
He has been definitively identified; he has a number, not a place; he is
stripped of his family, his profession, his network of friends, and his daily
habits; the practices of self-presentation available to him are significantly
reduced (to minimal washing of the person and of clothes; he can shave,
but his head is also shaven); and the company he keeps is as deplet-
ing as the food. He is physically unrecognizable and, in all social senses,
unrecognized. Self-recognition becomes crucial: this is the function of
the diary for Benjamin Schatzman.

Schatzman was a highly regarded dental surgeon, professor of dental ceramics and president of the Société d'odontologie before the outbreak of the Second World War. He was born in Romania, from where
his family immigrated to Palestine, and he received his schooling there
before going to France to pursue studies in agricultural science. The
presenters of the diary note that his somewhat non-standard French was

probably due to this history.[1] Later peregrinations took him to Algeria, back to Palestine, and to New Zealand, before his return to France and to new studies, this time in dentistry. He became a French citizen in 1907 and served in the Great War. He had not passed the baccalaureate so was not admissible to a university; for this reason, his qualifications were professional, not academic. Nevertheless, he read deeply and widely in the medical and biological sciences, and he authored scientific papers. His professorship was held in a professional institution, so did not carry the title of 'professor.' His recognized status was therefore somewhat ambiguous: on the one hand, he was rounded up along with university professors, judges, lawyers, and engineers in the *rafle des notables*, on 12 December 1941, and interned with them in *le camp juif de Royallieu-Compiègne*; on the other, a nurse in the hospital at Compiègne fails to recognize his expertise and refused to give him information about his medication, even though he had explained to her who he was (28 March 1942, 130). His indignation is palpable: 'je sais autrement mieux qu'elle la valeur des spécialités' (30 March 1942, 141; I know a bit better than she does what value these specialized medications have). Schatzman was held at Compiègne until 23 June 1942, when he was transferred to Drancy, thence to Pithiviers, then Beaune-la-Rolande and back to Drancy, before being deported to Auschwitz on 23 September. He did not return. The exact circumstances of his death are unknown; it may have occurred on the train.[2]

The first entry of his diary is dated 31 January 1942, six weeks after his arrest; the last extant entry is dated 30 August 1942, just prior to his transfer to Pithiviers, though there is some evidence that he continued to write it. His practice was to send instalments to his wife by any means possible – in bundles of laundry, or with comrades taken to hospital, who could receive visits, or with social workers able to travel to and from Drancy.[3] A letter dated 2 September tells her to expect one in a parcel containing his belongings, but the diary was missing from the package and never arrived; we can presume it was confiscated. Aside from the diary proper, the published volume of Schatzman's writings contains sections entitled 'Souvenirs et réflexions' (memories and reflections) and 'Feuillets épars' (scattered sheets) as well as letters to his wife, Cécile. The diary has been edited to standardize the spelling and the punctuation as well as to eliminate the *repentirs*, but not otherwise shortened or changed. All of Schatzman's papers, including the manuscript diary, are held in the Archives nationales de France. I quote from the published version, and shall draw on the other writings in that volume, as required.

I Am Unrecognizable

As far as we can judge, for the first six weeks of Schatzman's internment, he was in a state of shock, unable to process the event or its effects. It took on the quality of 'experience' in the full sense only when he started to write. This is evident in his reiterated lament, that he does not recognize himself: his internment has caused a radical discontinuity in his sense of self. 'Je ne me reconnais pas' (20 February 1942, 58; I don't recognize myself); 'je ne suis pas ce que j'étais' (25 February, 65; I'm not what I was); 'je ne me reconnais plus' (10 March 1942, 99; I no longer recognize myself); 'la souffrance par la faim transforme votre personnalité' (29 March 1942, 139; the suffering caused by hunger transforms one's personality). Writing the diary is very beneficial. From 'ne pas se reconnaître' (not recognizing himself) to 'rester avec moi-même' (spending time with myself), the diary is the principal means to rebuilding his sense of self and to its maintenance: 'je me sens revivre' (28 March 1942, 131; I come alive again).

Let us chart this change in greater detail. Schatzman writes of himself in his first diary entry: 'Je suis dans un état de déficience physique et morale d'autant plus surprenant que je me croyais plus riche en réserve de potentiel. Mon état d'âme et mon état moral ainsi que mental sont lamentables' (31 January 1942, 51; I am in a state of moral and physical deficiency all the more surprising because I believed I had greater reserves to draw on. My state of mind, my mental state and my morale are deplorable). However, the decision to write and the self-reflexion required for this description already imply a positive change, countering the change in himself that he records with evident surprise: 'Je sens en moi le même manque de courage et de volonté pour faire simplement ce que, dans ma vie habituelle, il m'aurait été impossible d'envisager, mais d'avoir la moindre hésitation' (n.d., 54; I feel the same lack of courage and willpower simply to do, things that I would not have imagined having the least hesitation to do); 'je n'aurais jamais cru cela si on me l'avait dit' (n.d., 55; I'd never have believed it if someone had told me). Indeed, the surprise itself is evidence of a state of consciousness other than total prostration and points to the very problem of continuity between the remembered self and the self of now.

Through February and early March, Schatzman was suffering increasing ill health, with a dramatic loss of weight (cachexia), a urinary affliction (pollakiuria), and edema of the legs and feet.[4] All these conditions were caused by malnutrition. He was sent to the neighbouring civil hospital on 11 March and discharged on 28 April 1942, his symptoms somewhat mitigated but by no means cured. On the day before his admission to hospital he writes:

> Enfin, malgré ma résignation, ma volonté flanche, mon découragement est quelquefois tel que la vie même m'est indifférente, et, à ce moment, je ne me reconnais plus, je ne retrouve pas mon attachement et l'intérêt en la vie, et tout ce qui m'est cher, et tout ce que pour quoi je désire vivre. Ceci est chez moi, optimiste incurable, est un événement qui marque la profondeur avec laquelle je suis atteint. (10 March 1942, 99)

> In the end, despite my resignation, my willpower fails, my discouragement is such that I am indifferent to life itself; at the moment, I no longer recognize myself, I have lost my attachment to life and the interest I take in it and everything that is dear to me, in everything for which I want to go on living. For the incurable optimist that I am, this is an event: it marks the depth to which I am affected.

This is the last time he writes 'je ne me reconnais plus' in the present tense: on 29 March, when he repeats the observation, it takes the form of a general truth posited of 'one' (139).

Schatzman's recovery began as soon as he started receiving medical care. Only two days after his admission to hospital, he is able to write about his decline in the past tense, as if it were already reversed: 'Toutes mes fonctions vitales me quittaient progressivement et cependant dans cette atmosphère d'égoïsme qui ne donnait libre cours qu'à une seule préoccupation, en vérité angoissante, manger, et, en second lieu, l'évolution de la guerre et les libérations' (13 March 1942, 109; All my vital functions were failing, and this in this atmosphere of self-centredness in which a single preoccupation, that of eating – an acute anxiety, it's true – and a second one, the progress of the war and of liberation, dominated everything). The next day, he is able to write, 'J'ai commencé dès ce matin à retrouver le besoin, le désir, et la volonté de m'occuper de moi' (112; This very morning I began to retrieve the need, the desire, and the will to take care of myself). This assumption of responsibility is a major change, with the reflexive verb and the tonic pronoun combining to extract 'me' from the position of passive victim. Then, following a visit from his wife, he writes 'Je me sens maintenant un autre homme' (15 March 1942, 114; I am a different man now).

The self Schatzman loses and needs to retrieve is a man for whom keeping the diary serves to counteract the fear that his usually very active brain will become 'stérile' (barren). The first entry of the diary notes his astonishment at the fact that he has neither the desire nor the capacity to read: 'Voici plus d'un mois que je n'ai pu non seulement me décider de lire, mais je n'ai eu ni le goût, ni le désir, ni le besoin de le faire. Je ne peux m'expliquer cela que par la souffrance de la faim' (31 January 1942, 51; It's more than a month since I could put my mind to reading; not only that, but I had no taste for it, no desire, no need to do so. I can explain this only by the suffering of hunger). He notes the same fact again, this time acknowledging that his expectations of himself are based entirely on normal times; is one still the same self, is the identity changed by abnormal circumstances? Taking cognizance of this threat is the key to self-knowledge; from it arises the possibility of continuity in the face of change. 'Est-ce que, par exemple, j'aurais pu rester pendant tant de semaines sans pouvoir et sans avoir envie de lire?' (12 February 1942, 54; Could I have remained so long without being able to read or wanting to?'), he asks. 'Je n'aurais jamais cru cela possible' (ibid.'I would never have believed it'). It proves that he had no experience of the effects of this kind of suffering. He must 'take note' of the fact (n.d., 54–5). As early as two days after his admission to the hospital, with better food and some medical care, he looks over his decline and repeats the shock he had expressed in January: 'je constate à mon grand étonnement, que voici deux mois que je n'ai pas lu une ligne, parce que je n'avais ni le goût ni la force, ni l'esprit pour cela' (13 March 1942, 109; I note with great astonishment that it is two months since I read a single line, because I had neither taste nor strength, no head for it'), but here the incapacity is written in the past tense. Now, 'il ne me reste plus qu'à me remettre vite, et à posséder quelque chose d'intéressant à lire' (ibid.; all I need is to get better quickly and to get hold of something interesting to read). From this point, reading will be the touchstone of his state of health (28 March 1942, 131). Two days later, having borrowed a book in English from an American who is also in hospital, he notes a far improved state of concentration; it's 'nearly' as good as he is used to, and will serve as a marker of his 'progress' (30 March 1942, 140–1).

English was a language he had picked up during his three years (1902–5) in New Zealand (a country he left because of the dearth of intellectual and cultural life there). In the course of the diary, we see him reading George Eliot, George Meredith, and Thomas Carlyle, and defending his books from threatened confiscation by giving them the status of 'books for study.' Pursuing the project of improving his competence, he is learning, and also teaching:

Autrement, rien de saillant à raconter. Je vais toutes les après-midi à l'infirmerie, y trouver Albert et deux médecins à qui cela fait plaisir d'être guidés

dans l'étude de la langue anglaise. Je leur suis souvent utile du point de vue prononciation. (1 June 1942, 257)

> Apart from this, there's nothing particular to tell. Every afternoon, I go to the infirmary to find Albert and two doctors who enjoy having guidance in their study of English. I am often useful to them from the point of view of pronunciation.

He also teaches English to his colleague Filderman (13 August 1942, 386). This is a way for him to fulfil his need to be useful to his co-detainees (1 March 1942, 74; also 20 May 1942, 227). The need for useful activity is evident throughout writings from the camps. In the following, 'des gens comme nous' (people like us) refers in the immediate context to the companions with whom he is sharing a room, who had been arrested in the *rafle des notables*; they were educated people, professionals.[5] Through his 'nous,' Schatzman claims this identity as his own, but it is undermined by inactivity:

> On ne peut pas imaginer, pour des gens comme nous, une vie plus déprimante moralement, cérébralement et physiquement! Se lever et se coucher avec l'oisiveté devant soi, sans aucun but, sans aucune activité utile possible, sans avoir ce qu'on pourrait faire pour occuper son temps et sans pouvoir occuper son temps de la façon qu'on désirerait, est une obsession très pénible et fortement stérilisante de sa personnalité. Même les conversations, les échanges d'idées ont un caractère agité, incomplet et sans suite. (4 May 1942, 172)

> You could not imagine a life more depressing for people like us, morally, intellectually and physically! Getting up and going to bed with nothing but idleness ahead, having no aim, no possible useful activity, with nothing to do to occupy one's time, not able to occupy one's time as one would like, this is a painful obsession, sterile and sapping of one's personality. Even conversational exchanges are agitated and incomplete, leading nowhere.

So it is that, when he is asked by a colleague to help with dental services in the camp, he must weigh this need against his need to persuade the authorities that he is sick enough to be released from the camp:

> Ma situation est très difficile en ce moment, puisque je dois concilier mon désir d'être utile, de rendre service, et ainsi m'occuper un peu, et mon besoin de repos et d'être considéré comme faible, ayant besoin d'être ménagé et de me soigner. (28 May 1942, 250; see also 23 June 1942, 233)

My situation is particularly difficult at the moment, because I have to recon-
cile my desire to be useful, to do favours for people, and thus to busy myself,
with my need to rest and to be considered weak, needing care.

Nevertheless, he accepts this work, as he accepts the offer of reading
material, and a kit of dental tools. 'Let's wait and hope,' he concludes,
recognizing that such calculations have no power over the situation
(28 May 1942, 250).

Professional recognition, being useful, and engaging in intellectual
pursuits: this is Schatzman as he has known himself. But, in the early
pages of the diary, he notes one further characteristic that he must
retrieve: his accustomed resolve and self-discipline. 'Ma volonté flanche'
(my willpower is failing), he writes on 10 March 1942 (99), and earlier, 'Je ne me reconnais pas, tellement je suis maintenant incapable
de tenir mes décisions concernant le rationnement de ce que je reçois
comme part' (20 February 1942, 58; I don't recognize myself, I'm so
incapable of holding to my decisions concerning the rationing and what
I receive as my share). This is his 'physical being' calling for help (ibid.).
Schatzman's self-understanding starts off by being deeply Cartesian,
his sense of who he is appearing to rest primarily on moral and intellectual criteria. However, in the camp, he comes to understand that all
aspects of the person are destroyed in the same process: 'Mentalement,
moralement et physiquement, cette vie [est] faite pour anéantir graduellement les forces vitales. C'est un fait plus qu'étonnant de voir que
tant de gens tiennent encore, en rapport avec le déchet qui se forme
tous les jours' (21 February 1942, 60; Mentally, morally, physically, this
life cannot but annihilate gradually all the vital forces. It's more than
surprising to see how many people keep going, in view of the day-by-day
decline). Although he thinks that, ultimately, the cold is the main cause
of his moral collapse (22 February 1942, 61), his primary needs are die-
tary: 'Sous le rapport de l'alimentation, les sensations sont différentes
et constamment les mêmes: besoin d'ingérer plus de nourriture et, plus
particulièrement, plus riche en protides et glucides' (ibid.; With regard
to eating, the sensations are always different, yet constantly the same:
the need to ingest more food and, more particularly, food that is richer
in protides and glucides). As a result, he discovers that the self is first a
body with needs. This is a radical change in his sense of who he is: 'En
toute sincérité, je dois reconnaître que je ne suis pas ce que j'étais. Mes
sensations et mes besoins se ramènent à ceux d'un animal quelconque.'
(25 February 1942, 65; Quite candidly, I must acknowledge that I am no
longer what I was. My sensations and my needs are reduced to those of
some sort of animal).

The primacy of food runs against the grain for Schatzman. An 'animal': he counts his preoccupation with food as some sort of moral failing unworthy of a man with his values and sense of priorities. He has a utilitarian view of food: it should be well prepared and tasty, but only so it can serve its purpose. Considering the body exclusively in terms of its healthy operation, for him the culinary arts have the status of untrustworthy decoration. While it is 'logical' to use them, they carry risks, above all that of disguising reality, just as rhetorical flourishes disguise the truth of unadorned scientific reason. The important thing is nutritional value: the diet should be balanced and devised to maintain the organism according to scientific findings (20 May 1942, 227). His exposition of these points takes the form of a lecture in which he would teach the principles of a healthy and rational diet. Otherwise, food is usually a subject of secondary importance. The somewhat puritanical Schatzman seeks to reassure his reader 'because I wouldn't want anyone to misinterpret my behaviour': the preoccupation with eating is due to the 'cruel and unjust circumstances' in which he is living (ibid.).

The shattering early months of his internment force Schatzman to admit the centrality of food and hence, the importance of physical well-being to the moral and intellectual self. Self-recognition, too, must have its physical dimension. In the disinfection shower, he sees his companions and himself naked for the first time: 'La majorité était d'une telle maigreur qu'on pouvait se demander comment ils tenaient debout. En me regardant, je ne reconnaissais pas mon corps' (5 March 1942, 92; Most [of the men] were so thin that you had to ask how they remained standing. When I looked at myself, I didn't recognize my body). 'Se regarder' (to look at oneself): this moment of self-consciousness mobilizes a central trope of diary writing. Here, Schatzman no longer recognizes his body; shortly hereafter, he accepts that his looks have changed.

He finds other ways of looking at himself. First in the barber's mirror, an image he would like to keep in a photograph:

J'ai oublié de noter un petit événement qu'il est bon de ne pas laisser dans l'oubli: jeudi dernier, le caporal infirmier allemand, qui est chargé de faire tondre les gens, que je n'ai pas pu éviter, m'a aussi fait tondre la tête. C'est dommage que je ne puisse pas me faire photographier car j'ai maintenant un faciès dont j'aimerai avoir l'image, ayant l'aspect d'un forçat. (10 May 1942, 195)

I forgot to mention a little event which I shouldn't forget: last Thursday, the German nursing corporal, whose job it is to shave people and whom I couldn't avoid, shaved my head as well. It's a shame I can't have myself photographed because I have the look of a convict: I'd like to keep an image of my appearance.

Second, a neighbour draws his portrait:

> Chaque fois que je me regarde dans la glace, je me trouve une tête désagréable à regarder. Mon voisin, Guermann, le violoniste, qui s'amuse à faire un peu d'aquarelle et de dessin, s'amuse aussi à faire au crayon des portraits au crayon. Il a commencé par moi et, si ce portrait ne me plaît pas, il donnera une idée de la tête que j'ai maintenant. (Ibid.)

> Every time I look at myself in the mirror, I discover how horrible I look. My neighbour, Guermann, who's a violinist and who also enjoys painting and drawing, likes to do pencil sketches of people. He started with me, and if I don't exactly like this portrait, it will give an idea of what I look like now.

The body has a history; in it are inscribed the privations of the camp, the experience that Schatzman must accept and then integrate into his self-understanding. A mirror, a portrait: while he doesn't like what he sees – his looks, his preoccupation with food – he must keep a record of it. The diary is a means of recognizing himself notwithstanding the changes, at the same time discovering how he can still be himself under these alien and alienating circumstances.

These means extend to the style of exposition. One of the most striking ways in which the diary serves as a means of self-recognition is Schatzman's prose: its discursive habits are borrowed from his scientific reading and writing. We might take as an example his explanation of hunger: 'Physiologiquement j'assiste à l'action des organes chargés de maintenir l'équilibre nutritif de tout l'être pour agir sur l'être psychique pour l'avertir qu'il manque de ce qu'il faut pour se maintenir dans la normale, après avoir épuisé les réserves intérieures' (20 February 1942, 58; On the physiological level, I observe the action of the organs whose task is to maintain nutritional balance for any being: they are warning the mind of that being that it lacks enough to maintain its normal state, having exhausted its internal reserves). This passage is part of a longer reflexion on his loss of willpower, which he seeks to explain; he understands it as 'une preuve évidente de mon état déficient et de l'appel au secours de mon être physique' (ibid.; an obvious proof of my deficient state and of my physical being's appeal for help). In turn, this is followed by an explanation of his usual self-control, which requires, as he puts it, that 'everything [be] in good working order' (ibid.).

Two levels of self-recognition are in play here: one, that of his body and its reactions; the other, his search for an adequate scientific explanation for the change. Once he can describe the physiology of his normal state, he can accept that his failure of willpower is not just a moral failing, but part of the normal processes of the body. He does so through an explanation of the norm, so as to deduce the causes of the abnormal. It is not simply the register of his lexicon – 'preuve,' 'organes,' 'équilibre nutritif' – but the explanatory procedure itself that is scientific. In this, he can accept not only that he is still himself, notwithstanding his unrecognizable behaviour, but also that his trained thought patterns are intact. Schatzman is again himself.

The need for physiological explanations and his capacity to draw on specialized knowledge are evident right from the start, when he is perplexed about 'l'explication physiologique et pathologique de la fonction anormale de mes organes rénaux' (12 February 1942, 52; the physiological and pathological explanation for the abnormal functioning of my renal organs'). We find the same habit throughout the diary: for his insomnia, for example, the cause of which escapes him (21 February 1942, 58), and for his urinary problems: 'J'ai surtout [réfléchi] sur mon cas du point de vue de la fonction rénale. Pourquoi et pour quelle raison, cette incontinence d'urine? Voici l'observation que j'ai faite sur moi' (16 March 1942, 116–17; Mostly I've been reflecting on my renal incontinence. Why and for what reason can I not contain my urine? Here are the observations I have made on myself). This is followed by a meticulous recording of what he has drunk and of other variables, and the conclusion that he was considerably better during the night after eating some sugar: 'Ce qui prouve bien que l'incontinence était due à une insuffisance de calories' (ibid.; this proves that my incontinence was due to insufficient calories) and was nothing to do with his prostate. Again we see good scientific practice at work: minute observation, measurement, the ruling out of one explanatory conclusion and the retaining of a more plausible alternative. And all this in a diary, as if he were writing a physician's report.

Indeed, acting as his own physician is the next step. In the early weeks, he has been told that his bladder problem is caused by his prostate, even though he has been assured that the gland is not enlarged:

D'ailleurs, j'ai décidé de l'étudier moi-même en l'étudiant dans les textes parce que je ne l'ai jamais bien connue [= cette question]. Dans les explications qu'on me donne ici il y a quelque chose d'obscur et qui fait qu'elles ne me contentent pas. J'ai hâte de me retrouver avec mes livres pour élucider cela. (20 February 1942, 57)

In any case, I've decided to study the matter myself by perusing what has been written about it, because I've never known a great deal about this question. In the explanations I am given here, there is something unclear, so they don't satisfy me. I'm keen to get back to my books to clarify this matter.

Very late in his internment, still very unwell as a consequence of his cachexia, he again consults a doctor, and again, to no avail: 'Mais, à mon regret, il n'a pas trouvé que j'étais un malade intéressant, et n'a pas satisfait ce que je voulais savoir sur moi, du point de vue des conséquences de ma cachexie' (7 August 1942, 376; But unfortunately, he didn't find me to be an interesting patient, and failed to answer my query concerning the consequences of my cachexia). He would undertake the diagnostic and therapeutic work more effectively himself:

Décidément, ces maîtres de la médecine ne se montrent pas capables de m'expliquer les symptômes que je ressens. Ils traitent ainsi à la légère ce qui a pour moi beaucoup d'importance. Je ne pourrai éclaircir, traiter et améliorer mon état que quand je serai de retour chez moi, du moins, j'espère pouvoir réunir les informations physiologiques et pathologiques qu'il me faut pour comprendre ces symptômes et m'appliquer le traitement rationnel qu'il faut. (Ibid.)

These masters in medicine are decidedly incapable of explaining my symptoms. So they take lightly things that have great importance for me. I won't be able to clarify, to treat, or to improve my state until I get home; at least I hope I'll be able to put together the physiological and pathological information I need to understand these symptoms and to treat myself rationally in the way I need.

Adding to his troubles, bad abdominal pain lays him low for several days; again, he receives no treatment, and again he acts as his own physician: 'Voici les symptômes que je ressens' (27 August 1942, 405; Here are my symptoms). This is because the doctors appear not to take him seriously (ibid., 405–6), until he meets one with whom he can behave as a colleague: 'Nous sommes tombés d'accord ... Le traitement conseillé est celui auquel j'ai pensé ... je me suis rendu compte que je faisais une faute en prenant des alcalins pour obtenir un soulagement, car je faisais plutôt de l'hypo-acidité' (28 August 1942, 407; We agreed ... The treatment he advised is the one I had thought of ... I realized that it was mistake to take alkalines to soothe the pain, because I was suffering rather from hypo-acidity).

Writing

Following the shock of his arrest – represented in the utter silence of the first seven weeks – keeping the diary gives Schatzman a way of being a self in time. 'Chaque jour, son histoire et ses vicissitudes' (12 February 1942, 52; each day has its story, each day its vicissitudes), he writes to open the second entry of his diary, thus outlining the content of his days and hence of his 'notes.' He insists he is not writing a diary – 'C'est moins un journal qu'un moyen de ne pas laisser stérile mon cerveau' (28 March 1942, 131; it's not so much a diary as a way of not letting my brain rot) – preferring to retain the term 'journal' to refer to the physical medium that contains 'mes impressions,' 'mes méditations,' 'mes observations,' 'mes réflexions,' 'mes pensées' (13 May 1942, 206; my impressions, meditations, observations, reflexions, thoughts). On one occasion, with a rare touch of humour, he calls his text 'la narration de mes faits et gestes' (5 June 1942, 269; the recital of my exploits). The range of terms for his entries does indeed point to the variety of their content: alongside reflections on relations with his fellow internees, we find long, reflective developments on topics such as eliminating the conditions for the outbreak of future wars, and scientifically inspired speculations on the causes of his symptoms. He tells us, however, that writing helps him focus his thoughts, and that achieving this focus is the principal function of the diary:

Le fait, dans mon isolement, que j'écris ce à quoi je pense, au lieu de rester simplement avec ces pensées plus ou moins vagabondes, me fait passer bien mieux mon temps, celui-ci s'écoule plus vite ainsi, m'obsède moins, et mon ennui est certainement beaucoup atténué [...] Je suis content d'avoir l'idée d'écrire tout ce qui me passe par la tête et tout ce que je fais, cela m'a rendu jusqu'ici service. Le temps, entre les repas, est long, c'est ainsi que les gens sont tentés de boire et de manger. (27 March 1942, 125)

In my isolation, the fact that I write what I am thinking, instead of allowing my thoughts to wander, helps me spend my time much better; time passes more quickly, less obsessively, and my boredom is considerably diminished [...] I am glad I thought of writing down everything that goes through my head and everything that I do, it has served me well. Time goes slowly between meals, that's what tempts people to eat and drink.

The variety of content, and the disciplining of his *pensées vagabondes* (wandering thoughts), helps him avoid thinking about painful topics. 'Il ne faudrait pas que je pense à cette souffrance, que je ne regarde pas en arrière puisque cela ne sert qu'à me faire du mal, sans aucun effort utile. Quand je peux m'évader de cette peine, je suis mieux'[6] (5 May 1942, 176; I must not think about this suffering, I must not look back to the past; that only makes me feel worse, without benefit. I am better when I can escape the pain). He is not fully absorbed by reading, he continues in the same passage: 'Seule l'écriture de ces pages m'éloigne plus complètement de mon état de tristesse et de désespoir' (only the writing of these pages takes me out of my state of sadness and despair).

Rather than to document the conditions of the camp or the events that take place in it, Schatzman's focus is to record the effort of remaining himself under those conditions. Not only a means of self-recognition, the diary is also a means of distancing himself from the experience through the mediation of description. On the other hand, the immediacy of the conditions is directly registered in the diary by the care Schatzman takes to record the material and emotional conditions under which he writes. These are far from being the mere context of a more substantive content. They index the here and now of the writing body – his hands, his levels of energy, his posture, how he makes a space and a time for writing amid the jostling promiscuity and preoccupations of the camp. They tell us how he can, why he must, and, at times, why he cannot, go on writing. There could be no more eloquent testimony to the details of survival in the French camps.

The first notation concerning the writing of the diary is made early in the period he spent at Compiègne, when he describes the material conditions of the writing body: 'Ici, pas de siège, pas de table, pas d'éclairage. Je ne peux écrire qu'assis sur une paillasse, avec mal au dos et les [mains] engourdies par le froid' (25 February 1942, 65; Here there is no seat, no table, no light. I can write only when I'm sitting on a palliasse, my back aching and my fingers numb with cold). A little warmth makes all the difference:

> Nous venons de finir de manger la soupe, et je suis disposé à noter mes méditations sur moi-même, mais surtout qu'on a fait un peu du feu, et, pour la première fois, depuis huit à dix jours, il y a du soleil, ce qui fait que j'ai moins froid aux mains. (1 March 1942, 73)

> We've just finished our soup, so I feel like writing down my meditations concerning myself, particularly because we've got a bit of a fire, and for the first time in a week the sun is shining, so my hands are less cold.

But it is all too short-lived: 'je m'arrête, ne pouvant écrire à cause de mes mains engourdies' (7 March 1942, 95; I'll finish up now because my hands are numb so I can't write). With a little care in the hospital, a little more comfort, he can write to pass the time: 'Le temps passe pendant que j'écris, car j'attends avec impatience le tilleul qu'on a promis il y a une heure' (11 March 1942, 105; Time passes while I'm writing, for I'm waiting impatiently for them to bring the linden-flower tea they promised an hour ago). But frequently, the conditions preclude this activity: 'Il est 20h 20, j'écris avec un éclairage du jour juste suffisant pour deviner ce que j'écris, d'ailleurs je m'arrête' (26 March 1942, 121; It's 8.20 p.m., I'm writing in barely sufficient daylight to make out what I'm writing, in any event I'll stop). The following is written at 7:15 p.m.: 'il fait encore grand jour, le calme complet règne dans la salle' (27 March 1942, 127; it's still full daylight, it's totally calm in the room). Especially at this time 'la longueur du temps est le plus insupportable' (time is intolerably slow), and he would like to use the time writing, but he cannot do so for long. He explains why:

> À partir de 20h, ou 20 h 15, il ne fait plus assez clair pour lire ou écrire et il n'y a pas d'autre éclairage que celui qui tombe de l'ampoule électrique, entourée d'un abat-jour, sur la table, au milieu de la salle, devant mon lit. Mais il n'y a pas de chaise, et je ne tiens pas encore à fatiguer mes jambes. (Ibid.)

> From about 8 or 8:15 p.m., there's not enough light to read or write; there's no other lighting but what falls from the light-bulb with its shade above the table in the middle of the room, in front of my bed. But there's no chair, and I'm still concerned not to tire my legs.

The physical arrangements of the room conspire with his body: his legs are still weak, and he is also worried about the edema in his feet. Nevertheless, he ends this entry optimistically, noting improvements in his state: 'nous verrons comment le temps agira' (ibid., 128; we'll see the effect of time). He needs his body to sustain his diary, as he needs his diary to sustain him.

It is in this entry that he defines the purpose of the diary as a means of not letting his brain rot. And yet, as he goes on to explain, it is important to him for two further reasons. One is that his loved ones may be interested: 'Peut-être, tout de même, les miens trouveront un intérêt à lire ce que je leur aurais probablement raconté si je les avais vus tous les jours ou s'ils avaient pu me soigner' (28 March 1942, 131; Perhaps, all the same, my loved ones will find some interest in what I would probably have told them if I were seeing them every day or if they had been able to look after me). The second is that – we have seen this with Lambert – his observations will be forgotten if he does not write them down. The diary is 'la cristallisation d'un événementimportant de ma vie, et tout ce qui se passe avec moi, en moi, pendant que je suis loin et qu'on se demande ce que je fais, comment je vis et dans quel état je suis (ibid.; the cristallization of an important event in my life, of everything that is happening to me and within me while I am far away and they are wondering how I am, how I am living, and what state I am in). Note that he projects his presence into his loved ones' lives, as well as theirs into his (see also 8 March 1942, 188). The very writing of the diary creates an interlocutor who wants to know. Besides, the materiality of writing consigns to paper his 'impressions' and 'crystallizes' them, guarding their fleeting nature from oblivion, for a future that otherwise would have ceased to care. He lives, he will have lived.

It is not only the body, its accommodation in space and light, but his nervous state that affects his writing. He explains:

> Par ma façon d'écrire, on peut reconnaître mon état psychique et nerveux au moment où j'écris. Quand je suis un peu plus calme, je peux écrire régulièrement, comme maintenant, pendant les heures d'excitation et d'agitation inérieures, il m'est très difficile d'écrire droit et de trouver les mots qu'il me faut. (3 May 1942, 166)

> My handwriting reveals my psychological and nervous state at the time I am writing. When I am calmer, my writing is regular, as it is now; when I feel agitated and overwrought, it is very difficult for me to write straight and to find the words I need.

By May, he had returned to the camp from the hospital and is already feeling the deleterious effects of the reduced diet and the impossibility of rest. Besides, he is surrounded by people who are speculating about the length of their internment and indeed, of the war. It may go on and on. He entertains thoughts of suicide:

> Je recommence à sentir les signes de faiblesse d'avant mon évacuation. C'est une raison pour que je me sente moins résistant à l'envahissement de la démoralisation et au dégoût. Je me lève et me couche avec le chagrin, et dans la nuit je me réveille avec l'angoisse que donne l'insécurité et que m'a donnée cette cruelle déception.
>
> Qu'est-ce que je peux espérer maintenant et à quel espoir puis-je m'accrocher? (2 May 1942, 165)

> I'm beginning to feel the same signs of weakness as I did before I was evacuated. This is one reason why I am more vulnerable to being overwhelmed by

demoralization and disgust. I get up in the morning and go to bed at night
in sorrow, and during the night I wake in the state of anxiety that provokes
insecurity and that was caused by this cruel disappointment.
  What hope is there for me now, what hope can I hold on to?

Again, the very act of verbalizing his demoralization, of explaining the
reasons for it, gives him some distance; it allows him to imagine an
interlocutor who has no idea what he is going through: 'On ne peut
s'imaginer et se représenter une pareille souffrance' (ibid., 166; One
cannot imagine or represent this kind of suffering). Addressing this
same interlocutor, he writes the next day: 'je me sens énervé et impatient et mon écriture s'en ressent, je ne peux pas écrire droit' (3 May
1942, 168; I'm nervous and impatient and it shows in my writing, I can't
write straight). Again, it is the indexicality of the manuscript that is
most eloquent; nevertheless, by drawing his reader's attention to it, he
ensures an accurate interpretation: this is not mere untidiness, but a
symptom. His reader is one who understands that the body is an instrument of writing. As is a good pen and good ink. Schatzman is fussy
about such things: 'je reprends mon encre violette car, vraiment, l'écriture est plus nette, plus lisible. J'ai écrit avec l'encre bleue à cause de
la finesse de la plume' (26 June 1942, 320; I'm writing again with my
purple ink because the writing is truly neater and more legible with it.
I was writing with blue ink because of the fine nib). For the sake of his
reader, the manuscript must be clean, and clear; perhaps, too, he recognizes himself in a neat hand.
  Let us return to the matter of posture. He is back in the camp at
Compiègne, and has just changed rooms. He is more comfortable; there
are fewer people and better spatial arrangements; the *chef de bloc* finds
him a little table:

> Pour être tranquille, je m'asseyais sur mon lit, et le papier appuyé sur un
> livre, et celui-ci posé sur ma cuisse pour écrire. Mais, ce matin, il y a deux
> heures (il est midi et demi), Miaskowski a apporté une petite table, meuble
> plus haut qu'un tabouret et plus bas qu'une table. Je m'en suis emparé
> pour écrire dessus, tout en étant assis sur le bord de mon lit, et, ainsi, je
> peux écrire d'une manière plus commode. (5 May 1942, 174)

As a way of remaining undisturbed, I was sitting on my bed, with the paper
resting on a book, and the book resting on my thigh. But this morning, two
hours ago (it is now half past midday), Miaskowski brought in a little table,
higher than a stool and lower than a table. I took possession of it to write
on, sitting on the edge of my bed; this is more comfortable for writing.

Only four days later, the little table seems to have disappeared, so 'j'écris dans des conditions bien fatigantes, assis sur le bord du lit, tenant le papier sur un livre, penché sur le lit voisin' (9 May 1942, 191; the conditions for writing are very tiring: I'm sitting on the edge of the bed, holding the paper on a book, and bent over the neighbouring bed). This is uncomfortable, and he is frequently disturbed.

The following passage concludes an account of visits he has been making to another room, where he finds compatible company; these men are interesting, and interested in what he has to say on subjects he knows something about, so he forgets his miseries when he is with them. But he is not sure he can continue these visits because 'toute activité me coûte, et je tiens surtout à ne pas négliger cette habitude que j'ai prise d'inscrire mes impressions et ce que je fais' (30 May 1942, 255; all activity saps my energy, and above all I am concerned to maintain my habit of writing down my impressions and everything I do). He is worn out and will reduce his activities when he needs to conserve his strength. But he is conserving it *for* his diary: this 'above all' he will not give up.

Shortly after this, having agreed to provide dental care, he is moved to the infirmary with the other health care workers (mainly doctors).

Il est maintenant 20h15. J'ai passé le reste de l'après-midi après 16h30, c'est-à-dire après avoir fait le lit, installé mes paquets et ma valise, à me reposer et à écrire.

Vers 17h30, ces messieurs avec des invités ont fait un bridge, j'ai pu avoir un coin de table pour lire et écrire. (5 June 1942, 269)

It's 8:15 p.m. now. The rest of the afternoon, after 4:30 – that is, after I had made my bed and put away my packets and my suitcase – I spent resting and writing.

At about 5.30 p.m., these gentlemen had guests in for bridge. I was able to use a corner of the table for reading and writing.

However, the relative comfort of his new accommodation has disadvantages: the bridge players are sociable. The timid, self-effacing Schatzman, who dislikes spending time in futile activities such as card games and ignorant conversation, has difficulty making and holding the space he needs for his writing:

Mon lit fut envahi par eux [ces messieurs] et des visiteurs, et cette petite pièce n'était plus abordable. J'ai pu me réfugier dans la pièce où se fait la consultation, mais je n'avais plus de chaise. Et ce n'est que très timidement que j'ai pu obtenir que ma chaise soit restituée, et en proposant que mon

lit serve de siège, j'ai pu ainsi m'asseoir pour écrire ces méditations. (7 June
1942, 281–2)

My bed was invaded by these gentlemen and their guests, and there was no
more space in this little room. I took refuge in the consultation room, but
there was no chair. With utmost timidity I got them to give me back my chair
by suggesting that they use my bed to sit on, that's how I could sit down to
write these meditations.

It is clear from these entries that having one's own space was both imperative and close to impossible in the camp. Even in the medical quarters,
his bed is not his own: the card players use it to sit on, and even though
he has room at the table, 'the bed is jolted around by the fellow beside
me (the anti-Semitic lawyer) who can't sit still' (10 June 1942, 290); this
too compromises his handwriting.[7]

Let us add to the matters of physical comfort, energy, and supple
hands, the need to obtain a supply of paper. He has attempted to use
wrapping paper (4 March 1942, 90) (later, in Drancy, this is confiscated),
and has begged and borrowed writing paper from other internees.[8]

Cette habitude que j'ai prise pour inscrire mes pensées me donne un
grand soulagement. Elle[s] navigue[nt] bien moins dans le vide et [elle]
donne à l'écoulement du temps une facilité agréable. Mais même ceci allait
bientôt disparaître à cause du manque de papier. Il n'y avait pas moyen
d'en acheter, et je n'en trouvais plus chez mes compagnons. (13 March
1942, 110–11)

This habit I've adopted of writing down my thoughts is very comforting.
It gives my mind a focus, and helps pass the time more readily and more
pleasantly. But even this was going to diappear soon because of the lack of
paper. There was no way of buying any, and there was none to be found
among my companions.

Eventually he asks a nurse to buy him paper, and he also obtains ink
(19 March 1942, 118). Following his wife Cécile's first visit, he starts to
make detailed requests for equipment from her. Paper and ink are constant items (letters of 15 March, 540; 10 April, 544; and 19 May, 585). For a
time, she was able to send writing materials in the authorized parcels, but
paper was an unauthorized item in both camps. On 3 June, he writes that
he has been allowed to keep some paper 'à ma grande surprise' (259) but
the next day notes that the rule has been formally reiterated (261). On
2 July, some sheets were missed in a search of his parcel (331); at other

times, Cécile sent paper with people who were free to travel to and from the camps. Max Filderman was a professional colleague of Schatzman and a family friend who seems to have worked in the social services:

> [Filderman] devait aussi demander [à Cécile] du papier pour moi, et finalement il ne m'en a pas apporté, et fut obligé de me donner un peu de papier de sa réserve, papier sur lequel j'écris et que j'aurais aimé être de meilleure qualité. Cela m'est agréable d'écrire sur un papier de bonne qualité, et sur lequel la plume glisse avec facilité et sur lequel l'écriture apparaît très nettement. Mais les circonstances dans lesquelles je vis ne se prêtent pas à une semblable satisfaction. (30 June 1942, 324; see also 336)

> Filderman was also supposed to ask Cécile for paper for me, but finally he brought none and was obliged to give me some from his personal stock. I'm writing on it now, but the quality is not as good as I'd have liked. It's a great pleasure for me to write on good quality paper on which my pen moves easily and the handwriting appears clearly. But my current circumstances do not lend themselves to that kind of satisfaction.

Not only is Schatzman fastidious in his personal habits and concerned with the appearance of his manuscript; he is also fussy about the quality of the paper he writes on. Given all the discomforts he records in the diary, taking pleasure in the fine accommodation of pen to paper takes on a special importance. But paper, like many other commodities, was in short supply under the Occupation; it is not surprising that Filderman was not able to fulfil the request.

Light, and time to write; pen and paper; supple hands; the corner of a table and a place to sit: these are the minima for keeping a diary. Schatzman also needs peace of mind, and for this he shuts out much of the activity of the camp, the conversations and the bridge games, and the bad behaviour of the guards. However, in the second half of July and the first weeks of August, he witnesses the mass arrivals and deportations subsequent to the *rafle du Vel d'Hiv*,[9] which was the biggest single round-up in France under the Occupation. In terms of quantity and detail, he focuses less on the events themselves or their implications than on the disruption caused. Yet it is of considerable interest to probe his entries from this period.

The internees at Drancy had wind that something major was about to happen on 15 July, when they were moved around the camp to make room for the new arrivals. This entailed transferring residents from one block to another and increasing the number of people to a room: three people were consigned to a two-person bunk, two on the bottom and one on the top. 'Il en a résulté chez tous la désolation, la répulsion, le désespoir' (15 July 1942, 348; The result was that we all felt distress, disgust and despair).

During the move and, writes Schatzman, due to the exertions it entailed, a man died of cardiac arrest; he is left unnamed at first, then we learn that his name was Goldman. This 'sad event' provoked 'apparently little emotion' (353), because finding a bed and getting settled was an urgent imperative; Schatzman comments that 'la vie d'un compagnon compte bien peu au milieu de cette profonde misère morale et materielle' (ibid., 353; the life of a companion counts for little in the midst of physical and moral misery of this depth). Yet Schatzman gives the dead man three pages: they are an intensely personal memorial to a man who was entirely alone.[10]

Schatzman's entry on this date ends by returning to the imminent mass arrests, of women as well as men. Their arrival at the camp was scheduled for the next day:

> Tout le monde était angoissé. Beaucoup se demandaient s'ils n'allaient pas voir arriver leurs femmes et leurs filles. Les mesures prises pour vider les escaliers de leurs habitants étaient bien en prévision de nouveaux internés.
>
> On ne voulait pas croire que des femmes seraient arrêtées et séparées de leurs enfants. (Ibid.)

> Everyone was anxious. Many wondered if they weren't about to see their wives and daughters among the arrivals. The measures to empty the stairwells had been undertaken in view of the need to accommodate new internees.
>
> We couldn't believe that women would be arrested and separated from their children.

On the next day, the first ones arrived, *with* the children, who had been included in an attempt to reach the target of 22,000 arrests set by the Nazis.[11]

> Cette foule de femmes était constituée par des êtres de tous âges. Beaucoup de jeunes filles, entre treize ou quatorze ans, dans la mesure où on peut apprécier l'âge, jusqu'à vingt ans ou plus, pas mal de femmes vieillies par le travail, maigres et bossues, ainsi que rachitiques, rien que des figures exprimant l'effroi et la douleur et des yeux qui n'ont fait que pleurer. Des hommes, déjà internés, ont pu voir leurs femmes et leurs enfants, à leur tour emprisonnés. On peut s'imaginer ce qui se passait dans le coeur et dans l'esprit de ces êtres innocents. L'effet douloureux sur moi était tel que

je n'ai pu rester longtemps mêlé à cette foule, et suis monté dans la chambre, intensément angoissé. (16 July 1942, 354–5)

There were women of all ages in the crowd. Girls of thirteen or fourteen, supposing one can guess their age, up to twenty and more, women prematurely aged by work, bent and hunched, some with rickets, nothing but faces expressing terror and grief, eyes that could only cry. Some men, already interned, saw their wives and children imprisoned in turn. You can imagine what was going on in the minds and hearts of these innocent people. The effect on me was so painful that I could not stay in the crowd; I went up to my room, intensely upset.

The passage is remarkable for its failure to maintain the mode of objective reporting with which it begins. Starting with 'la foule des femmes' and noting the evident emotion of their faces, it moves to consider the men, another 'foule': these are his fellows; the new prisoners are their wives and children. Their suffering is unimaginable. Yet to say so is, paradoxically, to imagine it, and then to feel it. Schatzman has been drawn into the crowd, and into the anguish.

His decision to leave the crowd of onlookers should not be attributed to a lack of solidarity; he is only too ready to imagine their grief and their horror. He simply cannot bear it: he seeks solitude and some means of self-protection. Then, when the deportations start two days later (18 July 1942, 356–7), Schatzman leaves his diary for nearly a week. This is a witness who cannot speak, his silence all the more eloquent for all that. When he takes up his pen again, it is to note the emotional effect these events have had on him. Mentioned with an uncharacteristic succinctness, these 'arrivées et départs' (arrivals and departures) register as events that he can barely write about. They 'seriously perturbed' him, but he puts off writing about the 'thoughts and feelings' awoken in him by the 'arrivals and departures' he has witnessed (25 July 1942, 357–8). 'La seule chose que je tiens à inscrire, c'est l'effet produit sur mon moral,' he had written on 17 July. 'Nous sommes en présence d'un inconnu tout ce qu'il y a d'inquiétant' (356; The only thing I'm keen to record is the effect on my morale ... We are facing something unknown, deeply disquieting). And the next day: 'Le coeur vous saigne devant le spectacle de tristesse et de désespoir que nous voyons pendant la préparation des départs. Il y a déjà eu deux suicides et il est probable que d'autres se produiront' (26 July 1942, 360; Your heart bleeds at the spectacle of sadness and despair when we watch the preparations for the departures. There have already been two suicides and no doubt more will follow). He will speak about them 'une autre fois' (another time). Note the impersonal 'you': addressing his interlocutor, it also generalizes his personal reaction, as if to protect him in another crowd.

However, these events have a direct, material effect on him as well: the disruption of several moves from one room to another. Even when the bulk of the arrivals and deportations is over, the moving around continues (30 July 1942; 361). Schatzman is moved to a room that had been used for temporary occupation; those who had occupied it were there so briefly that they had not been assigned cleaning duties, and it was filthy. This is his fourth move since arriving at Drancy: while a friend helps him with his suitcase, he must still go upstairs and down several times to retrieve all his belongings, and then to find planks for the base of his bed as well as a mattress. It was a day, he says, filled with vexations and exhaustion (362–3). The next day, with a neighbour, he dismantles the whole structure to kill the lice.

It would be hasty to interpret his focus on himself as a replication of the reaction of his room-mates to Goldman's death. Indeed, I think, something more profound is at stake. Exactly how to write about these distressing events is deeply problematic; we have seen him unable to maintain the position of detached onlooker – the position natural to his scientific bent – but at the same time overwhelmed by the position of implicated witness. He cannot, of course, entirely turn away: nevertheless, 'j'aime autant m'abstenir pour le moment' (3 August 1942, 372; I prefer to abstain for the moment).

He leaves expanding on what he has seen for 'later': 'j'en parlerai longuement une autre fois' (5 August 1942, 374; I'll talk about it at length another time), he promises; 'je raconterai plus tard' (later I'll tell) how the new arrivals are treated (8 August 1942, 377), and again:

> Grande préparation de départs. Enfants, femmes et hommes.
>   Nous sommes tous profondément émus et bouleversés devant ces spectacles et par l'inconnu qui nous attend [...] Il y a toujours beaucoup d'incidents et de cas intéressants à noter et il y en a même de plus en plus, mais je dois laisser pour plus tard leur narration. (15 August 1942, 388)

> Large-scale preparations for departures. Children, women and men.
>   We are all profoundly moved and upset by these scenes and by the unknown that awaits us [...] there are always numerous incidents and interesting details to note, indeed more and more, but I must leave telling these stories for later.

When was 'later' going to be? There is some indication that it refers to writings other than the diary – 'à la suite des notes' (26 June 1942, 316;

following these notes). No doubt these are the 'souvenirs et réflexions' collected and reproduced with the diary (414–514). However, nothing in these corresponds to an expansion of what Schatzman writes in the period following the *rafle du Vel d'Hiv*. It may be – since the diary for this period exists – that this material was (among) the pages of his 'mémoires' that, in his words, were 'fauchés' (filched) from the parcel he left to be sent on to his wife (letters of 2 September and 18 September 1942), but there is no way of knowing. What we do know is that he 'abstains' (3 September 1942, 372) from writing until another occasion and another place. That place, or that time, would allow him to write 'plus longuement' (5 August 1942, 374; at greater length) than he can here and now, in the diary.

If the diary is a means of mediating events into experience, the camp subjects him to events too intense, too traumatic, for him to (re)constitute himself as subject of reflection on them. Referring to the actual writing of the diary, Schatzman says that it keeps him busy. It makes a space and time for him to maintain his sense of self, giving him the separateness in which his individuality can be asserted and confirmed against the erasures inflicted by the context in which he writes. It is not implausible to suggest that that assertion simply could not withstand the spectacle of thousands of people being funnelled through Drancy toward their death. As we see when his fellow internees find their loved ones in the crowds and when he goes to bed in fear for his own family and friends, it was impossible to resist identification: 'Nous sommes tous profondément émus et bouleversés devant ces spectacles et par l'inconnu qui *nous* attend' (15 August 1942, 388; emphasis added; we are all profoundly moved and upset by these scenes and by the unknown that awaits *us*). And so he waits until he can write about it, hoping – I have no doubt – that he can do so at some time when he is no longer afraid for himself.

However, that fear increases as August proceeds. For a time, it stops him from writing: 'J'ai laissé passer tous ces jours, sans avoir la disposition d'esprit nécessaire pour inscrire mes méditations et mes observations' (21 August 1942, 388; I've let these last few days go by, without being in the necessary frame of mind to record my meditations and observations). His morale is fortified by reassuring rumours concerning the immediate future, but there are ups and downs that are 'very depressing'; nevertheless, he writes, 'je considère que toute semaine de passée est autant de gagné' (ibid., 395; a week passed is a week gained). The diary resumes its usual habits until 29 August, when he learns of the imminent transfer of 'tous les internés français' (408; all the French internees); in response to further rumours concerning conditions in other camps, 'l'agitation est très grande' (ibid.; there's a lot of agitation). The next day, he records his preparations for the move, and completes his final entry thus:

> Pithiviers ... sera bien pénible, mais comme nous n'y pouvons rien, il n'y a qu'à se résigner, et accepter le sort tel qu'il se présente. Maintenant, on dit aussi [que] notre séjour sera provisoire, parce que ce ne sont que des dispositions prises pour les déportations des gens qu'on amène ici de plus en [plus]. (410)

> Pithiviers will be very trying, but since we can do nothing about it, we can only resign ourselves and accept our fate. Now people are saying that our stay there is only temporary, because these are arrangements made for the deportation of the ever greater numbers of people who have been brought here.

For the next three weeks, resolutely himself among the thousands awaiting deportation, his individuality persists in his letters if not in his diary, the last of which is written from the train. Even here, we note his concern with self-presentation:

> Je m'efforce de maintenir mon moral et à moins que je sois trop sous-alimenté je suis décidé de tout supporter avec calme et patience. Je ne pourrai plus me raser et serai peut-être obligé de me laisser pousser la barbe. (Letter, 23 September 1942; 625–6)

> I'm doing my best to keep up my morale, and unless I am too severely underfed, I have decided to put up with it all calmly and patiently. I won't be able to shave, so no doubt I'll have to let my beard grow.

In the train, no longer solitary, both onlooker and part of the unseen spectacle, he writes 'we,' and then, with his customary precision, bears witness to his fellows:

> Nous sommes à Châlons-sur-Marne. Il est 14h 30. Je me dépêche de terminer pour qu'on puisse glisser la lettre à quelqu'un sur la voie. Dans ce wagon nous sommes 42, dont 22 femmes et enfants (15 enfants dont 9 sans parents). (Ibid.)

> We are at Châlons-sur-Marne. It is 2:30 p.m. I'm hurrying to finish so I can slip the letter to somebody on the track. There are 42 of us in this wagon, of whom 22 are women and children (15 children, 9 without parents).

There is no further trace of Benjamin Schatzman, either among the living or the dead.

Making It Last

As I hope to have shown, the frequent notes Schatzman makes about the very activity of writing the diary are themselves replete with information concerning the material conditions of camp living. However, reading a diary such as this should not stop at its indexicality. I have argued that a major function of the diary for Schatzman is self-recognition, and that the product of the writing – the manuscript, its neatness and clarity – as well as the activity, is intrinsic to this function. However, the pre-condition of this function is that there exist both subject and object of self-recognition, cognisant and able to undertake the activity required. Throughout, Schatzman reports his illnesses and the signs of his recovery, his failing strength, his hunger and fatigue: his survival. He writes of the body in time; this is the ultimate place of the self – not just its place, but its ground, its condition.

The body suffers, and it resists. 'Je vis dans un état de besoin de manger continuel' (31 January 1942, 51; I spend my life in a constant need to eat), he writes in his first entry; the rations are paltry: 'après chaque repas ... ma souffrance de la faim est, en vérité, plus grande par la sensation bien pénible de la mise en appétit seulement' (ibid.; after each meal, the suffering of hunger is increased by the sensation of merely having had one's appetite stimulated). With tea in the morning and soup at midday – an almost entirely liquid diet – the internees receive one-fifth, at times, one-sixth, of a *boule de pain*: 'Représentez-vous cette sensation, quand je vous dirai que cette quantité de pain suffirait à peine pour le goûter' (ibid. 52; You can imagine this sensation when I tell you that that quantity of bread would barely be enough for afternoon tea); they must make it last for twenty-four hours. Nevertheless 'ma santé semble resister aux conditions défavorables du froid, et le reste' (12 February 1942, 52; my health appears to be resisting the unfavourable conditions, the cold and all the rest). From the beginning until the end, we read the narrative of this body, beset by the conditions, and yet, for eight long months, withstanding them.

We learn of his bladder problems, which prevent him from sleeping (ibid., 53), and the persistance of cold weather: 'Ce froid tardif persistant accroît beaucoup mes souffrances [...] Si la température avait été plus clémente, j'aurais été un autre homme' (20 February 1942, 56; This persistant cold so late in the season increases my suffering a great deal [...] If the temperature were more benign, I would be a different man). It's raining, and his shoes are unsuitable. The rations cause constipation, but his bladder is incontinent (ibid., 57). Again we see him separate himself from the experience of his fellows: they are displaying a state of collapse against which he must defend himself; he is already very weak, but he has a 'method' (ibid.) At this stage, we do not know what it is. What we do know is that he is determined not to deteriorate like those he sees around him, although he is unable to resist the fear that he will: 'On voit graduellement augmenter le nombre de gens qui flanchent soit par la maladie, soit autrement. Ce qui provoque, malgré soi, une crainte intérieure inévitable' (ibid., 60; We see a gradual increase in the number of people who break down either through illnesses or other causes. Despite oneself, this provokes an inevitable inward fear). He resists their fate, and he resists their behaviour, and while he suffers from the same privations, he is determined to describe the reactions of his fellow internees as if he were not one of them:

> En vérité, le besoin de manger prédomine, il est une occupation immédiate et urgente, puisque les conséquences de cette insuffisance se sont déjà fait sentir chez beaucoup sous la forme de faiblesse extrême et de maladie, et chez les autres, l'amaigrissement plus ou moins fort est nettement visible, la crainte règne que les conséquences déplorables constatées autour d'eux se montrent assez vite chez eux. (24 February 1942, 64)

> Truly the need to eat dominates everything; it's an immediate and urgent [pre]occupation, since the consequences of this inadequacy are already being felt by many in the form of weakness and illness, and for others, a more or less significant loss of weight is quite visible; everybody fears that the deplorable consequences that they see around them will soon afflict them.

Despite the unclarity of the syntax in this passage, it is clear that Schatzman sets himself apart from 'eux' (them). Likewise, he does not have the money to indulge in 'la course aux denrées' (ibid.; the race to buy goods): 'Si j'étais obligé de faire comme eux pour me conserver la vie, je n'aurais plus qu'à me préparer à mourir, parce que mes moyens ne pourraient absolument pas me le permettre' (26 February 1942; 67–8; If I had to do what they do to preserve my life, I'd be better off getting ready to die, because my means simply could not allow it). He relies on his own as yet unexplained 'method' of resistance, which others view as an excentricity: 'À ce propos, personne ne me comprend et ils sont convaincus que j'ai tort d'agir ainsi' (ibid., 57; On this point, nobody understands me; they're convinced I'm wrong to take this action). On reflexion, he comes to understand that 'on n'a pas le droit... de se particulariser' (2 March 1942, 77; one has no right to stand out). In this entry, he explains that part of his method is to take a vigorous four-kilometre walk 'malgré l'inconvénient d'une dépense de calories trop grande pour la quantité ingérée' (ibid.,

78; in spite of the disadvantage of expending more calories than I ingest) because it is good for his muscular strength and his circulation.

Yet this valiant method does not defend him against the cold and the privations. Obliged to wait in the unseasonal snow to be photographed, 'j'avais du mal à me tenir debout' (25 February 1942, 66; I had trouble staying upright); 'Je souffre et suis abattu sous tous les rapports' (26 February 1942, 68; I am suffering and cast down in every respect). He is beset by the recurrent symptoms of previous illnesses and accidents (ibid., 69), his continuing urinary problems, and a rash (28 February 1942, 71). By early March, 'je dois avouer et reconnaître que ma faiblesse est bien grande, que je ne suis pas solide sur mes jambes, et que j'ai du mal à monter des marches' (2 March 1942, 80; I must confess and acknowledge that I am very weak, that my legs don't hold me up, and that I have trouble climbing steps); yet he resolves to resume his walks, whatever the weather. When he sees himself in the shower, he asks the crucial question:

> Suis-je arrivé au maximum, et peut-[on] espérer que la quantité d'aliments ingérés me permettra de stabiliser mon état actuel, ou la perte en musculature va continuer, et alors, me restera-t-il assez de forces pour revenir si la libération tarde encore à se faire? (5 March 1942, 92)

> Have I reached rock-bottom, is there any hope that the amount of food I take in will allow me to stabilize my current state, or will the wasting of my muscles continue? and then, will I have enough strength to return if my liberation is further delayed?[12]

Many of Schatzman's notations on his body to this point are couched in the punctual present. 'Today,' sometimes 'yesterday,' is specified by the dating convention of the diary, which in this way inscribes the body in time. By contrast, the passage above focuses on processes: *arriver, stabiliser, perdre, continuer, rester* (reach, stabilize, lose, continue, remain). Has his strength reached its nadir, or is there worse to come? Is the loss of condition ineluctable, or will it stop before the end? Can he hold out until he is freed? Through these processes, time is inscribed in the body. The body in time – time in the body: this double inscription is the central preoccupation of this diary.

Schatzman's condition does indeed get worse: 'Pour l'appel de 17 h, obligé d'y être présent,[13] je n'ai pu supporter cette nouvelle fatigue; j'ai failli me trouver mal, si deux compagnons n'avaient pas été priés de m'aider à aller jusqu'à mon lit' (10 March 1942, 98; Roll-call at 5 p.m., I had to be there, I couldn't cope with this new fatigue; I almost passed

out, if two companions hadn't been asked to help me back to my bed).
This event is a sign, not only that the loss of condition continues to
worsen, but that it is doing so dramatically: 'je sens que la glissade sur la
mauvaise pente ne peut s'arrêter, ma faiblesse augmente' (ibid.; I sense
that the downhill slide cannot be arrested, my weakness is greater). Note
the processual verbs with their adverbs – *décliner brusquement plus encore,*
baisser progressivement, s'accentuer de plus en plus, ne peut s'arrêter, augmenter
(suddenly declined further, going down progressively, becoming more
marked, cannot be stopped, getting worse):

> Voici environ dix jours que ma santé a brusquement plus décliné encore.
> Jusque-là, j'avais senti mes forces baisser progressivement [...] Mon amai-
> grissement et mon asthénie s'accentuent de plus en plus [...]
>   ... Ma santé a plus décliné parce que j'ai des ennuis avec les voies respira-
> toires. (Ibid., 98–9)

> It's been ten days since my health suddenly declined further. Until then,
> I had felt my strength going down progressively [...] My loss of weight and
> my debility are more and more marked [...]
>   ... My health is worse because my bronchial tubes are giving me trouble.

The next day, still more fatigued, he asks for a doctor, and, following
the intervention of a friend of his son, he is sent to the civil hospital of
Compiègne. The following passage precedes that decision. In it, we should
note the narrative he sets up. We should also note that the sentence collapses the relation between clauses, notably telescoping 'me remettre assez
vite' (recover quickly enough), as if he is hoping for a prompt liberation,
with 'me remettre assez pour être capable de faire le voyage' (to recover
enough to undertake the the return trip). 'J'espère enfin obtenir l'évac-
uation dans une infirmerie où l'alimentation est plus substantielle, avec
un moral meilleur, et me remettre assez vite pour être capable de faire
le voyage de retour en portant au moins ma valise (11 March 1942, 103;
At last I can hope to be evacuated to a hospital where the food is more
substantial, [and] with a better morale, [I can hope] to recover quickly
enough to undertake the return trip while carrying my luggage).

Hoping that this is the first step on the way to release, he does not
expect total recovery. Rather, he hopes to get to a point where he is strong
enough to walk to the station with his suitcase. This hope is the practical
future to which he looks forward throughout the diary. He has already
voiced it in the form of acute fear: 'J'ai eu peur pour la première fois,
j'ai pensé à la possibilité de faire une maladie grave et de ne peut[-être]
pas sortir vivant d'ici' (26 February 1942, 66; For the first time I was

frightened, I thought that I might be so gravely sick that I might not get out of here alive). 'Que faire et quoi espérer et je vis avec une appréhension terrible' (10 March 1942, 98; What can I do and what can I hope for, I'm living in terrible apprehension). Again the articulation of the prose is faulty,[14] as if his state of health was manifesting itself in a failure of syntax. Gradually, 'la glissade sur la mauvaise pente' (the downhill slide) will be arrested in the hospital, and then, he hopes, reversed:

L'alimentation ici, tout en étant beaucoup plus abondante, n'est néanmoins pas suffisante pour me faire remonter assez vite la dangereuse pente sur laquelle je glissais vers une issue fatale, si je me rapporte aux nombreuses morts survenues déjà dans le camp, trente-huit, à des gens qui seraient encore vivants s'ils n'avaient pas été arrêtés. (13 March 1942, 110)

Even though the food here is a great deal more plentiful, it is still not enough to move me back up the dangerous slope I was slipping down toward an outcome – fatal, in view of the numerous deaths that have already occurred in the camp. [There have been] thirty-eight, people who would still be alive if they hadn't been arrested.

The important thing is to avoid being one of the already dead. Regaining weight, getting out alive, avoiding the fatal outcome, will now become his principal objective. His symptoms demonstrate the severity of his malnutrition; a fortnight in the hospital has not changed them visibly: his feet are still swollen, and he has gained no weight (27 March 1942, 124). We note the constant monitoring of his health, both in the diary as he logs his progress, or the lack of it, and with the appropriate instruments if scales, for example, were available. Nevertheless, he is beginning to feel better:

En dehors de mes jambes qui restent faibles, je peux dire qu'une sensation générale de bien-être commence à se faire sentir. Ainsi, cette nuit, j'ai remarqué que c'est la première fois depuis longtemps que j'ai senti un envahissement de chaleur intérieure [...] Être à nouveau capable de fabriquer aussi de la chaleur intérieure en abondance est une grande nouveauté à retenir comme fait et comme date. C'est un signe de l'arrêt de la déficience. (Ibid., 128)

Apart from the persistent weakness in my legs, I can say that I am beginning to feel a general sense of well-being. For example, last night, I noticed that for the first time for ages I felt internal warmth suffusing my body [...] I must note this fact and this date: it is new, this capacity to generate ample internal heat. This is a sign of the end of undernourishment.

In the days and weeks after his return to the camp, he continues to monitor his progress. Although his loss of condition has been arrested by the hospital regime, this will be reversed as soon as he returns to normal rations:

> Il est certain que j'ai repris des forces, que j'étais en bonne voie de guérison, tout en n'ayant pas atteint l'équilibre, avoir regagné mon état antérieur, mais je n'étais donc qu'en voie de guérison, ce qui fait que quatre jours de retour à la fatigue et à une alimentation moins abondante pour que je recommence à sentir les signes de faiblesse d'avant mon évacuation. (2 May 1942, 165)

> I certainly regained some strength, and was on the way to restored health, although I had still not retrieved [a suitable] balance, [which would mean] retrieving my former state; but then I was only on the way to health, so four days after my return to fatigue and inadequate meals I have begun to feel the same signs of weakness as before my evacuation.

As the weeks go by, he is back to where he started: 'en fin de journée, mes jambes fléchissent comme au début de mon arrivée' (28 May 1942, 251; at the end of the day my legs give under me as they did when I first arrived).

It is instructive to consider the addressivity of this aspect of his diary: 'En écrivant donc que ma santé se maintient, je veux dire que je réussis à rester dans le même état de faiblesse, celle-ci ne s'aggrave pas pour le moment' (25 May 1942, 239; When I write that my health is steady, I mean that I remain in the same state of weakness, that it is not getting worse for the moment). He hesitates between writing as if to his wife, whom he must reassure, and to his 'inner' doctor, to whom he must make a scrupulously accurate report. However, as we see elsewhere, he has a certain investment in not appearing too robust. The rhetoric of the body treads a fine line between ensuring adequate care and being ill enough to be released. Besides this, self-monitoring is a form of 'control' both in the French and in the English sense: by 'checking,' he is taking control of the 'patient,' the passive body that suffers the ill effects of camp life. We recall that he wrote nothing under the effect of the initial shock of internment, and that deciding to keep a diary was a way of reacting against that passivity. Furthermore, resist as he might, Schatzman has failed to defend himself against the 'effondrement' (prostration) that he observes around him. This has frightened him, and his diary demonstrates both his terror that it will recur and a determined effort to prevent that. To monitor himself is to act out the doctor-patient relation, to enact a daily consultation in which he cares for himself.

In practice, caring for himself is his way of ensuring that he can hold out until the end. This involves rationing the material care he receives in the form of medication and food supplements. In turn, this provokes two forms of anxiety – that he may not receive supplies and that they not last for as long as necessary. If he has no control with respect to the former, he can exercise at least some control over the latter. A clear example is the story of the solution to his bladder problem. During this period, he is prescribed Mictasol (1 May 1942, 159); the symptoms are immediately alleviated, but he is anxious in case its effects are not durable (4 May, 169). How long, he worries on 9 May, will he have to wait until he receives more (190)? A parcel comes without the precious potion: 'je [le] désire avec une fiévreuse impatience' (21 May, 229; I'm looking forward to it with feverish impatience). The next parcel brings the drug, but it is confiscated (29 May, 251–2). He gets it back, and its effects are astonishing (30 May, 255), contributing to a strong improvement in his morale (1 June, 257), so he decides he must make it last: 'Pour économiser le Mictasol, je m'en suis passé' (6 June, 271; To save the Mictasol, I did without it).

Schatzman spent from 5 June to 22 June 1942 working as a dentist attached to the health care services; as a result, he was transferred to the infirmary and hence was both better fed and more comfortably housed. Again he notes an improvement in the symptoms of his pollakiuria and in his morale (14 June 1942, 300 and 301). His oedema is worse (17 June 1942, 307), but overall, the state of his health is 'stationary' (16 June 1942, 306). When he undergoes a medical check-up on arrival at Drancy, he notes his weight (49kg), his temperature (36.4°), and his blood pressure (7/16).[15] This is not a well man. By the end of July, he notes that he feels stronger; he is sure that his health will be entirely restored when he is again living under 'normal conditions' (26 July 1942, 260). Nevertheless, maintaining his current weight is a concern. As a result of his abdominal trouble, he eats nothing for nearly a week, and his blood pressure goes down further (to 7/13) (28 August 1942, 407). With the medication he is prescribed, he 'hopes' to get back to his normal state: getting out alive remains his constant concern.

Dr Lubicz has 'saved his life' in Compiègne by sending him to hospital (104). From then on, he must make that life last. He does so by adhering to a strict discipline: 'Je me maintiens dans mon programme: laisser des temps à mon tube digestif de se reposer, digérer d'abord ce qu'on a mangé et, après seulement, prendre à nouveau de la nourriture' (27 March 1942, 123; I adhere strictly to my programme: I leave time for my digestive tract to rest, to digest what I have eaten first, then to take food again only later). Eating slowly is a means of getting the

greatest benefit from his food. It is more abundant in the hospital, and
he has started receiving food parcels from home, so he can supplement
the camp meals:[16]

> Il me faudrait manger encore un peu plus, c'est-à-dire faire un autre repas,
> plus petit, vers 21 h, au moment où on nous apporte le tilleul à boire, mais
> je n'ose pas encore, d'une part, et je ne suis encore assez riche en provi-
> sions, d'autre part. Je tiens à conserver un peu plus ce que j'ai de façon que,
> s'il me prend la fantaisie de manger un peu plus, surtout en gâteaux, que je
> n'en manque pas. (Ibid., 126–7)

> I need to eat a little more, that is, have another small meal, at about 9 p.m.,
> at the time when they bring us the the hot drink, but I dare not yet, on one
> hand because I don't have a big store of provisions, and on the other, I want
> to keep back some of what I have in case a little snack takes my fancy, espe-
> cially of cake, to be sure of having some left.

Notice the anxiety implicit in 'je n'ose pas' and the fear of having nothing left; at the same time, he is tempted to indulge himself 'surtout en
gâteaux.'

Time and again, we will see him calculating the best way of improving his condition by eating a little more, without thereby running down
his provisions: 'Aujourd'hui, j'ai mangé une ration de pain plus grande
que celle qu'on nous donne et, si je devais ne rien recevoir demain, ma
réserve de pain serait vite épuisée' (28 March 1942, 132; Today I ate
more bread than the ration they allow us, and if it happened that I was
to receive none tomorrow, my stock of bread would run out quickly).
He details what he has eaten that day, hoping that, if his intake continues to be so good, it will result in 'une maigreur moins accentuée'
(less marked emaciation). Then he goes on to explain what it is to be
as thin as he is:

> Je suis si amaigri que toute la peau, particulièrement des fesses, du dos, de
> tout le tour du bassin me fait mal la nuit aussi bien que le jour puisque,
> pendant que je suis couché, elle est pressée, pour ainsi [dire], directement
> sur les os. Je n'ai plus le minimum de petite couche de musculature pour
> constituer, pour ainsi dire, un matelas. (Ibid.)

> I am so emaciated that all of my skin, especially on my buttocks, my back,
> and around my hips, hurts me at night as well as during the day, because
> while I'm lying down, it is pressed directly against the bones. I no longer
> have the minimum layer of muscle to form, so to say, a cushion.

This meticulous exposition concludes with his hope for improvement in his physical state: greater strength and at least a return to his former weight. Elsewhere, he explains that 'former' does not mean 'normal' in this context; it just means his weight before the crisis.

> Donc, en plus de mes forces, je désire au moins reprendre mon poids antérieur. Une journée, du moins un début de journée comme aujourd'hui, est déjà un bon signe. Et, pour pouvoir continuer ainsi, il faudrait que ma réserve ne s'épuise pas. (Ibid.)

> So what I want, beside my strength, is at least to recover my former weight. A day, at least a day beginning like today, is already a good sign. And in order to continue in this way, I must not exhaust my stocks.

Hence, his reserves must not run out. He ensures this by rationing himself: 'Mon appétit est bon, exigeant même cette semaine, et c'est parce que je me retiens et me rationne que je ne mange pas plus' (21 April 1942, 146; I have a good appetite, demanding indeed, and it's because I hold myself back and ration myself that I do not eat more). This is a means of controlling the immediate future. The inner doctor reappears in 'si je ne m'écoutais' (if I did not listen to myself), and in the supplementary rationale of his advice to himself not to overeat.[17]

> Mon appétit redevient tel que je mangerais encore plus si je ne m'écoutais et si je ne tenais pas à faire des réserves de façon à ne pas en manquer. Au fond, cela me rend service parce qu'il vaut mieux que je mette de la modération dans ma suralimentation. (4 April 1942, 148)

> With this appetite, I'd eat even more if I did not listen to myself, and if I were not concerned to stock food so as not to run out. This is actually a good thing because it's better to moderate my feeding up.

Heeding himself, he gives a careful accounting of what he has left: 'Pour le moment, j'ai à ma disposition pendant cette semaine une bonne ration de petits pois et aussi du fromage, que j'économise' (8 April 1942, 150; For now, I have available for the rest of the week a good ration of green peas and some cheese, which I'm saving).

The above passages, dated late March and April, are written in the hospital. Back in the camp, where the rations are again minimal, he revises his original method of maintaining his health. He has understood that walking four kilometres simply used up more calories than were available to him, so his new method relies on rest and on continuing to put food aside. 'Pour ne pas user trop vite la petite réserve que j'ai faite à l'hôpital, je me fatigue très peu. Je ne fais aucune marche et ne sors même pas en dehors des heures d'appel' (4 May 1942, 171; So as not to use up the small reserves I kept [or, built up?] at the hospital, I tire myself very little. I don't walk and don't even go outside except for roll-call). (Note that, in this quote, 'la petite réserve que j'ai faite à l'hôpital' may refer to food, or to his own body.) The important concern now is to get to the end: the end of his suffering, the end of his internment, the end of the war. His priority is to preserve himself as best he can:

> Voici mon état d'esprit ce matin au réveil: après tout, qu'il arrive ce qui pourrait, je vais avant tout faire en sorte de vivre, de supporter le mieux possible toutes ces misères et toutes ces souffrances, afin d'arriver à leur fin dans un état de conservation le meilleur possible, tant pis ce temps perdu, ce vide dans ma vie, car, ce qui compte, c'est la vie tout court et la vie telle qu'elle peut être au retour de la paix! (Ibid., 169)

> This is how I am this morning: after all, whatever happens, I'm going to do everything to get out of here alive, tolerate as well as possible all this misery and suffering, so I can last the distance as intact as possible, never mind all this wasted time, this gap in my life, for what counts is life, nothing else, life such as it can be when peace returns.

On 7 May, when the camp authorities at Compiègne allowed a select group including Schatzman to receive food parcels, he was deeply relieved that his fear of hunger would be alleviated (8 May 1942, 187). Beyond survival, food is important for life in the fullest sense: 'Je désire tant pouvoir revenir avec mes facultés conservées' (12 May 1942, 205; I so much want to return with my faculties intact). But his terror of starvation is such that hoarding becomes a habit: 'Nous sommes ici, en ce moment, bien fournis en confitures, je peux même faire une réserve pour les autres jours, en revanche, depuis quatre jours, nous ne recevons plus de margarine' (21 May 1942, 229; We're well supplied with jam at the moment, I can even put some aside for other days, but on the other hand, for the last four days, we have received no margarine). His determination to take control of his present situation means he must continually choose between hoarding and eating. One reason for this is a conflict between two imperatives: one is to eat enough – 'me nourrir le mieux possible' (feed myself as well as possible) in view of 'le besoin de manger' (the need to eat) – and the other is to convince the German doctors that he is ill: 'a pathological state could influence the German doctor.' 'I would like to point out,' he writes (but to whom?) 'how ambiguous my situation is at the moment.' He makes calculations like those we have seen previously:

> Je ne peux adopter qu'une ligne de conduite intermédiaire: me nourrir assez pour ne pas trop me débiliter et souffrir, et m'abstenir suffisamment pour que ma mine ne soit pas florissante, ce qui d'ailleurs de toute façon ne se produira pas de sitôt. (23 May 1942, 233)

> I can do nothing but adopt a middle course: eat enough so as not to become debilitated, and refrain from eating enough to guarantee that I don't look as if I am thriving – well anyhow that's not going to happen immediately.

He is choosing between trying to get out as soon as possible and ensuring that he gets out alive. This attempt to calculate the rhetoric of the body is a constant preoccupation, but he knows that he has little control over his fate:

> Je suis décidé à me tourmenter le moins possible à cet égard, et attendre les événements comme ils vont se dérouler, sans chercher à m'en défendre. En dernière analyse, ce sont des soucis inutiles, car je sens qu'il vaudrait mieux ne rien faire pour les hâter ou les changer. (14 May 1942, 208)

> I've decided to torment myself as little as possible in this respect, and to await events as they occur, without seeking to protect myself from them. In the final analysis, these are futile concerns, because I have the sense that it would be better to do nothing to hasten them or change them.

The second source of conflict is that some of what he receives is perishable; now that the weather is warm, once a can is opened, the contents must be eaten promptly. This runs counter to the discipline of making his provisions last as long as possible (3 June 1942, 260). However, his provisions are not so plentiful that they are likely to be wasted. Earlier, we saw him looking toward the long term: he must live long enough, in good enough condition, to get to the end of his internment intact. By June, the future is closer: he must ration his consumption in such a way as to make his supplies last until the next parcel. He itemizes what he has finished and what he has left (13 June 1942, 300). If it is fresh, he must cook it before it spoils, but this is not always possible. A solution to this problem – accepting that his comrade who cooks for the doctors will cook for him – also presents him with the possibility of saving his fuel (ibid.).

Food remains an obsession, constantly liable to provoke dramas. Schatzman is moved to Drancy in late June. On the first night there, in new surroundings, his habits leave him vulnerable:

> J'ai oublié de raconter qu'avant qu'on serve la soupe, j'ai coupé quelques tranches de pain, j'en ai mangé une, et laissé deux autres sur la table qui est près de mon lit. Quand on a commencé à servir la soupe, je suis donc parti pour me faire servir et, en revenant, j'ai constaté la disparition des deux tranches de pain. (26 June 1942, 322)

> I forgot to say that before the soup was served, I cut several slices of bread, eating one, and leaving the others on the table near my bed. When they began to serve the soup, I left to get mine, and when I came back, I noticed that the two slices of bread had disappeared.

He cannot lock his suitcase, so he worries that food will be taken from it (2 July 1942, 331). Despite the arrival of a food parcel with (fly-blown) cheese and fruit in it, he records the classic signs of systemic malnutrition:

> Mais, en vérité, mes joues et ma figure sont pleines à cause de l'œdème que j'ai partout. J'en ai la preuve par le fait que mon abdomen est plus gras qu'avant puisque mon vieux pantalon me serre maintenant, quand, au contraire, il devrait être trop large. Mes cuisses n'ont pas du tout un aspect normal. Et puis, ce qui montre bien que ma grosseur n'est pas due à de la graisse et des muscles, c'est la persistance de ma faiblesse. Je ne peux absol- ument pas encore marcher vite, et j'ai toujours du mal à me relever quand je suis accroupi. (3 July 1942, 336)

> But it's true that my cheeks and my face are full because of the swelling in all parts of my body. The proof is the fact that my abdomen is fatter than it was before, because my old trousers are tight on me, when on the contrary, they should be looser. My thighs don't look at all normal. And then – and this is what shows that my bulk is not due to fat and muscle – my debility is persistent. I cannot walk fast at all, and I still have trouble getting up when I've been squatting.

He is worried that his health is declining again; it is certainly not improving. But the doctors cannot discern the symptoms (9 July 1942; 346–7), so the diary continues the self-portrait above: 'il n'y a qu'à regarder mon cou pour voir que la peau est bien ridée et flottante' (one need only look at my neck to see that the skin is wrinkled and loose). Evidently, he just looks like an old man with a fat belly, with pain in his swollen feet that cannot be demonstrated to others. What he really wants is 'mon complet rétablissement' (ibid.; a complete restoration of my health), but that depends upon 'la fin de ces horribles misères' (3 July 1942, 339; the end of this horrible misery) – surely every passing week must bring it closer.

These are his hopes, but in practice the horizon of the short-term future is measured by the intervals between food parcels: 'J'ai pensé que le colis alimentaire me parviendra aujourd'hui, et j'étais un peu inquiet à ce sujet parce que, tout en rationnant le plus possible mes denrées, j'arrive tout juste à ne pas manquer le dernier jour' (18 July 1942, 357; I thought that my parcel was due to arrive today, so I was somewhat worried because, even though I ration my supplies as much as possible, I only just make them last until the last day). He is living from parcel to parcel, at times not managing to make it last until the end of the week (26 July 1942, 359), at others recording the satisfaction of having enough to get through the next seven days (2 August 1942, 370). However, the overall quantity is not the only concern: his calculations involve a daily struggle to divide his provisions into equal portions: 'Je dois chaque jour me faire un menu de façon à bien répartir les aliments reçus afin de manger à chaque repas une portion égale, et ne pas en manger trop' (ibid.; Every day, I need to devise a menu so as to [...] eat an equal portion at each meal and not to overeat). The provisions he receives from his wife are a nutritious supplement, but he must be careful of his continuing hunger and 'greed.' 'Mastering hunger and greed is not easy' particularly when he is so underweight (ibid.); his aim is to lose no further weight. His regime involves careful self-monitoring to this end:

L'essentiel, pour moi, c'est de ne pas perdre de poids et cela m'étonnerait. J'ai d'ailleurs l'intention de me re-peser pour contrôler. Il ne faut pas croire que ça est si facile, car la balance se trouve dans la salle de consultation du médecin-chef. (2 August 1942, 371)

It is essential for me not to lose any weight, and I would be surprised if I did. In any case, I mean to weigh myself again to check. Not that it's easy to do so, because the scales are in the consultation room of the head doctor.

Toward the middle of August, he receives two food parcels in quick succession. This, too, provokes a conflict. The perishable goods need to be used 'too quickly' and hence may disturb the strict control of the quantity he eats. He is avoiding the temptation of getting used to more: 'Je vais avoir à lutter contre la tentation' (12 August 1942, 385; I'm going to have to fight against temptation). Besides, if he does not eat the contents and has to move again, he will have more to carry, and he worries that there may be a third parcel on its way (ibid.). He does not want too much choice, satisfying himself with just enough to maintain his current state of health (4 August 1942, 373). Hope, with its constant shadow, fear: 'Quant à moi, je ne suis que résigné à ces conditions et me console en me disant: pourvu que je n'en meure pas' (3 August 1942, 372; As for me, I'm resigned to these conditions, nothing else, and console myself by thinking: as long as I don't die from them).

Drancy was known as the anteroom of Auschwitz, but Schatzman did not fear, because he did not know, that death from something other than 'these conditions' was likely. While he was waiting for release and healing, or for the fearsome unknown, he wrote his diary. The bare necessities were pen and paper, undisturbed time, a modicum of light and warmth, the corner of a table and a place to sit. The diary kept him, as he kept it, scrupulously, assiduously. Thanks to its cautious concealment in bundles of laundry, it outlasted him. He did not make it home, but it comes to us, fulfilling its promise: 'tout cela sera raconté et publié' (30 March 1942, 142; all this will be told, all will be made public).

Chapter Four

Narratives of Time

Demain, s'il en est un pour nous, quel sera-t-il?

Tomorrow, if there is such a thing for us, what will it hold?
— Jacqueline Mesnil-Amar, 17 August 1944

Vivre ... sans penser ... ni au passé ni à l'avenir

Living ... without thinking ... either of the past or the future
— Jean Oppenheimer, 2 April 1945

Introduction: The Experience of Time

Unlike autobiography, which is a remembering and a reconstruction (however unreliable this may be), writing a diary is an archiving activity. Diaries look forward, their writing a prophylaxis against the oblivion of history. Particularly in the case of diaries written in dramatic circumstances, the 'I' is caught up in the moment, in the urgent need to record the events of the day, in its commitment to bear witness and its struggle for survival. However, if it were caught up exclusively in discrete moments, it would disintegrate.[1] How does it maintain a sense of self against the experience of discontinuity? I have asked this question in chapter 1, proposing what we might term an existential answer in terms of the 'slender threads of memory' at work in stitching together the two parts of Jean-Claude Stern's life story. I ask it anew in terms of a technical discursive problem, in that the 'I' who speaks is reinvented every time it is uttered. At the same time, language locates the self in time: the writing and speaking subject avails itself of the infinitely adaptable mechanisms of tensed reference to situate itself in a world that both endures and changes constantly. This is particularly clear in the fragmentary and punctual composition of a diary, where the entry itself – its writing on this day, recording, reflecting, looking forward – displays, indeed enacts, a solution to the problem of continuity.

We can illustrate this solution with an early entry from Raymond-Raoul Lambert's diary, where he writes that he has decided to keep his diary in order to 'regain [his] awareness of the passage of time.'[2] What does this mean? Lambert uses writing to refer back and to look forward. Looking back, he forms a sequence from disparate events, thus distilling the story from the engulfing emotions they have generated, and he places this story in personal memory now structured by the conventions of the calendar. Time, recorded in the dates – the dates of the writing and the dates of the episodes – anchors his experience. This happens anew with each entry.

Nevertheless, in their very sequentiality, diaries recount an on-going present that may extend over a relatively long period. This characterizes 'both the communicative situation and the existential situation of the author'[3] – the 'now' at which we say things, the present in which we live. This fact is crucial to an understanding of the time of diaries. Following William James, I will call this now the 'specious present'; James coined this expression to refer to the durative yet transient time that is the time of experience. If 'the present instant' is merely 'the conterminous of the past and future,' James writes that it 'melt[s] in our grasp, [flees] ere we [can] touch it, [goes] in the instant of becoming.'[4] As against this, James posits the specious present, which is 'practically cognized,' 'no knife-edge, but a saddle-back, with a certain breadth of its own on which we sit perched, and from which we look in two directions into time.'[5] This concept appears on the face of it to be eminently suited to the time spans recorded in diaries, which tell what has happened since the previous entry and anticipate the morrow. James observes that the perceived length of time varies experientially; it is felt as the time of waiting, fearing, suffering, or pleasure.[6] We can extrapolate from the latter observation that time is known in fragmentary accounts of experience.

In James's account of the experience of time, the specious present remains relatively undeveloped, but it has been elaborated in phenomenology. Writing in this tradition, Francisco Varela argues that the first givens of knowledge – not 'perceptions,' which are instantaneous, but 'appearances' – are 'aggregated' dynamically into 'incompressible but complete cognitive acts'; in turn, these are 'linked together to form a broader temporal horizon.'[7] For Varela, this temporal scale 'is inseparable from our descriptive-narrative assessments and linked to our linguistic capacities,' allowing for a flexible, extensible interpretation of the specious present.[8] This gloss converges with what James writes, that the 'specious present' is a '*duration*, with a prow and a stern as it were – a rearward- and a forward-looking end. It is only as parts of this *duration-block* that the relation of *succession* of one end to the other is perceived.'[9] Varela adds that it is 'a unity, an aggregate,' 'textural' not mono-dimensional, a 'network of intentionalities,' and not a point on a line.[10]

A second elaboration of the 'specious present' comes from historiography rather than philosophy. We owe it to the distinguished historian Carl Becker:

> This telescoping of successive events into a single instant philosophers call the 'specious present.' Doubtless they would assign rather narrow limits to the specious present; but I will willfully make a free use of it, and say that we can extend the specious present as much as we like. In common speech we do so: we speak of the 'present hour,' the 'present year,' the 'present generation.'[11]

Becker's argument has to do with the nature of historical knowledge, and with the imperative – this is the burden of his essay – for historians to acknowledge the 'now' of their research and writing; only thus can the profession account for the ongoing modification of knowledge of the past. He calls for a history that 'lives' to do 'work in the world.'[12] This work involves 'anticipating (not predicting) what is coming to us': 'from the specious present, which always includes more or less of the past, the future refuses to be excluded.'[13] 'Man' alone, he argues, 'has a specious present that may be deliberately and purposefully enlarged and diversified and enriched' by the 'artificial extensions of memory' on which historians rely.[14] He is referring to those enabled by the invention of writing (archives, documents, the writings of previous historians) as well as by other forms of traces from the past. This specious present is *collective*, it is not confined to individual acts of understanding.

On the one hand, then, we have a 'present' confined to the contents of an individual consciousness, and on the other, a 'present' whose contents consist of the formal or informal memory – where memory is held in stories, in books, and in archives – of a historically particular group. We need features of both to conceptualize the time of diaries, the textural, multidimensional nature of phenomenological time, and the expansive present of the historian who looks to the past for the sake of the future. Moreover, in the definition of 'experience' that underpins the argument of this book, I have followed the lead of phenomenology in stressing the work of reflective consciousness, and I have quoted Varela to the effect that reflective consciousness 'is inseparable from our descriptive-narrative assessments' and relies on 'our linguistic capacities.' This is self-evidently true for historiography, as well as for the writing of diaries. While it is important not to exaggerate the similarities of the two genres, since the acts of remembering that constitute a diary are based in personal experience and are not tested against other sources, diaries are not confined to the individual sphere, since they are written and hence available to collective understanding. Indeed, they are also *informed* by collective understanding, at least in these particulars: the presumption of a shared context; the relation between the lived present of the person writing and public calendrical time; the narrative or descriptive interpretive nature of the record; and the central reliance of that record on the linguistic mechanisms of tense. As Becker's title would have it, every 'man' is 'his own' historian.

I understand the specious present to be a down-to-earth intimation of the Heideggerian 'being *in* time.' As Varela writes, it is 'our abode in basic consciousness.'[15] The preposition is significant: we can only be 'in' time if the present is something like what James describes. Paul Ricoeur calls this 'within-time-ness': 'it is the present of preoccupation, which is a making-present, inseparable from awaiting and retaining.'[16] Ricoeur spells out the implication that the experience of time is the object of stories, whether fictional or historical: 'I take temporality to be that structure of existence that reaches language in narrativity and narrativity to be the language structure that has temporality as its ultimate reference.'[17]

If this is the case, it suggests a corollary to the general proposition concerning diaries, that in them we find a writer writing in time, of the times: the corollary is that he or she writes in the times, *of time itself,* insofar as time is the dimension of affective states such as hoping and fearing; and – wherever on the timeline of past to future the objects of these acts might lie – it is also the dimension of knowing, predicting, recalling, and telling. This dimension – Varela's 'reflexive awareness' of experience as temporal – is itself an object of apprehension and hence tellable in the form of narrative. I shall explore this corollary in three ways. The first is through the use of a single word that indicates the horizons of tensed experience – the two directions (prow and stern) open to the specious present. This word is 'déjà' in French, 'already' in English. The second consists of two stories of waiting. The third tells a story in which the biographical future is progressively blocked, giving way to the future of the diary.

An Adverb Tells Its Stories: 'Already'

In an analytic philosophical account of the experience of time that equates it with 'perception,' Robin Le Poidevin finds himself in a quandary: 'information that is *metrical* in nature (e.g. "the burst of sound was very brief") is derived from *tensed* information, concerning how far in the past something occurred. The question is how we acquire this tensed information.'[18] In response, I suggest that we acquire 'tensed information' from technical practices such as carbon dating and from the semiotic means necessary to turn those data into information for 'work in the world.'[19] I shall focus primarily on the mechanism of linguistic tense, allied with the conventions of dating. This provides me with the crucial assumption for taking my distance from Le Poidevin's own answer, which is formulated in terms of memory traces: 'If there is such a thing as a memory trace that persists over time, then we could judge the age of a memory (and therefore how long ago the event remembered occurred) from the strength of the trace.'[20] Evidently, 'the age of a memory' is a quite different problem for the historian than it is for the philosopher of consciousness and cognition. If a historian is to assess 'the strength of the trace,' they do so by testing the documentary evidence. If a diarist remarks that they 'must jot this down before [they] forget,' they are referring to Le Poidevin's concept of memory; if, as a reader of that diary, I characterize it as 'a gift of (or to) memory,' I am referring to the historian's concept of memory. Reading any diary entry, we read tensed anecdotes or descriptions, and the tenses used are closely tied to the dating conventions that serve to answer the question the historian might put: When did it happen?

Note that in the following, I limit my remarks to languages that have a system of tenses; those that do not, such as Chinese, handle the location of an event in time by other means. The mechanisms of tense and of all temporal and spatial reference are governed by deixis.[21] This is the dimensionless but structurally indispensable point from which any utterance proceeds. Only by positing this dimensionless point can we account for the relationality of now and then, here and there; and only by positing an 'I that utters' can we account for the dynamics of address (you) and of reference to 'third-person' things located in time and space. The 'meaning' of 'now' is thus dependent on acts of discourse; it cannot be defined without 'I' and 'here,' and the same is true reciprocally for each of these terms. To clarify this, let us note the difference between a simple dating system and an utterance in which a particular date counts as 'today' in relation with 'yesterday' and 'tomorrow.' On this view, the dimensions of now – and likewise the dimensions of here – are occasional and contextually determined. It follows that the tenses have not only *temporal reference* but also *deictic force;* this is also true for many temporal adverbs, and in particular the one that interests me here. 'Already' – in French, *déjà* – illustrates precisely James's definition of the specious present as having 'a rearward- and a forward-looking end.' Where we look from is the deictic centre of experience.

The following exposition consists of examples of *déjà* in context. More than mere illustrations, the range of examples elaborates the specious present and shows the relation between the now of the utterance and the present of living. With its opposite, *pas encore* (not yet), it is an adverb of brinks and thresholds, looking forward, looking back. The examples are numbered for ease of reference; they are drawn from a wide range of the diaries in my corpus. Each is a micro-story not only of the event but specifically of the experience of knowing and recording it as an event in time. In each case the affective dimension of the story is attributable to the function of the word *déjà.*[22]

In the first entry of Raymond-Raoul Lambert's diary, we find him envisaging the definitive defeat of the French by the invading German forces: writing *déjà*, he anticipates the inevitable. Lambert is looking forward, but the future is 'already' present. He writes of his experience on 10 June 1940:[23]

1

Le soir Paris se vide et les édifices publics sont morts. *Déjà* souffle le vent de la défaite. (12 July 1940, 68)

Evening: Paris is emptying and public buildings are dead. *Already* the wind of defeat is blowing.* (4)

This *déjà* anticipates by four days the German entry into Paris. Lambert is reading the signs, contained in 'disastrous and enigmatic communiqués' (*Diary,* ibid.): the past few months lead to this. As he looks back, reviewing the sense – the direction – of recent events, he finds himself envisaging the end. It is in that end that the future consists. On 12 June, Valentin Feldman, serving with the retreating French army in Normandy, echoes this experience:

2

Il n'y a *pas encore* de défaite. Mais *déjà* sévit la mentalité de défaite.[24]

The defeat has*n't* happened *yet*. But *already* the mentality of defeat is rife.

On the previous day, he had 'already' predicted the political catastrophe that lay beyond the defeat:

3

Ce commencement de défaite – qui ne signifie *pas encore* défaite – permet de voir comment se dessinent, *d'ores et déjà*, les principes du fascisme français, comment naissent les réactions des fascistes français. (11 June 1940, 172)

This incipient defeat – *not yet* defeat – shows, *right now, already*, the lineaments of French fascism, shows how French fascist reactions begin.

Both men are reading the signs, but their predictions are markedly different on one crucial point. Lambert was a man whose way of knowing and engaging in the world was imbued with military logic and, we must say, with the logic of mainstream politics; his habits of mind are those of an historian and a practical man, not given to speculation. Feldman was a committed communist, who already anticipating the end, had written two days earlier that his 'decision' for the future was clear: 'je sais ce qu'il me reste à faire' (9 June 1940, 171; I know what I must do now). This means that he will join the Resistance. For him the opposition between communism and fascism formed the ground of his inferences concerning the sense of history. The two men share the experience of the brink but do not share an understanding of what lies ahead.[25]

Feldman was forewarned by the lessons of Marxism; Lambert was not. The fact that the latter cannot see the fascist future means that he is surprised when it affects him directly. Thus when, on 14 August 1940, he notes that his apartment in Paris has been expropriated, he cannot 'yet' grasp the implications and is so shocked that he cannot 'yet' feel indignation (82). Again, when he learns of the *Statut des Juifs*, on 19 October 1940, he writes 'je *ne* puis *encore* réaliser' (85; I cannot take it in yet), repeating the same incomprehension later in the same paragraph.

'Not yet taking in' registers a moment in the processing of experience that refuses, yet heralds, the inevitable knowing. At the same time as Lambert 'cannot yet grasp' the fact that France has promulgated the *Statut des Juifs*, other people did grasp it, and despaired. Two days after the text of the *statut* was officially published, Jacques Biélinky records in his reporter's notebook:

4

J'apprends qu'il y a *déjà* sept suicides parmi les Juifs de Paris ...[26]

I have heard that there are *already* seven suicides among the Jews of Paris ...

Biélinky's use of the present tense forces us to consider the word 'suicides' as referring to the people, rather than their action. Killing themselves does not place them safely in the past; they, with their act, remain among the Jews of Paris. For these people, the future could not be faced; the writer bearing witness does face it: their act is a sign of things to come, and the word 'déjà' predicts that the suicide count will rise, which indeed it did. Living in the specious present is living with 'more or less of the past, [from which] the future refuses to be excluded.'[27] Compare Schatzman, watching the preparations for deportations from Drancy:

5

Le coeur vous saigne devant le spectacle de tristesse et de désespoir que nous voyons pendant la préparation des départs. Il y a déjà eu deux suicides et il est probable que d'autres se produiront.[28]

Your heart bleeds at the spectacle of sadness and despair that we see during the preparation for departures. There have already been two suicides and no doubt more will follow.

These suicides are past events, but they too predict the future.

As the second year of the Occupation opens, Valentin Feldman discovers that his position as a teacher has given him the 'illusion' of staying in one place; although he knows better, his employment appears to offer 'provisional stability' (6 January 1941, 229). This impression is immediately disturbed – its provisional quality confirmed – by the (premature) news that he has lost his position:

6

Et quand je me crois révoqué, je ne le suis *pas encore* tout en l'étant probablement. (Ibid., 230)

When I think I have been dismissed, I'm *not, yet*, but still I probably will be.

Again, he is not surprised: his prediction concerning his future is accurate. And again, we can contrast him with Lambert, who has rejoined the Comité d'assistance aux réfugiés (9 October 1940), in order to 'feed his children.' Both men are considering their professional futures. In July and again in October 1941, Lambert goes to Vichy to test the wind, and by the end of the year, he is in active negotiation with Xavier Vallat, commissioner for Jewish affairs, concerning the establishment of the Union générale des israélites de France. I would not wish to reduce this contrast to a crude opposition between the *Résistant* and the collaborator, nor even between the situation of Jews in the Occupied Zone and those in the Free Zone, although both interpretations have their value. My focus is on the experience of the brink: Feldman knows his situation is unstable, whereas Lambert is attempting to assure the stability both of his community work and of his family. Anticipation of the future – and hence the ability to plan – is informed by differing understandings of the formation by the past of the present.

Indeed, for Lambert, the present moment is confined in practice to his personal aspirations and the battles they entrain. On 30 November 1941 he writes:

7

Les philanthropes et ceux que j'appelle les 'princes juifs' s'agitent, me critiquent *déjà*. (133)

The philanthropists and those whom I call 'the Jewish princes' are hot and bothered, and are *already* critical of me. (76)

and again:

8

Quelle que soit l'issue de la guerre, la fonction de secrétaire général que tous m'attribuent *déjà* sera lourde, très lourde ... (2 December 1941; 134–5)

Whatever the outcome of the war, the job of general secretary which everyone *already* thinks is mine, will be onerous, very onerous ... (78)

Lambert is working on a future in which 'the outcome of the war' appears – oddly – to be secondary; his 'own' future is 'already' within his grasp.

These are anticipatory uses of *déjà*, in which the point of utterance acts as a pivot where knowledge of recent events and anticipation of the future coexist in the present. Anticipated, but not necessarily predicted, the future may be known, or unknown. François Montel is in Drancy:

9

Entre l'Allemagne et la France j'ai *déjà* 18 mois de captivité ... Combien de temps encore?[29]

Between them, I've *already* been in German and French captivity for 18 months ... How much longer will it be?

Montel measures his wait 'up till now,'and thinks ahead to ask how long it will last; his question implies that it will indeed end. But when? Will waiting, will his internment, continue? As it turns out, he was deported from Drancy to Auschwitz; the end of the story is not the one here envisaged. *Déjà* is capable of implying a narrative together with the affect – encouragement for Lambert (extract 8), discouragement for Montel (9), cynical resignation for Feldman (6), and foreboding for Biélinky and Schatzman (4 and 5) – associated with living through, knowing it, or telling it.

Meanwhile, in Paris, Jacques Biélinky observes the relation between the time of personal experience and that of administrative measures:

10

Les délais laissés par les syndicats pour la liquidation des maisons juives (de un à trois mois) ne sont pas officiels. Mais beaucoup de maisons sont *déjà* fermées. (24 January 1941, 95)

The deadlines for the liquidation of Jewish businesses (from one to three months) are not official. But many have *already* closed.

Déjà used in this way registers prematurity; likewise, in the following instances, which refer to the imposition of the yellow star:

11

On a *déjà* remarqué dans les rues et au métro des Juifs décorés d'insignes avant le terme. (Biélinky, 3 June 1942, 214)

In the metro and in the streets, we've *already* noticed Jews adorned with their insignia ahead of time.

12

À la cantine de la rue Richer ce matin sont venues deux jeunes filles qui ont *déjà* cousu leur *Magen David* découpé sur leur poitrine avant le terme 'légal' (Biélinky, 5 June 1942, 215)

At the canteen in the rue Richer there were two young girls who had *already* sewn their cut-out Magen Davids on their breasts, before the 'legal' deadline.

Without the word 'déjà,' the sentences it is in would describe the same situations; with it, they express the writer's reaction to the facts. That reaction is inexplicit, but it poses a question concerning the kind of

anticipatory obedience in evidence, in which the victims of this measure bring its implementation forward. Does it tell us something about
behaviour under an authoritarian regime? A similar behaviour produces
absurd situations such as the following, in which the ration-card people
have pre-empted the work of the bootmakers:

13

La carte de chaussures est *déjà* entrée en vigueur; il n'y a que la chaussure
nationale qui manque. (Biélinky, 9 February 1941, 97)

The ration-card for shoes has *already* come into force, the only thing missing are state-issued shoes.

Déjà carries irony in this case. Vichy France was not noted for meticulous administrative organization. Sometimes the failures of coordination
were laughable, but sometimes they were tragic:

14

Schulman, le gérant de la cantine de la rue Richer est *déjà* déporté en
Allemagne. Cependant, on vient d'obtenir sa libération. (Biélinky, 3 August
1942, 239)

Schulman, the manager of the canteen in the rue Richer has *already* been
deported. In the meantime, his liberation has just been approved.

We see similar administrative chaos in the camp at Drancy, where,
because of the influx of new arrivals, last-minute orders to move from
one dormitory to another frequently aggravated the discomfort of camp
life – not to speak of death, as in the case of Goldman recounted by
Benjamin Schatzman (see chapter 3). Saül Castro was picked up in the
rafle du XI arrondissement on 20 August 1941 and interned in Drancy. In
December he was moved from one block to another:

15

Je me dirige vers le bloc indiqué et c'est avec grande peine que je monte
mes bagages au 4e étage où je dois loger ; là je rencontre mes premiers
compagnons [...] ils sont *déjà* installés, il n'y a plus de lit.[30]

I go to the block I'm sent to and it's with great difficulty that I carry my
luggage up to the fourth floor where I am to to be quartered; there I meet
my first room-mates [...] they're *already* settled in, there are no beds left.

François Montel notes the haste that these forced migrations entailed when arrangements have to be made for the internment of the thousands who will be picked up in the *rafle du Vel d'Hiv* (16–17 July 1942):

16

Le camp est en ébullition. *Déjà* hier soir les hommes ont travaillé jusqu'à 22h 30 pour vider le bloc III et retirer du bloc I les bois de lits que l'on y avait entassés voici huit jours. Le temps manque, paraît-il, pour monter ces lits. Lundi le camp doit être plein. (10 July 1942, 75)

The camp is in turmoil. *Already* last night the men were at work until 10:30 p.m. to empty block III and to clear the bed frames from block I where they had been dumped eight days before. Apparently there isn't time to assemble them. The camp is to be full by Monday.

It is of some historical interest to note that this logistical planning started seven days before the round-up took place. Montel registers the upheaval in the camp routine again caused by the failure of coordination between two parts of the administration. *Déjà hier soir* – 'already last night': this notation suggests that the work required of the internees to accommodate this upheaval was demanded with unnecessary haste, and no doubt prematurely in relation with the practical requirements of the situation. Implied in this situation are the operations of three levels of the hierarchy: one timeline overtakes the next, thereby controlling a third, the time of the men who were put to work.

The drama of the regulation shoes (example 13), that of Castro's missing out on a bed (15), not to mention Schulman's deportation (14), and this one (16), resides precisely in the narratives of time. Coincidence and non-coincidence are the stuff of little stories. Lived time is constituted by multiple sequences of events. Lots of things happen at once: one person (or event) is too late, or too early, in relation to another. Missed opportunities, or opportunities seized, can be the result; Saül Castro has better luck in this episode:

17

Après l'appel le chef de bâtiment nous informe d'être prêt pour aller à la désinfection; enfin mieux vaut tard que jamais; bagages couvertures doivent restés dans la chambre; en vitesse je remet à un de mes copins qui a *déjà* passé à la désinfection tous mes papiers et autres objets et rejoins mes camarades qui sont *déjà* rassemblés dans la cour. (8 January 1942)

After roll-call the building chief tells us to be ready for disinfection; oh well, better late than never; luggage, and blankets are to be left in the room; in a rush I give all my papers and other objects to a friend who has *already* been through disinfection and join my mates who are *already* assembled in the yard.

A similarly helpful coincidence is recorded by Jean Oppenheimer, in a displaced persons camp in Poland:

18

Nous avons l'intention de faire vendre par lui, qui se trouve ici depuis plus de deux ans *déjà* et connaît toutes les ficelles, une de nos couvertures.[31] (18 March 1945, 38)

We mean to ask [a comrade] to sell a blanket for us; he's been here for two years *already* and knows the ropes.

The 'now' of the displaced person has lasted for two years. What is called 'the liberation' is itself made up of multiple sequences and multiple durations.

At the end of Oppenheimer's stay in the displaced persons camp, he is put in a new group for transportation. Here he experiences a further happy coincidence:

19

Je suis [...] avec tout le groupe 59, agréables garçons en majeure partie, pris en amitié *déjà* à la caserne où nous étions dans la même chambre. (23 April 1945, 219)

I'm [...] with group 59, mainly nice boys; we had *already* made friends at the barracks where we were in the same room.

And here, a third, in which *déjà* brings a third time into relation with the time of the coincidence:

20

J'ai rencontré par hasard et à ma très grande joie le docteur De Benedetti ce matin, avec lequel j'ai travaillé à Auschwitz en tant que secrétaire et interprète, et que j'ai connu au *KB* de Monowitz *déjà*. (Oppenheimer, 3 April 1945, 122)[32]

This morning by chance, to my very great joy, I met up with Dr De Benedetti, with whom I worked at Auschwitz as his secretary and interpreter, and whom I knew *already* at the infirmary at Monowitz.

The texture of time is not confined to events in a single linear series. Hélène Berr attempts to keep the timeline of her personal life separate from that of the political circumstances affecting her family, but coincidence is still the principal feature of her experience of time in the following passage. Nevertheless, while there are two events in play, we will see a further property of *déjà* emerge in this note:

21

Mais je ne veux pas faire de la peine à Maman. *Déjà* ce soir Papa a reçu un avis de spoliation, et Maman prend tout cela sur son dos, et cache tout.[33]

But I don't want to upset mother. *Already* this evening father received a notification of expropriation, and mother takes all this on her shoulders, hiding everything. (22)

It is not that the notification to Raymond Berr has been received prematurely, or before it might have been expected. Indeed, given the date, it is rather late. The *déjà* of this passage refers to Hélène Berr's calculation of how much her mother can cope with on this occasion; it entails accumulation: she cannot add this to the burden her mother already bears.

The difference between the temporal and the quantitative uses of *déjà* is clarified in two entries from the diary of Germaine Léon. Her husband had been arrested ten days before the first of these (written on 22 December 1941), in the *rafle des notables*:

22

Le temps passera, même lentement et un jour je relirai ces lignes en disant: *déjà* 2 ans de cela. Où serons-nous?[34]

Time will pass, even if it is slow; one day I will reread these lines and say to myself: it's *already* been two years. Where will we be?

Here Germaine Léon is looking forward to a time when this period will be recollected in tranquillity; it illustrates precisely James's proposition concerning fast and slow time: 'a tract of time empty of experiences seems long in passing, but in retrospect short.'[35] However, very shortly after, her courage fails her when she sees ahead nothing but a continuation of this experience of waiting:

23

Et je l'attends – je l'attends chaque minute: je guette les pas sur le trottoir, je guette l'ascenseur. Je ne vais pas pouvoir durer comme ça – je n'en peux *déjà* plus. (6 January 1942)

And I wait – I wait every minute: I listen for steps on the pavement, I listen for the lift. I won't be able to go on like this – *already* [I'm at the point where] I no longer can.[36]

Note that in both cases, she uses 'déjà': in 22, looking back (in imagination) on two years' of waiting, 'déjà' signifies that they (will) have passed quickly, whereas in the present looking forward (23), waiting seems to be without end. After only three weeks, it is 'already' intolerable. She has, she thinks, reached the limit of her endurance. History, of course, does not respect such limits: Jean Léon was held in Compiègne until 27 March 1942, then deported directly to Auschwitz in the first convoy; he was killed on 18 April 1942. Germaine Léon received this news in October 1946.

What is intolerable for her is an unchanging present. But the specious present is also experienced through processes of change, as in the accumulation of problems that Hélène Berr worries about. We may think of processes of exacerbation and magnification, of increase or decrease, of deterioration or heightening, of fading or intensification. In the following, the difficulties encountered by a 'prisoner of freedom' in the camp with Jean Oppenheimer have led to a minor misdeed:

24

Je suis curieux [de savoir] si l'on accepte ses explications et pour combien de temps il en aura (5 jours). Si *déjà* on ne comprend pas le langage, les ordres sont mal donnés, et souvent contradictoirement, ce qui ajoute à la confusion, voilà le résultat, il n'a sûrement pas été commis de faute volontairement (24 March 1945, 52)

I'm curious to know if they accept his explanations, and how much time he'll get (5 days). If *already* you don't know the language, the orders aren't clear, sometimes they're contradictory, all of that adds to the confusion, so this is the result. I'm sure there was no intention to do wrong.

Here, *déjà* marks the beginning of an accumulation; everything else makes the 'confusion' worse, with an undeserved punishment as the result. By contrast, *déjà* can mark the limit beyond which the process cannot be tolerated. The following two examples refer to the loss of physical condition consequent upon malnutrition:

25

Qu'est-ce que cela représente une assiette au ¾ liquide avec quelques bouts de légume, on est *déjà* des loques nos visages sont osseux, je ne m'y reconnais plus. (Saül Castro, 23 September 1941)

What does this add up to, a plate three-quarters full of liquid with a few bits of vegetable, we are *already* skin and bones, our faces are skeletal, I don't recognize myself.

26

En bref, je dois pouvoir résister à l'effondrement qui se produit parmi nous de plus en plus et qui va jusqu'à la plus grande gravité. Il faut donc se défendre et résister à tout prix. J'ai, jusque maintenant, l'impression que ma méthode de défense me réussit, en dépit de l'extrême faiblesse *déjà* atteinte. Il est certain pour moi que, si je n'avais pu faire ce que j'ai fait, je serais devenu encore bien plus faible et que je serais *déjà* tout à fait épuisé. (Schatzman, 20 February 1942, 57)

To sum up, I have to resist the collapse that is happening more and more among us and that is becoming extremely grave. It's imperative to protect oneself and to resist at all costs. To this point, I have the impression that my method of defending my health is being successful, despite the extreme weakness *already* affecting me. Certainly, had I not been able to do what I have been doing, I'd even weaker and would *already* be absolutely exhausted.

How long can the body last? The question that arises from *déjà* used in this way shows that the limit reached is not absolute, but that it registers the continuation of the process even beyond the point where the intensification, or accumulation, is intolerable. But sometimes the limits of endurance are reached. We have seen this in example 4, drawn from Jacques Biélinky's notebook regarding the number of suicides in Paris; he provides another in a report of what he's learned about the conditions at the Vélodrome d'Hiver:

27

Au Vel-d'Hiv sont entassés quinze mille Juifs arrêtés (hommes, femmes, enfants) qui couchent par terre et ne sont pas nourris. Il y a *déjà* plusieurs morts, car il pleut et fait froid. (19 July 1942, 234)

Fifteen thousand Jews (men, women and children) are piled up at the Winter Velodrome; they sleep on the ground and are not fed. There are *already* several dead, because it's raining and cold.

Only the writer looks ahead; the outlook is grim.

Whether or not the person writing was to perish or survive, the now of the witness collects the past and stretches far into the future. Looking back, looking forwards, like the specious present generally, and like the adverbs of brinks and thresholds, the witness recalls the past and calls to the future. But this is not easy speech. My final example foreshadows Primo Levi's account of the repeating dream he shares with others. It starts with the 'intense pleasure' of 'being at home, among friendly people' and having 'so many things to recount,' and ends with the anguish of 'the ever-repeated scene of the unlistened-to story.'[37] Exchanging stories with his fellow liberated prisoners from a transitional place between Auschwitz and home, even – especially – in company with those who know, Jean Oppenheimer too anticipates the incredulity of those who do not:

28

Assez souvent je raconte (quand le cœur est plein ...) l'histoire vécue de la vie au camp et des atrocités et des hypocrisies dont les Allemands nous ont si bien comblés. Je sens ici *déjà* se réaliser ma crainte, devant des gens qui ont senti par eux-mêmes et qui ont pu constater de leurs propres yeux la véracité de mes récits, de rencontrer de l'incrédulité. (19 March 1945, 42)

Quite often (when my heart is full ...) I tell stories of life in the camp, of the atrocities and hypocrisies bestowed on us by the Germans. Here, with those who experienced it themselves and with their own eyes can confirm the truthfulness of my stories, here *already* my fear of being met with incredulity is real.

The real present might be 'gone in the instant of becoming,' but our 'consciousness [of time] never shrinks to the dimensions of a glow-worm spark. The knowledge of some other part of the stream, past or future, near or remote is always mixed in with our knowledge of the present thing.'[38] *Ici déjà*: here already, before its time, 'already' brings into the present the waking nightmare of the witness. It is premature, yet the future that it envisages – that of the witness calling to be heard – is potentially endless.

The expansion and the contraction of the specious present that we observe in the use of *déjà*, the convergence and divergence of series and threads of events and processes, are registered by speaking subjects whose experience of time is not (yet) radically disturbed. There is some flexibility in moving around this space, making connections across its several dimensions, looking from one direction to another. With some exceptions, the diarists I have quoted in this section are – at least at the point at which the quoted passage is written – relatively unscathed, and their present is relatively rich. In the following stories this is not so. For this reason, I take my cue from trauma theory: under conditions of trauma and its aftermath, the experience of time shrinks to the present.[39] This is the time of survival, a protracted now with no access to the past before the traumatic event or any future that might follow. In two of the cases to be considered here, we have stories of the subjection to trauma. Saül Castro – like Bejamin Schatzman in the previous chapter – is finding ways to survive in a concentration camp; we can follow the progress of this shrinkage until he reaches the point where he can no longer write. To serve as a counterpoint, I tell the story of Jean Oppenheimer, who writes from the threshold of release; here, we can follow the progress of a gradual expansion of time in which he learns anew what it is to look both back and forwards. The third story is that of Hélène Berr, living the semblance of a normal life in Occupied Paris: over the two years of her diary, she experiences what we might call a 'foremath': in the present, she is progressively cut off from her past, and hence from the possibility of envisaging a future that would have gone on from there. She, like Castro, is confined to the present; she continues to record it until her arrest. To tell these stories is further to explore the specious present, to ask what it is to live in what Paul Ricoeur calls the 'radical structure of temporality,' the ultimate plot, which is governed by 'being-toward-death.'[40]

Stories of Waiting

Saül Castro's Worry Beads

Saül Castro was a naturalized Jew from Istanbul. The family had settled in Salonica following expulsion from Spain, so his cultural background was Greek. He migrated to France in 1923 as a way of avoiding Turkish military duty. On 20 August 1941, he was rounded-up in the XIe *arrondissement*, when over 4,000 Jewish men were sent directly to Drancy, then under Nazi control, but run on a day-to-day basis by the Vichy authorities. This was the second of the big round-ups of 1941; the third was carried out on 12 December of the same year, when the Germans collected some 700 prominent Jews in retribution for Resistance activities. This latter group was sent to the camp at Royallieu-Compiègne, run directly by the Nazis. The connection between these two round-ups is significant in the story of Castro. The Germans had demanded 1,000 prominent Jews, but the French police who were carrying out their orders came up with only 743; to make up the numbers, they transferred 300 men from Drancy, of whom Castro was one.

Castro's diary starts on the first day of his internment (20 August 1941) and ends with his liberation (23 March 1942). He makes strictly regular daily entries until the state of his health is so severely impaired that he no longer can. This daily regularity and its breakdown are therefore one of the ways in which this diary tells time. I shall return to this matter in due course.

We learn from this diary and others that time is formless in a concentration camp. With no difference between yesterday and today, no prospect of a change tomorrow, the interminable present is a kind of pure duration. To write a diary under these conditions, dating every day, is a way of keeping hold of the temporality of the outside world; it is also a way of registering the passing of time. Of all the genres of discourse, a diary insists that there is such a thing as the progression of the days. The dated entry particularizes the day and anchors the writing self in the telling of it.

In the major narrative genres in which he analyses the experience of time – novels and history – Ricoeur argues that time is given interpretable form by the 'configuration' of plot.[41] Diaries, by and large, are not emplotted in this sense. Saül Castro's, for example, reads like a chronicle of boredom. However, it does present a figure, not fictional, not a product of the imagination, not an analogy except in the reading. It is a useful object that he fashioned, as many internees fashioned things from lengths of string, nails, scraps of metal or hessian. The making of such objects whiled away the time, and the objects – spoons, plates, mending kits – served as the minutiae of survival. These men were bricoleurs, and they set up the rudiments of a system of necessary trades, paying each other in kind, or trading services for cigarettes and rations.

> Je me suis mis raccommodeur de chaussettes, je fais des réparations et en rémunérations on me donne une ou deux cigarettes suivant le travail qu'il y a à faire et en même temps je passe le temps; d'autres se sont mis cireurs, coiffeurs. (31 December 1941)

> I've set up as a sock mender, I darn the socks and I am paid in cigarettes, one or two depending on the work there is to do, and at the same time I pass the time; others have set up as shoe blacks and barbers.

Busying themselves in this ingenious industriousness, they also make things they need for themselves; they are preoccupied with things, and with their use in the care of the self. A length of canvas is frayed to serve as mending thread (19 October 1941) or to make different styles of footware: one man combines it with a piece of doormat to make slippers (22 October 1941), and Castro himself makes inner-soles for his shoes (15 October 1941). None of this precious material is wasted:

> Après l'appel je retourne dans mon lit; le camarade R me prie de lui faire pour son pyjama une ceinture; il me reste un peu de fil de la toile anglaise

et me suis mis à tresser et à confectionner cette ceinture; ainsi j'ai été occupé toute la matinée. (23 October 1941)

After roll-call I went back to bed; my friend R asked me to make him a belt
for his pyjamas; I had some of the canvas left so I set about braiding it for
the belt; that kept me busy for the whole morning.

Having something useful to do is the crux of the matter, because 'ce qui
nous mine ... c'est l'inactivité' (25 August 1941; idleness is what undermines us). Busy, creative activities help pass the time; even hunger can be
momentarily forgotten, morale is raised by working to an outcome, and
camaraderie is reinforced in reciprocal help and in conversations having
content other than the miseries of camp life. Such activities occupy time,
forming and informing it with starting points and end points. In these
circumstances, finishing something is both satisfying and problematic.

Apart from his shoe linings, Castro makes for himself an object that
is not, at first sight, utilitarian; it is more like a toy or an accessory. 'Je
m'amuse,' he writes – and the verb is noteworthy – 'à enlever les fils et les
tressant en nattes j'arrive à faire un chapelet, en introduisant des pièces
de un, 4 et 5 sous, ainsi je ne trouve pas la journée longue' (19 October
1941; I enjoy fraying the threads, and plaiting them; I end up making a
string of worry beads by inserting coins of one cent, four cents, and five
cents in the plait. In this way, the day passes quickly). This object, known
as *komboloí* in Greek, consists usually of an odd number of beads; it is
used variously for simple tactile pleasure, to calm oneself, or for display;
it is most commonly used as a device of patience, to pass the time.

Let us note to start with that the very making of the string of beads
demands 'une certaine patience' (ibid.; some patience), and, furthermore, that it is the handiwork itself that Castro finds entertaining.
Otherwise the days take eternity to pass (27 August 1941) because of the
enforced idleness (8 October 1941). 'On ne sait quoi faire de la matinée,
chaque jour c'est le même problème à résoudre; étant réduits à l'inactivité ... on meurt d'ennui' (3 September 1941; We don't know what to do
with ourselves, every day it's the same problem; we're kept in total idleness
so we die of boredom). There is only one solution, he concludes: 'il faut
s'ingénier afin de tuer le temps' (9 September 1941; you have to invent
ways of killing time). The making of the worry beads serves this purpose.

Then they are finished. But Castro is not quite satisfied with the design,
so he undoes it:

Mes copins me critiquent, entre autres D ... qui s'occupe trop du voisin,
parce que je m'amuse à défaire mon chapelet, il est vrai que depuis que je

l'ai terminé une idée me traverse et je le défais pour le refaire d'une autre façon : bref cela me regarde et cela m'amuse et en même temps je me repose. (19 October 1941)

My friends criticize me for undoing my beads, particularly D ... who pokes his nose into other people's business, because now I'm having fun undoing my beads; it's true that since I finished it, I've had another idea, and I'm undoing it and remaking it in a different way; well anyhow, it's my business, I enjoy it, and it's restful.

Unlike other forms of *chapelet* (Christian rosaries, or Islamic prayer beads, for example) the worry beads are not associated with religious practice, but, like them, they are cyclical. The two ends of the string are joined at a head-bead and a tassel. To use it, one starts with the first bead, moving it toward the head-bead; each bead is moved in turn in the same direction until they are all on one side. Then the process starts again in the other direction; it is repetitive and continuous. The gesture is soothing, tactilely pleasurable, and regular. A formless series becomes a temporal sequence with a starting point and an end point in a subconscious, corporeal rhythm; life is concentrated into the present as it passes, yet it bears the promise of an arrival, and thus an answer to the question: 'À quand la fin de notre malheur et de nos misères?' (19–21 December 1941; When will our misery end?). Yet, not content with the metaphoric richness of the object itself, Castro enjoys taking it apart in order to redesign it. Despite the exasperation of his comrades, he persists: the work is fun; it's my business; I find it restful.

What a boon! It is less the object itself that satisfies its inventor, less its inherent properties, than its making, the perfecting of its design, the time taken absorbed in the craft. Yet eventually it is finished, and it starts to serve its purpose as an artefact. We discover its daily value when there's an inspection:

J'ai les mains dans les poches et nerveusement j'ai pris mon chapelet dans ma main, tout en le tenant dans la poche; au bruit métallique que j'ai occasionné Laroquette s'approche de moi, me fouille et n'ayant pas trouvé du tabac et toujours avec un air moqueur, m'élève [*sic* – m'enlève?] le chapelet. J'ai peur qu'il ne l'emporte pas; et je ne peux rien; il me questionne et lui ayant répondu que c'est un souvenir, l'ayant fait au camps; il n'a pas l'air de me croire et me dis de prier Allah pour que je sorte d'ici, enfin il me remet le chapelet, et se dirige vers la sortie. (10 December 1941)

I'm fiddling with my beads with my hands in my pocket; Laroquette hears the noise and comes toward me, searches me, and not finding tobacco, takes them from me, mocking me all the while. I'm scared he'll take them away. At his question, I reply that I made it in the camp and it's a souvenir for me; he looks incredulous and tells me to pray to Allah to get me out of here; at last he gives me back the beads and goes towards the exit.

Counting his beads in his pocket to calm his nerves, Castro is caught out. The scene is typical of the petty brutalities of the camp. Let us set aside the absurdity of taking a Jew for a Muslim, an identity that would no doubt have protected Castro under the persecutory circumstances of the time. We have seen it previously, used as a racist slur by Jean-Jacques Bernard. Here the guard presumes that the function of the beads is supplication for release. Castro's retort – that it's a 'souvenir of the camp' – does not convince him. But nothing could be more mistaken about the value of the worry beads; prayer and the beads that facilitate it are teleological; they seek an outcome, redemption, salvation, or paradise. The worry beads are merely an aid to living in the present by telling the countable units of time – days, hours, minutes – and their cyclical predictability.

Besides its function as a teller of time, the string of beads is valuable to Castro as a proof of his cleverness and of the strength of his morale. It is part of his way of staying sane in the camp:

> J'ai le coeur gros et j'ai du chagrin, un tas de mauvaises idées traversent mon cerveau, on nous a atteint jusqu'à nos plus profondes entrailles, nous séparant brutalement de nos femmes et enfants. Je me ressaisi, et si je veux voir mes enfants et ma femme, il ne faut pas me laisser abattre, il faut tenir le moral intact. (2 September 1941)

> My heart is breaking with grief, I'm having all sorts of awful ideas, they've really got us where it hurts, separating us brutally from our wives and children. I pull myself together: if I want to see my children and my wife, I mustn't let it get me down, I have to stay positive.

Letting it all get him down is what he's struggling against. He is a practical man. Knowing that it is not Allah or anything similar that will help him through, Castro focuses on not being depressed. He achieves this with practical activities: 'Afin de chasser le cafard je me lève et je lave mon linge que je met à sécher à la fenêtre' (12 September 1941; To stop feeling depressed I get up and do my washing, which I leave at the window to dry). Better than this, the worry beads are the outcome of his creativity; he values them because they affirm his humanity against the intimidations and violence of a regime that treats its victims as less than animals (28 August 1941). If they are a souvenir, moreover, they project a future beyond the time that they help to pass.

The string of beads represents and structures time, breaking it into regular intervals and a predictable sequence. This is also the case with the diary. It follows the strict conventional discipline of its genre: each entry corresponds to a date, there is an entry for every day, and the beginning and end of each entry are defined by the daylight hours – I get up, I go to bed. In the period he spends at Drancy, Castro fails to make regular entries on only three occasions: on 10–12 and 14 October, he doesn't touch his diary for fear of searches; on 23 November he is too sick; and he doesn't bother making entries between November 26th and 30th, because nothing abnormal has happened.

The day is the basic unit of time, and of the diary, itself being governed by a strict routine that in turn governs the composition of the entries. The day starts when the internees are woken and receive their morning 'coffee' – 'le jus' – bitter and unpalatable, often undrinkable: 'le café de ce matin ... n'était que de l'eau noircie et bouillie, c'est une purge que l'on est forcé de boire faute de mieux' (22 August 1941; the coffee this morning was nothing but boiled black water, it's a purge that we are forced to drink since there's nothing better). Again 'à la place du café, c'est la soupe à l'oignon qu'on nous sert, je garite, il y a de quoi faire rendre un chien; je suis écoeuré c'est plutôt de l'eau de lessive et je renverse par terre cette eau puante, mes copains font autant' (24 August 1941; Instead of coffee, they serve us onion soup, I gag, it's enough to make a dog vomit; it's disgusting, more like washing water. I tip it out, so do my friends). Getting up, roll-call, an empty morning, followed by soup for lunch, an empty afternoon broken only by one hour walking in the yard, followed by the distribution of bread (200 grams for twenty-four hours), and the evening meal: this is a day.

The detained men are constantly hungry – 'ici on ne pense qu'à manger' (25 August 1941; here we think only of eating). Mealtimes are the regular events that govern the rhythm of the day:

On ne sait quoi faire de la matinée, chaque jour c'est le même problème à résoudre; étant réduits à l'inactivité et comme il nous a été interdit de sortir dans la cour sauf l'heure de la promenade, nous sommes obligé d'être enfermé dans nos chambre; on meurt d'ennui et le cerveau travail; on ne pense qu'à manger et c'est un supplice terrible de patienter jusqu'à l'heure de midi. (3 September 1941)

We don't know what to do with our mornings, every day it's the same problem; we're reduced to utter idleness, and since we are no longer allowed

to go out into the yard except for an hour's walk, we are confined in our
rooms; we are dying of boredom and our brains work overtime; we think of
nothing but eating, it's torture to have to wait for midday.

Between times – the mornings, the afternoons, the evenings – there
is nothing to fill the time except card games sometimes, and reading if
there is matter to hand. But since there is no electricity in the dormito-
ries, the evenings are the worst. Packs of cards are prohibited, although
some men find ways around this prohibition. 'You have to keep busy,'
writes Castro. 'It's dreadful having nothing to do, especially when you're
haunted by hunger' (8 October 1941). Indeed, hunger is a specific form
of waiting, and waiting on an hourly basis is waiting only for food: 'Le
moment le plus agréable à passer c'est vers 16h30, l'heure de la distribution du pain et du sucre; c'est amusant et cela passe le temps; cela ne
dure qu'une demie heure.' (ibid.; the best time of day is around 4:30 in
the afternoon; this is the time when bread and sugar are distributed; it's
entertaining and it passes the time; it only lasts half an hour). 'It's entertaining and it passes the time,' just like the making of the string of beads,
an activity requiring the exact distribution of portions.
   Hunger and waiting: there is one activity that meets both needs at
once. This is vegetable duty:

La corvée des carottes est formée dans la cour, il est 15h30, je descends avec
un copin et nous nous mettons à la suite de la corvée; le chef de la corvée
nous donne un couteau rouillé et sans manche à chacun de nous et nous
voilà au travail; le temps passera plus vite et on sera soulagé de cette hantise
de la faim qui ne cesse de travailler dans notre cerveau. (26 August 1941)

People waiting to do vegetable duty are in the yard, it's 3:30 p.m.; I go down
with a friend and we mingle with them; the leader gives each of us a rusty
knife without a handle and we go to work; it helps pass the time and we'll
be less haunted by the hunger that obsesses us.

Not everybody can be taken on, and the workers are strictly forbidden
from filching scraps. But, as in the case of the card-games, they find a way:

Autour de nous des internés font cercle et veulent se mettre dans la corvée,
ils ont faim comme nous, les malheureux, mais les hommes de corvée sont
déjà si nombreux, que l'interné surveillant refuse de les enrôler; je suis
intervenu auprès du surveillant, et les a fait accepté, avec seule condition de
ne pas manger les carottes; les voilà tout heureux et se mettent au travail et
de temps à autre, ils font disparaître un bout de carottes dans leur bouche,

ainsi tout en travaillant on arrive à calmer la faim un petit peu et le temps
passe inaperçu. (1 September 1941)

There are internees milling around wanted to join in, they're hungry, the
poor things, but there are already so many workers that the supervisor
refuses to take them on; I intervened with him and got him to accept them,
on condition that they didn't eat the carrots; now they're happily working,
and from time to time a bit of carrot disappears into their mouths. In this
way, hunger is kept at bay and time passes unnoticed.

Carrots or cabbages are the standard fare:

On nous sert à 6 ½ le bouillon chaud après l'appel je vais avec un copain
nous engager à l'épluche ainsi le temps sera moins long à passer; c'est des
choux qu'il y a à éplucher, on réclame un couteau et nous voilà au boulot.
    Avec mon camarade R on est arrivé à mettre de côté 40 trognons qu'à la
fin de l'épluche on les a emmenés dans la chambre et avons distribué aux
autres copins; ce n'est pas si mauvais que cela les trognons; j'épluche mon
trognon et je fais des tout petits morceaux que je mangerais tout à l'heure.
(25 September 1941)

At 6:30 a.m. we get our hot drink; after roll-call a mate and I go down to
enrol in vegetable duty as a way of spending time; it's cabbages; we ask for
a knife and get to work.
    With my friend R we manage to set aside 40 cabbage stems that we take
to our room after we've finished and distribute to our room-mates. Cabbage
stems aren't all that bad; I cut mine up into little pieces that I intend to eat
later.

A little extra to eat, and an activity among comrades. Notice in each of
the above passages that Castro stresses the value of vegetable duty in
helping to pass the time. Without it, the men escape the monotony in
sleep, which, they hope, also slows down their digestion, helping them
wait more patiently for the next meal (27 September 1941): 'after lunch
we go to bed; after the evening soup, we go to bed' (29 October 1941).
There's nothing else to do.
    The days in the camp are all the same: 'it's always the same scenes,
repeated day after day; we have got used to this sad unhappy life; [...]
we don't know what to do each day ... we go to bed straight after lunch'
(27 October 1941). As a result, camp life consists of a sequence of habits,
like the writing of a diary or the ritual manipulation of beads. If something different is in the wind, it provokes fear of a nasty surprise. The first

of these was the arrest, the second would be the transfer to Compiègne.
A third – transfer *from* Compiègne – would be a fearful prospect indeed:

> Après la soupe, des bobards courent de chambre en chambre; des gen-
> darmes français sont dans le camp les uns disent que c'est les français qui
> prennent la direction du camp d'autres insinuent que nous serons déportés;
> aussitôt cette nouvelle lancée quelques uns ont commencé à préparer les
> bagages et être prêt à tout emporter afin de ne pas être pris en surprise
> comme à Drancy. (17 March 1942)

> After the soup, rumours were doing the rounds. There are French police in
> the camp: some say this means that the French are taking over the running
> of the camp, others think we will be deported. As soon as we heard that,
> people started preparing their luggage, getting ready to take everything
> with them so as not to be taken by surprise as we were at Drancy.

Boredom is preferable. The habitual is also the familiar, and Castro's diary
records the process of familiarization as his internment goes on. He is stoical: 'I force myself to drink the soup, I must get used to it' (25 August 1941);
'the soup is always the same, we no longer notice it' (27 August 1941);
'we're getting used to these miserable meals' (7 September 1941); 'hunger
is not bothering me as much as before, my stomach is getting used to it,
even so, I do wonder how we'll get through the winter' (22 October 1941).
Habit is calming, regularity is predictable: 'we're beginning to know the
camp and getting used to this life' (22 August 1941); 'I go down to roll-call;
nobody says a word, everything is calm, we're used to it' (28 September
1941); 'life in the camp is regular and calm' (25 October 1941); 'life goes
on; it's sad and calm' (25 November 1941).

In the closed world of the camp, habit, routine, the reassurance of predictability, take on the calming properties of the worry beads. Outside,
major events are taking place, but it is not until the transferees get to
Compiègne that they have access to news, through the good offices of
the political prisoners. However, Castro is cut off from news of his family, notably his wife, who is pregnant. Stoical when he is focused on his
own survival, he finds this deprivation far more difficult. He has to pull
himself together and bolster his morale to keep going: 'Je reste triste
accoudé au balcon, pensant au triste sort de ma femme et du mien, je
me reprends et me dis en moi même, qu'il faut avoir du courage et de
la patience et il ne faut pas se laisser abattre' (24 August 1941; I spend
some time sadly leaning over the balcony, thinking of my sad fate and
that of my wife; I gather myself up and say to myself that I must have
patience and courage, that I must not let myself get dejected).

Four months after his arrest, the baby is born; his emotions all but defeat him:

> Je suis heureux d'apprendre la bonne nouvelle; je suis soulagé que ma femme et les enfants se portent bien; mais d'autre part quel malheur pour moi de ne pas assister à cette joie, et pouvoir embrasser mes enfants; j'ai les larmes aux yeux. Enfin je me reprends et descends dans la cour afin de donner plus libre cour à ma pensée; heureusement pour moi, je ne me laisse pas abattre et me remonte aussitôt. (8 December 1941)

> The news makes me happy, and I'm relieved that my wife and the children are well. But on the other hand, what misfortune not to be there to share the joy, not to be able to embrace my children. I have tears in my eyes. Eventually I pick myself up and go down to the yard to give myself space to think; luckily, I don't get dejected and feel better immediately.

He is all too aware that 'if I want to see my wife and children, I mustn't give up, I have to stay positive' (2 September 1941).

If hell is defined as the condition in which every day is the same, the camp is hell: Castro is totally cut off from his everyday life in which small and big personal events mark dates and make changes. This cutting off is the effect of his arrest, which brings about a radical change in his life story. The next unpleasant surprise occurs with the transfer to Compiègne. The prisoners are told only that they are being moved; the news 'n'est pas de bonne augure' (is not a good sign); 'nous avons le pressentiment que quelque chose d'anormal va se passer' (12 December 1941; we have the feeling that something abnormal is going to happen). In yet another petty gesture of power, the authorities have not revealed their intentions: 'Avec la précipitation qu'on nous a enlevés de Drancy, rien de bon ne me dis ce voyage forcé' (ibid.; Given the haste with which we were taken from Drancy, this forced journey doesn't look good).

Not only do the authorities exacerbate their anxieties by not telling them their destination or the purpose of the transfer – it could have heralded deportation – but they also foster an experience of time where the present itself emprisons them with no window to the future, let alone a door. Not knowing if he will be alive the next day, Castro distributes most of the contents of the food parcel he has received at Drancy. He then realizes that the voyage may take several days, so he keeps some of it back (ibid.). However, the move to Compiègne is not the final voyage; nor is it a change in the routine. It is a mere repetition of the first arrest, bringing more of the same: 'Pour ceux de Drancy qui avons déjà souffert pendant 4 longs mois et recommencer ces souffrances dans des conditions

plus effroyables, c'est un cauchemard mortel ... nous sommes effrayés'
(1 January 1942; For those from Drancy who have already suffered for
four months, it's a deathly nightmare to think that the same suffering is
to start again, in worse conditions. We're scared).

Their fear is justified because the conditions are indeed worse. That
winter was particularly severe, and along with the cold, the internees
are beset by lice and fleas: 'voici un misère de plus qui s'ajoute à nos
misères' (15–22 January 1942; yet another misery to add to our miseries). Even the rations are more meagre (ibid.), and hunger defines
their experience of time: 'À midi on a eu la soupe réglementaire, et le
soir nous dînons d'un bout de pain avec la margarine. Ainsi s'écoulent
les journées' (24 January 1942; At midday we had the regulation soup,
and in the evening we sup on a bit of bread with margarine. That's how
the days pass).

The pattern persists: the days pass in hunger and sleep. The men
exchange visits when their strength permits (26 January 1942), but by
March 'tout le monde ... est à bout ... Chacun reste chez soi, ce n'est
plus comme au début qu'on se rendait visite; chacun pense à soi, il n'y
a plus d'esprit de camaraderie' (1–17 March 1942; everyone is at the
end of their rope. We stay in our own places, it's not like it was at the
beginning when we could go visiting; everyone thinks only of themselves,
there is no spirit of camaraderie). This is change of sorts, the progressive
deterioration of the body, registered in expressions such as 'no longer,'
'less and less,' 'more and more': 'Plus que jamais on grelotte de froid
on est de plus en plus faible, on passe les journées à être allongés au lit
on n'a goût à rien; on crève de faim et les poux font leur apparition'
(1 February 1942; More than ever, we shiver with cold, we are weaker
and weaker, we spend the days in bed, without the will to do anything;
we're dying of hunger, and we've begun to see lice). 'Je me vois mourir
de jour en jour je m'affaiblis' (25–8 February 1942; I'm watching myself
die, I'm weaker by the day). We are reminded of Schatzman when we
read 'Par curiosité je me suis regardé dans la glace, je ne me reconnais
plus' (15 March 1942; Out of curiosity, I looked at myself in the mirror;
I no longer recognize myself).

The last three months tell of such physical weakness that Castro can
barely stand up. Survival consists in living only for the day: 'as long as
we're warm today, we no longer think about tomorrow' (12 January
1942). He continues to proclaim his courage, but his comrades are
worried (25–8 February 1942). Despair is the opposite. If he can artic-
ulate the sense of fading hope in January – 'nous restons oisif toute la
journée et sans grand espoir de sortir d'ici' (30 January 1941; we're idle
all day, with little hope of getting out) – by 17 March he has no sense of

desire ('Je n'ai goût à rien') and he is losing his memory ('je perds la mémoire'). Time is reduced to now.

This loss of memory is evident in dating errors: there are two entries for the 24 January, and again for the 28th. Twice he writes 3 January, the second time no doubt for 3 February. There is one entry for the period of 1 to 17 March, then, following it, entries dated 15, 16, and 17. This is a man who uses the expression 'on ne compte plus les jours' (30 September 1941; we can't keep count of the days) in order to sum up his sense of interminable waiting, yet who keeps meticulous count not only by dating but by numbering each entry. He gets to 86 (15 November), but sometimes miscounts: 1 November has three titles, twice '101' and the third '72.' The count is interrupted between 15 and 18 November, then ceases definitively following 7 December. For the rest of his internment, he 'no longer counts the days.'

Not only does Castro lose his memory, he also loses his grasp of the very mnemonic techniques he has used to track the days; counting and, notably, keeping his diary on a daily basis. There are brief interruptions in October, in November, and again in January. In February, there are only five entries. The first fortnight of March is a total blank, followed by four entries; then he continues regularly from 15 March until his release a week later. Despair, the expressed wish to die quickly rather than by the slow death of starvation, physical weakness, and the need to spend more time sleeping than conscious, these processes converge in these all too eloquent gaps. Then, in the final week, he is so sick that he can only hope for transfer to the infirmary and the better diet it promises: it is during this week that he again keeps his diary regularly.

As we know, he is not the only internee at Compiègne who hopes to be sick enough for a spell in the infirmary. This paradoxical hope allows him again to envisage an end, an end to hunger, if not to incarceration. Before then, what he had lost in the previous two months is everything that his beads had promised – moving them one by one along the string, getting to the end, then starting again – a regular rhythm that obliges the user of a *komboloí* to maintain a stoical patience, over and over again. For the person who makes it, then refashions it, there is a future: when he uses it constantly, the days might well be all the same, each structured by the same routine, but each has a beginning and an end. He counts the days as he tells his beads, one by one. This is no longer the case at Compiègne, where the need to get up for roll-call or for the meagre meals is nothing but an interruption to the oblivion of sleep. Days such as these have no end; there are no days.

Paul Ricoeur writes of the Heideggerian analysis of within-time-ness that 'it is defined by one of the basic characteristics of care – our thrownness among things – which makes the description of our temporality dependent upon the description of the things of our concern [... They are] the subsisting things which our concern counts on [and] utensils offered to our manipulation.'[42] Castro's string of beads is both: making it and manipulating it, its status as a future souvenir, demonstrate that relating with an object is yet another way of living in time. It also has the felicitous property of representing metaphorically the very point of Ricoeur's theory of narrative: 'the simplest story,' he writes, 'escapes the ordinary notion of time conceived of as a series of instants succeeding one another along an abstract line in a single direction.' A string of events is 'configured' into a story by eliciting 'a pattern from a succession.'[43] This pattern – an eternal return – its constant reiteration in manipulating the beads and in writing the diary, is broken when Castro himself is broken by the conditions; when he returns home, he takes the diary up again, casting the pattern into the fictional space of a nightmare and hoping thereby to plot its end.

Understanding Castro's string of beads therefore stands at the very centre of what it is to read and to write about a diary. Does it plot itself at the same time as recording its days? Or is it the reader who configures the record of those days, getting them to tell a story that emerges only because we know the ending? Ricoeur writes that 'retelling takes the place of telling'; the apprehension of the end implied in the beginning grasps the 'episodes as leading to this end.'[44] This is reading, but we should not lose sight of the process of the writing, the painstaking telling of the days.

As the manuscript of the diary attests, Castro reviewed and revised his text as he proceeded.[45] This reworking demonstrates a parallel with the remaking of the string of beads when he changed the design. Castro undertook his writing as he undertook this other task, in the spirit of a careful craftsman. The revisions he made are evidence that he expects the account he has written in the camp to be read. I summarize changes made to the episode of 10 December (see above; for the full text, see the appendix).[46] The reader will not have been present, so the logic of the events and the posture of the participants – not evident in the first draft – need to be made explicit. At the same time, Castro takes care to maximize the impact on the internees of the petty brutalities of the guard; he avoids a rhetoric of the emotions, instead achieving his goal by means of manipulating the relation between clauses and bringing out the parallels between the guard's humiliation of the veteran by sneering at his medals and his threat to Castro to confiscate the string of beads. This parallelism is the pattern he makes from the string of gestures recounted.

We watch in this passage the way Castro transforms a routine event into a story, engaging his reader in the sequence of events in order to reveal their meaning. The worry beads are doing their job – Castro plays 'nervously' with them in his pocket – and they are precious for this reason. They are also precious in themselves as a crafted item, something not to be lost but also, therefore, vulnerable to the petty actions of the guard. They must be protected, like the diary, which Castro hides carefully to ensure it is not confiscated during searches, in the same way as other internees hide their money and their watches. Protecting both beads and diary, polishing them, revising the narration of his diary, Castro stakes his claim to a future beyond the camp in which he communicates his experience of shrinking time to another place in a restored temporality.

Jean Oppenheimer's Tartine

Jean Oppenheimer was born in Germany but settled in France at the end of his secondary schooling. A resistance activist, he was arrested in September 1943 and taken to Drancy where, with others, he was involved in digging an escape tunnel. It was discovered by the Germans, with the consequence that he and his comrades were deported. He was taken to Birkenau and from there to the labour camp at Monowitz. On 9 January 1945, he was admitted to the infirmary, where he remained after the evacuation of Auschwitz. When Soviet troops arrived on 27 January, he was cared for in an improvised hospital, then transported to a displaced persons camp at Katowice, Poland, on 11 March.

Following this, Oppenheimer waits for months to be repatriated. He starts a diary, his *Journal de route*, recording his experience of the threshold between the living death of the concentration camp (where he had tried to suicide) and the gradual opening of his horizon to the future.

In the course of his diary, he starts to record his memories of the camp, among which we read his retrospective account of waiting: memories dry up and the future is blocked: 'À la longue, même entre amis intimes, les conversations languissent, la vie stupide façonne les hommes à son image, l'évocation de souvenirs tarit. Et faire des projets d'avenir serait absurde, quel sera notre avenir, en avons-nous seulement un?' (2 April 1945, 115; In the end, even among close friends, conversation flags, a life of stupidity forms men in its own image, memories dry up. And it would be absurd to plan for the future: what could it be? do we even have one?). Time is reduced to 'now' through the survival strategy of living only in the present: 'effacer les souvenirs afin de vivre, de vivre le moment présent, de ne vivre que pour le moment présent [...] sans penser à rien, ni au passé, ni à l'avenir' (ibid.; erasing memories in order to live, to live in the present moment, to live only for the present moment [...] thinking of nothing, neither of the future nor of the past). As in the radical shrinkage suffered by Saül Castro, the specious present loses its prow and its stern: now is all there is when you don't know if there will be another minute of life.

Waiting when nothing happens, even under more hopeful circumstances, when one is on the brink of a future but its advent is suspended, is not unlike this. It is under such circumstances that Oppenheimer starts his diary. There is nothing to note, just the day: 'Dès le matin, je prends mon journal pour y consigner pas grand-chose, car peu de remarquable se passe pour couper les journées' (23 March 1945, 49; As soon as I begin my morning, I take up my diary to write in it nothing in particular, because nothing remarkable happens to break up the days). Contrast this with his evocation of time under normal circumstances, where even minute variety serves to distinguish one day from the next: 'C'est le superflu qui est le plus nécessaire dans la vie, le piment qui assaisonne, le petit rien qui satisfait, le désir qui attire, le geste qui marque les jours et rompt leur succession, leur déroulement uniforme' (13 April 1945, 183; The most necessary thing in life is what is superfluous, the piquant spice, the little nothing that makes all the difference, enticing desire, gestures that mark the days and break up their monotonous succession). Gradually, as he and his comrades start receiving enough to eat, he can write: 'Les jours se suivent et ne se ressemblent pas. Il y a moins de quatre mois à l'article de la mort par famine et inanition, il y a deux semaines, il n'y avait pas assez, maintenant il y en de a trop' (30 April 1945, 234; The days follow one another and are not alike. Less than four months ago, [we were] close to death from famine and starvation, two weeks ago, there was not enough, now there is too much). If starvation all but eclipses time for Saül Castro, having enough to eat revives it for Jean Oppenheimer: the days no longer resemble one another; there is a future.

Well before these prisoners of the liberation become liberated prisoners, a false rumour gives him hope that he is reaching the end of waiting:

Tout arrive donc, même la réalisation du désir le plus cher de l'heure actuelle: le rapatriement à courte échéance. Quelles que soient la durée du trajet en wagon à bestiaux d'ici à Odessa, les fatigues et les inconvénients, tout est accepté sans rechigner puisqu'au bout on croit déjà apercevoir un coin de France, tant attendu, tant chéri. (25 March 1945, 56)

So anything can happen, even the fulfilment of one's dearest desire of the present moment: repatriation shortly. However long the journey in cattle wagons from here to Odessa, whatever the fatigue and discomfort, we'll accept everything without complaint because at the end of it all we glimpse already the cherished corner of France we have waited for for so long.

This premature glimpse of France, *déjà*, is like this other: he anticipates eating a *tartine*: 'Décidément, je me suis fait des illusions en croyant manger déjà une tartine épaissement garnie de beurre. Eh bien non, ce ne sera pas encore pour aujourd'hui' (20 March 1945, 44; Decidedly I have been deluded, believing I was already eating a piece of thickly buttered bread. Well no, not yet, that won't be happening today). In both, the anticipation of 'already' meets the disappointment of 'not yet.' The two converge also in the following: news of other released prisoners allows him to measure his experience against the timeline governing that of the more fortunate group. Their good luck is not ours, yet, but it contains a promise: 'On dit que ceux de Cracovie sont partis pour Odessa, que de là des convois partent pour la France et qu'il y en a qui sont déjà arrivés' (13 April 1945, 180; They say that the Krakow group have left for Odessa, and that from there the convoys are leaving for France; some have already arrived).

Oppenheimer's wait did eventually end. After many delays and disappointments, 'On tient le bon bout maintenant, c'est sûr, car nous sommes à bord.' (4 May 1945, 237; This time it's a sure thing, we're on our way, we're on board). Travelling through the Bosphorus in relative luxury, waiting takes on a quite different flavour: 'J'attends de voir la suite, mais je suis sûr de ne pas être déçu' (ibid., 239; I'm waiting for the sequel, but I'm certain I won't be disappointed). On Sunday 6 May, enjoying the leisure, the sunshine, and the food, waiting is reduced to a single week: 'Et dimanche prochain, on prendra l'apéritif à la maison' (244; And next Sunday, an *apéritif* at home). The final entry is written while the ship is waiting to dock. Waiting is such a deeply engrained habit that he continues to doubt that it will end, but he corrects himself immediately: 'Avec envie, j'ai regardé tout l'après-midi vers le port et la ville si proche – et si loin à la fois. Mais heureusement cela ne va pas durer' (9 May 1945, 249; Longingly I look all afternoon at the port and the city, so close, and so far away. But happily that will not last). At last, on the eve of his return home, he anticipates a future already stated in the present: 'Je suis heureux ... d'avoir enfin cet affreux cauchemar à l'état de souvenir' (ibid.; I am happy ... to put this frightful nightmare in its place as a memory).

However, we know from other survivors that the memory may haunt him. Saül Castro tells the story of his return, his little daughter's failure to recognize him, the distress of his wife and mother-in-law at his appearance, and his first night in his own bed:

> Impossible de dormir cette nuit j'ai eu des cauchemards mes souvenirs sont encore dans ma mémoire, je me vois parmi mes copins dans le camp, souffrant de la faim et du froid, je me reveille en sursaut et me tâte, me demandant ce qu'il m'arrive; quel horrible cauchemard! (23 March 1942)

> Sleep was impossible last night. I had nightmares, my memories are still in my memory. I can see myself among my mates in the camp, suffering from hunger and cold, I start up, wondering what has happened to me; what a horrible nightmare.

It is remarkable that Castro uses the dreamt nightmare as an attempt to reduce the lived nightmare to the level of fiction. He can wake from it. This is similar to Oppenheimer's attempt to put it in its place. However, Castro's nightmare does not stay in the past: 'mes souvenirs sont encore dans ma mémoire' (my memories are still in my memory). Haunting the present of memory, his memories were to remain in his body. He died barely three years after his release, from sudden cardiac arrest, almost certainly a consequence of the severe undermining of his system under the camp regime.

Oppenheimer's *tartine* recalls a childhood pleasure, no doubt, a memory of his *goûter* after school, a kind of reward for getting through the day, and a proof of the comfort of home. Remembered, it is nostalgically evoked to promise the end of the rigours of his recent existence. He did get out of the concentrationary universe and back into the reassuring space of home; no doubt he had his pre-dinner drinks and his *tartines*, if rationing and the shortage of butter allowed. There was white bread and butter on board the repatriation ship (4 May 1945, 239), and sweetened milk (*lait sucré*) sipped with a spoon (8 May 1945, 247): comfort indeed, and a taste of the future.[47] Unlike Saül Castro, he lived into his nineties, and until 2002, he was an active member of the national association of survivors.[48] This was another way, perhaps, of living in the present with his memories.

The Posthumous Life of Hélène Berr

Hélène Berr was born to a prominent assimilated French Jewish family whose ascendance can be traced to the early eighteenth century in Alsace and Lorraine. Like many others, her forebears moved to Paris after the Franco-Prussian war. She was a gifted violinist and student of English literature, with a promising future in post-graduate studies. The first entry of her diary is 7 April 1942; she was twenty-one years old. The last entry is dated 15 February 1944; she was arrested on 8 March 1944, just prior to her twenty-third birthday, and killed a little over a year later, at Bergen-Belsen, five days before it was opened.[49] The diary starts as a typical young girl's diary, recording the activities and preoccupations predictable for someone of her age and class. The 'Jewish diary' emerges slowly, at first appearing punctually among stories of bourgeois normality, then taking over as the raison d'être of the writing.

In the early months of her diary, Berr uses her entries to review the day, report on the moment of writing, and prospect the next day: the pattern is exactly that of the standard specious present. I shall illustrate this pattern with passages from the first few days during which the present and the immediate past are defined by entirely personal issues; under these circumstances, the future too lies very close to home. Yet even at the beginning, the future is the source of constant anxiety. Second, I shall follow the sequence of entries in her diary to tell the story of her life, focusing on what happens to her sense of the future.

The very first entry tells of her visit to the house of Paul Valéry, who, on her request, has left with the concierge a signed dedication in her copy of one of his books. She is thrilled by the dedication, and thrilled by bringing off a bold exploit: she has the feeling that 'the extraordinary is the real' (*Journal of Hélène Berr*, 7 April 1942, 16). She is waiting for her English teacher and observing the weather as she writes. On the next day, a picnic is planned: 'je pensais à demain avec joie' (7 April 1942, 18; 'I was thinking joyfully about tomorrow' [16]) and the whole evening is given over to the preparations. Following the outing, she gives us a splendid illustration of the presence of the past:

> Tout cela me semble à la fois étrangement près et étrangement loin. Je sais que c'est fini, que je suis ici, dans ma chambre et en même temps j'entends les voix, je revois les visages et les silhouettes, comme si j'étais entourée de fantômes vivants. C'est que la journée n'est plus tout à fait Présent, et n'est pas encore Passé. Le calme environnant est tout bruissant de souvenirs et d'images. (8 April 1942, 21)

> All that now seems strangely close and strangely distant. I know it's over, that I'm here in my bedroom, and at the same time I can hear the voices, see the faces and shapes, as if I were surrounded by living ghosts. It's because the day is no longer entirely Present but not yet quite Past. (18)

Filled with joy on going to bed, she nevertheless wakes up unhappy the next morning, having 'planned nothing beyond' the outing, and being

totally 'unprepared' for the immediate future, let alone for a future without a close friend who is leaving Paris: 'comment vais-je faire sans elle
maintenant?' (9 April 1942, 21; 'how will I cope without her?'* [19]).
This pattern – today, now, tomorrow – is confirmed in the entries that
follow. Her mood is volatile: 'Pour l'instant, cela va mieux. Mais il y a
encore demain à passer' (21 May 1942, 48; 'For the moment I feel better.
But there's still tomorrow to get through' [45]). Some of this volatility is
caused by a dilemma of the heart: 'l'avenir s'est éclairé subitement parce
que j'ai pensé à lui pendant un long instant' (48; 'the future suddenly
brightened because I thought about him for a long while' [45]).

The bright and the foreboding: almost immediately, the personal
future will be intertwined with the darker dimension of her life as a Jew
in France. I have noted earlier in this chapter her use of *déjà* in the
following passage: 'Mais je ne veux pas faire de la peine à Maman. Déjà
ce soir Papa a reçu un avis de spoliation, et Maman prend tout cela sur
son dos, et cache tout' (11 April 1942, 24; 'But I don't want to upset
Maman. Already this evening Papa got an expropriation notice, and
Maman is taking everything on herself and showing nothing'* [22]). It
is a moment where her personal life and the realities of the persecution
coincide, yet here she resists the intertwining, preferring to keep her
personal preoccupations to herself. Bestowing the responsibility of the
adult world on the adults, she uses the diary to settle her intimate feelings, then, drawing a line she writes: 'Pensons à autre chose' (11 April
1942, 25; 'Let's think about something else' [22]). What follows is the
evocation of remembered happiness, called on to block out the future.
University life also takes on this function, placing her, as she writes herself, in '[un] territoire enchanté' (16 April 1942, 29; 'an enchanted
land' [27]). Yet nothing can keep the grim realities at bay. A fellow student tells her that 'son père était mort au camp de concentration de
Pithiviers [...] La pensée de cette mort me hantait et rendait absolument
inexistant tout le reste' (4 June 1942, 54–5; 'her father had died in the
Pithiviers concentration camp. The thought of that death haunted me
and turned everything else into nothing' [51]). On the same day, the
decree imposing the wearing of the yellow star is proclaimed. The present is destabilized, demanding decisions in the immediate future and
opening into a speculation as to the longer term: 'Où cela peut-il nous
mener?' (11 April 1942, 54; 'Where will this lead?' [50]).

Later the same month, her father is arrested on the pretext that his star
is not appropriately attached. It needed to be permanent, whereas her
mother had attached it with hooks and eyes so it could be worn on different suit jackets (24 June 1942; *Journal*, 76): the provident housewife has a
different view of the future from that of the police. The law requires that

the badge of identity be permanently affixed. Visiting him in prison with her mother and sister, Hélène sets to work with needle and thread: 'mon esprit était occupé par le présent' (ibid., 80; 'my mind was busy with the present'* [75]), but, 'par moments, j'avais de vagues pressentiments du futur immédiat, de ce qui allait suivre ces deux heures' (80; 'in flashes, I had obscure misgivings about the immediate future and what would follow those two hours'* [75]). Until Raymond Berr is released three months later, present and future are consumed in waiting. 'Nous vivons heure par heure, non plus semaine par semaine' (2 July 1942, 96; 'we live from hour to hour, no longer from week to week').[50] During the same period, Hélène Berr must say goodbye to friends who are leaving Paris to escape the occupiers. Not only will the future be defined by absences; she has the sensation that they, like the properly sewn-on yellow star, are permanent, definitive. 'Françoise s'en va la semaine prochaine, et j'ai l'impression qu'elle ne reviendra pas. J'ai l'impression que l'irrévocable se produit, je ne sais pas si je reverrai aucune des personnes qui me quittent' (9 July 1942, 101; 'Françoise is going next week, and I have the feeling she will never come back. My sense is that the irrevocable is coming to pass; I don't know if I'll ever see again any of the people who are leaving me' [94]). The atmosphere around her is of a world ending (ibid.). This sense of the impermanence of ordinary life and the permanence of the current state of affairs comes to pervade the diary. Anti-Jewish decrees follow in quick succession, affecting every aspect of life – shopping times, riding in the metro, a curfew uniquely for Jews. The summer of 1942 was fearsome.

Information circulating on 2 July was the first the family heard of an intention to 'lock up all Jews'; the raids were expected for 15th. The rumours of massive round-ups continue:

Quelque chose se prépare, quelque chose qui sera une tragédie, *la* tragédie peut-être.

M. Simon est arrivé ce soir à dix heures nous prévenir qu'on lui avait parlé d'une rafle pour après-demain, vingt mille personnes. J'ai appris à associer sa personne avec des catastrophes.

Journée commencée avec la lecture de l'ordonnance nouvelle chez le cordonnier, terminée ainsi. (15 July 1942, 11 p.m.; 104–5; emphasis in original)

Something is brewing, something that will be a tragedy, maybe *the* tragedy.

M. Simon came over this evening at 10 p.m. to warn us that he'd been told about a round-up for the day after tomorrow, twenty-thousand people. I've learned to associate the man with disasters.

Day began by reading the new order at the bootmaker's, ended this way.*
(97; emphasis in original)

The rumours were confirmed in the police actions of the next two days;
the plan was indeed to arrest 20,000 Jews in what became known as the
rafle du Vel d'Hiv; in the event, the full count was something over 13,000,
of whom a third were children. Berr writes in her diary : 'Je reprends ce
journal aujourd'hui. Je croyais jeudi que la vie serait arrêtée. Mais elle a
continué. Elle a repris' (18 July 1942, 105; 'I'm resuming this diary today.
On Thursday I thought life would stop. But it went on. It resumed'*
[98]). We might note her repeated use of apocalyptic analogies in the
foregoing: 'the end of the world,' 'life would stop,' '*the* tragedy'; later we
will see her refer to 'the final act of a play.' Such expressions betoken the
inconceivability of a future beyond these dreadful events. Yet it is *ordinary* life that is ending; the persecutions continue. From this point, she
envisages the future in terms of the consequences of these events: 'Qui
va nourrir les internés de Drancy, maintenant que leurs femmes sont
arrêtées? Les petits ne retrouveront jamais leurs parents. Quelles sont les
conséquences lointaines de cette chose arrivée avant-hier soir, au petit
jour?' (18 July 1942, 106; 'Who is going to feed the internees at Drancy
now that their wives have been arrested? The children will never find
their parents again. What are the long-term consequences of this thing
that happened at dawn the day before yesterday?'* [99]). Note her inability to name the event – *cette chose* – at the same time as her readiness to
think of its practical consequences. These consequences converge with
the work she has volunteered for at the Union générale des israélites
de France (UGIF); inevitably it will increase. This is confirmed by no
other than the wife of the vice-president of the UGIF: 'Dans le métro,
j'ai rencontré Mme Baur,[51] toujours superbe. Mais elle était très abattue
[...] Elle m'a dit que nous aurions beaucoup à faire rue de Téhéran. Elle
ne m'a pas caché non plus que le tour des Françaises allait venir' (18
July 1942, 107; 'In the metro I met Mme Baur, splendid as ever. But she
was very dejected [...] She said that we would have a great deal to do at
headquarters. Nor did she hide the fact that it would soon be the turn of
non-immigrant women'* [99]). Many French-born Jews were under the
illusion that only the immigrant Jewish population would be subject to
internment and deportation; while this distinction did govern the *rafle du
Vel d'Hiv*, the protection it afforded was temporary at best. Interestingly
for any historical assessment of André Baur's role, Mme Baur shows here
that she was not deluded: the French-born women would be next.[52]

This prediction looks forward in the same way as Berr's question concerning the consequences of recent events. There is also a longer term:

'Je note les faits, hâtivement, pour ne pas les oublier, parce qu'il ne *faut pas* oublier' (18 July 1942, 106; emphasis in original; 'I'm noting the facts, in haste, so as not to forget them, because *they must not* be forgotten'* [98]). We might think that Berr is referring to a record for her personal use, yet it joins with what was to become the guiding project of her diary, the bearing of witness. This becomes plain in further entries of the same date: 'Je veux rester encore, pour connaître à fond ce qui s'est passé cette semaine, je le veux, pour pouvoir prêcher et secouer les indifférents' (108; 'I want to stay longer, to know everything about what happened this week, I want to, so I can preach and shake up people who don't care'* [100]). And again:

> Au moment où je fermais la lettre, Denise est remontée de chez la crémière et elle m'a dit, haletante: 'Ça y est, ils ont raflé toutes les femmes et les enfants, ne le dis pas à Maman,' mais je raconterai tout cela en détail – j'ai rajouté un P.S. à ma lettre pour dire cela. (108)

> As I was sealing the letter, Denise came up from the dairy; she was panting as she spoke: 'It's happened, they've rounded up all the women and children, don't tell Maman.' But I will tell it all in detail – I added it in a postscript to my letter.* (100)

She uses any means she can – letters, conversations – to spread knowledge of the events and what they mean; she wants to shake people out of their apathy, spread the word as in a sermon concerning good and evil: 'comment guérira-t-on l'humanité autrement qu'en lui dévoilant d'abord toute sa pourriture, comment purifiera-t-on le monde autrement qu'en lui faisant comprendre l'étendue du mal qu'il commet?' (10 October 1943, 169; 'how will humanity be cured unless we expose its rottenness, how will the world be cleansed unless we make it understand the full extent of the evil it is committing?' [157]). And this, she claims, is why she wants to stay in Paris when the talk around her insists on the advisability of leaving. Yet she also acknowledges that bearing witness is not the only reason: her personal desires motivate her. She has gone to the library to wait for the young man she is falling in love with: 'les journées que je passe avec lui sont les seules belles choses de la vie, je ne veux pas m'en passer' (18 July 1942, 109; 'the days I spend with him are the only beautiful things in life, I don't want to give them up'* [101]); they dispel the nightmare (ibid.). In this jumbled summer of 1942, Hélène Berr cannot envisage her future without Jean, yet, at the same time, her understanding of the future is pervaded by what she learns of the persecutions, her immediate responses to them (telling, writing), and ultimately, 'l'hypothèse de la catastrophe' (18 July 1942, 108; 'the prospect of catastrophe' [101]). In the immediate, however, her present consists of the work she is taking up at the UGIF – 'Enfin, j'ai trouvé quelque chose à faire qui m'empêchera d'être trop égoïste. Je suis contente' (22 July 1942, 116; 'at last I've found something to do that will stop me being too self-centred. I'm glad' [107]) – and her social life, progressively more dominated by her relationship with Jean: 'il y a quelque chose d'enchanté dans ma vie actuellement' (26 July 1942, 119; 'there's an enchantment in my life at present' [110]).

Through August and early September, the diary entries show Berr living for the moment; that's where love is. 'Je ne peux plus écrire ce journal parce que je ne m'appartiens plus entièrement' she writes on 12 September (139; 'I can no longer write this journal because I no longer belong entirely to myself' [129]). Insofar as she notes any sense of the future, it concerns the fate of her father, who is still in Drancy. But on 18 September, she notes that 'on a arrêté les Belges et les Hollandais – José? Je crois que tout va recommencer comme en juin' (141; 'the Belgians and the Dutch have been picked up – José? I think it's all going to begin again, just as it did in June' [131]), and, on the 20th, she is filled with foreboding. As it turns out, this foreboding is fulfilled by news of 'massive deportations': 'c'était donc cela' (141–2; 'so that's what it was' [132]). Later that evening, she reflects on the day, focusing precisely on the awareness of the future in the present. This future is imminent.

> Je me surprends à souhaiter que cette journée soit finie et que le temps passe; et brusquement, je m'aperçois qu'il n'y a *rien* à espérer et tout à redouter de l'avenir, de la journée qui va suivre.
>
> Par moments, ma conscience du malheur imminent s'atténue. À d'autres, elle est aigüe. (142; emphasis in original)

> I find myself wishing that this day would be over and that time would pass: suddenly I realize that there is *nothing* to hope for and everything to fear from the future, from the following day.
>
> At times my awareness of imminent misfortune is muted. At others, it's acute.* (132)

That, for herself; then, for others:

> Tout se prépare et tout attend, comme pour le dernier acte d'une pièce. Pierre Masse a été transféré vendredi de la Santé à Drancy. Il a dit, paraît-il, qu'il savait ce que cela signifiait. Tous sont donc groupés, préparés, pour cette chose horrible, pour cet événement qui va se traduire par le silence

angoissant, l'exil lointain, et une souffrance de chaque heure à partir du moment où il se sera produit. (143)[53]

Preparations are made, and everything is waiting, as if for the last act of a play. On Friday, Pierre Masse was transferred from the Santé prison to Drancy. Apparently he said that he knew what that meant. So they are all brought into one place and prepared for this horrible thing, for this event that will be lived in anxious silence, in distant exile, in constant suffering from the moment it takes place.* (133)

The last act of a play: Hélène Berr imagines the end as silence, exile, and suffering. She cannot imagine the fate that we now know awaited these deportees.[54] But she can imagine the next act of a scenario closer to Paris: she has been told that massive deportations from Drancy will have emptied the camp within a few days: 'Avec quoi le remplira-t-on maintenant?' she asks sardonically (20 September 1942, 143; 'What will they fill it with now?' [133]).[55] Spared at the last minute from inclusion in the deportation, her father is released, but she knows 'ce qui va se passer cette nuit et demain' (22 September 1942, 146; 'what is going to happen tonight and tomorrow' [136]) for the others. At the UGIF, the work necessitated by these events was frantic: 'nous avons travaillé comme si c'était *après* le jugement dernier' (146, emphasis in original; 'we worked as if the last judgment had already happened' [135]). The last act, the last judgment, 'la fin d'un monde' (23 September 1942, 148; 'the end of a world'* [138)]): 'J'ai failli perdre mon équilibre' (148; 'I nearly lost my equilibrium' [138]). The same afternoon, she receives a message from her professor at the Sorbonne:

Il m'a fait discuter sur l'avenir, alors que j'étais dans un état anormal. Tout ce dont il me parlait, ce qu'il me demandait semblait venir d'un autre monde où je ne rentrerai plus. Il y a une espèce de glas qui sonne en moi, lorsque j'entends parler de livres, de professeurs à la Sorbonne. (149)

He made me discuss the future, but I was not in a normal state of mind. Everything he talked about, everything he asked me seemed to come from another world to which I would never return. There's a kind of death knell that tolls inside me whenever I hear talk of books and of professors at the Sorbonne. (138)

The life story of Hélène Berr is on the verge of what Fiona Kaufman calls 'de-emplotment,' the disintegration of the 'familiar life paradigm' in which 'the causal story and causal mechanisms, [are] all woven together,

[to] produce an outcome.'[56] This is predictable: with de-emplotment, the past no longer predicts the course of the future. In Berr's account, above, this is represented by the metaphor of two separate worlds between which there is no solution of continuity. Each might have its own future, but she cannot envisage that of the familiar world; the requirement to do so, as if the persecutions were irrelevant, provokes a crisis – 'I was not in a normal state of mind.' In her writing, de-emplotment is represented by entries in which the review of the day and the feelings of the present block out any consideration of the future. This series continues through October, until 'brusquement, tout s'est déchiré' (29 October 1942, 160; 'then suddenly it all fell apart' [148]): Jean has decided to sign up for the Free French and is about to leave. At the same time, there is better news on the war front, 'c'est peut-être le commencement de la fin' (8 November 1942, 161; 'perhaps it's the beginning of the end' [150]),[57] and she returns to the Sorbonne for the the beginning of term.

Then nothing: she desists from keeping her diary until August 1943, when she gets it out to have it taken into safe keeping: the future of the diary itself is in jeopardy. To complete it, she notes simply the key events of the past ten months, closing on a question: 'Que se sera-t-il passé lorsque je reprendrai ce journal?' (25 August 1943, 167; 'What will have happened when I resume keeping this diary?' [155]). She sends the extant volumes away, then, in mid-October, she starts to write regular entries again. The reason is firmly planted in the future – not her own, but the work the diary will do in the world:

J'ai un devoir à accomplir en écrivant, car il faut que les autres sachent. À chaque heure de la journée se répète la douloureuse expérience qui consiste à s'apercevoir que *les autres* ne savent pas, qu'ils n'imaginent même pas les souffrances d'autres hommes, et le mal que certains infligent à d'autres. Et toujours j'essaie de faire ce pénible effort de *raconter*. Parce que c'est un devoir, c'est peut-être le seul que je puisse remplir. Il y a des hommes qui savent et qui se ferment les yeux, ceux-là, je n'arriverai pas à les convaincre, parce qu'ils sont dur, et égoïstes, et je n'ai pas d'autorité. Mais les autres, ceux qui ne savent pas, et qui ont peut-être assez de cœur pour comprendre, ceux-là, je dois agir sur eux. (10 October 1943, 169)

I have a duty to write, because other people must know. Every hour of every day there is another grievous experience of realizing that *others* do not know, do not even imagine, the suffering of other men, the evil that some inflict on others. And I persist in my attempts to fulfil this arduous task of *telling the stories*. Because it is a duty, perhaps the only one I can fulfil. There are men who know and close their eyes to it, I'll never convince people like that, because they are hard-hearted and selfish, and I have no authority. But there are others who don't know, and who perhaps have the heart to understand; those are the ones I must act on.* (157)

From this point, there are very few mentions of a personal future in the diary, except this negative reflection: 'Craindre sans cesse pour les siens, ne pas pouvoir faire le moindre projet d'avenir, même le plus proche' (29 November 1943, 237; 'fearing endlessly for your loved ones, unable to make the least plan for the future, even the immediate future'* [222]).

She has brief moments of revolt:

Est-ce que beaucoup de gens auront eu conscience à 22 ans qu'ils pou-vaient brusquement perdre toutes les possibilités qu'ils sentaient en eux – et je n'éprouve aucune timidité à dire que j'en sens en moi d'immenses, puisque je les considère comme un don qui m'est fait, et pas comme une propriété –, que tout pourrait leur être ôté, et ne pas se révolter ? (27 October 1943; 188–9)

Would many people at the age of 22 be conscious that they could lose all the possibilities that they feel in themselves – I feel no shame saying that mine are immense, because I consider them to be a gift and not a possession – and that everything could be taken from them, without rebelling?* (175)

Shortly after writing this, at the period of the *rentrée* of 1943–44, she makes plans: 'Maintenant, mon impression: je suis débordante de projets ... c'est un jalon dans l'avenir si sombre' (4 November 1943; 214–15; 'This is my impression now: I'm overflowing with plans ... this is a stake in the darkness of the future'* [199]),[58] but the plans are short-lived:

Il y a huit jours, j'étais pleine d'enthousiasme pour travailler. Mais ce n'était qu'un état passager. Je savais bien que c'était une illusion. Elle a été dissipée par un petit fait, sans grande importance en soi, mais qui a cristallisé beaucoup d'autres éléments [...] Et puis, sans beaucoup de peine d'ailleurs [...] j'ai renoncé à essayer de travailler mon agrégation. (12 November 1943, 222–3)

A week ago, I was brimming with enthusiasm for work. But it was just a pass-ing phase. I was well aware that it was an illusion. It was dispelled by a little event, unimportant in itself, but which crystallized a lot of other things [...] And then, without much difficulty in fact [...] I gave up working for my *agrégation*.* (208)

As a Jew, Hélène Berr was excluded from formal enrolment in the *agré-gation*, but she was authorized to attend lectures. She used this authori-zation to prepare for the examination, which she hoped ultimately to sit, on the assumption that the current state of affairs – Vichy, the decrees against the Jews, the Occupation, and the deportations – would end some time. But it is not over, nor likely to be. It continues 'all the time'; the awful events recur with 'diabolical regularity':

> Et penser que chaque personne nouvelle qui est arrêtée, hier, aujourd'hui, à cette heure même, est sans doute destinée à subir ce sort terrible. Penser que ce n'est pas *fini*, que cela continue tout le temps avec une régularité diabolique. Penser que si je suis arrêtée ce soir (ce que j'envisage depuis longtemps) je serai dans huit jours en Haute-Silésie, peut-être morte, que toute ma vie s'éteindra brusquement, avec tout l'infini que je sens en moi. (1 November 1943, 209; emphasis in original)

> And to think that every single person arrested yesterday, today, this very minute, is probably destined to suffer this dreadful fate. To think it's not over, that it continues incessantly, with diabolical regularity. To think that if I am arrested this evening (which is something I've been expecting for a long time now), in a week's time I'll be in Upper Silesia, maybe dead, and my whole life will be snuffed out in no time, with the infinity I sense in myself.* (194–5)

So Hélène Berr gives up hope that it would end, thus giving up her stake in the world of 'enchantment' and giving in to the realization that her reality is entirely dominated by what it means to be Jewish in this place and time. Her own life – literally – or her 'official' life (4 February 1944, 273) – now that she and her family are on the run – is at an end. Save for a brief glimmer of hope that the Allies will land before she is deported – 'Irai-je jusqu'au bout? La question devient angoissante. Irons-nous jusqu'au bout?' (10 January 1944, 255; 'Will I make it through? It's an ever more harrowing question. Will we make it through?' [237]) – the foreseeable future lies in anti-Semitic hands. Berr delineates it broadly in two ways. One concerns the daily events – arrests and deportations – while the other concerns the writing and the reading of this diary, which bears witness to them. The two converge as she envisages her personal fate: recording the former, the vocation of her writing *in the future* is to bear the burden of memory.

> Il faudrait donc que j'écrive pour pouvoir plus tard montrer aux hommes ce qu'a été cette époque. Je sais que beaucoup auront des leçons plus grandes

à donner, et des faits plus terribles à dévoiler. Je pense à tous les déportés, à tous ceux qui gisent en prison, à tous ceux qui auront tenté la grande ex-périence du départ. Mais cela ne doit pas me faire commettre une lâcheté, chacun dans sa petite sphère peut faire quelque chose. Et s'il le peut, il le *doit.* (10 October 1943, 171)

So I must write to show people later what these times are like. I know that many others will have more significant lessons to give, and more terrible facts to reveal. I am thinking of all the deportees, of all those put away in prison, all those who took the risk of leaving. But that should not make me a coward; each in our own little sphere can do something. And if we can, we *must.* (159)

Here she raises the problem of genre: what kind of thing could she write? For now, the diary will have to do; it will serve as an *aide-mémoire* for a later work of witness:

Seulement, je n'ai pas le temps d'écrire un livre. Je n'ai pas le temps, je n'ai pas le calme d'esprit nécessaire. Et je n'ai sans doute pas le recul qu'il faut. Tout ce que je peux faire, c'est de noter les faits ici, qui aideront plus tard ma mémoire si je veux raconter, ou si je veux écrire. (10 October 1943, 171–2)

The only thing is that I don't have the time to write a book. I don't have the time, or the necessary tranquillity. And I don't have the distance I'd need. All I can do is note down the facts in this diary; that will help me remember if I want to tell, or write, the stories.* (159)

The diary will 'conserver des souvenirs de ce qui devra être raconté' (27 October 1943, 197; 'preserve memories of what needs to be told' [183]), not hers alone, but those of other people: 'Je suis ouverte à tous les récits d'horreurs, je recueille toutes les tristesses' (12 November 1943, 221; 'I am open to all the stories of horror, I gather all the sad-ness'* [205]). Throughout January 1944, she recounts stories she has heard, reminding herself – and us – insistently that 'il faut que je note quelques faits, de ceux qu'il ne faudra jamais oublier' (24 January 1944, 265; 'I must note down some facts, the kind that must never be forgotten' [247]). Her mother confirms her determination (*Journal*, 14 February 1944, 274), but, she asks, 'Que suis-je pour le raconter, à côté de ceux qui y ont été, et y ont souffert?' (15 February 1944, 274–5; 'Who am I to tell the story in the place of those who were there and who suffered there?' [256]). Nevertheless 'j'ai demandé des détails précis' (15 February 1944,

274–5; 'I asked for precise details' [257]). But these stories will never be adequate to the responsibility she has taken on:

> Et même n'est-ce pas une insulte à la souffrance indicible de toutes ces âmes individuelles, dont chacune a la sienne particulière, que d'en parler sous forme de reportage? Qui dira jamais ce qu'a été la souffrance de chacun? Le seul 'reportage' véridique, et digne d'être écrit, serait celui qui réunirait les récits complets de chaque individu déporté. (15 February 1944, 278)

> Indeed, isn't it an insult to the unspeakable suffering of all these individual souls, each person with his or hers, to speak of them as if for a news story? Who will ever say what each person's suffering has been? The only truthful report worth writing would be one that could include the full story of each individual who is deported. (259–60)

The problem, as she well knows, is that the stories should be told by a survivor: '"Je reviens de Drancy." Qui en parlera?' (15 February 1944, 278; '"I've returned from Drancy." Who will speak of that?'* [259]). But the future is filled with the silence of the dead. Even as she stakes her claim on the future by writing, she dreads the nightmare of the witness: 'ceux qui ne l'auront pas vécu, même mes amis ... à qui je le raconterais, ne réaliseront pas. Ils nous plaindront *nous*, mais ils ne réaliseront pas la portée de ce fait et ces conséquences' (24 January 1944, 266; emphasis in original; 'people who have not had direct experience, even my friends ... who will hear it from me, will never grasp it. They will feel sorry for *us*, but they won't grasp the significance of it, or its consequences'* [248]). To challenge this despair, Hélène Berr devoted her final years to telling other people's stories, to counteract 'the silence of the dead.' However, telling 'the full story of each individual' is impossible. Those of us who study diaries from this period do so in the hope of filling a small part of the void.

On 13 November 1943, Hélène Berr wrote in her diary that she was leading a 'posthumous life.' The comment follows a review of her memories from the previous year, in particular those relating to her family's decision to remain in Paris, and her own, to commit herself actively to relief work under the aegis of the UGIF. In this passage, she rehearses the charge of self-interest levelled against the people who worked there, that they had joined to save their own skin, and alludes to the fact that only by chance was she away from the office when a round-up was conducted and all her friends deported. 'J'oublie que je mène une vie posthume, que j'aurais dû mourir avec eux' (13 November 1943, 227; 'I forget that I am leading a posthumous life, that I should have died with them' [212]). A simple, but reductive, even misleading, construal of this sentence might be that she feels she is living on borrowed time.

Berr is giving voice to an experience described by Susan Brison in her book on surviving trauma: 'The immediate psychological responses to such trauma include terror, loss of control, and intense fear of annihilation. Long-term effects include [...] lack of interest in activities that used to give life meaning, and a sense of a foreshortened future.'[59] To survive trauma, she writes, is often to 'outlive oneself,' to be dominated by such a severe break in the life narrative that there is no continuity between the self of before and the one that survives: 'The ability to form a life plan is lost when one loses a sense of one's temporal being,' she goes on, quoting Primo Levi's account of the shrunken present of the survivor.[60] Under constant threat, bearing witness to the death and suffering of others, appalled by what she knows, and living in grief, Hélène Berr is herself a survivor of trauma: she has 'outlived' her life.

All this is dead, she writes in the same passage, and so is she, since her life has no future. Yet, even as she loses her past and lives on the threshold of death, Hélène Berr's experience of the specious present expands. Her life is passing into history as she writes: 'C'est une question qui m'a toujours angoissée, cette différence entre l'actuel et le passé, le passage du présent au passé, la mort de tant de choses vivantes. En ce moment, nous vivons l'histoire' (25 October 1943, 181; 'This is a question that has always disturbed me, this difference between the present and the past, the movement from present to past, the death of so many living things. At present, we are living History'* [168]).

When the future is death, imminent death in the imminent future, life loses its meaning:

> Je pense à l'histoire, à l'avenir. *À quand nous serons tous morts.* C'est si court la vie, et si précieux. Et maintenant, autour de moi, je la vois gaspiller à tort, criminellement ou inutilement, sur quoi se baser? Tout perd son sens, lorsqu'on est à chaque instant confronté par la mort. (25 October 1943, 181–2; emphasis in original)

> I think about history. I think about the future. *About when we will all be dead.* Life is so short, so precious. And now that I see it being wrongly squandered, criminally or pointlessly all around me, what can I rely on? Everything loses its meaning with death constantly staring you in the face. (169; emphasis in original)

That life might have a meaning depends precisely on the relation of the
past with the present and future. Likewise, with the death of her grandmother, 'nous avons perdu la dernière amarre qui nous fixait notre
place dans le temps, entre le passé et l'avenir' (28 November 1943, 235;
'we have lost the last mooring that gave us our place in time, between
the past and the future'* [219]). It is difficult to avoid the thought that,
painful and personal as this loss was, it stands more generally for the
severing of past and future that Berr records in her diary. Yet even as she
loses her moorings in time, she looks forward:

> Si cela arrive, si ces lignes sont lues, on verra bien que je m'attendais à mon
> sort; pas que je l'aurais accepté d'avance, car je ne sais pas à quel point peut
> aller ma résistance physique et morale sous le poids de la réalité, mais que
> je m'y attendais.
>
> Et peut-être celui qui lira ces lignes aura-t-il un choc à ce moment précis,
> comme je l'ai toujours eu en lisant chez un auteur mort depuis longtemps
> une allusion à sa mort. Je me souviens toujours, après avoir lu les pages que
> Montaigne écrivait sur la mort, d'avoir pensé avec une étrange 'actualité':
> 'Et il est mort aussi, cela est arrivé, il a pensé à l'avance à ce que ce serait
> après,' et j'ai eu comme l'impression qu'il avait joué un tour au Temps.
> (27 October 1943, 190)

> If it [deportation] should happen, and if these lines are read, it will be clear
> that I expected my fate; not that I have accepted it, because I do not know
> how my physical and moral resistance will hold up under the weight of real-
> ity, but that I have expected it.
>
> And perhaps the reader of these lines will be startled at this very moment,
> just as I have been when reading in the work of a long dead author an allu-
> sion to his own death. I remember, when I was reading the passage in which
> Montaigne speaks about his own death, thinking with a curious sense of the
> present: 'And he did die too, it happened, he thought in advance about
> what afterwards would be.' And it seemed to me as if he had played a trick
> on Time itself.* (177)

She has indeed played a trick on time, speaking from the past of her
foresight to the future of our hindsight, at a time when the past is
sutured to the present in the moment of reading. So her claim, that she
is living – in the present tense – a posthumous life, a life after the end of
life, is not paradoxical. The 'I' of the diary writes as it lives, and goes on
living in its death.
   'I lead a posthumous life.' I read a posthumous life. The time of
reading has a stern and a prow: the stories told require us to face the

past, their telling steers us forward, moves us to pursue its purpose. The final entry of the diary retells a witness's story of the massacre of Katyn; Hélène Berr comments that it resembles a story told her by a child in the hospital. The last words she writes are a quotation from *Macbeth*: '*Horror! Horror! Horror!*' They are spoken by Macduff, on seeing the murdered body of the king; the single word repeated is an appalled expression of helplessness at the enormity of the deed. The retellings and the quotations in this diary transmit messages from the past, woven together in a text whose specious present extends to include our own. In Ross Chambers's words, 'intertextuality ... is a human survival device;'[61] each quotation and retelling gives its inherited texts a new point of utterance from which they reach further into an unending future. As mine, of Hélène Berr's, must do.

Coda: The Self in History

Diarists do not write history, if by that we mean formal history drawn from a wide range of documentary sources. Nor would it be possible for them to write the history of their own times, for they would have to know where the events of their experience were to lead, and to occupy a future from which they could trace that trajectory. The future for a diarist, in Jacqueline Mesnil-Amar's words, is nothing but 'the front of the train,' closed, leading no one knows where.[1] On the train, they are *in* history – in the other sense of this word – beset by events as they happen. So they write stories like this one:

> Place de la Concorde, rue Boissy-d'Anglas, de l'hôtel Crillon et de tous les autres organismes allemands s'échappent des petits morceaux de papier calcinés qui nous inondent, tombent sur nos visages, nos cheveux, nos bras. Ces messieurs brûlent leurs archives jour et nuit, en toute hâte, et fiévreusement se préparent au départ. (Mesnil-Amar, *Journal*, 9 August 1944, 73–4)

> At Concorde, in the rue Boissy-d'Anglas, from the Hôtel Crillon and from other German administrative offices, it is raining down little scraps of burnt paper; they land on our faces, our hair, our arms. These gentlemen are burning their archives all day and night, in haste, feverishly preparing for their departure.

Like the scraps of paper from the burning German archives falling onto the hair and bare skin of a woman wearing a summer dress, the events we now count as history touch the self in the most intimate of ways.

This account is appealing, but it is somewhat misleading: it suggests that the individuals are free-standing human beings, rained on by 'history' but not themselves historical. If it is true that the self is constitutively historical, then the diarists I have discussed in this book are not merely touched by the events of the dark years; they were *of* their times, not blank sheets waiting for the horror to be inscribed. Their place in history need not be reduced to that. Let us ask who they were.

One way of doing so without leaving the diaries is to look closely at the reflective passages that we find there. Such passages are not functionally different from the interpretive move in the constitution of experience, but they are elaborated, sustained, and take a more speculative or generalizing form. They 'step off the train,' as it were: what frame of understanding do these individuals use to reflect upon the history that carries them along? I have chosen passages from two diaries to suggest answers to this question, the first from that of a survivor, Jacqueline Mesnil-Amar, who had to find a way to face the future, the second from Benjamin Schatzman, who did not, but who used his diary to bequeath a vision for those he left behind.

I

In this book, I have stressed the specificity of diaries in order to show what kind of work they do that is not done by other first-person genres. The contrast is sharpest with autobiography where the retrospective narrative purports to answer the question 'how did I become who, or what, I am now?' Implied is a sense of having arrived at a provisional stability from which a coherent answer is possible. In diaries, we read the telling of lives not governed by a telos. This is particularly true of diaries written under fearsome circumstances. In time, of the times, and entry after entry, we have watched the writing of a diary used to stabilize and maintain a (sense of) self even as that self is continually subject to forces that undermine it.

However, at two points in her diary, Jacqueline Mesnil-Amar engages in memory writing in the way of autobiography. These two passages are remarkable: in the other diaries I have studied, experience and reflection on it are confined to the time of survival, without access to, or interest in, more distant memories. Unlike them, Mesnil-Amar's diary looks searchingly into the past to reflect on her own life story. It will teach her that Enlightenment universalism as it was translated into civic life under the Third Republic had effected a break with the Jewish past that both fulfilled the desire for emancipation for Europe's Jewish population, and blinded it to the continuities of what she calls the 'ancestral story.' Adumbrated in the diary, and explored in her post-war writings, is an arrival point, stabilized but conflicted; the conflict is never resolved.[2] Telling this story, she locates her experience of identity in a longer and deeper history than the four years of Nazi-occupied France.

Mesnil-Amar's diary was written in the last six weeks of the Occupation, starting when André Amar, her husband, was arrested with other members of his Resistance cell; it finishes with news of his escape from the last train to Auschwitz,[3] and the imminent Liberation of Paris. On the way toward this end, on 6 August 1944, Mesnil-Amar asks why she is invaded by memories on the very evening when she hears the news that the Allied advance is 'driving towards Paris' (54). The answer seems plain: memory is released only when waiting has an outcome, loosening the grip of the anguished present. The same is true of the second memory passage, which follows the first certain news of André, who is 'well' (17 August 1944, 83).

On 6 August, at midnight, the first passage of memory writing concerns the beginning of these four long years, the German advance, the exodus, political news, and Pétain's speeches on the radio along with gestures and scraps of conversation from the period she spent taking refuge in Bordeaux, her family dispersed on the roads: 'Comme je les entends ce soir, seule, ... toutes ces voix humaines qui mourront avec moi' (48; How clearly I hear them this evening in my solitude, ... all these human voices that will die with me). She recalls the first openly anti-Semitic sentiments addressed to her, the first vague news of the persecutory machinery in Poland and Germany, the first manifestation of what the Vichy government was about to bring down (50–1). These memories include the acute sense of betrayal she felt when she began to understand that neither she nor her family would be protected by the people who had constituted their milieu before the war, and the discovery that came with it, that in Vichy France, she was Jewish, not French. She evokes her life in hiding, that of her parents, her first sighting of the yellow star on her sister's blouse, the early days of her Resistance activities, the attempt to live a normal life with false papers, the continual anxiety: 'Mais, toujours, nous avons l'oreille tendue ... Mes nuits, nuits de tous les Juifs, nuits de la peur et des larmes, nuits de nos enfants! Me poursuivrez-vous jusqu'en cette nuit nouvelle?' (63; But we were always on the alert. My nights, the nights of all Jews, nights of fear and weeping, the nights of our children! Am I to be pursued by you into this new night?) The answer is yes, for she recalls 'pell-mell' the unceasing arrests of family and friends.

In the course of this flood of memories of the past four years, she writes that she and her circle had lived in false tranquillity (56) until the 'scandal' of the first arrests – Pierre Masse, Jean-Jacques Bernard – and then the mass round-ups (57): the process of alienation from 'our previous civic' life was gradual, although the calm illusion was 'shattered.' This is a key moment in her revised understanding of a longer past: they made us, she writes, 'Jews from the outside' (ibid.), because we had forgotten it since the Dreyfus affair had effectively been swept under the carpet. Marcel Proust is famous for his observations of the erasure of this memory in the milieu he depicts:[4] for M. de Charlus, for example, the affair was 'une mode vulgaire et fugitive' (a vulgar passing fashion); for others, the 'loathsome' memory of the affair had a vague afterlife.[5] Likewise, notwithstanding the 'oblivion' that had been 'granted' to it ('granted,' like a blessing), it was 'fashionable' – a precautionary measure, perhaps – to relegate it to a 'prehistoric' era.[6] This paradox – of a collective memory present in its very repression[7] – is evident in Proust's writing itself, where reminders of the affair persist throughout the last volume of a work devoted to the presence of the past, and in which errors of social forgetfulness are regularly corrected by the vigilant narrator. It is equally evident in Mesnil-Amar's evocation which points, rather, to the need among assimilated Jews to forget anti-Semitism and to believe in the promise of its defeat. Again, it is Proust who explains the paradox of Jewish life in the aftermath of the affair:

> des suites de l'affaire Dreyfus était né un mouvement antisémite parallèle à un mouvement de pénétration plus abondant du monde par les israélites. Les politiciens n'avaient pas eu tort en pensant que la découverte de l'erreur judiciaire porterait un coup à l'antisémitisme. Mais, provisoirement au moins, un antisémitisme mondain s'en trouvait au contraire accru et exaspéré.[8]

> As a sequel to the Dreyfus affair, there was a rise in anti-Semitism parallel to the increased presence of Jews in high society. The politicians had not been wrong to think that the discovery of the miscarriage of justice would deal a blow to anti-Semitism. But, *a contrario*, at least for a while, it fostered a growth of exasperated anti-Semitism in this milieu.

Mesnil-Amar explains of the Jews of her milieu that, seduced by their own acceptance in this rarefied society, '[their] bourgeois consciousness' was 'deaf to the rest of the world' (6 August 1944, 57). The 'rest of the world' might be represented by Jean-Claude Stern (see chapter 1), whose parents were only too aware, a decade after Proust's death, that the increased prominence of Jews in politics could only leave them vulnerable to a repetition of the 'parallel' to which Proust refers. It is a matter of class: 'nous nous sommes laissé prendre aux mirages de notre classe,' writes Mesnil-Amar, by 'cette culture patricienne' (17 August 1944, 100; we were duped by the illusions of our class, by [its] patrician culture): the hierarchy of the professions in the first part of the century placed the Stern family – engineers, architects – in the ranks of skilled technical workers, alongside dentists such as Benjamin Schatzman, well below the liberal professions, and a long way from the upper echelons of industry, the stock exchange, politics, and high finance, which was the milieu of Mesnil-Amar's father, Jules Perquel. It is also a matter of inclusion, or not, in the Jewish world, Jean-Claude Stern having attended a religious school, by contrast with Mesnil-Amar, who spent her childhood listening to stories of the catechism (17 August 1944, 88). The self is bound by its place in history, blind and deaf to the stories that place cannot know.

And yet the paradox of collective memory and collective amnesia characteristic of the Third Republic means that those stories are there for the learning. And it is a story of this learning that Mesnil-Amar tells us in the passages of memory writing in her diary. The people in whose name she speaks had forgotten that they were Jews (6 August 1944, 57): this was possible because their only memory of the Dreyfus affair was that the captain's exoneration had seemed – as Proust tells us – to put a definitive end to anti-Semitism in France. And hence, to a particular Jewish identity. Accordingly, their life was at peace, comfortable in a country they call 'theirs,' settled into their houses, their seats on directors' boards, their banks and boutiques (ibid.). Yet on the far side of this turning point, the whole messy business of the Dreyfus affair – standing in now for the decades dominated by Drumont's *La France juive*[9] – was waiting to be recalled as the home-grown episode of the ancestral story. Such a touchstone is the expression 'l'affaire Dreyfus' that the return of the repressed is both mysterious, and not. There was, writes Mesnil-Amar, a forgotten habit of living with anti-Semitism: 'Et comment je ne sais quoi de mystérieux et d'ancestral, presque d' "habitué" à cette sorte de malheur, a soudain levé au fond de nos âmes!' (ibid.; And how something mysterious and ancestral, almost habituated to this sort of ill wind, suddenly rose up in the depths of our souls!).[10]

Still believing in the truth of what she later describes as a 'mirage' (17 August 1944, 100), she writes that this was the end of our 'true life' (6 August 1944, 57), and the beginning of a life of wandering and hiding, in which, 'disguised' as pariahs, we begged for a scrap of homeland (ibid.). Yet this disguise made them recognizable as the stereotypical Jew: 'a species of foreigner in their own country, French but different, furtive and over-modest, or people apart, always on the alert' (55). The alternative was to carry unconvincing forged papers (58) and to look like everybody else (55), all the time hearing disgusting insults thrown in our faces while we were wearing 'the impeccable clothes of the pre-war bourgeoisie' (55). This leaves them open to episodes such as the following:

[assis près de moi] ... ce capitaine ... me dit: 'S'il ne tenait qu'à moi, tous ces Rothschild, tous ces Juifs qui s'enfuient, n'iraient pas loin! Je leur prendrais leurs visas, leurs passeports, et les forcerais à rester. Ce sont eux les responsables de la guerre! Tenez, regardez-les, moi, je les reconnais même de dos.' Et mon cri: 'En tout cas, pas de face!' (6 August 1944, 49)

Sitting beside me, this captain ... said: 'If it was up to me, all these Rothschilds, these Jews who are running away, wouldn't get far! I'd take their visas and their passports and I'd force them to stay. They're the ones who caused the war! I mean to say, look at them, I can tell them even from behind.' And my shouted retort: 'Not from in front, in any case!'

Mesnil-Amar is caught between two 'looks,' two ways of being identified, and, hence, two ways of knowing the society that offers her this choice. She, as do her parents, chooses the second, hiding in the open and risking recognition. Not only does this enable her participation in the Resistance, it also fosters her deepened understanding of the place of assimilated Jews in pre-war Paris society. This is the subject of the second long passage of memory writing, dated 17 August (84–103).

The memories are triggered by two things: the first is the story of a friend she is to visit, and the second, the part of Paris this takes her to. Her friend had escaped from Drancy; while there, serving as a nurse, she had cared for André's parents and his grandmother, all deported and killed. Much of André Amar's family, and many of Mesnil-Amar's own relatives, have suffered the same fate, so grief is the tenor of many pages of the journal. Notwithstanding their opening paragraphs, these pages are largely dry-eyed, because Mesnil-Amar, cycling through Paris towards the *beaux quartiers* where her family home was situated, subjects the 'mirage' she lived in as a young assimilated Jew to relentless critical revision. The passage is very 'written,' very 'literary'; it rests on the trope of the journey through memory. Starting with the 'étrange trajet à bicyclette' (84; a strange trip on the bike), it traverses the different parts of Paris she had lived in successively (ibid., 103), and ends when she reaches her destination. The beginning is worth quoting at length:

J'ai longé le bois de Boulogne dans le beau crepuscule, j'ai remonté le cours de ma vie en ces lieux d'autrefois, chimériques et absurdes, qui n'existent plus que pour moi. J'ai fait à bicyclette cette course à rebours, vers mon enfance, vers ma jeunesse, qui ne touchent plus que moi, ce raid interminable à l'envers de moi-même, dans [...] l'alternative épuisante où je me débats, et ce sang qui s'écoule de mes plaies cachées. (84–5)

I went along the edge of the Bois de Boulogne in the mellow dusk, up-river to the absurd, chimerical places of yesteryear that no longer exist for

anyone but me. I rode back towards my childhood, my youth, of concern to
me alone these days; I took my bike on an endless foray into my past [...] in
the exhausting inner conflict I keep going through, in the blood streaming
from my secret wounds.

I shall return later to the 'exhausting conflict'; for now, I attend to the
apparent paradox of any diary: while she claims that her memories touch
no one but herself, her childhood and her youth are facts of history, and
are explored as such in her reflexions.

The passage treats of time in every sense: it is the end of the last summer of the Occupation when she knows she is going toward an unfore-
seeable future, and yet is absorbed by her memories recent and distant.
It treats of a place that is inscribed with its own history – '[les] vieilles
fortifications de 70' (86; the fortifications that date from 1870) – of the
mysterious conversations of the adults during the first war, the names of
places, generals, and battles, including the battle of Chemin des Dames
in which Raymond-Raoul Lambert distinguished himself (see chapter 2).
It speaks of the sense of time of children, living in an 'eternal present'
(13 August 1944, 82), and the telescoping of the child she was with the
woman she now is. She is cycling in 'le bois de Boulogne magique d'autrefois, toute ma campagne et ma forêt d'enfant de Paris' (17 August
1944, 85–6; the magical Bois de Boulogne that used to be a whole countryside, a forest for a child) where she evokes her childhood games, and
the children she played with:

Je revois les petites filles de jadis, des petites filles Kahn, Weil ou Dreyfus
(du milieu des Israélites du haut commerce, de la banque ou de la Bourse,
du XVIe arrondissement) [...] Petites filles des beaux quartiers qui pen-
saient y être depuis toujours, pauvres innocentes, et y rester à jamais! Et
je revois aussi toutes les autres petites filles, Morel ou Verne, ou Lefort,
que sais-je [...] tous ces jeunes visages qui m'apparaissent ce soir, surgis de
cet âge lointain où l'on joue [...] sans se soucier des noms, des profils, des
familles ou des races (ibid., 87)

I see in my mind's eye the little girls of long ago, the little girls Kahn, or Weil,
or Dreyfus (all from the milieu of the 'Israelites' in commerce, in banking,
or in the stock-exchange, all from the XVIth *arrondissement*) [...] Little girls
from the chic districts who thought they'd been there for ever and would
stay there for ever, poor innocent creatures! And then I see the other little
girls, Morel or Verne, or Lefort, something like that [...] all those young
faces appearing to me this evening from that distant age where, indifferent
to names and profiles, to families and race, we played together.

A little older, she was 'mysteriously attracted' to these other children, now seen to be other (87–8), who were offspring of a centuries-long certainty (88); she needed to be like them, hankering after their sense of belonging, an attraction typical, she believes, of assimilated Jewish children and shared with 'nos générations d'Israélites qui ne sont plus des Juifs' (ibid.; our generations of Israelites who were no longer Jews). 'Étions-nous un peu différentes, nous, les petites filles juives? Je ne sais plus. Avions-nous un peu plus d'angoisse ... de conformisme dans notre vie?' she asks in the diary (89; Were we a little different, we, the little Jewish girls? I can't tell. Were we more anxious, more keen ... for our lives to conform?) This is a question that takes on the status of an assertion in an essay she was to write in 1950: 'Ainsi étions-nous naguère, enfants juifs sortis du ghetto depuis cent cinquante ans, enfants de France qui restions si peu Juifs mais juste assez pour se sentir à part, différents et parfois étrangers, élevés en pays chrétiens' (That's what we were like, we Jewish children that had left the ghetto 150 years before, children of France with so little left of our Jewishness, just enough to feel we didn't quite belong, to feel different, even foreign, brought up as we were in a Christian country).[11] Inheriting centuries of anxiety, there was no voice to save them from 'the temptation of similitude';[12] they longed for a stable world, a bulwark against time, and a house like those of their playmates, for their own, however beautiful, is like 'un frêle radeau trop exquis sur l'océan du réel, c'est une maison sans souvenirs, sans mémoire, et sans survivance' (a fragile raft, far too exquisite for the ocean of reality, a house without memories or memory, that could not survive).[13] Of her family home, she writes in the diary, '[elle] me semblait un bastion, quelque château de Versailles, quelque vaisseau de guerre ancré dans Paris loin des eaux mouvantes des angoisses ancestrales' (17 August 1944, 91; it was a bastion in my eyes, a sort of palace like Versailles, a warship at anchor in Paris, far from the troubled waters of ancestral anxieties). Yet the timeless palace existed only in the imagination of a child, and anchors give only temporary resting places.

Quel invincible mur nous gardait alors! À present nos maisons sont effondrées, refuges pour d'autres, les voix de jadis se sont tues, les bureaux paternels sont en cendres, misérables vestiges d'une puissance illusoire. (91–2)

What unbreachable wall protected us then! Now, our homes have collapsed, they serve as refuges for others, the voices of yesteryear are silent, our fathers' offices sacked, pathetic remnants of an illusory power.

This former life is finished (29 July 1944, 33); now, the raft she is drifting on is not a family home, but a series of safe-houses peopled by comrades

in the Resistance (6 August 1944, 43). The Jewish story she tells is one of
rupture and radical loss. History is rapid here. Though French for generations, the 'petites Israélites de vieille souche' (the little girls from the old
Israelite families) have been taken by 'un raccourci foudroyant' (a merciless shortcut) from the avenue du Bois to Auschwitz (17 August 1944, 89).

Her memories now are 'absurd' (93), yet they are a means of evoking
'une vie ouatée et tiède de jadis, vie d'enfant gâté qui prépare d'éternels
enfants' (90–1; a childhood wrapped in warm cotton-wool, the life of
a spoiled child, training us to be children forever). Childhood is more
than a mere period of life; it is a theme she was to develop in her later
writing: Jewish children are 'hyper-assimilated,' charmed by the world
that will one day injure them.[14] If Jewish children are the paradigm of
total assimilation, then total assimilation is a perpetual childhood, the
dream even of some post-war Jews whose aspiration to resemblance persists: 'Et dans quel but en définitive ce glissement vers la facilité? Ce refus
de porter un passé, impossible à lâcher?' (And in the end, what are they
after as they slip into their facile solutions? Why this refusal to shoulder
a past that is impossible to give up?).[15] That is what a child is, someone
who does not know her past, or even that she has one, albeit intergenerational. And if they lived in 'un paradis sur mesure, un peu ennuyeux
comme tous les paradis' (a customized paradise, somewhat boring, like
any paradise),[16] it is because paradise is not simply a space of sexual
innocence, it is the Beginning, with no past and therefore nothing to
remember: 'Juifs de l'oubli, nous, le peuple de la mémoire' (Jews of the
great forgetting, we, the people of memory).[17]

Hence the importance of her memories, each phase of which takes
her from her 'sheltered' childhood to the 'Destiny of Israel': 'nous voici
aujourd'hui, pauvres enfants sans abri' (17 August 1944, 92; here we
are today, poor unsheltered children). She evokes her dancing youth,
only to wonder what has happened to her friends from that time (94);
she evokes her father in hiding, dressed in the memories of 'both' his
pasts, looking in public like a retired military man (96) with his cane and
his decorations (6 August 1944, 59), and at home, wearing a cap and
a shawl, looking like one of Rembrandt's Jews (17 August 1944, 96–7);
and she evokes the betrayals of Vichy and her own desperate belief in
the people she had known (ibid., 97–8). Like trusting children, they
had no sense of the future: 'Nous n'avons pas prévu cette montée de
haine et d'horreur à l'horizon, ni senti déjà la trahison glacée, peureuse,
fardée de politesse, d'une grande partie de la bourgeoisie ... Trop tard,
nous avons compris' (100–1; We didn't foresee the hatred and horror
rearing up on the horizon; nor did we sense yet the cold and fearful
betrayal behind the polite exterior, of a large part of the bourgeoisie ...
We understood too late.). Like children, 'nous avons vécu sans vraiment

apprendre à vivre' (100; we lived without truly learning to live). If living means leaving paradise, if it means learning that even a childhood is lived in history, Mesnil-Amar's diary recounts this late and painful lesson.

She tells it as a story of identity. 'Mon être s'est déchiré en deux' (my whole being was torn in two), she writes early in the diary (26 July 1944, 25) as she wonders desperately if André's sacrifice and her own have been for France or for the Jews. In the generalized moral incoherence of wartime France, when the certainty of good and evil, guilt and innocence, is lost, she asks where truth lies: 'Où donc est la vraie vie? Celle où on serait enfin cohérent avec tous ses moi?' (29 July 1944, 34; Where is the truth of life, a life where all one's selves would finally find their coherence?). She has a public face and a secret face (8 August 1944, 73); as an outcast, she has lived in a series of different cities, all called Paris (17 August 1944, 102): 'Moi qui me suis trouvée entre deux mondes, entre deux destins, dans la série des hasards, quel Paris sera le mien?' (23 August 1944, 122; I discovered I was between two worlds, two destinies, which Paris would be mine in all this randomness?) This is 'l'alternative épuisante où je me débats' (17 August 1944, 85; the exhausting debate I have with myself) that she elucidates in the journey through memory of 17 August. Paradise was a false coherence; now she knows that assimilation was based on the loss of memory.

In this passage, she discovers that 'ce moi caméléon' (this chameleon self) has come through, certainly not unscathed, but able to face the future (ibid.). Her post-war life was based on a choice (29 July 1944, 34), not – ultimately – between her French and her Jewish selves, but to renew her commitment to Jewish learning and practice and a searching investigation of the work of French Jewish writers. She read the 'lost children,' those Jews whose duality sometimes exhausted them,[18] those eternal Marranos such as Max Jacob, 'serving mass at Saint-Benoit and dying at Drancy,'[19] or Simone Weil, who rejected Judaism because she recognized herself in it and whose choice was death.[20] 'What will we do with these missing people' she asks 'Where can we place them?'[21] She is determined not to lose them from Jewish understanding.[22] Her conclusion is that 'il est parfois aisé de quitter le judaïsme, il est moins aisé d'être quitté par lui' (it is sometimes easy to walk away from Judaism; it is less easy to have it leave you).[23] She reflects on Jewish humour in the country of Voltaire, discovering in it 'cette richesse des pauvres, cette victoire des vaincus' (the wealth of the poor, the victory of the vanquished).[24] She reads Proust, whose 'Jewish condition' became more explicit following the Dreyfus affair, discerning in both his sociological analyses and the investigation of his unconscious, an 'essentially Jewish inspiration.'[25] She revisits her life as a Jew in Passy, looking for the forms, the sources, and the consequences of their 'forgetting.' She reads Irène Némirovsky's

David Golder and the writing of Edmond Fleg, André Spire, Albert Cohen, André Schwartz-Bart. The lessons of experience have set her on a quest through books; there, she seeks a broader understanding of her place in a world, in a cultural moment that had seemed to be the golden age of French Jewry, and that she comes to understand as 'cette sorte de crise du judaïsme français des cinquante dernières années' (a kind of crisis in French Judaism over the past fifty years).[26] We have seen one form of this crisis exemplified in Jean-Jacques Bernard's denial (chapter 1), but Mesnil-Amar tells us that it took many forms:[27]

> Parmi les ...enfants juifs, beaucoup ont oublié; laissant la religion au musée des antiques [*sic*], vivant la tradition française du rationalisme et de la liberté, ils ont donné leurs forces et leur carrière, et toute leur ferveur inemployée à leur pays. D'autres ont été appelés par [...] le christianisme. D'autres, enfin, se sont perdus tout à fait [...] pauvres assimilés honteux, qui sont les seuls à croire que les autres ont oublié.[28]

> Among the Jewish children, many forgot; leaving religion in the museum of antiquities, living in the French tradition of rationalism and liberty, they gave their talents and their careers, all the fervour left idle, to their country. Others answered the call of [...] Christianity. And others, entirely lost, [...] assimilated and ashamed, poor things, the only ones who believed that the others had forgotten.

On the threshold of those fifty years, a precedent for Mesnil-Amar's critique of assimilation had been set by the current known as 'Jewish nationalism'; it was a minority movement, not accepted by the large majority of French Jews.[29] Mesnil-Amar's critique stands in anamnesic relation to it. In the course of those fifty years, thousands of people had sought in France the promised land of human rights, or simply a space of freedom in which their lives could flourish: we have met Saül Castro, Jean Oppenheimer, Benjamin Schatzman, Léo Lania, Valentin Feldman, Albert Grunberg. In the course of those fifty years, some Jews rose to unimagined heights in government or in their professions, among them Raymond-Raoul Lambert, who, following a distinguished military career – at a time after Dreyfus when the army needed its Jews (proving their patriotism, they all signed up) – gave up his career in the civil service in order to devote his efforts to the cause of Jewish refugees. In the course of those years, Hélène Berr and Josette Perquel – sister of Jacqueline Mesnil-Amar – were fellow students at the Sorbonne, both excluded from formal enrolment in the *agrégation d'anglais*, while only a few years earlier, Valentin Feldman, having studied with Victor Basch, had passed his *agrégation de philosophie* and had taken his place on the free-thinking left of that field. In the course of those years, Jean-Claude

Stern was at school, learning the ideals of the French national motto and seeing, but taking no heed of, the graffiti on the walls of Paris: 'Mort aux Juifs'[30] (death to the Jews). Like him, the Jews of Passy – caught in the trap of 'extreme assimilation'– failed to heed the warnings.[31] In her analysis of that heedlessness and that trust, Mesnil-Amar defines the past fifty years by means of two ruptures: under a certain model of assimilation, ties with the Jewish past were broken; under the Vichy laws, those with France.

In a critique that resonates with that of Hannah Arendt, she writes that people of her generation had relegated 'the Jewish problem' – and thus the problem of identity – to a space outside of history: 'au sein de la grande famille universelle et du mythe de "l'Humain." Ce qui est un leurre. Il n'y a pas d'homme à l'état pur, hélas, et chaque être relève d'une appartenance' (in the bosom of the great universal human family, lulled by the myth of pure uncluttered Humanity. It's a trap. There is no such thing as pure mankind, unfortunately; everybody comes from somewhere).[32] To 'come from': this is the bond of belonging. But where did they – who were ripped in two – come from?[33] The conjunction of 'Jewish' with 'French' would have to be reimagined, based on something other than forgetting:

Et depuis le grand choc [...] je crois que le fait d'être Juif s'est imposé. Qu'on le refuse ou qu'on l'accepte à nouveau en une espèce de retour, qu'on le supporte mal, qu'on s'y raccroche, ou qu'on l'esquive de toutes les plus subtiles façons, pourtant il est là. Le lourd fardeau d'être Juif, même diversement, est porté par chacun de nous.[34]

I believe that since the great shock, [...] the fact of being Jewish is inescapable. Whether we refuse it or accept it anew in a kind of return, whether we put up with it grudgingly or cling to it, or even if one dodges its demands, with whatever subtle casuistry, in any event it is there. The heavy burden of being Jewish in whatever way is borne by each of us.

This 'nous,' this 'we,' born of the experience of identity. Yet Mesnil-Amar's reading of the crisis of forgetting among France's assimilated Jews is based on her interpretation of her own autobiography. I have insisted throughout that this book is about diaries, and hence about personal experience, and I have defined 'experience' to include reflections on – and hence interpretations of – the events lived through by the individual. Mesnil-Amar's memory writing in her diary is the beginning of her life-long reflections on what the Vichy and Nazi persecutions meant for people like her, and what she could draw from that experience for the future. It continued to mean the discomfort of her 'duality,' the tension of her Jewishness with her Frenchness. It is important, therefore, to measure how deeply imbued this tension is by the very terms of Vichy anti-Semitism.

She was a woman of her times, not only because of the events that shaped her, but also because her reflections on them, her interpretive schemas, however thoughtful and elaborate these became, could not be freed of the informing discourse of assimilation on the French model.

Her autobiographical memories led her to draw conclusions she was tempted to generalize beyond her own experience. Perhaps, as her critics wrote, she was seeking to understand the whole story on the basis of the lives of the highly privileged Jews of Passy; her response to these critics was that the Jews of Passy were the paradigm case of French assimilation. But there were other selves who sought to understand their place in history in quite other terms. Vladimir Rabinovitch, for instance, does not once question his own secularism: for him, the crisis of the Occupation and the persecutions was an ethico-political one, and he sought in the post-war years to convince his fellow Jewish intellectuals that there were significant points of convergence between Jewish ethics and the Republican ideals of justice.[35] Nor does Hélène Berr; indeed, for her, Jewish particularism remained unacceptable, and her analysis of the dark years is cast very simply in terms of good and evil. Survival into the practical, day-to-day future is the only story for Saül Castro, Jean Oppenheimer, and Jean-Claude Stern, while for Valentin Feldman, as for Albert Grunberg, the dominance of fascism was provisional, and would inevitably give way to a Marxist utopia.

II

Let us close with Benjamin Schatzman, also a committed secularist, who sought to draw from the dreadful history he knew a different lesson. He did not do so in autobiographical writing; his genre was a manifesto, its gaze firmly fixed on the future. Yet it is no less inscribed in the historicity of his experience than Mesnil-Amar's conclusions. Furthermore, it bespeaks a sense of selfhood reached before his arrest, based on a stable set of beliefs that served to maintain him throughout his ordeal. This is his belief in science; it was unshakable.

Schatzman's usual way of envisaging the future remains on what had become for him, over eight months of internment, familiar territory. 'Je vis avec le sentiment que ce lieu d'internement est un tombeau jusqu'à la fin de la guerre' (I am living with the impression that this place is a tomb in which internment will last until the end of the war).[36] This is relatively optimistic; when he feels acute fear, it is of the unknown and the unexpected – 'qu'est-ce qu'on fera de nous d'ici ce soir, ou demain matin?' (14 June 1942, 302; what will they do to us here and now, or tomorrow morning?) – but in general, he adopts the stoical wisdom of fatalism: 'attendons et espérons' (30 March 1942, 140; let's wait and hope).

However, aside from the monitoring of his health, the waiting and the hoping, he writes 'meditations' of a more philosophical bent. In them, he allows himself to dream of a deeper future.

> Je voudrais tout changer, tout transformer, faire une humanité nouvelle où règne le progrès moral et scientifique, je ne trouve en moi aucun respect et aucune estime pour le passé, et je peux ajouter que je n'y ai que du mépris pour l'héritage moral qui nous vient de lui. (14 March 1942, 113)

> I'd like to change everything, transform the lot, create a new humanity governed by moral and scientific progress; I find in myself no respect, no esteem for the past, and I would add that I have nothing but scorn for the moral heritage it has bestowed on us.

The world he lives in, the present of the war and the camps and the persecutions, is inherited from the past. He despises this inheritance. In place of this, his interest in economics inspires a view of what must happen when a rational world order is restored:

> L'inconnue qui m'échappe et qui mettra tout le monde dans les mêmes conditions, c'est la façon [dont] l'économie européenne et mondiale sera organisée ou transformée. Il y aura bien probablement des changements dans la structure économique et il est impossible d'épiloguer là-dessus maintenant. (ibid.)

> What I don't know yet, and what will place everyone in the same conditions, is how the European economic order, indeed that of the world, will be transformed and organized. There are sure to be structural changes in it, but it is impossible to write a treatise on this now.

For Schatzman, the march of history is teleological: dystopia would inevitably give way to utopia. 'L'effroyable catastrophe dont nous souffrons si durement et si cruellement aura servi à activer la construction de cette nouvelle Humanité' (10 August 1942, 381; The dreadful catastrophe that is causing us such cruel hardship and suffering will serve to inspire the construction of a new Humanity). We may well share his sentiments about the moral inheritance that nourished Nazism, but with what is called the 'benefit' of hindsight, it is difficult to go along with his belief in progress:

> Si la paix est faite de manière à ce que des catastrophes semblables ne puissent plus recommencer, si certaines démences ne peuvent plus se manifester pour tenter de ramener l'humanité à la barbarie, et si l'évolution peut

se faire rapidement vers la liberté et le respect de la personne humaine, une ère nouvelle, dans laquelle les haines, les intolérances de races et de pensées [?], se constituera sans retour. (15 March 1942; 118)

If peace is concluded in such a way as to ensure that similar catastrophes cannot recur, if the demented behaviour cannot arise again to tempt humanity back into barbarity, if evolution toward freedom and respect for the human person can take place quickly, a new era in which hatred and intolerance of races and ideas, a new era will be established without reversal.

Schatzman's deep future is transgenerational, and can be understood now as a fantasy of modernity; it depends on a radical break with the past. He is convinced of 'the need to construct Europe on a new basis' (15 May 1942, 211–12), which will entail educating children without the 'contamination' of ideas inherited from the interwar years (ibid.). Bad social mores that have been sedimented through the ages must be eradicated:

Or, les générations se suivent et on constate vraiment peu de progrès éthique, spirituel et affectif. Avec une société humaine qui est encore dominée par des traditions et des conceptions opposées au progrès véritable, l'évolution dans le sens de l'élévation rapide de l'homme, sa transformation et son perfectionnement, ne peut être que très lente, d'où découle cette cristallisation dans des mœurs et des sentiments qu'on peut qualifier de barbares et criminels. (6 June 1942, 275 et seq.)

Now, generations follow one after the other, and there has been very little ethical, spiritual, or emotional progress. In a society that is still dominated by ideas and traditions that are opposed to true progress, any evolution of man toward his elevation, his transformation, and his perfecting can only be very slow. This is the source of the crystallization of mores and feelings that can only be considered barbarous and criminal.

The ground of barbarity is ordinary carelessness and individualism; he associates personal, moral responsibility with the structural change involved in 'la formation de générations complètement différentes' (ibid.; the formation of generations that will be completely different) from the current crop that has brought about the present catastrophe. Only in this way will future generations be formed in a spirit of responsibility quite different from the ideas of 'our ignorant ancestors.' Reversing the effects of these ordinary evils is not achieved by addressing the present generation of adults so much as by intervening in the upbringing of their children. He envisages reformed education, supported by economic reform. Shifting from a utopian teleology that would have us believe such change is 'inevitable,' he adopts a deontological form of argument. The financial regulation of Europe will have to be sorted out before a better future is possible:

> La structure économique capitaliste me paraît mortellement blessée. Les tentatives de la faire revivre pourront difficilement réussir [...]
> Je me dis donc que, de toute façon, cette question d'argent, de dettes sous toutes les formes, devra être réglée d'une façon urgente [...] le désespoir n'est pas de mise. (9 July 1943, 344–5)

> The capitalist economy appears to me to be fatally wounded in its very structure. I don't see how any attempt to revive it could succeed [...]
> In any event, my view is that the problem of money, of debts in any form will have to be sorted out urgently [...] there is no place for discouragement.

Progressivism and deontology converge in the lessons of history, one of which is that the peace concluded at the end of the First World War did not prevent, and probably contributed to, the outbreak of this one. Furthermore, both wars have lessons to teach:

> Je suis convaincu que ces peuples et leurs représentants ont enfin compris, riches de l'expérience de la guerre 14–18 et celle-ci, qu'il faut absolument faire la paix, c'est-à-dire réaliser des conditions de paix tells que le recommencement de ces criminels événements ne soit plus possible. (4 July 1942, 339)

> I am convinced that all peoples, and their representatives, will have finally understood from their experience of the war of 14–18 and this one, that peace must be made, and that this means a peace constructed in conditions that will render impossible the recurrence of these criminal events.

Though never abjuring his Jewish heritage,[37] Schatzman was a rationalist: the traditions and beliefs inherited with religion must be given up in favour of the scientific modernity in which he believed without reservation; this includes progress in the psychological sciences (6 June 1942, 278). Only in this way can the utopian vision be achieved: 'Les générations immédiates et à venir seront libérées de tous les préjugés et toutes les superstitions surtout religieuses. Les religions actuelles disparaîtront aussi, et une Humanité nouvelle éclora, qui n'aura aucun rapport avec la nôtre' (10 August 1942, 381; the coming generation, and those to follow, will be freed from prejudice and from superstition, particularly religion. So the religions we know now will disappear, and a new Humanity will blossom; it will be nothing like ours). But scientific modernity was more dangerous than he could know. Schatzman relied absolutely on scientific rationalism for his own survival, and it is of interest to note the similarities between his decisions concerning his personal regime and his recipe for a reformed world. Both rely on science, and on controlling the future. Yet survival and deep social change are different things, and it is disconcerting to read this gentle, thoughtful man expounding ideas that have a frightening resonance for us now. Once the inheritance of our ignorant ancestors has been eradicated, the practical problem will then be how to eliminate inadequate parenting. His answer is to move the children into institutions of care (ibid.). He even envisages eugenics and forced contraception (ibid., 276). He could not know that his utopian fantasies were cut from the same cloth as the dystopia to which he had been consigned. He could not know the full extent of that dystopia, or its reliance on scientific research, and he would not come to question modernity.

With hindsight, we understand that Nazism, as with many modern dictatorships, was no mere moral failing, but that it arose from a meta-historical fantasy very like that of Schatzman: change depends on eradicating the past and controlling the future. However, Schatzman's analysis is cast in moral terms, with the current catastrophe understood as the failure of moral sense, and this in turn attributed to superstition and religion; the solution he offers is rationalist: science discovers the truth, therefore science offers the certainties needed to correct the mistakes and errors of the past. Accordingly, Schatzman the scientist looks to remake the world in the future. His manifesto contrasts sharply with Mesnil-Amar's return to religion. Both draw lessons from their experience but where one relies on modernity to correct the evils of the past, the other discovers the ancestral story and the failed attempt to erase it in the Enlightenment utopia of assimilation.

In *Lessons of the Holocaust*, Michael Marrus argues that drawing lessons from history is a perilous business: interpretations are various, and the past is a different country in each of them, apt to be put to work in all sorts of political enterprises.[38] There is no generalization I can draw from the diaries I have discussed in this book, and therefore no generally applicable lesson, except this, perhaps: that personal experience, even when we collect it under adjectives such as 'Jewish,' from periods such as the Holocaust is infinitely varied, and accounts of it infinitely humbling about how little – but how precious, that little – we can know of the past as it was lived.

APPENDIX: SAÜL CASTRO'S DIARY, 10 DECEMBER 1941

Note: Revisions by the diarist are indicated in square brackets.

Les journées s'écoulent sans autres espoirs de libérations; [actuellement le camp présente] des malades attendent leur libération perdent espoir: par ci par là quelques petits incidents se passent. [Des inspecteurs en civils visitent les chambres à l'improviste c'est ainsi que beaucoup d'interné ont été pris.] Chaque jour des inspecteurs en civils [visitent les] font la visite dans les chambres à l'improviste; [nombreux sont les camarades qui ont été pris comme il a été interdit de jouer aux cartes dans beaucoup de chambrée ils nous interdisent] et voir si on fait du feu, ou si on joue aux cartes, et l'argent étalée sur le tapis est aussitôt raflé par les inspecteurs qui le mettent en poche, sans délivrer aucun reçu; c'est ainsi que plusieurs internés se sont vu dépouillé de leur argent; on ne peut réclamer et rien dire. [Ce matin vers 10h un camarade] Cet après midi [nous avons été surpris] un camarade vient nous donner l'alerte nous informant que Lar. passe dans les chambres; aussitôt nous mettons de l'ordre, et celui qui a du tabac et cigarette le [cache] met en lieu sûr afin de ne pas être pris, car c'est la tôle avec ce loustique. [Comme j'avais reçu mon colis de vêtements Ayant reçu mon colis de vêtement ma femme] Vivement je cache mon tabac et on se met à bavarder; [comme si de rien n'était Cinq minutes plus tard] quelques camarades entourent le fumiste qui est là en train d'arranger la tuyauterie.

... un camarade qui était en train de fumer avant cette visite, à l'annonce du garde à vous a éteint sa cigarette et l'a lancé par terre; Laroquette a-t-il remarqué ce geste, toujours est-il c'est qu'il s'avance sur [nous] l'interné en question et le fouille; il lui retire sa bague à tabac de sa poche dans laquelle il trouve 3 cigarettes que le malheureux venait d'acheter, et les met dans sa poche en faisant le malin; continuant à le fouiller il lui retire [la médaille militaire] de son porte feuille la médaille qui lui a été décerné au champ de bataille; c'est un ancien combattant 14–18; prenant dans sa main cette médaille Laroquette d'un air moqueur et indifférent l'applique sur la poitrine de cet [interné] ancien combattant et rigole avec son partenaire qui est à côté. [enfin il la lui remet]. Personne ne dit un mot, nous sommes [blême et furieux d'avoir] indignés de le voir agir ainsi envers un ancien combattant. [et du reste] enfin il lui remet la médaille et [continu] se met à l'interroger en qualité d'ancien combattant il a eu le sursis de la prison.

[J'ai les mains Je suis debout] J'ai les mains dans les poches et [sans me rendre compte j'ai fait du bruit avec] nerveusement j'ai pris mon

chapelet [entre] dans ma main, tout en le tenant dans la poche; au
bruit métallique que j'ai occasionné Laroquette s'approche de moi, me
fouille et n'ayant pas trouvé du tabac et toujours avec l'air moqueur,
m'élève/m'enlève? le chapelet. J'ai peur qu'il ne l'emporte pas; et je ne
peux rien; [c'est un souvenir pour moi et j'y tiens] il me questionne et
[me dit que je peux] et lui ayant dit que c'est un souvenir, l'ayant fait au
camp; [il me le rend et me dit de prier Allah] il n'a pas l'air de me croire
et me dit que je suis [en train] de prier Allah pour que je sorte d'ici;
enfin il me remet le chapelet, et se dirige vers la sorti.

Notes

Preface

1 See Carolyn Miller, 'Genre as Social Action,' *Quarterly Journal of Speech* 70 (1984): 163.

2 Ibid. See also Anne Freadman and Carolyn Miller, 'Reflections on Rhetorical Genre Theory,' forthcoming.

3 See Jacek Leociak, *Text in the Face of Destruction: Accounts from the Warsaw Ghetto Reconsidered*, trans. Emma Harris (Warsaw: Zydowski Instytut Historyczny, 2004).

4 Passages from the diary of Hélène Berr show her using the word 'thing' (*chose*) for round-ups and their doom-laden upshot. *The Journal of Hélène Berr*, trans. David Bellos (New York: Weinstein Books, 2008).

5 Amos Goldberg, *Trauma in First Person: Diary Writing During the Holocaust* (Bloomington: Indiana University Press, 2017).

6 Ibid., 10. He quotes as his authority for this point Peter Börner, *Tagebuch* (Stuttgart: Metzlerische, 1969). More recent work takes a different view, notably that of Philippe Lejeune, helpfully anthologized in English in *On Diary*, edited by Jeremy Popkin and Julie Rak (Hawa'i: University of Hawa'i Press, 2009), and Michel Braud, *La forme des jours: Pour une poétique du journal personnel* (Paris: Seuil 2006).

7 Goldberg, *Trauma in First Person*, 36. Diaries are 'a genre (if it can be called that) that allows contradiction and even antithesis'; they are thus adapted to 'articulating chaos' and suited to the disruption of 'continuity and coherence' (10–11).

8 Ibid., 39.

9 This discussion is adapted from Anne Freadman, 'Diaries,' in *Gender: Time*, ed. Karin Sellberg (New York: Macmillan 2018).

10 Hélène Camarade, *Écritures de la résistance: Le journal intime sous le Troisième Reich* (Toulouse: Presses Universitaires du Mirail, 2007), 21.

11 Goldberg, *Trauma in First Person*, 50, 41.
12 Ibid., 38.
13 For an indispensable elaboration of the notion of the 'trace,' see Paul
     Ricoeur, *Temps et récit*, vol. 3 (Paris: Seuil, 1985), 175 ff.
14 Berr, *Journal*, entry for 10 October 1943.
15 Alexandra Gabarini, *Numbered Days: Diaries and the Holocaust* (New Haven,
     CT: Yale University Press, 2006).
16 Jean-Jacques Bernard, *Le camp de la mort lente: Compiègne, 1941–1942* (1944;
     Paris: Éditions le Manuscrit, 2006); Léo Lania, *The Darkest Hour: Internment and
     Escape, France, 1940–1941* (London: Gollancz, 1942); Jean-Claude Stern, *Car-
     nets d'un héros ordinaire (1940–1944)*, ed. Viviane Koenig (Paris: Belin, 2006).
17 Bohny-Reiter, *Journal de Rivesaltes*; Françoise Siefridt, *J'ai voulu porter l'étoile
     jaune: Journal de Françoise Siefridt, chrétienne et résistante* (Paris: Robert Laffont,
     2010).
18 Extracts of Castro's diary have been published in Collectif, *Le camp juif de
     Royallieu-Compiègne, 1941–1943* (Paris: Éditions le Manuscript, Fondation
     pour la Mémoire de la Shoah, 2007), 199–305.

Introduction

1 The conditions in this camp, which was run directly by the Germans, were
    very severe. See Collectif, *Le camp juif de Royallieu-Compiègne, 1941–1943* (Paris:
    Éditions le Manuscrit et Fondation pour la Mémoire de la Shoah, 2007).
2 Albert Grunberg, *Journal d'un coiffeur juif à Paris sous l'Occupation*, ed. Roger
    Grimberg (Paris: Les Éditions de l'Atelier / Éditions Ouvrières, 2001), 166,
    entry for 6 May 1943. Subsequent references to Grunberg's diary in this
    section are cited in the text, with the entry date and the page number in
    this published volume. Unless otherwise indicated, all translations are mine.
3 He knew German, Romanian (his first language), and English, as well as
    French, and seems also to have been able to pick up information from
    Russian and Italian broadcasts.
4 Karski, a member of the Polish Underground, had arranged to be
    smuggled into Belzec and had witnessed first hand the processes of selec-
    tion and gassing. He had also been smuggled into the Warsaw Ghetto. His
    report was broadcast on the BBC on 8 July 1943. See Renée Poznanski, *Être
    juif en France pendant la Seconde Guerre mondiale* (Paris: Hachette, 1994), 626.
    Karski published his memoir in 1944: Jan Karski, *Story of a Secret State: My
    Report to the World* (London: Penguin, 2011).
5 Seventy-five thousand Jews from France were deported and killed; it follows
    that approximately 250,000 remained alive, though not necessarily in
    France. Zucotti gives the following figures: at least 50,000 escaped to Spain

or Switzerland; 20,000 to 30,000 were saved by Jewish rescue organizations; and 150,000 survived in hiding. Susan Zucotti, *The Holocaust, the French, and the Jews* (New York: Basic Books, 1993), 237.

6 Hélène Camarade, *Écritures de la résistance: Le journal intime sous le Troisième Reich* (Toulouse: Presses Universitaires du Mirail, 2007), 21.

7 Victor Klemperer, *I Will Bear Witness, 1933–1941: A Diary of the Nazi Years*, trans. Martin Chalmers (New York: Modern Library, 1999), 274, entry for 25 November 1938.

8 Peter Steinbach, 'Préface,' in Camarade, *Écritures*, 15.

9 Saul Friedländer, *Nazi Germany and the Jews, 1939–1945: The Years of Extermination* (New York: HarperCollins, 2007), xxv.

10 Ibid., xxvi.

11 Ibid., xxv–xxvi.

12 Amos Goldberg, 'Jews' Diaries and Chronicles,' in *The Oxford Handbook of Holocaust Studies*, ed. Peter Hayes and John K. Roth (Oxford: Oxford University Press 2010), 406.

13 *The New Shorter Oxford English Dictionary*, ed. Lesley Brown (Oxford: Clarendon Press, 1993).

14 In general, I prefer the term 'reflection' over 'interpretation' because the former can include the latter (i.e., 'reflecting on x, I think it means x'), and because of its lexical association with the reflective consciousness inherent in the phenomenological account of experience.

15 Friedel Bohny-Reiter, *Journal de Rivesaltes, 1941–1942*, trans. Michèle Fleury-Seemuller (1993; Carouges-Genève, CH: Éditions Zoé Poche, 2010), 57, entry for 16 December 1941. Bohny-Reiter was a Christian, working with the Swiss Red Cross at the Camp of Rivesaltes.

16 Ibid., 35–6, entry for 12 November 1941.

17 Raymond-Raoul Lambert, *Carnet d'un témoin, 1940–1943* (Paris: Fayard, 1985), 155–6, entry from 2 March 1942.

18 For example, Jacques Biélinky, *Un journaliste juif à Paris sous l'Occupation: Journal, 1940–1942*, ed. Renée Poznanski (Paris: CERF & CNRS, 1992). Biélinky wrote a detailed report on the conditions of life for Jews in the Occupied Zone, presumably using the same method. See 'Étude sur la situation des Juifs en Zone Occupée,' typescript held in the archives of the Mémorial de la Shoah, Paris (DLXXII-9).

19 See Jean-Jacques Becker, 'Napoléon et les Juifs,' in *Les Juifs de France, de la Révolution française à nos jours*, ed. Jean-Jacques Becker and Annette Wievorka, 30–42 (Paris: Éditions Liana Levi, 1998).

20 For a thoughtful investigation along these lines, see Kwame Anthony Appiah, *The Lies That Bind: Rethinking Identity* (London: Profile Books, 2018).

21 Lambert, *Carnet d'un témoin*, 135, entry for 2 December 1941, and 177, entry for 21 July 1942.
22 For 'disintegration,' see Janusz Korczak, *Journal du ghetto*, trans. Zofia Bobowicz (1957); Paris: Laffont, 2012.
23 William James, *The Principles of Psychology* (London: Macmillan, 1890), 609–10.
24 See Ross Chambers, *Facing It: AIDS Diaries and the Death of the Author* (Ann Arbor: Michigan University Press, 1998), 117, 129, and passim in ch. 6.

1. Narratives of Identity

1 For the provisions of the statute, see http://web.fdn.fr/~fjarraud/loivichy.htm
2 See Vicki Caron, *Uneasy Asylum: France and the Jewish Refugee Crisis 1933–1942* (Stanford, CA: Stanford University Press, 1999), 323. All the diarists I discuss were either born in France or had had citizenship conferred prior to 1927.
3 See Renée Poznanski, *Être juif en France pendant la Seconde Guerre mondiale* (Paris: Hachette, 1994), 23–46; Anne Freadman, 'From Assimilation to Jewish Identity,' *French Cultural Studies* 28, no. 1 (2017): 54–66.
4 See Saul Friedländer, *Nazi Germany and the Jews, 1939–1945*, vol. 2, *The Years of Extermination* (New York: HarperCollins, 2007), 175–8. For a striking instance of Jewish xenophobia, see Jean-Jacques Bernard, *Le camp de la mort lente: Compiègne, 1941–1942* (1944; Paris: Éditions le Manuscrit, 2006).
5 Philip Gleason, 'Identifying Identity: A Semantic History,' *Journal of American History* 69, no. 4 (March 1983): 910–31.
6 Ibid., 918.
7 Foote, qtd. in ibid.
8 Charles Lindholm, *Culture and Identity: The History, Theory, and Practice of Psychological Anthropology* (Boston: McGraw-Hill, 2002), 149–56.
9 Ibid., 150–1. The notion of habit in Peirce crosses the divide between the human and the natural sciences: inspired by the theory of evolution, it is his account of the capacity of 'laws' to perdure and yet respond to circumstances. See Anne Freadman, *The Machinery of Talk: Charles Peirce and the Sign Hypothesis* (Stanford, CA: Stanford University Press, 2004), and 'Does "Peirce" Have a History: A Contribution to a History of "the Moment of Theory,"' *Culture, Theory and Critique* 49, no. 1 (2008): 1–20.
10 Erving Goffman, *The Presentation of Self in Everday Life* (New York: Anchor Books, 1959).
11 Lindholm, *Culture and Identity*, 155.
12 Goffman, Presentation of Self, 15.
13 Judith Butler, *Gender Trouble: Feminism and the Subversion of Identity* (New York: Routledge, 1990) and *Bodies That Matter: On the Discursive Limits of 'Sex,'* (London: Routledge, 1993).

14 Gleason, 'Identifying Identity,' 925. Gleason calls attention to a connection between studies of Hitler's 'success in winning the loyalty of German youth' and the wartime concern in America with the 'national character.'

15 Erik Erikson, *Identity and the Life Cycle: Selected Papers* (New York: International Universities Press, 1959), 102.

16 Vincent Descombes, *Les embarras de l'identité* (Paris: Gallimard, 2013), 14.

17 Erikson, *Identity and the Life Cycle*, 102.

18 Erikson, qtd. in Gleason, 'Identifying Identity,' 914 (Gleason's emphasis) and n.12, citing Robert Coles, Review of *Dimensions of a New Identity* by Erik Erikson, *New Republic*, 8 June 1974, 23.

19 Valentin Feldman, *Journal de guerre, 1940–1941* (Tours: Édition Farrago, 2006), 324, entry for 3 December 1941; Feldman is commenting here on the formation of the Union générale des israélites de France.

20 Jacques Derrida, *Le monolinguisme de l'autre* (Paris: Galilée, 1996), 32ff.

21 Léo Lania, *The Darkest Hour: Internment and Escape, France, 1940–1941* (London: Gollancz, 1942), 115.

22 Bernard, *Le camp*.

23 After reading Bernard's memoir in 1946, Vladimir Rabinovitch remarked that 'l'expérience n'a servi à rien, sinon à confirmer chacun dans ses thèses premières: l'assimilateur à l'assimilation, le socialiste juif au bundisme, le communiste juif au communisme, le sioniste au sionisme' (experience has taught them nothing: they have remained true to their prejudices: assimilators are still assimilators, Jewish socialists are still bundists, Jewish communists are still communists, and Zionists are still Zionists). Vladimir Rabinovitch, *Journal de l'occupation*, vol. 3, *De la libération et de l'après-guerre, 1944–1947* (Val-des Près, FR: Éditions Transhumances, 2011), 82.

24 See Robert Badinter, *Un antisémitisme ordinaire: Vichy et les avocats juifs (1940–1944)* (Paris: Fayard, 1997).

25 Bernard, *Le camp*, 42. Further citations of this work in this chapter are indicated in the text by page references to this published volume.

26 See Jacques Adler, *The Jews of Paris and the Final Solution: Communal Response and Internal Conflicts, 1940–1944* (New York: Oxford University Press, 1987), and Michael R. Marrus and Robert O. Paxton, *Vichy France and the Jews* (Stanford, CA: Stanford University Press, 1995), 365ff. Some leading collaborationist intellectuals argued that there was no difference between assimilated Jews and immigrants, and that 'the Jew' was by definition unassimilable (Marrus and Paxton, *Vichy France*, 43). J.-J Bernard's view is close to this, but not quite identical: it is certainly possible that after some time, '[these foreigners] can be assimilated on condition that they abandon the ancient particularism of Israel. Those who hold to the traditional Jewish positions, and only they, we can say that they are not assimilable, because they are not French' (*Le camp*, 109).

27 Marrus and Paxton, *Vichy France*, ch. 3, argue that the significant issue for
the Vichy government was to assert its sovereignty against the German
authorities. This sometimes took the form of deciding on the categories of
people to deport (it was on a French initiative that children were included),
sometimes on administrative control, and, throughout the Occupation,
on control of the proceeds of the expropriations. Whereas the Germans
conducted a survey of the Jews in the Occupied Zone in 1940, Vichy did the
same for the Free Zone (see Adler, *The Jews of Paris*, ch.1). These censuses,
providing names and addresses, numbers of family members, dates of
arrival in France and country of origin (if applicable), profession, and
assets, were invaluable resources for all measures of persecution. See for
example the study by Annette Kahn of the file established and held by the
préfecture de police: *Le Fichier* (Paris: Robert Laffont, 1993).
28 'Ce fichier ... a été utilisé pour organiser les rafles de 1941 et de 1942'
(Kahn, *Le Fichier*, 11; this card-index was used to organize the round-ups of
1941 and 1942).
29 See Noël Calef, *Camp de représailles* (Paris: Laffont, 1997), ch. 5.
30 The question was live and forms the basis of a letter sent by Jacques
Helbronner to Pétain, in the name of the Consistory: 'our dignity as
French nationals, since as far as we know our status as citizens has not
been revoked, makes it our duty to protest [...]. The Law [the *Statut* and
the law on the Census] [...] takes cognizance only of a Jewish flock whose
nationality, even when it is *French*, is only an accessory fact and has no value
or impact.' Quoted in Raymond-Raoul Lambert, *Diary of a Witness*, trans.
Isabel Best, ed. Richard I. Cohen (Chicago: Ivan R. Dee, 2007), 64; the
letter is dated 1 July 1941.
31 Marrus and Paxton, *Vichy France*, 311.
32 Ibid., 90.
33 Victor Klemperer, *I Will Bear Witness, 1942–1945* (New York: Modern
Library, 2001). For example: 'Study of Herzl's Zionist writings. Very great
affinity with Hitlerism,' 85, entry for 23 June 1942.
34 We should recall the distinction in French between 'Juif' (the ethnic
category) and 'israélite' (the religion): it may be the case that Bernard
intended to repudiate only the former (*nous ne sommes pas juifs*). However,
the term was used in the very title of the *Statut des Juifs* without regard to
that distinction, so invoking it was a vain hope on the part of French-born
Jews. Bernard's later self-designation as 'un Juif chrétien' suggests that he
came to accept that 'Juif' denoted his ancestry.
35 For an illuminating discussion of the attitude displayed by Bernard, see
Susan Rubin Suleiman, *The Némirovsky Question: The Life, Death, and Legacy of
a Jewish Writer in 20th Century France* (New Haven, CT: Yale University Press,
2016), ch. 1, 'The "Jewish Question."'

36 'Je ne cesserai bien sûr jamais d'être juif. Ce n'est pas une fonction dont on puisse démissionner.' Mihail Sebastian, *Depuis deux mille ans*, trans. Alain Paruit (Paris: Éditions Stock, 1998), 329.

37 Jacqueline Mesnil-Amar, *Ceux qui ne dormaient pas: Journal, 1944–1946* (1957; Paris: Stock, 2009).

38 Ibid., 52; entry for 6 August 1944. Unless otherwise noted, subsequent citations of Mesnil-Amar's diary in this chapter are to this entry date; the page numbers in the text refer to this published volume.

39 The allusion is to Goffman's *Presentation of Self*.

40 Note that I have supplied the word 'own' in my translation. The context appears to justify this. However, the ambiguity of the French is extremely telling: were we turned into foreigners in their country, or in ours?

41 Stuart Hall, 'Cultural Identity and Diaspora,' in *Identity, Community, Culture, Difference*, ed. Jonathan Rutherford (London: Lawrence and Wishart, 1990), 225.

42 Jacques Helbronner, president of the Central Consistoire. His letter to Pétain is quoted *in extenso* by Raymond-Raoul Lambert, *Carnet d'un témoin* (Paris: Fayard, 1985), entry of 2 August 1941, 122–4.

43 Sebastian, *Journal*, 550, entry for 22 March 1943.

44 Lania, The Darkest Hour, 58.

45 'Since identity shifts according to how the subject is addressed or represented, identification is not automatic, but can be won or lost.' Stuart Hall, 'The Question of Cultural Identity,' in Stuart Hall, David Held, and Tony McGraw, *Modernity and Its Futures* (Cambridge: Polity Press with the Open University, 1992), 280.

46 I return to this issue in the Coda.

47 Goffman, *Presentation of Self*. Note that, in 1959, Goffman used the term 'self,' but in his later publications, he adopted the term 'identity': for example, *Stigma: Notes on the Management of Spoiled Identity* (Englewood Cliffs, NJ: Prentice-Hall, 1963).

48 Goffman, *Presentation of Self*, 15.

49 Ibid., 12, 17, 3.

50 Ibid., 13.

51 'Mesnil-Amar' was a *nom de plume*, later shortened to 'Mesnil.' Amar was her husband's name.

52 Goffman, *Presentation of Self*, 24 and 71.

53 Ibid., 71 and 254.

54 She was not to know it, but 'History' was indeed being made by the kind of apprehension recorded by Mesnil-Amar: the end of the war and the radical restructuring of women's identities that it brought about were no doubt crucial in the triggering of second-wave feminism.

55 Article reprinted in Mesnil-Amar, *Ceux qui ne dormaient pas*, 139–40.

56 Note the use of the term 'identity.' However, it does not stand as an exception to the history of usage I have adduced, since it dates from 1957, the date of the introduction to the collection of articles appended to the first edition of Mesnil-Amar's diary, thus coinciding with its emergence into both technical and general discourse in the 1950s. Nowhere do I find 'identity' used in diaries or memoirs of the 1940s.

57 Article reprinted in Mesnil-Amar, *Ceux qui ne dormaient pas*, 141.

58 Ibid., 143.

59 See Poznanski, *Être juif*, 670–5.

60 Ophüls began to make the documentary in 1969; it was first shown in 1971.

61 The authoritative account of this history is to be found in two works by Henry Rousso, *Le syndrome de Vichy de 1944 à nos jours* (Paris: Éditions du Seuil, 1987) and *Vichy: L'événement, la mémoire, l'histoire* (Paris: Gallimard, 1992).

62 Article reprinted in Mesnil-Amar, *Ceux qui ne dormaient pas*, 139.

63 The published edition of Feldman's diary has an informative introduction by Pierre-Frédérique Charpentier and contains a helpful chronological outline of his life: Valentin Feldman, *Journal de guerre, 1940–1941* (Tours: Édition Farrago, 2006). Subsequent references to Feldman's diary in this chapter are cited in the text, with the entry date and the page number in this published volume.

64 Martyrdom *with* faith is no doubt what he sought through his militancy; he is famous for shouting as he died, 'Imbéciles, c'est pour vous que je meurs!' (You fools, I die for you!)

65 Feldman spells out the rule in the following way: 'En zone non-occupée, les saboteurs de l'ordre – les communistes – subiront la peine capitale. Les Français arrêtés par les autorités allemandes sont considérés comme otages et répondront des vies allemandes (306, entry for 24 August 1941; In the non-occupied zone, those who undermine order – the communists – will be subject to capital punishment. French people arrested by the German authorities are considerd to be hostages, their lives will be taken in reprisal for German lives) – thus, capital punishment was used under both regimes. In general, Jews were not executed in France: they were deported and gassed. It is not possible to ascertain that this differentiation applied in all cases. In the case of Jewish members of the Resistance, there seems to have been little consistency: Feldman was executed, but André Amar and his colleagues from a Jewish resistance cell were deported and sent to Auschwitz (they escaped before arriving). The distinction made by Feldman takes no account of executions by the Milice, which was created in January 1943.

66 'Repères chronologiques,' in Feldman, *Journal de guerre*, 345.

67 Goffman, *Presentation of Self*, 17–18.

68 Butler, *Bodies That Matter* and *Gender Trouble*.

69 Stuart Hall and Paul Du Gay, 'Introduction: Who Needs Identity?' in *Questions of Cultural Identity*, ed. Hall and du Gay (London: Sage, 1996), 13.

70 J.L. Austin, *How to Do Things with Words*, 2nd ed. (Cambridge, MA: Harvard University Press, 1975).

71 Butler, ibid., *Bodies That Matter*, 32.

72 Butler, *Gender Trouble*, 145.

73 Ibid., 142.

74 Butler, *Bodies That Matter*, 230.

75 Ibid., 131.

76 Ibid.

77 Butler, *Gender Trouble*, 133.

78 Françoise Siefridt, *J'ai voulu porter l'étoile jaune: Journal de Françoise Siefridt, chrétienne et réistante* (Paris: Robert Laffont, 2010), 81, entry for 7 June 1942. Subsequent references to Siefridt's diary in this chapter are cited in the text, with the entry date and the page number in this published volume.

79 For more information regarding this protest, see the Postface to Siefridt's diary by Cédric Gruat (149–75), and Cédric Gruat with Cécile Leblanc, *Amis des juifs: Les résistants aux étoiles* (Paris: Éditions Tirésias, 2005).

80 See the preface to Siefridt's diary by Jacques Duquesne for a helpfully nuanced account of the history of the Catholic Church in relation to the persecution of the Jews under Vichy (7–77).

81 See Vincent Colapietro, *Peirce's Approach to the Self: A Semiotic Perspective on Human Subjectivity* (New York: SUNY Press, 1989), 90. Colapietro's exposition is a searching philosophical investigation of Peirce's fragmentary comments on this topic.

82 Goffman, *Presentation of Self*, 254.

83 Qtd. in Colapietro, *Peirce's Approach*, 90–1.

84 Ibid., 76, 93.

85 Ibid., 89.

86 Ibid., 69 (emphasis added).

87 Jean-Claude Stern, *Carnets d'un héros ordinaire: De Paris au maquis du Mont Mouchet (1940–1944)*, ed. Viviane Koenig (Paris: Belin, 2006), 125. Subsequent references to Stern's memoir in this chapter are cited in the text by page number in this published volume, along with time period, where relevant.

88 Nikolas Rose, 'Identity, Genealogy, History,' in Hall and Du Gay, *Questions of Cultural Identity*, 143.

89 In his introduction to the diary of Raymond-Raoul Lambert, Richard Cohen writes of the inter-war period: 'nothing could be more telling of French Jewish involvement in and support for the Republic than the impressive number of Jews in the French civil service and the army [...], not to mention their unparalleled (in comparison to other countries) representation in French politics as ministers, deputies, and senators. Léon Blum's election as prime minister [*sic*] in 1936 brought to an apex the rise of Jewish participation in the state apparatus.' Lambert, *Diary of a Witness*, xvi.

90 Les Éclaireurs Israélites de France had a distinguished role in the Resistance and were effective in rescuing thousands of Jewish children at risk of deportation. The Zionist tendency of the EIF became more pronounced in the latter years of the Occupation. See Johanna Lehr, *De l'école au maquis: La Résistance juive en France* (Paris: Le Vendémiaire, 2014), 38–58. For a first-hand account of the activities of one group supported by the EIF, and of their escape across the Spanish border on their way to Palestine, see Jacques Samuel, *Journal, 1939–1945: Une famille juive alsacienne durant la Second Guerre mondiale* (Paris: Éditions le Manuscrit, 2014).

91 In May 1942, his sister was arrested with her children; the children were returned to their grandparents with the help of the Red Cross, but with their 1943 arrest, the whole family was lost.

92 Hall, 'Cultural Identity and Diaspora,' 225.

2. The Place of the Self: The Diary of Raymond-Raoul Lambert

1 Jacques Derrida, *Le monolinguisme de l'autre* (Paris: Galilée, 1996), 53.

2 Renée Poznanski, *Être juif en France pendant la Second Guerre mondiale* (Paris: Hachette, 1994), 680; Richard I. Cohen, 'Preface,' in Raymond-Raoul Lambert, *Diary of a Witness, 1940–1943*, trans. Isabel Best (Chicago: Ivan R. Dee, 2007), vii; Vicki Caron, *Uneasy Asylum: France and the Jewish Refugee Crisis, 1933–1942* (Stanford, CA: Stanford University Press, 1999), 348; and Michael Marrus, 'Jewish Leadership and the Holocaust: The Case of France,' in *Living with Anti-Semitism*, ed. Jehuda Reinharz (Hanover, NH: University Press of New England, 1987), 381.

3 See Maurice Rajsfus, *Des juifs dans la collaboration: L'U.G.I.F., 1941–1944* (Paris: Études et documentation internationales, 1980). Jacques Adler moderates the tenor of Rajsfus's position but accepts the premiss of its judgments: see *The Jews of Paris and the Final Solution: Communal Response and Internal Conflicts, 1940–1944* (Oxford: Oxford University Press, 1987). In particular, Adler argues that the native French Jews, thus the consistory and the UGIF, sacrificed the immigrant and refugee population to protect themselves. See Marrus, 'Jewish Leadership,' 388ff, for a discussion of this argument. Adler's focus being on Paris, Lambert is not a major player in his account.

4 Marrus, 'Jewish Leadership,' 381–84; Caron, *Uneasy Asylum*, 320.

5 Julian Jackson, *France: The Dark Years, 1940–1944* (Oxford: Oxford University Press, 2001), 365.

6 Cohen, 'Introduction,' in Lambert, *Diary*, xxi. Most of the information I cite concerning Lambert's career is owed to Cohen's introduction.

7 Caron, *Uneasy Asylum*, see especially chapters 5, 11, 12, and 13.

8 The consistories (one in Paris, several in the regions) were set up by Napoleon to administer Jewish religious affairs and deal directly on behalf of the Jewish community with the government.

9 Lambert's opinion of Helbronner is coloured by the bitter dispute between the two men. For a sympathetic portrait of Helbronner, and an impersonal account of his activities under the Occupation, see Simon Schwarzfuss, *Aux prises avec Vichy: Histoire politique des juifs de France (1940–1944)* (Paris: Calmann-Lévy, 1998).

10 Caron, *Uneasy Asylum*, 115.

11 Ibid., 303 and passim.

12 Ibid., 303–5. The general political context was important in this transformation; a pro-refugee policy was supported by the Popular Front but again rejected by the Daladier government, which came to power in 1938 and was faced with a new influx of refugees after *Kristallnacht*. At this time, however, the moderate faction of French Jewry prevailed over the hardliners (ibid., 306ff). Their attempts to find long-term solutions for refugee settlement were obstructed by the 'protectionist demands of labor unions and ... of the middle-class professional associations of artisans, merchants, and lawyers and doctors,' to which the government deferred (ibid., 309).

13 Ibid., 317–19 and passim.

14 Ibid., 317, 320.

15 Ibid., 320.

16 See Marrus, 'Jewish Leadership,' 385: 'The UGIF never assumed the position of political preeminence among the Jews that Vichy and the Germans had originally intended. In this sense the identification of the UGIF as a *Judenrat* is inaccurate.'

17 See Cohen 'Introduction,' li. In Jacques Adler's view, the Jewish orphanages and old people's homes run by the UGIF provided direct assistance to the Gestapo; this is true only of the period from late 1943, after Lambert's arrest.

18 See Poznanski, *Être juif en France*, 619–25 for details of the differences (in both senses) between the two branches.

19 Caron, *Uneasy Asylum*, 319.

20 Cohen, 'Introduction,' xlvii.

21 Poznanski, *Être juif en France*, 624–5.

22 The relation between collaboration and resistance is now understood to be far more complex than the stark opposition would suggest. See for example R.O. Paxton, O. Corpet, C. Paulhan eds., *Archives de la vie littéraire sous l'Occupation: À travers le désastre* (Paris: Tallandier & IMEC Éditeur), 2009), and Jackson, *France*, esp. the introduction.

23 A note in the diary indicates that he had friends in London – that is, people who were active in the Gaullist resistance – and that he would have joined them had he not had a wife and children, and 'graves to care for' (9 October 1940, 22).

24 On the topic of Lambert's relation to Resistance activities, recent scholars concur that the loosely federated structure he maintained in the UGIF-sud (by contrast with the tightly unified structure of UGIF-nord) allowed it to provide a cover for those organizations that engaged in clandestine work

such as providing false papers and helping people to cross the border into Spain or Switzerland. See in particular Poznanski, *Être juif en France*, 623–4. It appears that, in the struggle over money between the two branches in 1943, Lambert's concern was to hold on to his capacity to continue funding these covert operations.

25 The overt policy of the UGIF was its determination to save the charitable agencies under its umbrella; for some of those left in charge following the arrest of André Baur and R.-R. Lambert, this entailed saving the organization itself. Jacques Adler argues that they adhered unwaveringly to this priority even when the situation evolved to the point where it demanded more supple strategic thinking. This is shown in the case of the orphanages and old people's homes run by the agencies; they were soft targets because they concentrated vulnerable people. By late 1943, the UGIF was constantly threatened with closure if there was any move to disperse their occupants. The matter was bitterly disputed but left unresolved, with the result that thousands of children were collected from these homes and deported along with their carers. See Adler, *The Jews of Paris*, ch. 7. Lambert took the view that it was better to scuttle the organization but, by the time the German blackmail had started to take effect, he was in Drancy and his view did not prevail (see letter of 26 October 1943 in *Carnet*, 244; *Diary*, 205).

26 Raymond-Raoul Lambert, *Carnet d'un témoin, 1940–1943* (Paris: Librairie Arthème Fayard, 1985), translated as *Diary of a Witness, 1940–1943*, by Isabel Best, ed. Richard I. Cohen (Chicago: Ivan R. Dee, 2007). In this chapter, I generally cite Lambert's diary in the text by referring to the French text first, with the translation, taken from the published English volume, following in parentheses. Where necessary for clarity, I refer to the French version as *Carnet* and the English as *Diary*. Note that the introduction to the translation differs in minor respects from that of the 1985 publication of the diary; when referring to the introduction, I use the updated one Cohen provided for the translation in 2007.

27 Bergson, correspondence, *Le Monde*, 19 May 1954; the clause is discussed in Philippe Soulez and Frédéric Worms, *Bergson: Biographie* (Paris: PUF, 2002), ch. 11.

28 The codicil and volume were published in Geneva because, although Pétain had granted an exemption to Bergson from registration in the census of Jews, news concerning him and his work was vulnerable to censorship. Lambert tells us that, 'when Bergson died, it was forbidden to print in the obituaries that he was a Jew of Polish origin who was naturalized as a special favour after his admission to the École Normale Supérieure' (22 June 1941, 48), and Valentin Feldman notes that, although Bergson's works continued to be sold until the print run was exhausted, they were not allowed to be republished. Feldman, *Journal*, 214–15.

29 Typescript, first published in *Hillel*, organ of the Union Mondiale des Étudiants Juifs, 5/6 (1947).
30 Léon Baratz, *Bergson et ses rapports avec le Catholicisme et le Judaïsme*, typescript, held by the Bibliothèque nationale de France.
31 The codicil stipulated *inter alia* that all of Bergson's private papers and notes should be destroyed, including his letters; he wished to be represented only by his published work. However, a will is by nature a public document, and the political context seems to have dictated a modification to the execution of this stipulation.
32 Maurice Barrès, *Les diverses familles spirituelles de la France* (1917; Paris: Plon, 1930), 61–2.
33 Ibid.
34 Ibid., 53.
35 Ibid., 61.
36 According to Cohen, 'Barrès' book took on mythic proportions and remained a sacred text for Lambert and other native Jewish leaders in the succeeding generations.' See Cohen, 'Introduction,' xx.
37 Translation modified. Such modifications will be marked by an asterisk in the text.
38 Lambert's dream of communal 'solidarity' and 'mutual assistance' could not be achieved by the UGIF, but he identified the need for Jewish unity, which was ultimately to be recognized by Jewish resistance groups and the Consistory, leading in January 1944 to the formation of the Conseil représentatif des israélites de France (CRIF). The UGIF had lost all credibility by then, and could have a place neither in this organization nor, more generally, in French Jewish politics after the war. See Poznanski, *Être juif en France*, 635–68.
39 The exception to this generalization is his quotation of a letter from a friend: 'thus we, Jews of France ...' (*Diary*, 6 November 1940, 24).
40 See Lambert, *Carnet*, 267n50 (*Diary*, 73n5), which quotes a letter from Lambert to Vallat proposing a limited role for himself in effecting the liaison between the government and the Jewish leaders; also, the entry for 11 December 1941: 'It was I who, for personal reasons and because of my experience (I have been known to the ministry people for ten years), was summoned by Vallat to act as an unofficial liaison agent or technical expert' (*Diary*, 80). These two texts are contradictory with respect to which of the partners to the negotiation took the initiative, but not with respect to the proposed parameters of the role. However, the administrative structure was subject to intervention from the Commissariat, and, following Vallat's dismissal, all the roles were changed. See Diary, 25 May 1942, 119–20.
41 *The New Shorter Oxford English Dictionary*, ed. Lesley Brown (Oxford: Clarendon Press, 1993).

42 A misprint in the French edition reads: 'le 16 juillet 1941.' Since it precedes the entry for the 7th, I have restored the 6th, in conformity with the English edition.

43 Bloch had made contact with Vallat to protest against the *Statut*. He was a prominent member of the Free French.

44 With the Commissariat sidelined in all but the measures of expropriation, and the Southern Zone occupied from November 1942, French and German police took charge of 'the Jewish question.' See Michael R. Marrus and Robert O. Paxton, *Vichy France and the Jews* (Stanford, CA: Stanford University Press, 1995), 304ff.

45 Lambert, *Diary*, 178–9n1.

46 Commonly known as 'the Joint,' this refers to the Joint Distribution Committee, which 'brings together all the Jewish aid organizations in the United States' (ibid.).

47 Lambert, *Carnet*, 282n151; *Diary*, 144n3.

48 'Stiffening' is characteristic for him: cf. the 'emotional farewells' with his family during the retreat of the French troops: 'The sight of my little Tony [his son] was heartrending for me, and I cut the farewells short' (*Diary*, 21 July 1940, 14). The entry refers to events of 16 June.

49 Donna F. Ryan, *The Holocaust and the Jews of Marseille* (Urbana and Chicago: University of Illinois Press, 1996), 9.

50 Cohen 'Introduction,' liv.

51 Lambert, *Diary*, 143n1.

52 During this period, he reads no German writing, and some, but little, English writing.

53 In his preface to the diary, Richard Cohen tells us that Lambert had kept a diary since 1916; the previous volumes have been lost, presumably as a result of the plunder of his library. See Cohen, 'Preface,' viii–xix.

54 Henri Bergson, *Oeuvres* (Paris: Presses Universitaires de France, 1963), 498.

55 Ibid., 495.

56 Ibid., 498.

57 André Gide, *Journal* (Paris: Gallimard, 1951–4), 507, entry for 26 September 1915.

58 Ibid., 386, entry for 23 November 1912.

59 Lambert, *Carnet*, 283n156; *Diary*, 151n8.

60 The published translation gives the following for the last sentence: 'It's by the light of his friendship that he sees this.' I have used a more literal translation of the verb, and brought out the implications of the tense; the French carries the suggestion that Empaytraz had not understood this previously.

61 Gide, *Journal*, 537, entry for 7 February 1916. The edition of the diary available to Lambert stopped in 1935.

3. Making It Last: The Diary of Benjamin Schatzman

1 Benjamin Schatzman, *Journal d'un interné: Compiègne, Drancy, Pithiviers, 12 décembre 1941–23 septembre 1942* (Paris: Fayard, 2006). The published journal is presented by Evry Schatzman and Ruth Schatzman. Subsequent references to Schatzman's diary in this chapter are cited in the text with the entry date and the page number in this published volume. Sometimes Schatzman's syntax is a little contorted, and sometimes he uses several words where one would do. In my translations of these eccentricities, I have sometimes simplified, sometimes inserted extra punctuation, and sometimes placed words in adjacent clauses or sentences. I have tried on all occasions to clarify, not to distort, the sense.

2 Information concerning the life of Benjamin Schatzman is drawn from the preface, introduction, and notes in the volume containing his diary.

3 At Drancy internees were allowed to receive parcels from their families containing food supplements and fresh linen; in turn, they sent their washing home and were able to send requests. For details of the régime, see Renée Poznanski and Denis Peschanski, with Benoît Pouvreau, *Drancy: Un camp en France* (Paris: Fayard, le Ministère de la Défense, 2015), 72–7. This apparent kindness was designed to minimize the expense of running the camp, which was eventually entirely provisioned by the Jewish community. No contact with the families was allowed at Compiègne, except in the hospital, which was not under the control of the camp.

4 For a contemporary medical account of these problems, see Schatzman, *Journal*, 654–6. The symptoms of the urinary problem were a constant need to urinate and the passing of abnormally large amounts of urine.

5 It seems that he is referring to the companions with whom he is currently sharing a room; they are generally pleasant company. He gives pen sketches of them in the following entry (5 May 1942, 172–3).

6 The syntax is confused here. I assume that sentence should read 'Il faudrait que je *ne* pense *pas* à cette souffrance, que je ne regarde pas en arrière.'

7 He is referring to François Montel, a converted Jew, whom he describes in detail (5 May 1942, 173) and mentions on several other occasions. Montel also kept a diary, in which Schatzman is mentioned: the antipathy between them was mutual. François Montel, 'Notes du matriculé 6137,' in François Montel and Georges Kohn, *Journal de Compiègne et de Drancy*, edited by Serge Klarsfeld (Paris: FFDJF, 1999). See also the *notice* concerning Montel in Schatzman, *Journal*, 664–5, which quotes Christian Lazard's account of Montel's selection for deportation.

8 See also in the *Feuillets épars*: 'J'ai vite épuisé et le peu de papier que j'ai eu l'idée d'emporter et l'encre dans mon stylo. C'était alors pour moi une privation qui me causait un ennui insupportable. Je me suis mis à mendier

chez l'un un bout de papier, chez l'autre quelques gouttes d'encre, je me
suis servi de papier d'emballage' (497; I quickly used up both the little
paper that I had thought of bringing and the ink in my pen. This was an
unbearable privation. I begged paper from this one, some drops of ink
from that, and I used wrapping paper).

9 The mass round-up (of 13,152 Jews, including 4,000 children) took place
   on 16 and 17 July. They were held in the velodrome for five days, then
   sent to Drancy, Pithiviers, and Beaune-la-Rolande (see Michael R. Marrus
   and Robert O. Paxton, *Vichy France and the Jews* [Stanford, CA: Stanford
   University Press, 1995], 250–2 ff.). The round-up resulted in terrible
   overcrowding in the camps and frantic transfers of internees between
   the French camps before deportation to Auschwitz. Schatzman's transfer
   to Pithiviers, then Beaune-la-Rolande, then back to Drancy before being
   deported is part of this history.

10 François Montel also mentions this death: 'Death of [Conrad] Goldman.
   He was 71 years old and had taken refuge near Dax. A few days ago, he was
   given an hour to get ready; then he was brought here. He had nobody in
   the world, and spoke little French' (Montel, 'Notes,' 15 July 1945, 78).

11 Some of the people arrested in this massive round-up were not sent to
   the velodrome but directly to Drancy.The actual number of arrests in this
   operation fell well short of the target. The inclusion of children is variously
   attributed to a decision by Adolf Eichman, who already envisaged the total
   eradication of the Jewish population of Europe; to Pierre Laval, who was
   determined to display his willingness to collaborate, and for whom the
   concern not to separate children from their mothers served as a convenient
   excuse; and to René Bousquet, chief of police, who used them as a bargain-
   ing chip against arms for his forces.

12 There is some ambiguity in this sentence due to the use of 'revenir': does
   he mean 'get [come] back to health,' or 'go [come] home'?

13 He had been let off the morning roll-call because of his age, but was
   obliged to attend in the evening.

14 I was frightened for the first time / for the first time I thought I might be
   gravely ill and perhaps not get out of here alive.

15 This measurement is given in a form that is no longer usual in terms of modern techniques for taking blood pressure. It seems that a pre-war technique,
   invented by Dr Pachon, used during the Great War, and widely used until
   the late 1940s, is being used here. Schatzman appears to be familiar with it.
   The measurements for systolic pressure given in descriptions of this apparatus resemble those given by Schatzman; if the normal systolic pressure for an
   individual was 18, then anything between 17 and 20 was considered normal,
   while anything below 17 was considered to be an indication of hypotension.
   (P. Loodts, 'Les médecins de la Grande Guerre prenaient-ils la tension des

soldats?' http://www.1914-1918.be/tension_arteriel_soldat.php, accessed 30 June 2017.)

16 Receiving food parcels was a privilege for patients in the civil hospital. It was also encouraged at Drancy, a policy deliberately designed to minimize the costs of running the camp.

17 See also a note among the *Feuillets épars*, apparently written in the hospital (hence, contemporaneously with the quoted passage): 'Le problème le plus urgent pour moi maintenant à résoudre, c'est une suralimentation assez forte et rapide sans provoquer des troubles graves dans le tube digestif. On peut compter maintenant pas mal de morts de gens qui n'ont pas pris les précautions nécessaires. Je suis tous les jours en lutte avec la faim et fais mon possible pour ne pas m'exposer à être atteint de diarrhée (*Journal*, 498; The most urgent problem for me is that I must feed myself up quickly without causing problems for my digestive tract. A lot of people have died because they did not take the necessary precautions. I spend my life struggling with hunger and do my best to avoid getting diarrhea). Schatzman's interest in nutrition is attested several times both in the *feuillets* and in the *souvenirs et réflexions* (see 459 ff.). It is probably based on his professional expertise and seems well ahead of its time.

4. Narratives of Time

1 As Bergson writes, 'notre durée n'est pas un instant qui remplace un instant: il n'y aurait alors que du présent, pas de prolongement du passé dans l'actuel, pas d'évolution, pas de durée concrète' (Henri Bergson, *Oeuvres* [Paris: Presses Universitaires de France, 1963], 498; our self perdures not in the replacement of one instant by the next: there would be only the present, the past would not prolong itself in what is happening now; there would be no evolution, no concrete duration).

2 Lambert, *Carnet*, 67, entry for 12 July 1940.

3 Jacek Leociak, *Text in the Face of Destruction: Accounts from the Warsaw Ghetto Reconsidered*, trans. Emma Harris (Warsaw: Zydowski instytut Historyczny, 2004), 19.

4 William James, *The Principles of Psychology* (London: Macmillan, 1890), 609.

5 Ibid., 608.

6 Ibid., 622.

7 Francisco J. Varela, 'The Specious Present: A Neurophenomenology of Time Consciousness,' in *Naturalizing Phenomenology: Issues in Contemporary Phenomenology and Cognitive Science*, ed. Jean Petitot, Francisco J. Varela, Bernard Pachoud, and Jean-Michel Roy (Stanford, CA: Stanford University Press, 1999), 277.

8 Ibid., 277.

9 James, *Principles of Psychology*, 609–10.
10 Varela, 'The Specious Present,' 269–81, passim.
11 Carl Becker, 'Everyman His Own Historian,' *American Historical Review* 37, no. 2 (January 1932), 226.
12 Ibid., 234.
13 Ibid., 227.
14 Ibid.
15 Varela, 'The Specious Present,' 269.
16 Paul Ricoeur, 'Narrative Time,' *Critical Inquiry* 7, no. 1 (1980), 173. For the full elaboration of the argument in support of this view, see Paul Ricoeur, *Time and Narrative*, 3 vols., trans. Kathleen Blamey and David Pellauer (Chicago: University of Chicago Press, 1984–88).
17 Ricoeur, 'Narrative Time,' 169.
18 Robin LePoidevin, 'The Experience and Perception of Time,' in *The Stanford Encyclopedia of Philosophy* (Summer 2015), ed. Edward N. Zalta, https://plato.stanford.edu/archives/sum2015/entries/time-experience/, accessed 12 July 2016.
19 The inclusion of technologies of representation under 'signhood' is an important component of Charles Peirce's semiotics. See Anne Freadman, *The Machinery of Talk: Charles Peirce and the Sign Hypothesis* (Stanford, CA: Stanford University Press, 2004). The expression 'work in the world' is drawn from Carl Becker, Everyman His Own Historian,' 234.
20 Le Poidevin, 'Experience and Perception,' n.p.
21 The classic authority on these matters is Emile Benveniste, *Problèmes de linguistique générale*, 2 vols. (Paris: Gallimard, 1966–74), see vol. 1, part 5 and vol. 2, part 2). See in particular 'L'appareil formel de l'énonciation,' vol. 2 part, 2, ch. 5 and 'Les relations de temps dans le verbe français,' vol. 1, part 5, ch. 19.
22 This assertion can easily be tested by restating the relevant sentence without this adverb. Note that the translation of *déjà* into 'already' has no effect on this fact.
23 Raymond-Raoul Lambert, *Carnet d'un témoin, 1940–1943* (Paris: Librairie Arthème Fayard, 1985), translated as *Diary of a Witness, 1940–1943*, by Isabel Best, ed. Richard I. Cohen (Chicago: Ivan R. Dee, 2007). Throughout this discussion, I refer to the French text first, with the translation, taken from the pubished English volume, following in parentheses. I mark with an asterisk translations that I have modified. I refer to the French version as *Carnet* and to the English as *Diary*.
24 Valentin Feldman, *Journal de guerre, 1940–1941* (Tours: Édition Farrago, 2006), 173, entry for 12 June 1940. Subsequent references to Feldman's diary in this chapter are cited in the text by the entry date and the page number in this published volume.

25 This experience of the brink is recorded retrospectively in this entry by Lambert, but this is not so for Feldman. Feldman's prescience is confirmed in an entry from 14 June 1940: 'Vivrions-nous les dernières journées, les dernières heures de la République Française?' (ibid., 174; Could it be true that we are living through the last days, the last hours, of the French Republic?).

26 Jacques Biélinky, *Un journaliste juif à Paris sous l'Occupation: Journal, 1940–1942*, ed. Renée Poznanski (Paris: CERF & CNRS, 1992), 62–3, entry for 21 October 1940. Subsequent references to Biélinky's journal in this chapter are cited in the text by the entry date and the page number in this published volume.

27 Becker, 'Everyman His Own Historian,' 227.

28 Benjamin Schatzman, *Journal d'un interné: Compiègne, Drancy, Pithiviers, 12 décembre 1941–23 septembre 1942* (Paris: Fayard, 2006), 360, entry for 26 July 1942. Subsequent references to Schatzman's diary in this chapter are cited in the text by the entry date and the page number in this published volume.

29 The diary is edited together with that of Georges Kohn. See François Montel, 'Notes du matriculé 6137,' in François Montel and Georges Kohn, *Journal de Compiègne et de Drancy*, ed. Serge Klarsfeld (Paris: FFDJF, 1999), 54, entry for 21 May 1942. Subsequent references to Montel's diary in this chapter are cited in the text by the entry date and the page number in this published volume.

30 Ricoeur, *Time and Narrative*, vol. 2. The quote is taken from the typescript transcription of a manuscript of Saül Castro's diary held by the family, entry for 1 December 1941. Extracts from this manuscript were published in Castro et al., *Le camp juif de Royallieu-Compiègne, 1941–1943* (Paris: Éditions Le Manuscrit and Fondation pour la Mémoire de la Shoah, 2007), 199–30. The quotations from Castro in this chapter are taken from the typescript and are accompanied by the date of the entry.

31 Jean Oppenheimer, *Journal de route: 14 mars–9 mai 1945* (Paris: Le Manuscrit, 2006), 38, entry for 18 March 1945. Subsequent quotations from Oppenheimer's journal in this chapter are to the entry date and the page number in this published volume. The translations are mine.

32 Ibid., 122n1 identifies Dr De Benedetti as a long-time companion of Primo Levi. They had met when they were first rounded up, had maintained contact during their internment at Auschwitz-Monowitz, and together wrote a medical report on the conditions in the camp. This is the Leonardo of *The Truce* (ch. 4); see Primo Levi, *If This Is a Man, and The Truce* (London: Abacus, 1987).

33 Hélène Berr, *Journal, 1942–1944* (Paris, Tallandier, 2008), translated as *The Journal of Hélène Berr*, by David Bellos (New York: Weinstein Books, 2008), entry from 11 March 1942 (p. 24 in the French edition; p. 22 in the English translation). Throughout this chapter, I refer to the French text first, with the translation, taken from the published English volume, following in parentheses. Translations in which I have made minor modifications are

marked with an asterisk. I refer to the French version as *Journal* and to the English as *Journal of Hélène Berr*.

34 Entry from 22 December 1941. I thank Mme Markoff for granting permission to quote from and discuss the diary of Germaine Léon (Jean Léon and Mme Jean Léon, Archives du Mémorial de la Shoah, Paris, DCCCXXIX-1). Jean Léon was deported in March 1942 and did not return.

35 James, *Principles of Psychology*, 624

36 In most contexts, 'already' cannot be used with a negative, whereas in French some combinations of 'pas' with 'déjà' are admissable; in the translation, I have inserted a positive clause to handle this grammatical non-equivalence.

37 Levi, *If This Is a Man*, 66.

38 James, *Principles of Psychology*, 606.

39 Susan Brison, *Aftermath: Violence and the Remaking of a Self* (Princeton, NJ: Princeton University Press, 2002), 53.

40 Ricoeur, 'Narrative Time,' 182.

41 Paul Ricoeur, *Temps et récit*, vol. 2.

42 Ricoeur, 'Narrative Time,' 172.

43 Ibid., 174, 178.

44 Ibid., 179.

45 I thank Franck Berthelet for sending me a scanned copy of this page of the typescript.

46 For a narratological study of these changes, see Anne Freadman, 'The Word and All Things in It,' *Journal of Language, Literature and Culture* 16, no. 2 (2018): 117–33.

47 Since it was sipped with a spoon, this may have been sweetened condensed milk.

48 L'Union nationale des associations de déportés, internés et familles de disparus (UNADIF). See Oppenheimer, *Journal de route*, 269–73).

49 The exact manner of her death is revealed in Jacqueline Mesnil-Amar, 'Des temps tragiques aux temps difficiles,' in *Ceux qui ne dormaient pas* (Paris: Stock, 2009), 168.

50 This sentence is omitted from the published translation.

51 Mme Baur is the wife of André Baur, vice-president of UGIF-nord; rue de Téhéran refers to the headquarters of the organization.

52 I presume the specification of 'women' is due to the context of the conversation. See the previous quoted passage.

53 Pierre Masse was the brother of Mme Léon Lyon-Caen, whose son, Gérard, figures frequently in the early part of Hélène Berr's diary as the young man with whom she is falling out of love. The two families were close; hence, this intimate information concerning a very prominent member of the pre-war ruling class.

54 In 2009, Robert Badinter wrote of Pierre Masse: 'Nous connaissons par les archives allemandes la composition du convoi 39 partant de Drancy pour Auschwitz. Le nom de Pierre Masse et la qualité avocat y figurent. Cette mention est la dernière trace de Pierre Masse sur cette terre' (The German archives disclose the composition of convoy no. 39 that left Drancy for Auschwitz. The name of Pierre Masse and his profession, lawyer, are noted. This note is the last trace of Pierre Masse on this earth) Robert Badinter, 'Mort d'un israélite français: Hommage à maître Pierre Masse," *Le Débat* 158 (2010–11): 101–7. However, there is a mention of Pierre Masse in the diary of Jean Oppenheimer (*Journal de route*, 60). If this information can be corroborated, it would put his death much later than October 1942, the date usually cited. According to Oppenheimer, they were together at Auschwitz for the new year of 1944, and had 'long and lively conversations.'

55 We have seen François Montel answer this question, as does Benjamin Schatzman (see ch. 3). Georges Kohn's diary also provides information on this subject: see Kohn, *Journal de Compiègne* in Montel and Kohn, *Journal de Compiègne et de Drancy*.

56 Fiona Lisabeth Kaufman, 'By Chance I Found a Pencil: Holocaust Diary Narratives of Testimony, Defiance, Solace and Struggle' (PhD diss., University of Melbourne, 2011), 22, 20.

57 Two things happened in early November: one was Mussolini's resignation. The excitement in response to that event was quickly dispelled by the takeover of Italy by the Nazis and the Occupation of the Southern Zone of France on November 11. The other was the fall of Algiers to the Resistance and the Allies, on exactly 8 November.

58 In the published translation, this appears in a passage included under the date of 3 November 1943.

59 Brison, *Aftermath*, 39–40.

60 Ibid., 52, 53.

61 Ross Chambers, 'Significant Others, or Textual Congress,' *Australian Journal of French Studies* 55, no. 3, 2018, 235.

Coda

1 Jacqueline Mesnil-Amar, *Ceux qui ne dormaient pas: Journal, 1944–1946* (Paris: Stock, 2009), 101, entry from 17 August 1944. Subsequent references to Mesnil-Amar's diary in this chapter are cited in the text by the entry date and their page number in this published volume. Where it is necessary to distinguish the diary from her other writings, the former is cited as *Journal*.

2 My discussion will be based primarily on Mesnil-Amar, *Journal*. However, it will also draw heavily on her post-war writings, anthologized, together with writings by her husband, in André Amar and Jacqueline Mesnil-Amar,

Parcours d'écriture (Paris: Alliance israélite universelle, collection 'Repères,' 2005), which are cited by essay title in the notes.

3 See Jean-François Chaigneau, *Le dernier wagon* (Paris: Julliard, 1982).

4 See, for example, Marcel Proust, *À la recherche du temps perdu*, ed. Jean-Yves Tadié, vol. 3, *Le Temps retrouvé* (Paris: NRF-Gallimard, Bibliothèque de la Pléiade, 1989), passim.

5 Ibid., 800 and 728.

6 Ibid., 958.

7 See Elisheva Rosen, 'Littérature, autofiction, histoire: L'Affaire Dreyfus dans *La recherche du temps perdu*,' *Littérature* 100 (1995): 64–80.

8 Proust, *À la recherche du temps perdu*, vol. 3, *La Fugitive*, 574–75.

9 Published in 1886. For a study of this notorious book, see Michel Winock, *Edouard Drumont et Cie.: Antisémitisme et fascisme en France* (Paris: Seuil, 1982), ch. 5. Winock writes of Drumont that he gave definitive impetus to French anti-Semitism (36). A specialized study of the relation between the Dreyfus affair and assimilation in France is Michael Marrus, *The Politics of Assimilation: A Study of the French Jewish Community at the time of the Dreyfus Affair* (Oxford: Clarendon Press, 1971), ch. 8.

10 Compare this to Primo Levi in the internment camp on the eve of deportation: 'We experienced within ourselves a grief that was new for us, the ancient grief of the people that has no land, the grief without hope of the exodus which is renewed every century.' Levi, *If This Is a Man* (London: Penguin Books, 1979), 22.

11 Mesnil-Amar, 'De l'enfant perdu à l'enfant prophète,' in Amar and Mesnil-Amar, *Parcours d'écriture* (hereafter *Parcours*), 137. This essay is a reading of a story by Edmond Fleg.

12 Ibid. Cf. 'la soif obscure de resemblance,' in *Journal*, 88.

13 Mesnil-Amar, 'De l'enfant perdu à l'enfant prophète,' 136.

14 Mesnil-Amar, 'Le message des enfants perdus,' in *Parcours*, 146. This essay concerns writers of Jewish origin who converted or were otherwise 'lost' to Judaism: Marcel Proust, Max Jacob, and Simone Weil.

15 Mesnil-Amar, 'Être Juif à Passy,' in *Parcours*, 249.

16 Mesnil-Amar, 'Nous étions les Juifs de l'oubli,' in *Parcours*, 257.

17 Ibid., 263.

18 Mesnil-Amar, 'Le message des enfants perdus' in *Parcours*, 144.

19 ibid., 153.

20 Mesnil-Amar, 'Simone Weil, l'auteur de *L'Enracinement*,' in *Parcours*, 117, and '*La pesanteur et la grâce* de Simone Weil,' in *Parcours*, 127.

21 Mesnil-Amar, 'Le message des enfants perdus,' in *Parcours*, 143.

22 Ibid.

23 Ibid., 145.

24 Mesnil-Amar, 'L'humour juif au pays de Voltaire,' in *Parcours*, 184.

25 Mesnil-Amar, 'Marcel Proust, les juifs et le monde,' in *Parcours*, 201 and 205.

26 Mesnil-Amar, 'De l'enfant perdu à l'enfant prophète,' in *Parcours*, 134.

27 Mesnil-Amar, 'Le message des enfants perdus,' 146.

28 Mesnil-Amar, 'De l'enfant perdu à l'enfant prophète,' 139.

29 See Marrus, *Politics of Assimilation*: 'Jewish nationalism exalted the quality of being Jewish, stressed Jewish distinctiveness, and was committed to Jewish preservation' (164). Essentially a rejection of assimilation and an internal French political position, it should not be conflated with Zionism until, following the Zionist congresses of the late 1890s, the two tended to converge.

30 Jean-Claude Stern, *Carnets d'un héros ordinaire: De Paris au maquis du Mont Mouchet (1940–1944)*, ed. Viviane Koenig (Paris: Belin, 2006), 19.

31 Mesnil-Amar, 'Être juif à Passy,' 245.

32 Ibid., 252 and 241.

33 Ibid., 251.

34 Ibid., 248.

35 See Vladimir Rabi, *Anatomie du Judaïsme français* (Paris: Les Éditions de Minuit, 1962) and *Un peuple de trop sur la terre?* (Paris: Les Presses d'Aujourd'hui, 1979).

36 Benjamin Schatzman, *Journal d'un interné: Compiègne, Drancy, Pithiviers, 12 décembre 1941–23 septembre 1942* (Paris: Fayard, 2006), 337. Subsequent quotations from Schatzman's diary are accompanied by the entry date and the page number in this published volume.

37 Schatzman devotes several pages of his *souvenirs et réflexions* to the 'question of anti-Semitism,' focusing in particular on the opinions he hears around him (*Journal*, 464ff).

38 Michael Marrus, *Lessons of the Holocaust* (Toronto: University of Toronto Press, 2016).

Bibliography

Unpublished Primary Sources

Baratz, Léon. *Bergson et ses rapports avec le Catholicisme et le Judaïsme.* Typescript, 1954. Bibliothèque nationale de France.

Biélinky, Jacques. 'Étude sur la situation des Juifs en Zone Occupée.' Typescript, Archives of the Mémorial de la Shoah, Paris: DLXXII-9.

Castro, Saül. *Journal.* Typescript held by the family.

Germaine, Léon. *Journal* et Jean Léon *Lettres.* Archives du Mémorial de la Shoah, Paris: DCCCXXIX–1.

Published Primary Sources

Amar, André, and Jacqueline Mesnil-Amar. *Parcours d'écriture.* Paris: Alliance israélite universelle, collection 'Repères,' 2005.

Bernard, Jean-Jacques. *Le camp de la mort lente: Compiègne, 1941–1942.* Paris: Albin-Michel, 1944. Reprinted, Paris: Éditions le Manuscrit, 2006.

Berr, Hélène. *Journal, 1942–1944.* Paris: Tallandier, 2008.

– *The Journal of Hélène Berr.* Translated by David Bellos. New York: Weinstein Books, 2008.

Biélinky, Jacques. *Un journaliste juif à Paris sous l'Occupation: Journal, 1940–1942.* Edited by Renée Poznanski. Paris: CERF and CNRS, 1992.

Bohny-Reiter, Friedel. *Journal de Rivesaltes, 1941–1942.* 1993. Translated by Michèle Fleury-Seemuller. Carouges-Genève, CH: Éditions Zoé Poche, 2010.

Calef, Noël. *Camp de représailles.* Paris: Laffont, 1997.

Collectif [Saul Castro et al.], *Le camp juif de Royallieu-Compiègne, 1941–1943.* Paris: Éditions le Manuscrit and Fondation pour la Mémoire de la Shoah, 2007.

Feldman, Valentin. *Journal de guerre, 1940–1941.* Tours: Édition Farrago, 2006.

Grunberg, Albert. *Journal d'un coiffeur juif à Paris sous l'Occupation.* Edited by
   Roger Grimberg. Paris: Les Éditions de l'Atelier / Éditions Ouvrières, 2001.
Karski, Jan. *Story of a Secret State: My Report to the World.* London: Penguin, 2011.
Klemperer, Victor. *I Will Bear Witness, 1933–1941: A Diary of the Nazi Years.*
   Translated by Martin Chalmers. New York: Modern Library, 1999.
– *I Will Bear Witness, 1942–1945.* New York: Modern Library, 2001.
Korczak, Janusz. *Journal du ghetto.* 1957. Translated from Polish by Zofia
   Bobowicz. Paris: Laffont, 2012.
Lambert, Raymond-Raoul. *Carnet d'un témoin, 1940–1943.* Paris: Fayard, 1985.
   Translated as *Diary of a Witness,* translated by Isabel Best, edited by Richard I.
   Cohen. Chicago: Ivan R. Dee, 2007.
Lania, Léo. *The Darkest Hour: Internment and Escape, France 1940–1941.* London:
   Gollancz, 1942.
Levi, Primo. *If This Is a Man, and The Truce.* London: Abacus, 1987.
Kohn, Georges. *Journal de Compiègne.* In François Montel and Georges Kohn,
   Journal de Compiègne et de Drancy. Edited by Serge Klarsfeld, 129–226. Paris:
   FFDJF, 1999.
Mesnil-Amar, Jacqueline. *Ceux qui ne dormaient pas: Journal, 1944–1946.* 1957.
   Paris: Stock, 2009.
Montel, François. 'Notes du matriculé 6137.' In François Montel and Georges
   Kohn, *Journal de Compiègne et de Drancy.* Edited by Serge Klarsfeld, 49–97.
   Paris: FFDJF, 1999.
Oppenheimer, Jean. *Journal de route: 14 mars–9 mai 1945.* Paris: Le Manuscrit, 2006.
Proust, Marcel. *À la recherche du temps perdu.* Édition établie par Jean-Yves Tadié.
   Paris: NRF-Gallimard, Bibliothèque de la Pléiade, 1989.
Rabinovitch, Vladimir. *Journal de l'occupation.* Volume 1, *1940.* Val-des-Près, FR:
   Éditions Transhumances, 2008.
– *Journal de l'occupation.* Volume 2, *1942–1944.* Val-des-Près, FR: Éditions
   Transhumances, 2009
– *Journal de l'occupation.* Volume 3, *De la liberation et de l'après-guerre, 1944–1947.*
   Val-des-Près, FR: Éditions Transhumances, 2011.
Samuel, Jacques. *Journal, 1939–1945: Une famille juive alsacienne durant la Second
   Guerre mondiale.* Paris: Éditions le Manuscrit, 2014.
Schatzman, Benjamin. *Journal d'un interné: Compiègne, Drancy, Pithiviers,
   12 décembre 1941–23 septembre 1942.* Paris: Fayard, 2006.
Sebastian, Mihail. *Depuis deux mille ans.* Translated by Alain Paruit. Paris:
   Éditions Stock, 1998.
– *Journal, 1935–1944.* Chicago: Ivan Dee, 2000.
Siefridt, Françoise. *J'ai voulu porter l'étoile jaune: Journal de Françoise Siefridt,
   chrétienne et résistante.* Paris: Robert Laffont, 2010.
Stern, Jean-Claude. *Carnets d'un héros ordinaire: De Paris au maquis du Mont
   Mouchet (1940–1944).* Edited by Viviane Koenig. Paris: Belin, 2006.

Secondary References

Adler, Jacques, *The Jews of Paris and the Final Solution: Communal Response and Internal Conflicts, 1940–1944*. Oxford: Oxford University Press, 1987. Originally published as *Face à la persécution: Les organisations juives à Paris, 1940–1944*. Paris: Calmann Lévy, 1985.

Appiah, Kwame Anthony. *The Lies That Bind: Rethinking Identity*. London: Profile Books, 2018.

Austin, J.L. *How to Do Things with Words*, 2nd ed. Cambridge, MA: Harvard University Press, 1975.

Badinter, Robert. *Un antisémitisme ordinaire: Vichy et les avocats juifs (1940–1944)*. Paris: Fayard, 1997.

– 'Mort d'un israélite français: Hommage à maître Pierre Masse.' *Le Débat*, 158 (2010–11): 101–7.

Baratz, Léon. 'Deux "juifs-chrétiens": Henri Bergson et J.-J. Bernard.' *Hillel* 5/6 (1947).

Barrès, Maurice. *Les diverses familles spirituelles de la France*. 1917. Paris: Plon, 1930.

Becker, Carl. 'Everyman His Own Historian.' *American Historical Review* 37, no. 2 (January 1932): 221–36.

Becker, Jean-Jacques. 'Napoléon et les Juifs.' In *Les Juifs de France, de la Révolution française à nos jours*, edited by Jean-Jacques Becker and Annette Wievorka, 30–42. Paris: Éditions Liana Levi, 1998.

Benveniste, Emile. *Problèmes de linguistique générale*. 2 vols. Paris: Gallimard, 1966–74.

Bergson, Henri. *Oeuvres*. Paris: Presses Universitaires de France, 1963.Brison, Susan. *Aftermath: Violence and the Remaking of a Self*. Princeton, NJ: Princeton University Press, 2002.

Butler, Judith. *Bodies That Matter: On the Discursive Limits of 'Sex.'* London: Routledge, 1993.

– *Gender Trouble: Feminism and the Subversion of Identity*. New York: Routledge, 1990.

Camarade, Hélène. *Écritures de la résistance: Le journal intime sous le Troisième Reich*. Toulouse: Presses Universitaires du Mirail, 2007

Caron, Vicki. *Uneasy Asylum: France and the Jewish Refugee Crisis, 1933–1942*. Stanford, CA: Stanford University Press, 1999.

Chaigneau, Jean-François. *Le dernier wagon*. Paris: Julliard, 1982.

Chambers, Ross. *Facing It: AIDS Diaries and the Death of the Author*. Ann Arbor: University of Michigan Press, 1998.

– 'Significant Others, or Textual Congress.' *Australian Journal of French Studies* 55, no. 3 (2018): 223–36.

Colapietro, Vincent. *Peirce's Approach to the Self: A Semiotic Perspective on Human Subjectivity*. New York: SUNY Press, 1989.

Derrida, Jacques. *Le monolinguisme de l'autre*. Paris: Galilée, 1996.

Descombes, Vincent. *Les embarras de l'identité.* Paris: Gallimard, 2013.

Erikson, Erik. *Identity and the Life Cycle: Selected Papers.* New York: International Universities Press, 1959.

Freadman, Anne. 'Diaries.' In *Gender: Time,* ed. Karin Sellberg. Chicago: Macmillan, 2017.

– 'Does "Peirce" Have a History: A Contribution to a History of "the Moment of Theory."' *Culture, Theory and Critique* 49, no. 1 (2008): 1–20.

– 'From Assimilation to Jewish Identity.' *French Cultural Studies* 28, no. 1 (2017): 54–66.

– *The Machinery of Talk: Charles Peirce and the Sign Hypothesis.* Stanford, CA: Stanford University Press, 2004.

– 'The Word and All Things in It.' *Journal of Language, Literature and Culture* 16, no. 2 (2018): 117–33.

Friedländer, Saul. *Nazi Germany and the Jews, 1933–1939.* Volume 1, *The Years of Persecution,* New York: Harper Perennial, 1998.

– *Nazi Germany and the Jews, 1939–1945.* Volume 2, *The Years of Extermination.* New York: HarperCollins, 2007.

Gabarini, Alexandra. *Numbered Days: Diaries and the Holocaust.* New Haven, CT: Yale University Press, 2006.

Gide, André. *Journal.* Paris: Gallimard, 1951–4.

Gleason, Philip. 'Identifying Identity: A Semantic History.' *Journal of American History* 69, no. 4 (March 1983): 910–31.

Goffman, Erving. *The Presentation of Self in Everday Life.* New York: Anchor Books, 1959.

– *Stigma: Notes on the Management of Spoiled Identity.* Englewood Cliffs, NJ: Prentice-Hall, 1963.

Goldberg, Amos. 'Jews' Diaries and Chronicles.' In *The Oxford Handbook of Holocaust Studies,* edited by Peter Hayes and John K. Roth. Oxford: Oxford University Press, 2010.

– *Trauma in First Person: Diary Writing during the Holocaust.* Bloomington: Indiana University Press, 2017.

Gruat, Cédric, with Cécile Leblanc. *Amis des juifs: Les résistants aux étoiles.* Paris: Éditions Tirésias, 2005.

Hall, Stuart. 'Cultural Identity and Diaspora.' In *Identity, Community, Culture, Difference,* edited by Jonathan Rutherford, 222–37. London: Lawrence and Wishart, 1990.

– 'The Question of Cultural Identity.' In Stuart Hall, David Held, and Tony McGraw, *Modernity and Its Futures.* Cambridge: Polity Press with the Open University, 1992.

Hall, Stuart, and Paul Du Gay, eds. *Questions of Cultural Identity.* London: Sage, 1996.

Jackson, Julian. *France: The Dark Years, 1940–1944.* Oxford: Oxford University Press, 2001.

James, William. *The Principles of Psychology*. London: Macmillan, 1890.

Kahn, Annette. *Le Fichier*. Paris: Robert Laffont, 1993.

Kaufman, F. 'By Chance I Found a Pencil: Holocaust Diary Narratives of Testimony, Defiance, Solace and Struggle.' PhD diss., University of Melbourne, 2011.

Lehr, Johanna. *De l'école au maquis: La Résistance juive en France*. Paris: Le Vendémiaire, 2014.

Leociak, Jacek. *Text in the Face of Destruction: Accounts from the Warsaw Ghetto Reconsidered*. Translated by Emma Harris. Warsaw: Zydowski instytut Historyczny, 2004.

Le Poidevin, Robin. 'The Experience and Perception of Time.' *The Stanford Encyclopedia of Philosophy* (Summer 2015), edited by Edward N. Zalta, https://plato.stanford.edu/archives/sum2015/entries/time-experience/, accessed 12 July 2016.

Lindholm, Charles. *Culture and Identity: The History, Theory, and Practice of Psychological Anthropology*. Boston: McGraw-Hill, 2002.

Loodts, P. 'Les médecins de la Grande Guerre prenaient-ils la tension des soldats?' http://www.1914-1918.be/tension_arteriel_soldat.php, accessed 30 June 2017.

Marrus, Michael. 'Jewish Leadership and the Holocaust: The Case of France.' In *Living with Anti-Semitism*, edited by Jehuda Reinharz, 380–96. Hanover, NH: University Press of New England, 1987.

– *Lessons of the Holocaust*. Toronto: University of Toronto Press, 2016.

– *The Politics of Assimilation: A Study of the French Jewish Community at the time of the Dreyfus Affair*. Oxford: Clarendon Press, 1971.

Marrus, Michael R., and Robert O. Paxton. *Vichy France and the Jews*. Stanford, CA: Stanford University Press, 1995.

Miller, Carolyn. 'Genre as Social Action.' *Quarterly Journal of Speech* 70 (1984): 151–67.

Paxton R.O., O. Corpet, and C. Paulhan, eds. *Archives de la vie littéraire sous l'Occupation: À travers le désastre*. Paris: Tallandier et IMEC éditeur, 2009.

Poznanski, Renée. *Être juif en France pendant la Seconde Guerre mondiale*. Paris: Hachette, 1994.

Poznanski, Renée, and Denis Peschanski, with Benoît Pouvreau. *Drancy: Un camp en France*. Paris: Fayard et le Ministère de la Défense, 2015.

Rabi, Vladimir. *Anatomie du Judaïsme français*. Paris: Les Éditions de Minuit, 1962.

– *Un peuple de trop sur la terre?* Paris: Les Presses d'Aujourd'hui, 1979.

Rajsfus, Maurice. *Des juifs dans la collaboration: L'U.G.I.F., 1941–1944*. Paris: Études et Documentation Internationals, 1980.

Ricoeur, Paul. 'Narrative Time.' *Critical Inquiry* 7, no. 1 (1980): 169–89.

– *Temps et récit*, 3 vols. Paris: Seuil, 1983–85.

– *Time and Narrative*, 3 vols. Translated by Kathleen Blamey and David Pellauer. Chicago: University of Chicago Press, 1984–88.

Rose, Nikolas. 'Identity, Genealogy, History.' In Hall and Du Gay, *Questions of Cultural Identity.*

Rosen, Elisheva. 'Littérature, autofiction, histoire: L'Affaire Dreyfus dans *La recherche du temps perdu.' Littérature* 100 (1995): 64–80.

Rousso, Henry. *Le syndrome de Vichy de 1944 à nos jours.* Paris: Éditions du Seuil, 1987.

– *Vichy: L'événement, la mémoire, l'histoire.* Paris: Gallimard, 1992.

Ryan, Donna F. *The Holocaust and the Jews of Marseille.* Urbana: University of Illinois Press, 1996.

Schwarzfuss, Simon. *Aux prises avec Vichy: Histoire politique des juifs de France (1940–1944).* Paris: Calmann-Lévy, 1998.

Soulez, Philippe, and Frédéric Worms. *Bergson: Biographie.* Paris: PUF, 2002.

Suleiman, Susan Rubin. *The Némirovsky Question: The Life, Death, and Legacy of a Jewish Writer in 20th Century France.* New Haven, CT: Yale University Press, 2016.

Varela, Francisco J. 'The Specious Present: A Neurophenomenology of Time Consciousness.' In *Naturalizing Phenomenology: Issues in Contemporary Phenomenology and Cognitive Science*, edited by Jean Petitot, Francisco J. Varela, Bernard Pachoud, and Jean-Michel Roy, 266–329. Stanford, CA: Stanford University Press, 1999.

Winock, Michel. *Edouard Drumont et Cie: Antisémitisme et fascisme en France.* Paris: Seuil, 1982.

Zucotti, Susan. *The Holocaust, the French, and the Jews.* New York: Basic Books, 1993.

Index

community, 16, 22, 23, 24–5, 72, 75,
78–9, 82
Compiègne camp: conditions, 34,
222n1, 235n3; deportations and,
96; internees, 3, 19–21, 24, 25–6,
167, 178, 179–81; and *rafle des
notables*, 170; Schatzman at, 116–24,
126–33, 142–9
concentration camps, 8–9, 30, 53–5,
176–7, 135, 171. *See also specific
camps*
Consistoire central des israélites
de France, 80, 90–1, 106–8, 230n3,
230n8, 233n38
continuity, viii, 12; diaries and, 153–4,
221n7; for diarists, 86, 103, 117,
119, 194, 199; and memory, 55–6,
60, 61–4; and the self, ix–x, 199
courage, 92, 93, 94, 100. *See also*
heroism
cowardice, 85, 98, 104, 197

Darquier de Pellepoix, Louis, 90, 91
death(s): 'being-toward,' 170;
at concentration camps, 134,
136, 164, 168, 188, 236n10;
and 'posthumous life,' 199–
201; statistics, 222n5. *See also*
executions; suicide(s)
'de-emplotment,' 193–4
deixis, ix, x, 157–8
déjà (already), uses of, 158–70,
240n36; anticipatory, 158–61,
169, 185; and limit, 167–8;
and prematurity, 162–3, 169;
quantitative vs. temporal, 166–7
deportations: Berr and, 192–3,
197; of children, 54, 75, 226n27,
232n25; Lambert and, 93, 94, 95–8,
105; Schatzman and, 116, 135–6,
137–8, 236n9; statistics, 222n5. *See
also* round-ups

Derrida, Jacques, 13, 14, 17, 50, 65–6
Descombes, Vincent, 16
diaries: as archival, vii, 112, 153;
concepts of, viii–ix, x; and
continuity, 153–4, 221n7 (*see also*
continuity); and experience, 9,
11–12, 31, 218; function(s), 5,
9, 31, 106–7, 128–9, 197 (*see also*
memory); and history, viii, 39–40,
81, 104–5, 106–7, 109, 199; vs. other
genres, vii–viii, 65, 156, 202, 203; as
rehearsal, 30, 65, 81–2, 89, 93, 106,
113, 198 (*see also* performance); and
the self, 6–7, 55, 65, 137 (*see also* self,
the); and survival, 178, 201, 203,
214; and temporality, vii–viii, 5, 171
(*see also* time); and thinking, 108,
111–14, 126; typical composition
of, 9, 175. *See also* Jewish wartime
diaries; witness/witnessing; writing
difference, ix, 22, 40, 60, 199, 206,
209, 225n26
disintegration, viii, 11, 153, 193–4
disruption, 10, 57, 133, 136, 210, 213
diversity, 20, 41, 73, 74
'drama of the Jews,' 27, 106, 109
Drancy camp: conditions, 175–7,
235n3, 237n16; death of Goldman,
134, 136, 164, 236n10; diary
accounts, 133–7, 145, 150–2, 161–2,
163, 164–5, 170–9, 183; internees,
22, 52–5, 192–3; and round-ups, 19,
133–5, 190, 236n9, 236n11
dreams, 6, 61, 75, 79, 100, 169, 210,
215. *See also* illusion(s); nightmares
Dreyfus affair, 28, 31, 58, 77, 204,
206, 242n9
Drumont, Édouard, 206, 242n9
du Bellay, Joachim, 76
duration, 8–9, 55, 165, 171, 237n1
duty, 101, 194, 226n30. *See also*
responsibility

honour/dishonour, 77, 81, 86, 102
hope: Berr, 192, 196; Castro, 180–1;
    Lambert, 75, 77, 85, 90, 97, 99, 101,
    110, 113; Lania, 17; Schatzman,
    121, 125, 130, 141, 142–3, 147,
    151–2, 214. *See also* morale
humanity, 24, 174–5, 191, 213,
    215–18
humour, 46, 47, 49, 126, 211

'I' (*je*): and identification, 16, 18,
    24, 28, 80–4; and 'posthumous
    life,' 200–1; reclaiming of, 118;
    time and, x, 153, 157. *See also* first
    person
identification: concepts of, 28–30,
    36, 38–9; diarists and, 50, 51, 53–4,
    57, 59–60, 63, 77, 82, 106, 137; and
    identity, 10–11, 13, 14–15, 227n45;
    with the past, 41; as relational,
    16, 18 (*see also* language, analysis
    of: pronouns). *See also* identity
    practices
identity: administrative, 44–6, 53, 54,
    60; ancestral (*see* ancestors); and
    appearance, 34–5; categories of,
    70, 72, 115, 226n27; collective, 21,
    120, 137, 213 (*see also* community);
    concepts of, ix, 14–15, 16, 49,
    50–1, 52, 55, 65–6, 80; cultural, 21,
    36; disaggregated, ix, 72–3; dual,
    29, 32, 33, 34–5, 39, 51–2, 211, 213;
    and identification, 10–11, 13, 16,
    227n45; mixed, 51, 70; 'narratives
    of the past' (Hall), 29, 41, 63–4;
    national accounts of, 15, 19, 20–1,
    23–5, 29, 30, 33, 41, 73–4, 76, 102;
    as performance, 35–8, 39–55,
    63, 65, 190, 193; professional,
    37, 62, 88, 115; '*topoi* of,' 36, 55,
    63–4, 66; vs. wandering, 19. *See also*
    belonging; Jewish identity

identity practices, 36, 37, 40, 48,
    50–2, 53–4, 115. *See also* labelling;
    performance
illusion(s), 76, 85, 160, 185, 194, 204,
    205. *See also* dreams
immigration. *See* refugees
indifference, 93, 100, 118, 191, 208
internment. *See* concentration camps
internment diaries. *See* Castro, Saül
    (diarist); Montel, François (diarist);
    Oppenheimer, Jean (diarist);
    Schatzman, Benjamin (diarist);
    Siefridt, Françoise (diarist)
interpretation, 8, 31, 154–5, 213, 218,
    223n14
Israel, 'children of': 30, 32, 211,
    212; 'israélite,' 33, 208, 209, 210,
    226n34; as term for the Jews, 72,
    73. *See also* Zionism
Israelite Central Consistory of
    France, 80, 90–1, 106–8, 230n3,
    230n8, 233n38

Jackson, Julian, 67
James, William, 12, 154, 155, 158,
    166, 169
'Jewish community,' 16, 22, 23, 24–5,
    78–9
Jewish Guides and Scouts of France,
    60, 230n90
Jewish identity: belonging and, 20, 24,
    209; Bernard and, 33, 65, 70; diarists
    and, 40, 43–5, 60, 72–3, 209; history
    and, 71, 206, 213–14; 'trouble,' 10,
    11, 13–17, 28, 29, 30, 31
'Jewish nationalism,' 212, 243n29. *See
    also* Zionism
'Jewish question,' 41, 99, 234n44
Jewish wartime diaries: about the
    corpus, 5–6, 9, 224n2; author's
    approach to, vii–xi; hiding of,
    116, 183; historical study of, vii, 7;

9 781487 525194